84139

D1002138

The Online Writing Classroom

edited by

Susanmarie Harrington
Indiana University-Purdue University

Rebecca Rickly
Texas Tech University

Michael Day
Northern Illinois University

HAMPTON PRESS, INC.
CRESSKILL, NEW JERSEY

Printed in the United States of America

Library of Congress Cataloging-in-Publication Data

The online writing classroom / edited by Susanmarie Harrington, Rebecca Rickly, Michael Day.
     p. cm. -- (Instructional and information technology)
  Includes bibliographical references and indexes.
  ISBN 1-57273-271-7 -- ISBN 1-57273-272-5 (pbk.)
   1. English language--Rhetoric--Study and teaching--Data processing.
2. English language--Rhetoric--Computer network resources. 3. Report writing--Study and teaching--Data processing. 4. English language--Computer assisted instruction. 5. Report writing--Computer network resources. 6. Online data processing--Study and teaching. I. Harrington, Susanmarie. II. Rickly, Rebecca. III. Day, Michael. IV. Series.

PE1404.045 2000
808'.042'0285--dc21

00-021407

Hampton Press, Inc.
23 Broadway
Cresskill, NJ 07626

Contents

Contributors

Michael Day is Assistant Professor of English at Northern Illinois University, where he teaches advanced composition and composition pedagogy. Previously, he was chair of faculty development at the South Dakota School of Mines and Technology, where he taught composition, technical communications, and computers in society. His research interests include the rhetoric of computer-mediated communication, teacher training in technology, and faculty development. He has served as chair of the NCTE Assembly on Computers in English, co-chair of the Great Plains Alliance for Computers and Writing, and chair of the Fifteenth Computers and Writing Conference in Rapid City. His work has appeared in edited collections as well as *Computers and Composition* and *Kairos*.

Susanmarie Harrington is Director of Composition and Associate Professor of English at Indiana University-Purdue University, Indianapolis. Her research interests include writing assessment, and technology and teacher training. Previously visiting Associate Director of Composition at Texas Tech University, her work has appeared in the *Journal of Basic Writing, WPA: Journal of the Council of Writing Program Administrators,* and in edited collections.

Rebecca Rickly is an Assistant Professor at Texas Tech University where she serves as Associate Director of Composition. Previously, she coordinated the University of Michigan's Online Writing and Learning (OWL). Her research interests include gender studies, technology and the writing process, and applications of methods and methodologies in composition research. She has served on the CCC Committee on Computers and Composition, the NCTE's Assembly on Computers in English, and is currently chairing NCTE's Instructional Technology Committee. Her work has appeared in edited collections as well as *Computers and Composition, CMC Magazine,* and *Kairos*.

John Barber is the Paladin Professor of Literature at Texas Woman's University and a professor of writing at Southern Methodist University. He is co-chair of the Computers and Writing 2000 Conference. His primary research and applied interests are directed toward pedagogical and cultural issues raised by the intersection of literacy, technology, and society. His publications and presentations often address the use of technology in teaching, learning, and teacher training. He brings wide experience in business, professional, and free-lance writing to his work. With Dene Grigar, he is editing *New Worlds, New Words: Exploring Pathways for Writing about and in Electronic Environments* (forthcoming, Hampton Press).

Betsy A. Bowen is Associate Professor of English and Director of Composition at Fairfield University. Her research examines adult literacy and the effects of technology on education.

Kate Coffield is Writing Instructor and Lab Coordinator in the Department of English and Comparative Literature at American University in Cairo. Her research interests include instructional technology; the effects of computing technology on writing, research, and professional development; collaborative writing; de-centering in the classroom; resistance and technophobia; and building an interdisciplinary, user-focused computing culture on campus.

Bill Condon is Director of Washington State University Writing Programs. In addition to supervising campus-wide assessment and writing across the curriculum programs, he supervises WSU's Writing Center. He also participates in the development of Online.WSU. Condon is co-author of *Writing the Information Superhighway* (Allyn & Bacon, 1997), and with Liz Hamp-Lyons, *Assessing the Portfolio: Principles for Practice, Theory and Research* (Hampton Press, 2000).

Sharon Cogdill teaches at St. Cloud State University in Minnesota, where she has taught in and administered her department's computer classroom for many years.

Terry Craig is professor of English at West Virginia Northern Community College.

Joe Essid directs the Writing Center at the University of Richmond, where he teaches composition, composition theory, and the interdisciplinary first-year core course. His research interests include computers and writing and the history of technology.

Pamela Gay is Associate Professor of English and Women's Studies and Director of Writing Across the Curriculum at Binghamton University, State University of New York. She has published a textbook *Developing Writers: A Dialogic Approach* (1995); articles in the *Journal of Basic Writing, Computers and Composition,* and *Issues in Writing;* and an essay in *Portfolios: Process and Product.* As part of a larger pedagogical project on "De-colonizing Our Pedagogical Practices," she is teaching writing in an interactive, Internet environment where she is exploring expanding notions of literacy and the classroom. Gay and her students have been experimenting with two cross-cultural inquiry projects via the Internet, one with students in New Zealand and a full-course project with students in the Czech Republic. See http://bingweb.binghamton.ed/~rhet380m or contact pgay@binghamton.edu.

Linda K. Hanson, Associate Professor of English at Ball State University and Director of the Indiana Writing Project, teaches writing (basic writers to graduate students), Romantic studies, 19th century rhetorical theory, literary history, and a seminar in Theory, Pedagogy and Research in Basic Writing. She links her teaching and research interests in rhetoric and composition and British Romanticism through epistemological inquiry. Publications have appeared in the *Journal of Basic Writing, Computers and College Writing, Assessment Update, Good Practice in Assessing Higher Education Outcomes, Major Field Assessments 1994,* and *Computers and Composition.*

Leslie D. Harris is Decker Chair of Instructional Technology at Goucher College. He was formerly Instructional Technology Facilitator at Plattsburgh State University of New York and an Assistant Professor of English at Susquehanna University. He was also Project Director of the Annenberg/CPB "Composition in Cyberspace" Project. His research interests include instructional technology, computer-mediated communication, computer-based pedagogy, and collaborative learning.

Fred Kemp, Associate Professor of English, serves as an Associate Director of Composition and Rhetoric. After teaching English and language arts in public schools for 9 years, he received his Ph.D. in Rhetoric and Composition, with an emphasis in Computer-Based Rhetoric, at the University of Texas at Austin in 1988, where he was instrumental in founding and directing UT's Computer Writing Research Lab. He is currently a member of the NCTE Instructional Technology Committee and is a past chair and current member of the CCC Computers in Composition Committee. He is co-director of the Alliance for Computers and Writing, and is co-author of DIWE, the "Daedalus Integrated Writing Environment" (1990 EDUCOM/NCRIPTAL award winner for best writing software). The Internet email discussion lists he has founded include Megabyte University (MBU-L), ACW-L, and WCENTER. He has written and presented extensively about computer-based writing pedagogies

Beth Kolko is an assistant professor of English at the University of Texas at Arlington where she also co-directs an advanced technology lab. Her recent research and teaching has been primarily in the area of technology and culture; her other fields include cultural studies, feminist theory, and composition. She is the founder of MOOScape, a text-based virtual world dedicated to studying race as a component of virtual identity, and she is co-editor of *Race and Cyberspace,* forthcoming from Routledge.

Steven D. Krause is Assistant Professor in the Department of English Language and Literature at Eastern Michigan University in Ypsilanti, Michigan. He teaches writing classes at all levels, from first year composition and rhetoric to graduate courses. Besides writing pedagogy (particularly the teaching of writing with computer technology), his interests include rhetorical theory and history, the rhetoric and discourse practices of the Internet, and writing program administration. His publications have appeared in outlets such as *Pre/Text, Computer Mediated Communication,* and *Writerly/Readerly Texts.*

Jane Lasarenko is Assistant Professor of English at Slippery Rock State University. Originally a specialist in critical and narrative theory and the novel, she re-directed her career when computers hit the mainstream in education. She has investigated and used computer technology in her writing and literature classes for the past 4 years, and has published in technology and pedagogy. She has also directed the writing across the curriculum program at West Texas A&M University.

Carrie Shively Leverenz is Assistant Professor of English at Florida State University, where she directs the Reading/Writing Center and Computer Supported Writing Classrooms. Her research interests include collaboration, writing program administration, TA training, multicultural pedagogy, writing center theory and CAI.

Gail Matthews-DeNatale is the Projects Manager for the Educational Technology Center at Northeastern University. Prior to Northeastern, she served on the faculty of the Institute for Educational Transformation at George Mason University and previous to that she taught as adjunct faculty of the Anthropology Department at the University of South Carolina. Matthews-DeNatale graduated Phi Beta Kappa from Kenyon College and holds a Ph.D. from Indiana University. Her multimedia productions include videos and web sites for the Gorbachev Foundation, South

Carolina Educational Television, and the Annenberg/CPB-funded Epiphany Project.

Ruth Mirtz is an assistant professor at Ferris State University in Big Rapids, Michigan. Formerly Director of the First Year Writing Program at Florida State University, she is currently working on writing program administration research, TA preparation issues, and questions concerning student writing as a genre. She co-authored *Small Groups in Writing Workshops: Invitations to a Writer's Life* (NCTE, 1994) with Robert Brooke and Rick Evans.

Linda Record is an English instructor and chairperson of the Institutional Technology Committee at College of the Sequoias in Visalia, CA. She may be contacted at lindar@giant.sequoias.cc.ca.us.

Richard Selfe is the Director of Computer-based Instruction in the Humanities department at Michigan Technological University. He directs the Center for Computer-Assisted Language Instruction, a communication-oriented computer facility and teaches computer-intensive first-year English technical communication and graduate computer studies courses. His interest is in communication pedagogy and the social/institutional influences of electronic media on that pedagogy.

Robert McClure Smith is Assistant Professor of English at Knox College in Galesburg IL. His research interests include computers and composition, American literature, and cultural studies. He has published in *Narrative, Contemporary Literature, ATQ,* and *Journal of Narrative Technique.* He is also the author of *The Seductions of Emily Dickinson* (University of Alabama Press, 1996).

Hugh M. Stilley is an Associate Professor of Communications at Kettering University. He is interested in the editing process, literature, and distance education.

Barbara Stedman, assistant professor of English at Ball State University, has taught writing, literature, and interdisciplinary courses at Indiana colleges and universities for most of the last 17 years. In addition to writing and technology, her research interests lie chiefly in cultural studies and environmentalism. Currently she is a fellow at the Center for Energy Research, Education, and Service at Ball State, where she is exploring Indiana's history of environmental literature.

Megumi Taniguchi is a junior specialist at the University of Hawai'i at Manoa. She serves as a program assistant to Dr. Margit Misangyi Watts for two freshman programs, the Rainbow Advantage Program and

Freshman Seminars. She also teaches English composition for the Rainbow Advantage Program.

Margit Misangyi Watts is the Director of Rainbow Advantage and Freshman Seminars, two learning community programs for beginning students at the University of Hawai'i at Manoa. Although her PhD in American Studies, with a specialization in feminist theory, led her to teach and publish in that arena, she has spent the last 7 years delving into educational philosophy and the challenges facing higher education today. She directs an international project, Collaboratory, which brings together museums, communities, and students in grades K-16. Synchronous gatherings occur on Walden3, a virtual community that she runs. Believing in the possibilities of technology, but not blinded by them, Margit has written about educational changes, technology as a catalyst, and is editing a book called *Necessary Conversations* in which she challenges others to develop a philosophy of technology.

Robert Yagelski is assistant professor of English at the State University of New York at Albany, where he directs the Writing Center and teaches undergraduate courses in writing and tutoring and graduate courses in rhetoric and composition and literacy. His research focuses on understanding literacy and the uses of technology in literacy instruction.

Introduction to the Online Writing Classroom: Supporting Teachers Who are Beginning to Use Technologies to Expand Notions of Literacy, Power, and Teaching

Susanmarie Harrington
Rebecca Rickly
Michael Day

BACKGROUND: AN INTRODUCTION TO THE FIELD

The field that has come to be known as computers and writing is at an odd juncture in its development. In recent years, it has become firmly established as a subfield in rhetoric and composition, and some of the most prominent figures in composition publish regularly on technology issues. Three of the last four chairs of the Conference on College Composition and Communication, for instance, have made important contributions to scholarly thinking about technology and writing. The annual Computers and Writing Conference is now in its 13th year, and draws more and more submissions and attenders each year. *Computers and Composition*, a successful journal, now in its 14th volume, has moved from a small, university-published journal to larger, international journal published by a major publishing house. The Alliance for Computers and Writing (ACW), formed in 1993, serves as a central organization for teachers, publishers, and developers committed to using computers and networks in teaching writing, and regional ACWs hold annual conferences in several parts of the country. Some of the leaders of ACW are directors of the Annenberg-CPB funded Epiphany Project, a coalition of teachers committed to training and support for computer and networked writing instruction now affiliated with the American Association for Higher Education's Teaching and Learning with Technology (TLT) group. Both ACW and Epiphany are essentially superstructures set up to focus and organize grassroots curriculum and faculty development efforts; both organizations also allow teachers to pool their resources nationally. This network of scholarly and professional activities has enabled teachers to draw on an increasingly sophisticated body of scholarly literature for classroom and program development, and in 1996, the first history of the field appeared (Hawisher, Selfe, & Moran, 1996).

As these academic developments have progressed, attention to computers and the Internet in popular culture has become commonplace. The media is full of predictions about the spread of networked technologies, and the "information superhighway," once an exciting new development, has become a rather stale metaphor. The graphically rich, seamlessly linked and instantaneous World Wide Web has eclipsed e-mail as the hottest new technology, used for communication, commerce, as well as information. With the rapid pace of technological change, software and hardware can seem dated even before they come to seem familiar. The public awareness of technological change, coupled with the increase in scholarly attention to technological issues, has helped writing teachers who were early adapters of technology—once marginalized in their departments and their profession—to move toward center stage.

Considering all this progress, it would seem that teachers interested in computers and writing would have a wealth of resources from which to choose, and that teachers and scholars moving into the field would find it a welcoming place. Yet some problems persist. The rapid spread of technologies, and popular media's often underinformed excitement about the Internet, obscures the fact that many students and teachers have little, or no, access to these technologies. Furthermore, most schools must pay for Internet access, and computers once bought need to be upgraded and maintained. Without training in the new or upgraded technologies, teachers are somewhat helpless when it comes to integrating them into the curriculum.

Because teachers are often not in control of computer technologies—these being often bought by a central district or campus authority—they may be handed software or hardware that is not ideal for writing classrooms, or they may have access to labs that are not designed for student interaction or collaboration. This physical complexity can be complicated by the increasing complexity of new theoretical applications. As the field of computers and writing has become more established, and thus more theoretical, new teachers can be overwhelmed as they look at hyper-textual, postmodern representations of life in a writing classroom and ask, "But what should I do on Monday?" The purpose of this book is to help answer that question. The contributors have all successfully integrated technology into their writing curricula, and their focus is on practical pedagogical applications grounded in current composition theory.

COMPUTERS IN THE CLASSROOM: PANACEA OR POISON?

The most current scholarship on computers and writing reminds us that technology itself is neither savior nor destroyer, but rather an element in classroom and curriculum design that, when implemented well, can have beneficial effects, and when implemented badly, can have disastrous effects. This nuanced, contextual view of technology has developed as the field of computers and composition has matured, and as computers and composition scholars have moved from narrative accounts of classroom experiences to more broadly theorized explorations of teaching, writing, and learning.

The first wave of attention to any new technology is usually replete with "lore," personal testimonials about the technology and its positive uses, and teachers often make broad predictions about the hopeful changes that the technology can bring. The next wave of scholarship takes a more critical view, exploring how the technologies in use can be shaped by teachers, and how constraints on technology use and development can have a range of effects (Barker & Kemp 1990; Barton, 1994). And as teacher-scholars continue to study the effects of writing technologies, technology itself continues to develop, often straining our ability to keep up. In many cases, the problems caused by poor technical support, anxiety surrounding technology, or unequal access coexist with the promises of new pedagogies, literacies, and online communities. Our contention in this volume is that through reflective practice, teachers can shape the forms and uses of technology in their own schools and departments. But to do that, teachers need support—ideally from a school or department that values technology and a campus that provides a good infrastructure for technical support. Absent that, teachers can still create their own support networks, forming informal and formal groups to discuss teaching strategies.

The chapters in this volume go beyond the success stories of early adopters and offer a more critical examination of pedagogical practices in the age of technology. Collectively, we argue that in order to effectively use computers in the classroom, we need to first carefully articulate course goals, then consider the ways in which technology use will help students meet those goals. Planning is essential to any pedagogical enterprise, of course, but it is even more crucial for a computer-based course, where it is easy to assume that the technology will simply take over and "work," unproblematically. Lack of planning, as all the contributors to this volume will attest, often leads to the most unproductive use of class time and poor instructor evaluations.

TURNING STORIES INTO GUIDING THEORIES

This book is thus designed for writing teachers who teach in online environments—primarily networked computer labs and the Internet—and for writing teachers who would like to teach in such spaces. Teachers who are new to teaching online, or who are refiguring their teaching goals and practices, face a bewildering array of technological possibilities. They also encounter students with varying experiences with and attitudes about technology. These teachers can be quickly overwhelmed with choices and decisions, not to mention doubts and fears. In this volume, we address these overwhelming choices and emotions with reflective examples. All of the contributors are writing from their own teaching, research, or administrative experiences, and all tell their stories in a rich theoretical context that will allow readers to see the relation between theory, context, and practice. With further reflection, these stories provide the basis for the theories that ground us as a field. We offer these chapters not as prescriptive guides for practice, but instead as descriptive guides to new teaching practices in hopes that they will help the readers of this book find ways to use online activities to further their own pedagogical goals within their own specific contexts. And we offer them, finally, to challenge readers to examine their pedagogical goals in light of the claims that critical pedagogy and networked pedagogy make about writers and writing classrooms: that the best writing environments are those that offer writers a chance to develop informed critical consciousness about the approaches and technologies they can use in a variety of rhetorical situations.

THE NECESSITY FOR TEACHER TRAINING

Like many other educators, we want to respond to recent political initiatives such as the "Bridge to the Twenty-First Century" that will create robust networks connecting computer-equipped schools, businesses, and households. In the 20th century, U.S. schools have seen ever-increasing gaps between rich and poor districts (Kozol, 1986), and we fear that these increasing gaps will create a permanent underclass lacking economic and social opportunities (Faigley, 1997). Initiatives like "NetDay," which will provide computers in public libraries and in more classrooms, are welcome attempts to correct this imbalance. To meet the needs of the 21st century, it is crucial that we invest in new computers for schools and towns that have been left out of the first wave of computer technology—and that we invest in teacher training and curriculum development that will bring the benefits of networked, interactive, and critical pedagogy to all classrooms, not only those located in wealthy school districts and universities.

But investments in technology are worthless without accompanying investments in teachers. New technology will go to waste unless teachers are trained to use it in educationally sound ways and are given opportunities to develop their theories as technologies develop. We have only to remember how so much of the computer equipment donated in the 1970s and 1980s went to waste because many school systems and institutions had neither the budget nor the expertise to train faculty to use the sophisticated machines and complicated software. However, these days software and user interfaces are becoming more user-friendly (just look at the friendliness of software like Netscape, as compared with the old command-line interfaces Internet users once had to learn); with some encouragement in the form of reward, released time, inservice and professional workshops, and positive promotion and tenure reviews, along with help in the form of training and workable models, writing teachers can and will learn to use the new technologies for their teaching and research.

Teachers need to be trained not only to use technology, but to use it in pedagogically sound ways. We have often heard the expression "where technology is taking us." Simply put, as teachers we should maintain that technology is not going to take us anyplace we do not already want to go. That is to say, technology such as the Internet should not be used simply because it is there, but rather because it can further existing educational goals, such as allowing students to receive feedback from distant audiences, allowing students from vastly distant backgrounds to teach each other, helping students read and write through engaged practice for real audiences, or helping students find communities with whom they can discuss issues and learn communication conventions. Experiences with technology can also help teachers extend their educational goals, allowing for new definitions of literacy, new forms of collaboration, and even new notions of teaching and classrooms.

CRITICALLY EXAMINING TECHNOLOGY

In all cases, pedagogical goals should determine whether and what technologies are used, not vice-versa. Ultimately, our choices become more difficult in a pluralistic society facing ever more complex technologies. The most outspoken critics of technology, writers such as Clifford Stoll, Mark Slouka, and Sven Birkits, caution us not to enter the networked world because of important ethical issues raised by the move headlong into technology and cyberspace. Birkits (1994), for instance, contends that the shifting cultural and social terrains created by technologies are profoundly changing, even eliminating, reading as we know it. Online, he contends, the "pace is rapid, driven by jump-cut increments, and the basic movement is laterally associative rather than vertically cumulative" (p. 122), leading to what he called "language erosion" (p. 128).

One of Slouka's (1995) major concerns is also that much of what now passes for communication on the network is banal, inflammatory, and certainly not respectful of others. Even worse, according to Slouka, cyberspace removes the common ground of worldly experience that rhetoricians from Aristotle to Burke have called crucial to effective communication:

> human culture depends on the shared evidence of the senses, always has; we can communicate with one another because a hurled rock will always break skin, a soap bubble will always burst. A technology designed to short-circuit the senses, a technology capable of providing an alternate world—abstract, yet fully inhabitable, real to our senses yet accessible only through a computer screen—would take away this common ground and replace it with one manufactured for us by the technologists. And this is not a good thing. . . . Virtual systems, by offering us a reality divorced from the world, from the limits and responsibilities of presence, offer us as well a glimpse into an utterly amoral universe. (pp. 12-13)

Similarly, Birkits (1994) argues that the rise of computer networks will change—for the worse—"the idea of what it means to be a person living a life. . . . The figure-ground model, which has always featured a solitary self before a background that is the society of other selves, is romantic in the extreme. It is ever less tenable in the world as it is becoming" (p. 130). The demise of private space, and the decline of the barriers between public and private, means that the very notion of individualism is threatened. According to these critics, then, the online world would be inappropriate for writing instruction, as well as any other human interaction because the shift from the physical world into "one manufactured for us by the technologists" implies a move away from the value systems of our everyday lives into a place where rules and conventions do not apply.

At the close of *The Gutenberg Elegies*, Birkits (1994) realized the following:

the question I face is not, as some would have it, whether I should get myself a computer, find myself a network, do whatever one does to be in step. To me it is more a question of how I want to position myself as history makes a swerve, not only ushering in new circumstances and alignments, but changing its own deeper nature as well. (p. 214)

Birkits positioned himself in resistance to technological changes (the closing line of his book is "Refuse it" (p. 229). The contributors in this volume, however, take another approach, positioning themselves squarely in the midst of technological changes, arguing that the participation of thoughtful teachers who seek to create democratic, communal writing spaces is the only act that can counter the elements of technology that promote addiction, dehumanization, and disinformation.

Furthermore, the contributors argue, computer networks in and of themselves will cause neither harm nor benefit; the consequences of networks are the consequences of the activities that occur on them, and when thoughtful teachers and students work together, positive effects are produced. Rather than blurring the boundaries between public and private, networks can create a new sense of shared public space in which healthy and respectful debate can flourish; these vigorous debates are essential to a critical pedagogy and a successful democracy. All the chapters in this volume are evidence that good teaching, good learning, and good writing can emerge from networked spaces. If we draw a divide between teachers and technologists, as did Slouka, or between technopolists and teachers, as did Postman, we are left with no choice than to see computer networks as problematic and threatening. However, if we see teachers (and students) as those with a great stake in the development of networks, and we provide a solid theoretical rationale for technological development, we construct a critical position from which teachers can develop and critique new pedagogies and new softwares.

Cyberspace is not going to vanish, no matter how pointed the criticism of it may be, and writing teachers need to be aware of its continuing evolution. Furthermore, they need to be actively involved in the construction of software, cyberclassrooms, and pedagogical sites on the Internet. Without teacher involvement, we will have no control over the educational resources that are developed. As large corporations and government institutions create growing presences in technology and on the Internet, we should have a stake in the development of software and the Internet, in order to keep this technology ethical, human (and humane), and available to all. We owe it to our students and colleagues to provide good examples of the activities most beneficial to humankind, those that build community, generate good ideas, and foster new kinds of communication.

HOW THIS BOOK CAN HELP

The chapters that follow examine a variety of approaches that allow teachers to get beyond the "two by four" approach to education; that is, learning that must take place between the two covers of a book or inside the four walls of a classroom (McDaniel, McInerney, & Armstrong, 1983). These online activities help writers by providing a variety of contexts and audiences; they can also widen students' understanding of different cultures and life experiences by allowing interactions that previously would never have taken place.

Teaching online privileges writing in ways that traditional classrooms cannot; in online environments, much more communication takes place through writing, as class discussions, for instance, are conducted in writing. Students tend to write more when class activities move online, as written communication replaces some (but rarely all) oral communication. Furthermore, students who publish on the Web or who engage in list "conversation" find out first hand what it is like writing for a real audience. The presence of potential readers beyond the teacher and members of the class can give students a sense of purpose that the seemingly artificial assignments in the traditional writing class cannot always provide. Communicating entirely in text can be challenging because channels such as facial expression and tone of voice are missing, but it is precisely that challenge that, with the appropriate teacher guidance, can spur students to become more aware of and eventually improve their rhetorical strategies in writing.

Textual communication such as e-mail has caused a resurgence of emphasis on the power of the written word, resulting in what has been called a New Electronic Epistolary Movement (Day, 1997). Among the literate, letter-writing was once a primary vehicle for communicating thoughts and ideas; the intellectual circle of Samuel Johnson is a good example. Now, families, friends, and circles of teachers and students are finding that the ease of using e-mail makes it possible to communicate more frequently and at greater length. Through online communication, writing is enjoying a renaissance.

The most adventurous electronic pioneers have found ways to make interactive worlds on Internet-connected computers, in which they create environments described solely in text. Once the playgrounds only of role-playing gamers, these environments, known as MUDs or MOOs, are inhabited by writers, both teachers and students who, like poets, make use of the power of words to evoke imagination. Here they can collaborate on real-world or cyberspace projects, while at the same time combining practical communication with the aesthetic of the well-turned phrase or the most evocative textual description. Granted, without guidance, students can slip into bad habits, ignore expectations for standard usage, and communicate in the textual equivalent of grunts, but when combined with guidance and more traditional practices, the potential for growth and breadth in writing skills in MOOs is great. At the same time, the fact that writers online communicate largely through writing, often in well-defined communities that have produced their own varieties of language, offers writing classrooms enormous potential. Real-time audiences for writing help students see ways in which texts immediately affect others; the playfulness and possibility of online language opens up fruitful areas of rhetorical analysis. Teachers and students can explore the ways in which new terms are coined, the ways in which language is used to build (or break down) community, and the ways in which language itself is both medium of communication and object of study.

None of the contributors to this volume proposes that completely online classrooms ever supplant face-to-face teacher-student and student-student interactions. Except when distance or disability prevents physical proximity, most educators feel it is important for writing classes to be able to come together in physical space, to develop social skills and the sense of a class community so important to writers who need to share and freely discuss their works in progress. Like many other activities for the writing classroom, these online approaches meet specific pedagogical needs that complement other activities. Furthermore, we know that software packages and Internet functions, similar to any other technologies, can unintentionally exclude certain kinds of students or privilege certain learning styles (Kaplan, 1991; the essays in Selfe and Hilligoss, 1994, explore this point in various settings).

Therefore, a single online approach, or a set of exclusively online approaches, will not address the needs of all students. As can be seen by the diverse set of practices included here, an effective writing classroom is one in which students are encouraged to try a range of approaches to writing in a variety of contexts, for various audiences and purposes, with as many tools as we can effectively show them how to use. Many successful classes have a balance of online, face-to-face, and paper-based activities, with students often choosing which approaches to take on a given day.

Finally, with the introduction of online classroom approaches, we encourage a reflective, critical pedagogy (Hawisher et al., 1996; Shor, 1980) that encourages students and teachers to question the motives and results of such approaches, along with the power relations these approaches engender. In the metadiscursive realm, students should be able to look back at e-mail messages and logs of real-time written conversation to identify rhetorical strategies; to see who responded to whom, how, and why. In the metacognitive realm, writing classes might encourage students to go back through transcripts of online tutoring and peer-response sessions to identify the processes through which collaboration and revision take place. Only then, as students and teachers of writing and rhetoric, can we discuss, internalize, and practice those approaches that help us grow as writers.

THE POWER OF CRITICAL REFLECTION

As the chapters in this volume illustrate, critical reflection on the nature of reading and writing, the relationships between authors and readers, and the role of technology in developing relationships in the classroom is a rich and rewarding process. It is also hard work. But it pays off in many ways: It offers a chance for teachers to renew their commitment to pedagogical principles, to develop new ways of teaching, and to encourage a variety of learning styles. It also offers teachers a chance to renew their commitment to existing practices. Reflection may lead to change, but it does not necessarily do so. Reflection can help teachers see where technology use would not be helpful, or where more traditional face-to-face activities may be the most effective use of classroom time. In many ways, current calls to consider technology may provide teachers with institutional support and time to reflect on teaching in broad ways that extend beyond practical technological issues.

The contributors to this volume assume, however, that critical reflection on technology will contribute to changes in particular dimensions of teaching. All the chapters in this volume promote what many writing teachers have long recognized: Students learn more when the classroom is not a quiet place in which the teacher's voice dominates. The radical pedagogy advocated by Paulo Friere, who contrasted the banking model of education with the problem-posing model of education, found easy acceptance among composition theorists who were seeking to find ways to put students' meaning-making activities in the center of the classroom (see, e.g., Berthoff, 1981; Bruffee, 1984; Trimbur, 1988). The idea of the classroom as a community, with responsible, participating members now replaces the lecture-based, teacher-led model. Interactive, networked technologies make it easier for classrooms to function as active communities, and the the uses of technology can affect the ways students and teachers function in and out of computer classrooms.

One of the most important articles in the early development of computers and composition was a study of networked pedagogy by Barker and Kemp (1990), which stressed the value inherent in networked classrooms; the computer network can decenter the classroom, literally moving the classroom beyond its physical location. This decentering can be surprising, frightening, and unexpected. As the classroom moves, at least partially, online, notions of public and private space in the classroom are changed. In the traditional classroom, much student writing was private; online, much student writing becomes public. However, teachers must recognize the change in the rhetorical context, help students understand it, and respect their decisions about which writing should be public and which private. Often, this can mean keeping some communications and drafts private, limited to the student and teacher, or the student and a small group.

Many of the contributors here examine shifting boundaries between what has traditionally been viewed as private experiences. Online activities allow us to generate public discussion quickly, to generate ideas rapidly; the Internet connection between the classroom and other resources, such as outside library catalogues, Web pages, and e-mail contacts with outsiders, can bring a very public sense into the classroom. Collaborating teachers can also use distance collaborations to make the classroom a very public space. At the same time, electronic private spaces can be created, with individual contact between teachers and students and between students. These public and private spaces can be extended with paper activities, as well, and as we refigure our classrooms we should pay special attention to shifting boundaries between public and private.

These shifts in classrooms and communities raise a host of questions. Although current theory would hold that decreasing the instructor's authority is desirable, what of the old mentoring model, in which the experienced, knowledgeable instructor guides the less-experienced students? Are students truly adequate mentors for one another? Furthermore, how do we deal with the "authority" of a student's own race, ethnic background, gender, age, or socioeconomic reality? If, as some claim, these elements of authority are lost or de-emphasized in cyberspace, is it always a positive change? What are the trade-offs, and how do we foreground changing notions of authority in the online classroom?

These questions extend to the very notion of literacy itself. Shifting notions of authority and classroom boundaries lead to shifting notions of text and language. Kaplan (1995) used the term *E-literacies* to discuss two dimensions of the impact technology has had on literacy. In one sense, she used the term to denote the "social-economic elites whose interests might be served by electronic literacies of one sort or another, or who might come to be elites by virtue of their ability to shape electronic literacies." In another sense, she used the term "to mean those reading and writing processes specific to electronic texts (by texts, I mean a whole range of digitally encoded materials—words, sounds, pictures, video clips, simulations, etc.)." The multiplying array of literacies that face teachers and students is staggering. In 1996, the National Council of Teachers of

English (NCTE) passed a resolution calling for the inclusion of visual literacy in English programs, but teachers working with technology must also contend with shifting conceptions of text, as well as the incorporation of visual elements in texts. Hypertexts and Web pages create new possibilities for text form; as texts become more fluid and less stable, writing and reading processes can adjust. Yet the conservatism of many literacy practices means that teachers and students must explore more traditional practices as well as these innovative practices. Business and professional writing instructors increasingly find themselves called on to teach about the uses of electronic texts in "real-world" settings.

The proliferation of technologies and new text forms means that writers must re-examine the ways in which authority is inscribed and evaluated. These issues are key not only in professional uses of technology, but in personal uses as well. Several years ago, a *New Yorker* cartoon carried the now familiar caption "On the Internet, nobody knows you're a dog," underneath a picture of a dog working away at its computer. The wide array of information available on the Internet raises complex questions for students conducting the research so frequently a part of writing classes. After all, how is one to verify the information obtained on the Internet? What kinds of clues are embedded in the text about the author's credibility and ethos? What other methods can students use to determine whether the content they see is accurate and trustworthy?

The following chapters explore these and other issues by providing a number of models and scenarios for online classrooms, with suggestions based on practical experience grounded in theory. It is our hope that the critical reflection of these chapters will help readers incorporate new online activities in their own writing classes. But more than anything, it is our hope that this collection will enable teachers and students to take up the challenge offered by Selfe in her keynote address at the 1998 Conference on College Composition and Communication: that we must *pay attention* to the ways in which technology and literacy have become increasingly entwined in an educational system that has increasingly large divides between rich and poor. As Selfe (1999) argued, "when we take technology for granted, when it becomes invisible to us, when we forget technology's material bases—regardless of whether or not we use technology—we participate unwittingly" in a system that distributes educational resources horribly inequitably (p. 429). It is our hope that readers of this book will take up Selfe's challenge, and consider carefully the ways in which technology is used, or not used, in shaping their own and their students' visions of what kinds of literacies are possible, and what kinds of changes language use can bring about in their classrooms and in their world.

REFERENCES

Barker, T., & Kemp, F. (1990). Network theory: A postmodern pedagogy for the writing classroom. In C. Handa (Ed.), *Computers and community: Teaching composition in the twenty-first century* (pp. 1-27). Portsmouth, NH: Boynton/Cook.

Barton, E. L. (1994). Interpreting the discourses of technology. In C. Selfe & S. Hilligoss (Eds.), *Literacy and computers: The complications of teaching and learning with technology* (pp. 56-75). New York: MLA.

Berthoff, A. (1981). *The making of meaning: Metaphors, models, and maxims for writing teachers.* Portsmouth, NH: Heinemann/Boynton-Cook.

Birkits, S. (1994). *The gutenberg elegies.* New York: Fawcett Columbine.

Bruffee, K. (1984). Collaborative learning and the "converation of mankind. *College English, 34,* 635-652.

Day, M. (1997). Humanities and the internet: Strange bedfellows? In T. Gasque (Ed.), *Silver anniversary humanities anthology* (pp. 159-169). Brookings: South Dakota Humanities Council.

Faigley, L. (1997). Literacy after the revolution. *College Composition and Communication, 48*(1), 30-43.

Hawisher, G., Selfe, C., & Moran, C. (1996). *Computers and the teaching of writing in American higher education, 1979-1994: A history.* Norwood, NJ: Ablex.

Kaplan, N. (1991). Ideology, technology, and the future of writing instruction. In G. Hawisher & C. Selfe (Eds.), *Evolving perspectives on computers and composition studies: Questions for the 1990s* (pp. 11-42). Champaign/Urbana IL: NCTE Press.

Kaplan, N. (1995). Politexts, hypertexts, and other cultural formations in the late age of print. *Computer-Mediated Communication Magazine, 2*(3). http://www.december.com/cmc/mag/1995/ mar/kaplan.html

Kozol, J. (1986). *Illiterate America.* New York: New American Library.

McDaniel, E., McInerney, W., & Armstrong, P. (1993). Computers and school reform. *Educational Research Technology and Development, 41*(1), 73-78.

Selfe, C. (1999). Technology and literacy: A story about the perils of not paying attention. *College Composition and Communication, 50,* 411-436.

Selfe, C., & Hilligoss, S. (1994). *Literacy and computers: The complications of teaching and learning with technology.* New York: MLA.

Shor, I. (1980). *Critical teaching and everyday life.* Boston: South End Press.

Slouka, M. (1995). *War of the worlds: Cyberspace and the high-tech assault on reality.* New York: Basic Books.

Trimbur, J. (1988). Consensus and difference in collaborative learning. *College English, 51,* 602-616.

PART • I

FOCUS ON PEDAGOGY

Part I of this volume explores the actual practice of teaching in a networked computer classroom. All the training in the world does not completely prepare teachers for what goes on in the computer classroom, especially for the wide range of eventualities—from a wonderful, cooperative, collective class synergy to chaos, with angry, frustrated students wishing that the class had never gone online. We hope that the following scenarios in their chapter form offer a sense of the potentials and pitfalls of the online classroom by providing examples of pedagogical approaches and possible solutions to some of the more common problems of online pedagogy.

In "Hooked on Tronics, or Creating a Happy Union of Computers and Pedagogies," Stedman shifts attention to synchronous computer conferencing, a type of real-time chat in which students can communicate directly in text with others across the Internet. Stedman has a cautionary tale: If teachers embrace technology with uncritical enthusiasm, without effective pedagogical goals, students will not see the reasons for the use of the technology, and may rebel. Central to Stedman's reconfiguration of the pedagogy of synchronous communication is the notion of appropriate use, and of balance among the several online and face-to-face activities of the writing classroom.

Kolko, in "Cultural Studies In/And the Networked Writing Classroom," makes the shrewd observation that the pedagogy of cultural studies and the pedagogy of the computer classroom share much in common. Indeed, as Kolko points out, online conversations in the computer classroom not only allow increased participation by diverse kinds of students, they also provide a rich set of texts for students to discuss and analyze on the road to seeing themselves in relationship to their prose, in relationship to others, and, ultimately, as producers of cultural artifacts. If we

15

reconceive students' relationships to each other in the online classroom, using the technology to restructure the hierarchies and question the assumptions we make when we communicate, we may be able to use a social constructionist approach to create class communities in which students better understand their position "as subjects who act—discursively, socially, and politically." In the second half of the chapter, Kolko provides a practical series of online assignments designed to help turn the writing classroom into a site of cultural inquiry by stimulating "recursive and rigorous thinking and writing."

Condon's "Virtual Space, Real Participation" offers a vision of what such careful planning can bring about. Drawing on his experiences as a teacher in a three-institution introductory writing course, Condon argues that virtual classrooms can be "far less intimidating and far more accessible than most people believe." Condon's redefinition of classroom space invites exploration of the ways in which written texts create a discursive world for new college students, requiring teachers to reconfigure what and how they teach. Students become their writing in Condon's virtual classroom, and this experience offers them a rich and invigorating introduction to the world of college writing. Condon challenges teachers to reconceive the kinds of assignments they use as well as the assessment strategies they use in order to make students the center of their teaching lives.

In "Teach Us How To Play: The Role of Play in Technology Education," Matthews-DeNatale revisits a concept that we have all, at one time or another, associated with computers and networks: the concept of play. Associated with video arcades or young adolescents glued for hours at a time to stand-alone or interactive computer games, play is often thought of as counterproductive to education, which should be a kind of work. However, as educational theorists from Piaget to Papert have noticed, play can be very educational, and the computer can be a compelling medium for play. Central to Matthews-DeNatale's chapter is the notion that play can be engaging and motivating for students in online writing classes, and can help to make both machines and classmates more familiar and easier with which to interact. Play can make the difference between a bored class, with little willingness to write, and a class in which the fun leads to greater class community, more writing, and increased consciousness of the meaningful contexts for communication. In the last part of her chapter, Matthews-DeNatale offers a great example of what she means by play with her description of her class activity "Cyber-Rescue," a Web-based adventure game. Through the participatory role-playing drama of Cyber-Rescue and the reflective writing assignments that followed it, Matthews-DeNatale's students learned how to search out, make use of, and communicate information, how to interact through and with computers, and how to be comfortable with not knowing—with not having a "right answer."

In "Indiscipline: Obscenity and Vandalism in Cyberclassrooms," Cogdill deals with a teacher's worst fears: How to handle the situation when students in online writing classes, for unfathomable reasons, become hostile, counterproductive, offensive, and even abusive. If they act out, become offensive, or make threatening statements to their classmates, teachers, or even outsiders, how is the decision made as to what must be dealt with as harmful and counterproductive, and what can be ignored as a by-product of constructive discussion and inquiry? What obligations do teachers have to protect students and colleagues, and even the perpetrators? What can or should teachers say or do to the class and the offenders? How do teachers prevent their colleagues and administrators from blaming computers and the Internet (and the teachers who would use them in writing classes) instead of the student offenders themselves? In discussing these complicated questions, Cogdill offers writing teachers some concrete principles both for understanding the problems and their origins, and for dealing with these problems effectively.

Krause demonstrates several practical applications for the World Wide Web in the writing classroom, in his aptly titled chapter "'Why Should I Use the Web?' Four Drawbacks and Four Benefits to Using the World Wide Web as a Pedagogical Tool for Writing Classes." The Web is a relatively recent phenomenon, but it has rapidly become the most popular online tool for communication and dissemination. Krause argues that the Web is an effective teaching tool, not only for disseminating class materials, but for research, and for student collaboration and publication. The most up-to-date teachers are creating Web pages for their classes, with class materials and links to a wealth of outside resources available at a mouse click. With proper introduction to the Web and effective training in navigating and evaluating webbed sources, students can use evidence from the Web for their projects in writing classes. Similarly, with proper training in HTML and hypertext design, students can use the Web to share their work with outside audiences, and to receive feedback on that work. However, Krause shows several ways in which using the Web can be a setback. Not only is searching the Web often frustrating and time-consuming, the information gleaned is often low quality, unsubstantiated, partial, and biased. Furthermore, students and teachers alike face a steep learning curve with regard to search strategies and the skills needed to create good Web pages. Finally, not everyone has access, especially regular access, to the more modern high-powered computers that can access the Web and provide the most user-friendly web-composition tools. Keeping these benefits and drawbacks in mind, Krause recommends that teachers proceed with caution in using the Web in their writing classes.

Together, these five chapters offer both theoretical grounding for and practical approaches to the online writing classroom. Hopefully, the ideas and examples they provide will inspire readers to strike out on their own, to create new innovative approaches to online pedagogy.

Chapter • I

Hooked on 'Tronics, or Creating a Happy Union of Computers and Pedagogies

Barbara Stedman

Many teachers who have adopted the use of computer technology in the English classroom sometimes fall into an automatic assumption that computer technology can enhance students' learning in nearly any situation. My experience has proven the pitfalls of such an assumption. I have learned, through trial and error, that I must consciously create and have students engage in computer-based activities that are compatible with my pedagogical goals.

Early in the fall of 1985, Marion College, where I was teaching, acquired its first writing center computer lab: 21 Apple II-e and four Apple Plus terminals. With two 5-1/4" disks in hand (one of them my word processing program, AppleWriter), I made my first foray into word processing. And the writing process, especially revision, seemed easier than I had ever thought possible.

My writing habits changed in those weekend hours spent in the computer lab, and I knew that word processing would change my students' habits, too. I took my composition and journalism classes into the lab, gave them a few simple instructions for formatting, saving, and printing, and did, in fact, see word processing change the way many students wrote, particularly writing majors who had known the drudgery of retyping draft after draft.

Several years later, when I began teaching at Ball State University, the English Department there acquired its first networked computer lab: 25 Zenith 286s, running Novell software in a LAN configuration. The lab came equipped with the Daedalus Instructional System, a program that included not just word processing, but invention heuristics, a bulletin board, synchronous conferencing (InterChange), and other tools for the writing classroom.[1]

With the same enthusiasm that I had brought to word processing, I took my freshman composition classes into "LAN-land" and found that not only did synchronous electronic discussions place the responsibility for learning firmly on students' shoulders by allowing them to educate one another, but they also enabled my quieter students to finally have a voice in the class discussion. The computer seemed to have unlimited potential in my classroom. I was ready to move beyond the LAN.

That opportunity came when Becky Rickly, a colleague with whom I taught basic writing classes on a collaborative basis, proposed that we have our students explore virtual community formation on Internet Relay Chat (IRC).[2] She had found IRC to be a valuable means of community formation, as she and other "techno-rhetoricians" discussed professional concerns each Monday evening. And, like her, I shared the belief that writing itself is, on at least one level, a social act and that students are members of the community of academic discourse. This assignment, we hoped, would make them more aware of the workings of communities formed through words on a computer screen alone. With Becky's encouragement, I began to explore channels that related to my own interests, and Becky began introducing her students to IRC during the first semester of this two-semester basic writing program, just to familiarize them with the medium. Together we worked to create a project that required our four classes of basic writers (two classes each) to engage their skills in observation, critical thinking, and analysis. What we came up with was a type of participant-observation project that asked students to explore at least five IRC channels, paying particular attention to the ways in which communities were or were not formed.

The results of this computer-intensive assignment were primarily positive, although I found myself at times wondering if the technology was not overshadowing my ultimate purpose of helping the students become better writers. I found myself spending an inordinate amount of time and energy coaching and reassuring students who could not type the correct command to gain IRC access, or who were unable to find a server

---

[1]The Daedalus Instructional System has since been renamed the Daedalus Integrated Writing Environment.

[2]IRC consists of hundreds of "channels" where users may come to chat about the topic indicated by the channel operator (e.g., #christian, #singapore, #motocross). In essence, each channel becomes an interactive electronic community where participants can carry on a synchronous discussion (or discussions), the content of which is solely determined by the users and the channel operator.

that would let them in to IRC, or found themselves repeatedly being "burped" off the system. Still, the final products—students' essays—soothed my fears adequately, demonstrating that students were, in fact, exploring important ideas of community and communication through IRC activities. Many came to the realization, for instance, that jargon and shared information are instrumental in creating community boundaries (which not only hold members in but also serve to keep nonmembers out).

Encouraged by the results of our IRC assignment, I forged ahead with our collaboration the following year, bringing yet another Internet-based activity into our basic writing classrooms. We established writing consultant trios, joining a basic writing student from each of our classes with one high school student from Mike Benedict's advanced placement class at Fox Chapel Area High School in Pittsburgh. Students shared limited personal introductions with their writing consultants, yet the lack of face-to-face contact lent a feel of anonymity to their communication. Our minimal guidelines to the students began with this instruction: "Communicate with your Pittsburgh student (or, conversely, your Ball State student) at least once a week, via e-mail, to discuss your current writing assignment—ideas, problems, questions, and so forth." Because our student writers were already learning the value of oral and electronic feedback from their classmates via InterChange and e-mail, we assumed they would do the same just as easily by "talking" to these long-distance sounding boards. We also expected that the relative anonymity of this communication would free them up even more to give honest feedback.

We were wrong.

The hints of technophobia that had come out in the IRC assignment were magnified a hundred-fold. Students did not have to enter a long alphanumeric command one time only, as they did with IRC; here they had to enter the long Internet address every time they communicated with their Pittsburgh partners, and they had to remember to send a copy of the message to themselves each time, too. For these students, at least, that attention to seemingly picayune detail was a major hurdle.

More important, however, was the obvious fact that students did not feel motivated to learn and follow through with the project requirements. We continually had to remind them, urge them, coax them to communicate with their Pittsburgh partners each week. Many suffered from "amnesia," needing frequent one-on-one reteaching of the basics for sending Internet mail (despite the fact that all possessed what Becky and I considered a very simple self-paced handout). The messages that did get sent often consisted of little more than a line or two (e.g., "Sorry I haven't written, but I've been busy. I'll try to write next week"), or contained the latest news about a girlfriend or boyfriend, rather than the essay assignment at hand.

Many of them let us know, repeatedly, that they saw no reason for carrying on this communication. It wasn't "graded," per se, nor was it an official part of their semester-end portfolio; therefore it did not seem worth their time and energy. And because the project extended throughout an entire semester—unlike the IRC project, which forced students to solve problems and find help in a limited time frame—they seemed slow to address, and "solve," their difficulties with the medium and given discourse context. In short, students were frustrated, as was I.[3]

At the beginning of the new semester, as Becky, Mike, and I reassessed the project, we tried to provide greater structure by creating similar assignments and more meaningful tasks for each week's communiqué. In one assignment, for instance, we asked both of our classes to examine the same poem and carry out a character analysis; this tighter structure did provide somewhat more satisfying results. We tried being more insistent in our reminders—but verged on nagging. We tried spreading our enthusiasm for the medium (something that Becky was able to do better than I was at this point) by reassuring them that communication with their writing consultant could be valuable and fun—but found our contagion limited. Students complained of communication that seemed empty because it was forced. They complained about the lack of response from their partners; or when response to an idea or draft did come, it was often outdated and thus of little use.

Eventually, despite our best efforts, I concluded that the majority of students were not profiting from electronic communication. And the question that students asked most often was the question I was asking myself: Why are we doing this? What's the point? How will these student writers profit by communicating on the Internet?

My answers, like the project itself, fizzled out. Instead, the problem that I had begun to sense during the IRC project was now ablaze: An enormous amount of computer lab time was spent telling students for the

---

[3]At this point, Becky was frustrated, too, although not nearly to the degree that I was. As we discussed our different levels of frustration, I learned another important lesson about designing computer-assisted writing assignments: The instructor must be fully committed to the project. At the time our writing consultant project began, Becky (like Mike) had long been a member of professional communities created through IRC and other Internet "chats" devoted to computer-mediated communication (CMC) concerns. Her membership in these computers-and-composition communities had thus brought her personal satisfaction and scholarly growth. I, on the other hand, was open to the prospect of developing such avenues of communication, but had not experienced the rewards firsthand. When "storms" arose in our writing consultant communication, I didn't possess the same broad context that Becky did in order to patiently ride the waves of frustration. Soon I realized that such a project required a level of personal confidence and commitment that I had not brought to it, and therefore could not pass on to the students either.

umpteenth time how to send a message or how to recover and resend a message that had not been successfully sent the first time. Like many other writing teachers, I found that energy and time that could and should have been spent developing students' writing skills were spent on minuscule logistics of Internet mailing. Ultimately, I realized that the old saw—"Why climb a mountain? Because it's there"—does not translate into "Why use a computer lab? Because it's there."

What had happened in my evolution as a computer user and composition and literature instructor was, in Hawisher and Selfe's (1991) words, an "uncritical enthusiasm" for the medium—a failure to develop carefully a pedagogy for this clumsy marriage of computers and classrooms. Instead, I had operated with the philosophy that "computers are good for me; surely they'll be good for my students." My hazily sketched-out CMC-based learning goals were soon outweighed by my increasing sense that I was trying too hard to justify my employment of computers. As the technology and the writing projects increased in their complexity, my lack of a clear pedagogy for computer-based instruction became an unavoidable reality.

Rather than scrapping everything that I knew to be good about the use of networked computers in the classroom—both through LANs and the Internet—I returned to the basics of what I consider my pedagogy for composition in general. That is, I embrace a pedagogy of eclecticism, which combines different teaching styles and learning environments, including technology, in recognition that different students learn and write in different ways. Although I do not attempt to learn what students' specific learning styles may be by administering, as many teachers do, the Meyers Briggs Type Indicator (MBTI), I do heed Jensen and DiTiberio's (1989) fundamental message of the MBTI for writing teachers: We need to offer a variety of learning contexts as we take students through the writing process. Some students need solitude; others need sounding boards from start to finish. Some need to free write in the process of generating ideas, then find shape and order later; others need a sense of tentative structure from the start. And so on. In the "regular" classroom, I had provided a mix of activities that recognizes diversity of learning styles, and I had, in fact, first integrated computer lab time to further account for such diversity. But somewhere along the way I had allowed computer time to limit that diversity, rather than capitalize on it.

Perhaps most important in deciding how to effectively utilize computer technology in my teaching was a reminder to myself that I believe in what Hillocks (1986) called an "environmental mode" of writing instruction, one that uses "materials and problems selected to engage students with each other in specifiable processes" that are relevant to "clear and specific objectives" (pp. 122-123). The writing consultant project was doomed for failure from the start because I imbued it with neither "specifiable processes" nor relevance to "clear and specific objectives." I had simply thrown my students into the electronic mix, and hoped they would come out swimming.

Later, however, as I refashioned my composition pedagogy, I returned to several pieces of scholarship that had originally inspired me to use the computer in the classroom as more than a glorified typewriter. Most important were two edited collections—Hawisher and Selfe's (1989) *Critical Perspectives on Computers and Composition,* and Handa's (1990) *Computers and Community: Teaching Composition in the Twenty-First Century*—and Eldred's (1991) article "Pedagogy in the Computer-Networked Classroom." Together, these texts reminded me that each computer-based activity needed to have a direct correlation to the learning I hoped to see accomplished.[4]

Today, several semesters wiser, I am still using the networked computer in my classroom, but with an actual pedagogy at work—one with identifiable learning goals that can be best met through the computer, not one that (as with some earlier disasters) tried to force my "square-peg" students into "round-hole" computer activities. I have continued to rely on synchronous conferencing activities in various English classes, because they meet my specific learning objectives. For instance, when I want students to brainstorm for essay topics and collectively sift their "chaff" from their "grain," I employ synchronous conferencing (InterChange) in order to achieve these specific goals:

1. Presentation of every student's ideas to an audience of 18 to 24 peers.

For example, as a first step to writing a letter to the editor of the campus newspaper, each student is asked to send a message on InterChange that briefly describes three possible topics to argue, and how he or she would support each argument.

2. Immediate response to those ideas.

After posting their own possible topics, students are then asked to give feedback to at least three other students, commenting on the potential strengths and weaknesses of each letter's argument.

---

[4]The Web site http://www.louisville.edu/groups/english-www/cai/bibliography. html offers a helpful online bibliography that includes these as well as more recent publications on the subject of computers and pedagogy.

3. Safety in the relative distance afforded by the medium.

While presenting ideas, and receiving feedback, about potentially controversial topics may be intimidating to some students in a face-to-face classroom setting, responding to ideas on a screen may relieve some of their anxiety and apprehension.

The LAN is equally valuable as a medium for students to provide feedback on essay drafts, for similar reasons, but again the instructor needs to design particular tasks that will achieve particular goals.

On the other hand, however, I have finally admitted that not all groups of students derive equal benefit from synchronous conferencing. Some groups, for example, depending on the particular mix of personalities, may be highly verbal, and the artificiality of conversing through a network server only impedes their exchange of ideas. Therefore, I now ask students to decide for themselves how much they want to participate in electronic discussion. After the first two or three conversations via the computer, I let students vote where they would like to be during their weekly lab day: in the computer lab, as scheduled, or in the regular classroom. I honor the majority, but give proportionate time to the minority vote as well, perhaps by scheduling our class in the computer lab but allowing students to push their keyboards aside and work alone or in a small face-to-face group. And although I have retained certain networked activities in modified form, I have eliminated others altogether. Internet writing consultants, for instance, are no longer a part of my basic writing classroom, because my specific objectives can usually be better met in face-to-face interaction. However, this is not to say that I would rule out integrating a similar arrangement in an upper level writing classroom, or for groups of motivated basic writers. The more mature learning styles of advanced students, and their typical willingness to take responsibility for their own education, would, I suspect, make the writing consultant assignment, via the Internet, a useful resource for them.

At the same time, I have tapped into other Internet capabilities that fit with my learning goals. In a cultural studies course, for instance, one of my primary goals is to engage students in cross-cultural communication that is both interactive and immediate. I, therefore, require students to spend an allotted amount of time on the Internet during the course of the semester, but give them total freedom in deciding which part or function of the Internet they find most valuable. They have these four options:

1. Mailing lists that deal with cross-cultural issues. On a staggered schedule throughout the semester, each student subscribes to two lists (EWD-L and XCULT-L) for a minimum of 4 weeks, then regularly receives, in his or her mail account, messages that are posted to the lists by their subscribers.

2. Usenet newsgroups. Specifically, I give students direct access to a selected list of approximately 100 newsgroups that deal with non-Western cultures.
3. Gopher. Students learn how to access gopher sites relevant to world news and cultures, including the CIA World Fact Book, which gives them easy access to demographics and other such information about nearly every nation.
4. The World Wide Web. Using Yahoo and various other search engines, students learn how to access information regarding world cultures.[5]

Rather than asking students to "surf the Net," just because it's there, I consider the Internet capabilities a means of extending my classroom to include the entire world—which is precisely where I aim to take these students in the course of each semester. The Internet becomes a place to gain information (primarily through Gopher and the Web), as well as a place to ask questions and enter the marketplace of idea exchange (primarily through Usenet and the two mailing lists, to which students are required to post two questions or comments by the end of the semester, with the goal of actively engaging them in cross-cultural discussion). Students know exactly what is required of them, and how Internet activity will enhance their understanding of cross-cultural issues.

Such clear and specific objectives for Internet use have come into view in my writing classes as well. The Web, for instance, has become a tremendous research tool for my students. Cathy, a pre-med major, wanted to write a research paper on adrenoleukodystrophy (ALD), a disease of the immune system made famous in the film *Lorenzo's Oil*. Despite such fame, however, the disease is still relatively rare, and therefore little discussed in the library research this student had turned up. When she searched for relevant information on the Web, however, she found extensive information posted by Dr. Axel Wrede, one of the leading ALD researchers in the world. Not only did Cathy get firsthand accounts from Wrede, but she also obtained his phone number in Germany and his e-mail address from one of his research reports that had been published on the Web. Rather than reading about the authority, she went directly to him and asked the questions that were important to her research.

Thanks to the kind of excitement experienced by students like Cathy, I am no less hooked on electronic communication than I was when

---

[5]By the time this book has reached publication, a homepage devoted to cross-cultural issues, now under construction, will have eliminated the need for students to access Usenet and Gopher. The homepage will provide one site of entry for all the Internet resources I ask my students to explore. See Krause (chap. 6, this volume) for information on using the Web as a pedagogical tool.

computers first entered my world. But no longer do I assume that because I find LAN and Internet activities fascinating and profitable, students will too; instead, I consciously create and apply computer-based activities that are compatible with my pedagogical goals and are appropriate for both the course and the students.

Those who hope to avoid my mistakes might profit from these suggestions:

- Believe in the value of your CMC assignment before you ask students to carry it out.
- Know your medium and your software, rather than trying to learn it along with your students.
- If you don't have firsthand knowledge of the kind of learning you expect your students to do (as I did not have with electronic community building), draw on other instructors' experiences. Teacher-training workshops and forums for sharing information can be an excellent means of finding out what does and does not work, given your institution's particular equipment and resources.
- Gauge the activity and technological demands to suit the level of learners. Consider degrees of independence, self-motivation, and willingness to take responsibility for their own education.
- Give students precise directions not just for the logistics of maneuvering around a LAN or the Internet, but for the kinds of questions and observations they should be making about the subject matter or context at hand. For instance, in the IRC project, Becky and I asked students to pay special attention to seven specific aspects of community formation on IRC channels (e.g., the way that newcomers are received in a particular discussion). Such specificity is especially crucial at the beginning of the semester, when students are still feeling their way through a new medium.
- Be patient, both with yourself and with your students, when introducing a networked activity into your classroom. No matter how well you plan, things will not always go as planned, and you need to be willing to change directions midstream. Have a "Plan B" ready when the network server suddenly fails.
- Solicit students' advice for improvement, and feedback on the degree to which they find networked activities profitable.
- As much as your course schedule and the physical layout of your computer classroom allow, try to plan different kinds of

activities for different kinds of students. If some students prefer working alone or in small face-to-face groups, try to provide an area where they can do so.
- Finally, in the worst case scenario, do not be afraid to bail
out when necessary. If things are not working, and clearly no
degree of "adjustment" will make them work, your students
are the ones who will be most harmed by your doggedly pursuing an unprofitable path.

Above all else, the best advice I can give is this: Know your pedagogy, find those points where pedagogy and technology genuinely meet,
and develop highly specific goals, tasks, and instructions that facilitate
such a union. With care, the love affair with networked computers can be
turned into a productive, and eventually indispensable, avenue of communication for your students.

REFERENCES

Eldred, J. M. (1991). Pedagogy in the computer-networked classroom.
Computers and Composition, 8(2), 47-61.
Handa, C. (Ed.). (1990). *Computers and community: Teaching composi-
tion in the twenty-first century.* Portsmouth, NH: Boynton/Cook.
Hawisher, G. E., & Selfe, C. L. (Eds.). (1989). *Critical perspectives on
computers and composition.* New York: Teacher's College Press.
Hawisher, G. E., & Selfe, C. L. (1991). The rhetoric of technology and the
electronic writing class. *College Composition and Communication,
42,* 55-65.
Hillocks, G. (1986). *Research on written composition: New directions for
teaching.* Urbana, IL: NCTE.
Jensen, G. H., & DiTiberio, J. K. (1989). *Personality and the teaching of
composition.* Norwood, NJ: Ablex.

Chapter • 2

Cultural Studies In/And the Networked Writing Classroom

Beth E. Kolko

Cultural studies is one of those labels that evokes both enthusiasm and loathing. For some, cultural studies has transformed the landscape of disciplines and classrooms, opening up heretofore unexplored terrain and possibility, calling to audiences previously ignored or bypassed. And, for others, cultural studies is a marker of, if not sloppy thinking, then the onslaught of the persistently trendy in academia. The goal of this chapter is to show how cultural studies theory, in conjunction with networked computer pedagogy, can sharpen the focus of the writing classroom and draw students into a relevant and nuanced writing community.

Compositionists have been at times almost anxious to claim cultural studies as a transformer of and, in some respects, a savior for tired pedagogy. All too often, the adoption of cultural studies in writing courses has translated into using popular culture readings, incorporating reception studies into assignments, or similarly piecemeal classroom strategies. These tactics ignore the theoretical complexity and power of cultural studies, and thus prevent substantial transformation of classroom practice. What follows here is an explication of cultural studies-informed pedagogy in a networked computer classroom that attempts to incorporate the richness of production as well as reception studies that form the basis for cultural studies inquiry. In particular, I show how the focus of cultural studies on production dovetails with social constructionist composition theory and, consequently, how each can be used to mutually strengthen the pedagogical possibility of the other. The site for this exploration is the networked classroom, precisely because communication technologies facilitate the kinds of community building that are central to the blending of cultural studies and social constructionism. In particular, a computer classroom allows sustained peer-to-peer conversation and simultaneous conversations. Researchers have documented how computer classrooms allow students increased participation, and although this effect is far from uniform, it does affect the tenor of the classroom (Bump, 1990; Cooper & Selfe, 1990; Slatin 1992).

The series of assignments presented in this chapter was developed for a networked writing class that is based on the principles of social constructionist and cultural studies theory; these assignments aim to turn the classroom into a site of cultural inquiry, involving students in a process of recursive and rigorous thinking and writing. Ultimately, the assignments that are presented focus on a series of linked activities that restructure students' relationship to their prose and to one another, instructing them in reading texts, seeing themselves as an interpretive (reception) community, and also, finally (or perhaps primarily), as producers of cultural artifacts.

How we envision the classroom matters to our practice. The pedagogical architecture of the classroom affects what develops within the space. One of the central claims made regarding networked computer classrooms is that they restructure students' relationships to each other and to the instructor. However, as Jessup (1991) illustrated in "Feminism and Computers in Composition Instruction," teachers in networked classrooms face strong temptations to recreate old pedagogical models with computer technology. Takayoshi (1994) cited Ohman and Janangelo making similar arguments, and she emphasized the need for feminists to examine how computer-mediated communication (CMC) can further marginalize women in the classroom. Meanwhile, Jessup urged teachers to consider the technology, the students, and their own pedagogical practice if any substantial refashioning of classroom practice is to occur. Indeed, changing the pedagogical shape within a networked classroom requires a singularity of vision. In many ways, the challenges facing teachers who venture into networked classrooms are similar to those that confront instructors who wish to move their courses into a cultural studies framework. That is, even with utopian promises by now muted, each transition appears at first rather seductive, and the possibility of concrete transformation is a powerful draw. However, both shifts—adopting a cultural studies-based pedagogy and moving to a networked classroom—require structural and theoretical changes in one's pedagogical stance. Jessup's by now several-years-old-warning remains a reminder that neither Macintoshes nor television in the classroom guarantee substantive change in the educational enterprise.

The changes that are possible, however, are significant. Much remains of the networked classroom's initial promise to upend hierarchies and reposition teachers and learners. The technological picture is still a compelling one, if slightly more sophisticated. Joyce (1995) argued that his goal is "to suggest that the challenge of hypertext to traditional structures can take on commonplace dimensions and that disenfranchised students, like expert learners, can use such tools to empower themselves in transforming knowledge to their own ends" (p. 50). Although Joyce focused on one component of the kinds of discourse allowed by computer-based teaching, his claim echoes many of those put forth by teachers of electronic discourse during the last decade. This continuity, I argue, indicates the extent to which CMC, appropriately or not, retains a hold on our field's collective pedagogical imagination. The assignments introduced in this chapter tap into that continuity, and they function as a component of the ongoing conversation regarding how the non-utopian setting of a networked classroom can substantially transform the educational experience of students. The empowering that Joyce referred to is an element of the process, but the assignments discussed later also push students to a version of critical awareness that dovetails with the theoretical goals of cultural studies. Joyce, like many of those publishing in the field of computers and writing, seizes on the seductiveness of CMC and demonstrates the ways in which technologies transform communicative acts. The nature of that transformation is not completely understood, however, and this is precisely where cultural studies provides an effective framework for understanding some of the changes that CMC brings to the classroom.

Sirc and Reynolds (1990) put forward an argument impressive in its directness. "If one accepts current theories of the social construction of meaning," they argued, "then one has to believe that a LAN will allow students a broader, richer, more pluralistic view of writing, and that it will help them to conceive of writing as a collective activity. If the network has an interactive dialogue function, the rationale is even more compelling" (p. 53). While Sirc and Reynolds subsequently critiqued these very assumptions in their conclusion, as they discussed the "repositioning" required by social constructionist theory, they focused on the way their basic writers used LAN-based technology to change the focus of the "act" in which they were engaged. Interestingly, they used cultural studies theorist Hebdige (1979) as a way of understanding their students' activity as subcultural, resistant, marginal, and part of what I would characterize as an attempt to read networked classrooms within the framework of cultural studies work. One might also argue that cultural studies, in this version of LAN-based pedagogy, focuses on tangible and substantial changes in the theoretical underpinnings of the classroom, rather than allowing a kind of facile optimism to gain purchase. As Sirc and Reynolds combined social constructionist theory with cultural studies, they illuminated how cultural studies most effectively informs writing pedagogy. That is, one of cultural studies' central concerns is the question of subjectivity and the ways individuals construct themselves within, and are constructed by, the wider world. It is through production that composition approaches this question, and production is an integral part of cultural studies methodology.

Faigley (1992) effectively mapped out how questioning the notion of a coherent self is a cornerstone of social constructionist composition theory; it is this same question that forms the basis of much cultural studies inquiry. Indeed, the shared concern of the construction of selves, of subjects, of agents links both composition and cultural studies in an additional concern with the political sphere. In fact, I argue that the primary connection between cultural studies and composition is that both consider the act of production as a site where individuals actively engage language in order to carve out a place for themselves within the world; text production, then, becomes charged with the promise of political efficacy as the act of a subject, in Smith's (1988) schema, working increasingly at determining itself, rather than being determined. This very connection between production and agency has led CMC-related scholarship to focus on by-now-qualified claims regarding technology and student selves. Sirc and Reynolds (1990) combined social constructionism with cultural studies precisely in order to discuss how the self-subject productively fragments in CMC. The assignments I discuss later are designed to allow students to engage in a questioning of the self and a form of cultural critique that branches out from an initial examination of the self in relation to society—a kind of response to inevitable fragmentation. The assignments use the capabilities of CMC to facilitate larger pedagogical goals predicated on exposing the process of constructing (or attempting to construct) coherent selves.

Teachers' and researchers' discussion of CMC within the writing classroom quickly reveals a central vocabulary. The dispersed subject, the displaced body, the liberated voice, the awareness of multiple positions on a topic, within a conversation, the realization of classroom discourse as public discourse, of the classroom space as public space: these concepts are all central to the shape of the field (Daisley, 1994; Faigley, 1992; Landow, 1992; Madden, 1993; Miall, 1990; Romano, 1993; Slatin, 1992; Taylor 1992). I would like to claim that the argument regarding CMC in the writing classroom resonates with the argument about cultural studies in the writing classroom. I should add, here, that I am not referring to the perspective that equates cultural studies with popular culture. Rather, I focus on the versions of cultural studies that place considerations of subjectivity and political action at the center of inquiry. In other words, the goals of CMC that are articulated in current scholarship resonate with the goals of cultural studies. Furthermore, a social constructionist classroom is predicated on the kinds of inquiry focused on by cultural studies theorists.

CMC shares substantive epistemological background with cultural studies, and it can be envisioned in such a way as to encapsulate the claims of social constructionism in general, and cultural studies in particular.

Cultural studies is about the interrogation of culture. It is not, in Grossberg's (1995) words, simply about the popular, nor is it simply about politically charged projects. Rather, cultural studies is about a particular interrogation of the subject in relation to the larger culture, and it is about questions that take issue with the ways in which the society constructs individuals. In many ways, cultural studies is about the tension between the determined subject and the determining individual—the agent. Social constructionism is predicated on a belief in epistemic rhetoric; a belief that knowledge is constructed rather than delivered lays at the root of social constructionist pedagogy. Social constructionism positions students as readers and writers in dialogue with the world surrounding them. Thus, a social constructionist classroom necessarily incorporates the goals of cultural studies. The kinds of classroom practice, the assignments, and the larger vision of the classroom from the perspective of a social constructionist teacher dovetails with the perspective of cultural studies theorists. One might make the claim, then, that social constructionist writing teachers are those best poised to instantiate a cultural studies pedagogy. If we add CMC to this equation, we would find that social constructionist composition teachers in a networked classroom are those instructors who are most versed in developing cultural studies-based curricula. The irony here, of course, is that although social constructionist writing teachers labor under the marginalized conditions of writing programs, they are, in fact, performing the activity of English departments that currently holds the greatest cachet.

Given, then, that CMC in the writing classroom is used to accomplish the same goals as cultural studies in both its theoretical and pedagogical formulations, it is worth taking the time to examine some assignments that utilize a cultural studies theoretical positioning, and that also ascribe to the formulations of social constructionist composition pedagogy. Essentially, what I argue here is that a perspective on CMC that comes out of a social constructionist composition perspective is the same as a cultural studies-informed pedagogy, and that together they can be combined to form a compelling pedagogical restructuring. Clearly, both cultural studies-based pedagogy and social constructionism can be effected without the use of computer technology. However, the goals of each are similarly met by specific uses of computer technology within classroom settings.

I delineate those goals at this point and show the specific ways in which I think cultural studies and networked pedagogy overlap. That is, I argue for networked pedagogy as a subset of social constructionist composition theory. I realize that there is more to composition than social constructionism, and that there is more to networked pedagogy than the version that emphasizes synchronous conversation software, the focus of this chapter. However, this narrowed conversation has the advantage of sharply focusing on two component elements that might help avoid some of the dangers Takayoshi (1994) and Jessup (1991) associated with the networked classroom.

The series of assignments on which I base the discussion in this chapter evolved over several years of teaching a variety of writing classes. I offer the assignments as guidelines rather than recommendations; they illustrate what kinds of work can be done with a progression of assignments that build on one another and are woven into not just the fabric of the syllabus, but into the contours of the classroom environment as well. I explain a step-by-step series of assignments that, I believe, can accomplish a number of tangible and intangible goals in the writing classroom. The tangible goals include making the classroom space one of public discourse; instructing students to see their peers' words are worthy of weight and citation; providing evidence that their words, rather than being disposable, will be used recursively as the semester proceeds; allowing them to collaborate not on a particular formal, graded document, but, rather, in the intellectual process of brainstorming, refining, and challenging arguments; and providing them with opportunities to examine their concepts of their selves in relation to the larger culture. The intangibles are more difficult to enumerate. Namely, this series of assignments establishes the classroom as a site of cultural production. In so doing, it sets the basis for a pedagogy that sees students as creators of culture and meaning. Such a pedagogy also seeks to establish the ever problematic notion of community. And, finally, it brings cultural studies into a writing classroom in such a way that defies hierarchizing English studies and, rather, shows how social constructionist composition pedagogy in many ways anticipated the articulated goals of cultural studies. Conceptualizing the classroom as public space, composition theorists in many ways corroborate Benhabib's (1992) breakdown of private-public boundaries, and allow a consideration of the political embedded in the act of writing. Compositionists have refined a variety of instructional techniques that seek to create a public forum within classroom space. The voices of Harris (1989, 1992), Trimbur (1989), and Brodkey (1987, 1989) join with Faigley (1992) in asserting such a function for the writing classroom. Additionally, contemporary writing pedagogy incorporates collaborative and group-based work in an attempt to fashion student voices as expert voices, providing another facet to the classroom as site of public discourse. Peer critiquing is perhaps an activity that most obviously represents practitioners contributing to the conversation of experts within the writing classroom. When students read and comment on their classmates' drafts, they are providing another perspective on what constitutes effective writing for a particular assignment. In some sense, it is a redistribution of influence that provides the student voice a space from which to speak. Students' voices being heard through the form of peer critiques is a pedagogical move that stands to change the classroom in productive ways.

The work of Shaughnessy (1977) and Rose (1989) has addressed ways to position students in classrooms so that they have space from which to speak. Fox (1990) built on their work as he described a pedagogy that "see[s] students as people, with experiences, with backgrounds, with linguistic resources" (p. 20). Such a pedagogy posits students as agents, as participants in culture, as valuable contributors to the conversation. Fox described a course he taught as an attempt to "draw extensively on students' social knowledge, a usually untapped source of student knowledge" (p. 21). Brodkey (1987) emphasized the importance of the kind of moves Fox chronicled as she asserted the materiality of language and its concurrent power. She was eloquent in her characterization of writing as an act with material consequences, and she focused our attention on the need to make this explicit within our classrooms. Brodkey wrote the following:

> Writing is something people do with language. At the very least, what one wants to know about writing is who writes what to whom, under what circumstances, and to what avail. These questions seem not only fundamental to an intellectual understanding of writing but the kinds of questions anyone who writes or teaches writing might ask. It is no easy matter to study the experience of writing, not least because most of our attention has been directed not to the act of writing (what people do as writers), but to written artifacts (what they produce as writers). Moreover, when writing processes have been studied, research has concentrated on specifying writers' cognitive processes while in the act of writing things down on paper. Yet the social circumstances under which people write would obviously influence how people conceptualize the act of writing as well as what gets written . . . writers are socially circumstanced. (pp. 82-83)

In its move to separate writing instruction from entrenched individualism and authentic voice, Brodkey's approach considers writing as a social act and allows us to transform our classrooms into sites of cultural inquiry. By examining the social forces that impinge on writers, we can conceptualize the classroom as a site of intervention. On the other hand, Cooper (1989) traced the same development and noted "a growing awareness that language and texts are not simply the means by which individuals discover and communicate information, but are essentially social activities, dependent on social structures and processes not only in their interpretive but also in their constructive phases" (pp. 4-5). Cooper, like the others, claimed that our conception of subjectivity influences curriculum. The public-private split, and the awareness that writing is a social activity, correlates with cultural studies' push to redefine boundaries of public and private. Cultural studies theorists like Garber and McRobbie (1976) illustrated how such a redefinition identifies a wider and more diverse range of activity that speaks to public discourse and political action. Rather than construct writing sites such as classrooms as boundaried spaces with few exchanges with the larger world, and inhabitants as unified (and apolitical) subjects, a formulation that explicitly links the classroom to the public sphere acknowledges the complexity of participants' identity, and in so doing is more able to view them as agents. The following assignments are influenced by these theorists and others who focus on writing sites generally, and networked writing classrooms particularly, as sites of active engagement with, and creation of, culture.

I present the series of steps included within the assignment, and then discuss the rationale for each component, and the results I have observed. The assignments themselves were developed based on research in the field and conversations with colleagues. Although the assignment was generated for English classes, the goals are applicable across disciplines. The central idea in the assignment concerns asserting a particular culture of teaching and learning within the class; this aspect is far more important than a specific disciplinary perspective.

I have used this assignment in two different institutions, and with a wide range of courses, including first-year writing courses, a Writing in the Disciplines-based course, an advanced first-year writing course, and an advanced topics-based writing course. I have found that this particular series, which I use beginning on the first day of the class, allows for the creation of a classroom culture that facilitates the goals of a social constructionist composition pedagogy and that meets the aims of cultural studies inquiry in the way it is predicated on students' questioning of their selves within and outside of the classroom environment.

THE ASSIGNMENT

On the first day of class, students log on to a synchronous conversation software program (such as the Daedalus Integrated Writing Environment's InterChange program or a MOO), and the entire class discusses a question along the lines of: "What is culture?" It is, of course, an unanswerable question, but students generally are able to talk around it for quite some time; several attempt definitions, and others speculate wildly.

When students return for the second class, I have transcripts of the previous day's conversation ready for them. A few minutes are spent reviewing the conversation; students then log back on and continue the conversation by choosing one comment from the transcript from which to begin talking. The class will generally gravitate toward a handful of comments to investigate further. At the end of class, students are given a transcript of the discussion to bring home and review. The homework assignment requires them to analyze the conversation further and come to class with a claim prepared regarding what culture is. Often they will be drawn to selected comments; during other semesters students have come in with an unfathomable variety of claims drawn from the session. The reactions of not unpleasant shock as they read while classmates cite their words are early indications of how this assignment can affect a class.

During the third class, the students address the claims, again via the synchronous conferencing software. Either a few students may be designated to offer their claims to the class, or everyone can contribute. Students may also be broken into smaller groups to focus on a particular claim. Clearly, there are different advantages to large versus small groups in this exercise. Depending on the focus of the course, slower moving chat and more studied comments might be the goal. Alternatively, if time allows flexibility and protracted brainstorming sessions before students revise into more polished prose, a few more large-group multithreaded exchanges can add to the textual record of the class.

In either a large or small group, choosing volunteers to coordinate discussion focuses the conversation further and pushes students to talk around the same ideas. By the fourth class they are into the rhythm of using the previous transcripts (i.e., theirs and other class members' comments) as the evidence with which they support or refute claims. Some threads will drop out, but others will form the basis around which the groups collaborate to build more complex arguments.

Eventually, students break into smaller groups online and have more focused conversations with four or five in each group. This allows students to focus more definitively on strengths and weaknesses of arguments in the transcripts they have helped create. By this time, as well, the class has begun to discuss elements and strategies of argumentation, and students use this material to critique the transcripts, and also to revise arguments presented in earlier online discussions.

The students' first paper assignment is in some way based on this series of assignments, and they use passages from the transcripts both as material from which to draw on for their papers, and as evidence with which to support or refute claims. The paper can be supplemented with outside research that supports or critiques classmates' discussion. Alternatively, if the online conversations have been substantive enough, students might use the transcripts alone as texts to analyze.

The series of class activities is designed to provide the students with an opportunity to engage in meaningful conversation with one another, to have different types of writing activities, and to see their contributions to the classroom community as something other than ephemeral and peripheral. Each of these goals dovetails with a major movement within social constructionist composition theory as articulated by Brodkey (1987), Faigley (1992), Harris (1989), and others. Each also correlates with conceptions of cultural studies held by a variety of scholars. The first day of the series, for example, is designed to give students an opportunity to interact with the technology of the classroom from the very beginning. It becomes important to integrate the technology into the pedagogy at this level in order for students to see the computers within the room as something that *facilitates* the learning process, rather than distracts or takes away from. The use-from-the first-day dictum reflects ways teachers have talked about the importance of making the first day student-centered if one desires a student-centered pedagogy for the semester. That is, compositionists have written of how important it is to begin the class in the direction one wishes to pursue; once students are directed down a particular path (i.e., listening to the teacher lecture), it becomes that much more difficult to shift focus and change direction on subsequent class days.

The introduction of the technology works within a cultural studies perspective in that it seeks to demystify the classroom and the machines that lie within. When cultural studies critics invoke Foucault, for example, in order to argue that there is no central power that remains any longer, they are making the claim that it is imperative that we not locate power within traditional centers of control. Whether power is reinforced structurally or personally (through an authoritarian teacher), the locus of power needs to be dispersed in order to provide the potential for political movement (Poster, 1990). What becomes crucial, then, is that introducing students to the technology at the beginning of the semester begins to develop a matrix of power that branches out more than in a traditional classroom. Instead of the teacher standing (or sitting) at the front of the room, the teachers' presence is mediated by computers, thus displacing the symbol of authority—although by no means effacing that symbol. Additionally, students have the opportunity to posit themselves as experts. Indeed, students increasingly come better prepared, and more acquainted with, technology than the roster of instructors that maintain so-called control over the classroom. Allowing students to lay claim to the machines on the first day of class, then, provides them with the possibility of claiming some expertise in the classroom.

The context of this assignment cannot be ignored, for the conditions surrounding students' labor in the classroom has significance. In addition to contextual issues, however, are the content ones, and the unanswerability of the question ("What is culture?") used in that first discussion is crucial. Although "What is culture?" may not be appropriate for all students, all classes, or all schools, it is the kind of question that produces the most effective variety of work. The desired result is a chaotic multithreaded conversation that serves as a brainstorming session. And even though this conversation occurs at the beginning of the semester, prior to any actual course instruction, the level of, for example, argumentation sophistication is less important than the generation of a variety of ideas, half formed though they may be.

When students return for the second class, it is imperative to have a transcript from that first session available to them. At times I have chosen to have the transcript online; when resources are available I prefer to have a hard copy of the transcript available for reading and notating. It is useful for students to continue writing in large groups for this class session. Although the discussion will almost inevitably spiral out of control and generate multiple threads that remain unexplored, the production of valuable raw material that the students will use at later points remains the important activity. Some students will fall behind in the discussion, and, indeed, as the teacher I found that I did as well. When 25 people are typing simultaneously on a topic as fluid as this, a great deal of text is produced. I suggest emphasizing to students that reading every comment made by classmates is not the goal of the assignment. Rather, encourage them to concentrate on specific comments that interest them. As they respond to specific comments, perhaps prefacing their remarks by invoking the name of the person to whom they are responding, a series of subconversations will emerge. Although this can also be accomplished by splitting the students into smaller groups in subconferences, one benefit of the more messy large group discussion is that students have more opportunity to see what others are saying, even if they do not have the time to engage with those comments.

As in previous classes, when this session is complete, students are given a copy of the transcript (depending on local constraints, copies of the transcript might have to be made available for students to pick up a few hours later). The homework assignment, to find a claim in the large transcript, seems relatively uncomplicated. And, indeed, it does not require students to do reading outside of the transcript. However, I would like to emphasize that this series of assignments is not one that will necessarily lead to tangible improvements in students' phraseology at this point; nor will it even necessarily lead to greater rhetorical awareness—at least not on its own. It will, however, establish from the beginning of the semester a version of classroom culture that resonates with the political and pedagogical goals of social constructionism. When the class returns for the next period, they will have examined the words of their peers in order to extract meaningful class discussion-sparking items. This is the beginning of a process that can shape the remainder of the semester. There are a variety of options at this point. Students can join a large group discussion where each types in the claim he or she extracted from the transcript and then a general discussion ensues; this model will produce yet another rapidly scrolling dense transcript. Depending on the shape of the class, this may be effective. If it does not seem particularly promising, another option is to designate a few students to type in their claims and have the class discuss those selected arguments. Alternatively, split the students into smaller groups, and each collection of four or five can discuss a smaller group of claims; this approach allows more focused discussion, however, it also narrows the kind of feedback generated. For example, if students remain in a large group but only three or four students put forth their claims, the class has the advantage of hearing a wider range of responses to these claims. Similarly, students then have the opportunity to show how their claim (as yet not presented to the class) correlates with those that were entered at the beginning. This affects students' investment level for the session, and, eventually, for the course as a whole. The most important aspect of the class at this point is that students see that their words are used as the basis for discussion, and that their ideas are not disposable. Instead, the teacher is very specifically according those ideas importance and dwelling on them through repeated class periods, lending them a certain weight and durability. This, I argue, is the beginning of transforming classroom culture, and it is the utility of this series of assignments.

As students propose their claims and argue with one another, discounting some ideas, encouraging others, developing, challenging, and refining, they become involved in a process that encourages them to occupy different roles in the classroom; simultaneously, the product of their conversations leads them to question their roles in another fashion. That is, by interrogating culture, students begin to articulate their sense of self, but they also challenge that sense of self as the classroom is destabilized and reformed according to the parameters of CMC and synchronous conversation. From the perspective of cultural studies, students have begun to see how their assumptions are shaped by others, and how they make choices to move among varying positions—their initial position on the first day, the claims they drew from the transcripts, the expanded arguments they made in tandem with classmates.

When students finally do break into smaller groups for sustained conversation regarding the claims generated and critiqued within previous class sessions, they are equipped to consider the words of their peers as worthy of weight and consideration. By this time, students have also learned that their contributions might very well appear in a classmates' work. Comments, then, tend to be more thoughtful and considered. It is important to make these small group sessions available, in transcript form, to all of the students. Those in one group can make use of the comments of another group, and it is possible that an intraclass thematic weaving can emerge.

The final component of the assignment series is integral to the progression. The focus of these assignments is the combination of exploratory, brainstorming activities, and the formal assignments that evolve from the materials. The presence of the formal assignments is a recognition of Fishman and McCarthy's (1995) assertion that classroom practice must culminate in a reasonable exigence for writing. Fishman and McCarthy's argument centers on the necessity of balancing internal motivation with external motivation. "[T]here are at least two ways I establish teacherly authority," Fishman wrote of his expressivist classroom. "There are . . . ways in which I contract to deliver certain grades to individual students for certain kinds of work. . . . But there are also . . . ways in which I motivate students to work, not for individual gain like grades, but for communal ends that benefit all members of the group" (p. 65). The small group work in this series of assignments is an example of that internal and external motivation. If students do not participate meaningfully in the subsequent conversations, they know that they will not have viable transcripts at the end of the sessions; it also eventually becomes clear that an impoverished small group transcript will impoverish the papers of each of the students. The formal essay, then, that is generated from this weekslong series of activities is the final internal motivation—the individual grade for which students are used to striving. The external motivations, however, the ability of class members to draw on a rich and insightful transcript for the paper itself, may be what is most new to students.

It may seem a leap from this point back to the theoretical discussions at the beginning of this chapter; the topic of subjectivity has faded into the background. However, the series of assignments described is an attempt to embody the theoretical discussions with which the chapter opened. During these class periods, students are pushed to reexamine their roles as learners in the classroom, but also as participants in the culture. They are posited as agents embedded in a web of relations, and their definitions of seemingly reified concepts are challenged. They use the synchronous conversation capabilities of technology to work through a fluidity of identity that is encouraged by the assignments, and they are given ways to see fragmentation as a workable position. Finally, as students move from intervening in the chaos of the first large discussion to situating themselves with respect to their classmates in order to make a sustained argument, they come to realize how their selves relate to those around them. The focus provided by cultural studies frames this class as an inquiry into the role of discourse in creating subjects, a construction that highlights the ways CMC strengthens the pedagogical goals of the social constructionist writing classroom. Ultimately, then, these assignments seek to position students as subjects who *act*—discursively, socially, and politically.

REFERENCES

Benhabib, S. (1992). *Situating the self: Gender, community and postmodernism in contemporary ethics.* New York: Routledge.

Brodkey, L. (1987). *Academic writing as social practice.* Philadelphia: Temple University Press.

Brodkey, L. (1989). On the subjects of class and gender in "the literacy letters." *College English, 5,* 125-141.

Bump, J. (1990). Radical changes in class discussion using networked computers. *Computers and the Humanities, 24,* 49-65.

Cooper, M. (1989). The ecology of writing. In M. Cooper & M. Holzman (Eds.), *Writing as aocial action.* Portsmouth, NH: Boynton/Cook.

Cooper, M., & Selfe, C. (1990). Computer conferences and learning: Authority, resistance, and internally persuasive discourse. *College English, 52,* 847-859.

Daisley, M. (1994). The game of literacy: The meaning of play in computer-mediated-communication. *Computers and Composition, 11,* 107-119.

Faigley, L. (1992). *Fragments of rationality: Postmodernity and the subject of composition.* Pittsburgh: University of Pittsburgh Press.

Fishman, S., & McCarthy, L. P. (1995). Community in the expressivist classroom. *College English, 57,* 62-81.

Fox, T. (1990). *The social uses of writing: Politics and pedagogy.* Norwood, NJ: Ablex.

Garber, J., & McRobbie, A. (1976). Girls and subcultures. In S. Hall & T. Jefferson (Eds.), *Resistance through rituals: Youth subcultures in post-war Britain* (pp. 209-222). London: Hutchinson

Grossberg, L. (1995). Cultural studies: What's in a name (one more time). *Taboo: The Journal of Culture and Education, 1,* 1-37.

Harris, J. (1989). The idea of community and the study of composition. *College Composition and Communication, 40,* 11-22.

Harris, J. (1992). The other reader. *Journal of Advanced Composition, 12*(1), 27-37.

Hebdige, D. (1979). *Subculture: The meaning of style.* New York: Methuen.

Jessup, E. (1991). Feminism and computers in composition instruction. In G. Hawisher & C. Y. Selfe (Eds.), *Evolving perspectives on computers and composition studies: Questions for the 1990s* (pp. 336-355). Urbana: NCTE.

Joyce, M. (1995). *Of two minds: Hypertext pedagogy and poetics.* Ann Arbor: University of Michigan Press.

Landow, G. (1992). *Hypertext: The convergence of contemporary critical theory and technology.* Baltimore: Johns Hopkins University Press.

Madden, E. (1993). Pseudonyms and interchange: The case of the disappearing body. *Wings, 1*(1), 4.

Miall, D. (1990). Rethinking English studies: The role of the computer. In D. Miall (Ed.), *Humanities and the computer: New directions* (pp. 49-59). Oxford: Clarendon.

Poster, M. (1990). *The mode of information: Poststructuralism and social context.* Chicago: University of Chicago Press.

Romano, S. (1993). The egalitarianism narrative: Whose story: Which yardstick? *Computers and Composition, 10,* 5-28.

Rose, M. (1989). *Lives on the boundary: A moving account of the struggles and achievements of America's educational underclass.* New York: Penguin.

Sirc, G., & Reynolds, T. (1990). The face of collaboration in the networked writing classroom. *Computers and Composition, 7,* 53-70.

Shaughnessy, M. (1977). *Errors and expectations: A guide for the teacher of basic writing.* New York: Oxford University Press.

Slatin, J. M. (1992). Is there a class in this text? Creating knowledge in the electronic classroom. In E. Barrett (Ed.), *Sociomedia: Multimedia, hypermedia, and the social construction of knowledge* (pp. 27-51). Cambridge: MIT Press.

Smith, P. (1988). *Discerning the subject.* Minneapolis: University of Minnesota Press.

Takayoshi, P. (1994). Building new networks from the old: Women's experiences with electronic communication. *Computers and Composition, 11,* 21-35.

Taylor, P. (1992). Social epistemic rhetoric and chaotic discourse. In G. Hawisher & P. LeBlanc (Eds.), *Reimagining computers and composition: Teaching and research in the virtual age* (pp. 131-148). Portsmouth, NH: Boynton/Cook.

Trimbur, J. (1989). Consensus and difference in collaborative learning. *College English, 51,* 602-616.

Chapter • 3

Virtual Space, Real Participation: Dimensions and Dynamics of a Virtual Classroom

William Condon

Ever since the advent of networked computers, much has been said and written about the potential for teaching writing via computer networks, in virtual space, in a virtual classroom. Even though virtual writing classrooms began with Electronic Networks for Interaction (ENFI), early in the 1980s (Batson, 1988) and have been the subject of numerous articles and books since, for most people the phrases *virtual classroom* and *virtual space* conjure up images of students wearing high-tech goggles and special gloves, of technicians coordinating tens of thousands of dollars of complicated equipment located in special rooms, and of the kind of technology that only a laboratory filled with computer scientists could possibly manage. And yet, if the definition is kept simple and direct, virtual classrooms turn out to be both far less intimidating and far more accessible than most people believe. Essentially, a virtual classroom occurs whenever teachers and students interact in a sustained way via a computer network. The interaction might occur over the space of 30 minutes or it might last for a semester or more. The key factors are group interaction and duration in time, not the technological means of supporting the interactions over time. The interactions can occur among people sitting in the same computer-equipped, networked classroom at the same time or among people located literally anywhere in the world, communicating at times that suit their own schedules, as long as they can gain access to a computer that can access the

Internet. Although virtual classrooms can require sophisticated technology, in most cases, virtual classrooms employ relatively familiar hardware and software: e-mail, conferencing software such as Daedalus InterChange, Houghton Mifflin's Commonspace, Lotus Notes, World Wide Web sites that enable class members to exchange comments or interact in other ways (e.g., via HyperNews, WebChat, links to MOOs, and so on), all of which students can access from a desktop computer that is linked with a network to other students' computers. Viewed this way, virtual classrooms are practical, flexible, and familiar tools, rather than expensive, overdetermined, and exotic toys. At the simplest level, anyone whose class has access to e-mail and who can set up any kind of e-mail group can teach in a virtual classroom.

Most of the literature on virtual classrooms that has arisen to date is exploratory in nature, describing both successful and problematic attempts to employ networked computer environments to support the teaching and learning of writing. And most of that literature describes e-mail-based virtual classrooms. Hawisher and Moran (1993) noted that e-mail is "pan-disciplinary" (p. 629), which, they argued, legitimates its use in first-year college writing courses. Spooner and Yancey (1996) pointed out that e-mail-based virtual spaces promote greater democracy and expand the means of interaction. E-mail, they argued, presents a different opportunity to learn, a collaborative resource that incorporates into writing a group's shared knowledge and experience; practice at a genre that increasingly is becoming more a part of intellectual and workday experience. And Selfe and Cooper (1990), discussing the use of asynchronous conferencing to extend class interactions beyond class space and class time, noted that "we have begun to recognize the need for non-traditional forums for academic exchange, forums that allow interaction patterns disruptive of a teacher-centered hegemony" (p. 847). Selfe and Cooper argued for "the importance of discourse in learning, the importance of students talking and writing to one another as well as to the teacher as they attempt to come to terms with the theories and concepts raised in their courses" (p. 847).

As these scholars described it, the mechanism of the virtual classroom provides a different kind of forum from the traditional classroom, and its advantages include more than the ability to extend class time and class space. In virtual learning environments, students "[bring] up ideas and topics and questions we would never have thought of addressing and [interact] with one another and with us in astonishingly frank and open ways" (Selfe & Cooper, 1990, p. 848). Selfe and Cooper noted that computer-mediated communication (CMC) helps students become more active learners because it encourages them to participate in shaping their roles as learners and directing their learning so that it more closely addresses their needs. They also note that the atmosphere in the CMC classroom is more egalitarian, less teacher-centered. Palmquist (1993), too, noted that "rather than simply extending [the classroom], [access to computer networks] transforms the classroom" (p. 25). Agreeing with Hawisher's (1992) observation that some of the benefits of networked classrooms flow from the fact that students are immersed in writing, Palmquist (1993) also attributed the success of network-based learning spaces to the fact that "access to computer networks allows students to receive more timely feedback on their writing, to create and subsequently review transcripts of network-based brainstorming and peer-review sessions, and to communicate more easily with their teachers and classmates" (p. 26). To this list, Selfe and Cooper (1990) added, "the success of computer conferences as non-traditional academic forums is due to three influences: the synergistic effect of written conversation, dialogue, and exchange; the shift in power and control from a teacher-centered forum to a student-centered one; and the liberating influence of the electronic medium within which the conferences occur" (pp. 857-858).

For the most part, reports and studies on adventures into virtual classrooms have so far focused on the contrast between the traditional and the computer-equipped classroom, a contrast that, as Slatin (1994) pointed out, is only possible because of the existence of newer classrooms, real and virtual, that incorporate computer technologies into the process of teaching and learning. As those who have tried the conversion from traditional to computer-assisted classrooms have discovered, the change involves reconceiving most of what we think we know about effective teaching, and it often involves adopting new paradigms of learning (see, e.g., Selfe & Selfe, 1995; Spooner & Yancey, 1996). Indeed, Palmquist (1993) argued that "network-based communication and classroom and curricular context are *inter*related." Thus, the network shapes the curriculum, and the curriculum, in turn, determines class members' willingness to use this means of communication. Thus, "In cases where a curriculum designer sees clear benefits to using network-based communication programs, care should be taken to create a curriculum that encourages that use" (Palmquist, 1993, p. 27). If that kind of curricular transformation takes place, Palmquist's study demonstrates that participating in some kind of virtual classroom experience leads to better academic performance.

The shift from the *physical* computer-assisted classroom to the virtual classroom—which might be thought of as a computer-*enabled* classroom—involves this kind of reconception and makes similar demands for change in habitual approaches to and methods for teaching and learning writing. In order for a change of that magnitude to be worthwhile, its advantages must be clear, the differences in teaching and learning that occur in virtual space must be explained, and some of the benefits the research just described has claimed for this new forum for learning must be demonstrated—as well as allaying fears about effects stemming from gender and class, differences in levels of access, and so forth (Selfe & Selfe, 1995). As a contribution to the process of evaluating the effectiveness of virtual classrooms, this chapter examines three principal attributes of an actual virtual class, one that involved students from the University of Michigan (U of M), The Ohio State University at Columbus (OSU), and the University of Illinois at Chicago (UIC) in producing collaborative essays online. But first, I provide a description of the project.

WHAT IS A LIBERAL ARTS EDUCATION?: A COLLABORATIVE PROJECT

The virtual classroom experience I explore took place in the fall term of 1993, and it involved students in three writing classes, my own at the U of M's English Composition Board (ECB), one supervised by David Jolliffe at UIC, and one team-taught by Theresa Doerfler and Rob Davis at OSU. The students in these classes never met together in one place. Instead, they communicated and collaborated in virtual space, using an asynchronous conferencing program developed at Michigan and called Confer. Confer arranges discussions by item, so that each item could be conceived as a workspace for an interscholastic team of students. In addition, the program retains all entries in chronological order within items, so that at any time the entire transcript of the work that has taken place there is available to all the participants.

The team of teachers met in August and identified a 5-week window that would allow courses at institutions on three different academic calendars—quarters, semesters, and trimesters—to "gather" and work together on a project that would invite the students to explore the meaning of "liberal arts education" as it was put into action on each of the campuses. We then devised the following sequence of activities:

> Week 1: Each class member was assigned a partner on each of the other campuses and a CONFERence item to work in. Each then posted a two-page summary of a literacy autobiography essay, based on readings common to all three classes, as an introduction to their partners, and then responded to questions from those partners.
> Week 2: By Monday, each class member posted a quotation about literacy from some sort of university document or publication. The potential sources were unlimited, but quotations were to represent, in some way, an official declaration that focuses on literacy. Students posted the institutional

texts to their own Confer "items" and to an item where all the texts from all three classes were listed—an archive item. The electronic peer groups began to form ideas about these texts and to generate questions to ask in the following week's interview of a panel comprising a university administrator, a senior professor, and an upper division undergraduate student.

Week 3: Each class interviewed its own panel, using the questions generated about the institutional texts each class gathered. Each class member took notes on the interviews and posted a summary of it to their electronic peer group early in the week. Later that week, work centered on generating subtopics for a collaborative essay.

Week 4: Early in the week, each student posted her or his section of the collaborative essay, and the groups began discussing how to combine the sections into the body of an essay. This process continued through the week, and students used the weekend to write introductions.

Week 5: On Monday or Tuesday, students posted their introductions for peer review. By Wednesday, reviewers had responded to the posted introductions, and writers then posted revised versions.

After the 5-week period was finished, each member of the class revised the group essay as she or he saw fit. The essay then became part of the student's graded work.

The transcript of all the interactions for this 5-week project amounts to more than a megabyte of ASCII text. That much material presents many aspects for exploration. Some of these potential directions confirm work that has been cited earlier in this chapter. Other directions have already been explored elsewhere (Doerfler & Davis, 1998). For the present, I expound on three factors—they can be called benefits—that strike me as most important about the virtual classroom.

The Virtual Classroom is a Written Classroom, Not Just a Writing Classroom

Whether the class uses synchronous or asynchronous conferencing software, this classroom's very presence resides in the writing students and teachers do there. The mechanisms of the classroom are identical with the agents in the classroom. This factor, I contend, is the key to the transformative nature of the virtual classroom that both Palmquist (1993) and Selfe and Cooper (1990) noted. In the traditional classroom, the elements are separate and identifiable—the chairs, the chalk and chalkboard, the walls, the door, and so on. The classroom exists separate from and independent of the class members—and, more important, independent of their writing. In the virtual classroom as it exists in most cases, if there is no writing, there is no classroom. The participants are what they write. In the project described here, for example, the classes—teachers, students, interviewees, and so forth—existed in three different physical spaces separated from each other by hundreds of miles and by different academic calendars and class schedules. They gathered and worked together only in the online environment. They introduced each other with text, they became friends in text, they advised each other in text, they—well, you get the idea. No writing, no classroom.

This factor goes beyond Hawisher's (1992) observation that "When participants in an electronic conference communicate with one another . . . they are totally immersed in writing" (p. 84). Indeed, when participants in a virtual classroom communicate with each other, they *are* their writing. The only way a writer can make his or her presence known in a virtual classroom is by writing there. In most composition classes, teachers struggle first to convince writers that they should be present in their texts and then to help writers discover ways to create that presence. Online, writers quickly discover that they must be present in their texts, and the environment itself—the fact that interaction is constant, that readers are processing writers' texts and negotiating misunderstandings, omissions, abstractions, ambiguities, and so forth—means that writers are always conscious of the fact that their texts embody not only their ideas, but their purposes and their personae as well. In traditional classrooms, these negotiations occur relatively infrequently, and they are limited to transactions among small groups of writers or between the writer and the teacher. Moving a class into virtual space creates a writing situation in which the focus on rhetorical concerns is a natural part of the desire to communicate. Writers cannot separate form from content as they can in physical classrooms or in paper texts. Form, content, purpose, audience, occasion, context, all these and more matter in every "utterance," primarily because they have no existence outside the utterance. Virtual space may be hard to locate, but it provides a powerful environment for helping students see themselves as writers, for helping them understand all that is involved in addressing an audience, and for helping them see how multifaceted a thing writing in any context really is.

The real question is how to make the best use of this space, how to re-envision the curriculum so that the class derives the maximum possible benefit. Planning the virtual classroom involves finding ways to take full advantage of the fact that virtual classrooms are *written* classrooms:

- *Inviting frequent opportunities to write there.* Students should be online often, daily if possible, interacting in a variety of ways. Virtual space exists on a 7/24 basis: It is accessible at any time. Given reasons to interact there, students will interact there. They will write there.

- *Incorporating writing that ranges from online chat up to formal, academic prose.* Our project began and ended with relatively formal writing, but in between, writing ranged from very casual, informal chat to businesslike reporting to journalistic reportage. Students wrote in order to build trust, give personal advice, review classwork, develop materials, plan, revise, and so on.

- *Involving students in meaningful collaborations that produce resources that are useful to the students, individually and collectively.* This space is made of the collected writings of all the participants. It cannot help but be collaboratively constructed, negotiated space. In order to take advantage of this capacity, we designed our project so that students would create resources that only existed as a result of their work. They collected chunks of text that addressed the ways their home institutions conceived of and carried out the mission of the liberal arts degree. They interviewed panels of administrators, senior faculty, and advanced students in order to test how those written formulations worked when applied to their own institutions. They first created an extensive resource, a large data set, and then they set out to make meaning from it, to interpret the data first for each other and then for a more public audience and purpose. In short, our virtual classroom was, in part, a place for getting a job done, a strongly transactional space. (It was not solely transactional, however, as I demonstrate later.) Students had a job to do, and they had to rely on each other for the data needed to get it done.

- *Providing a space in which students can re-create, in microcosm, the intellectual "conversations" academics have in their face-to-face conferences, their books, and their journals.* In the end, all three classes shared the purpose of introducing students to the academy in general and to academic writing in particular. Thus, the environment was designed to reinforce that curriculum. Asynchronous conferencing, mixing face-to-face contact with working at a distance, and creating knowledge that must be negotiated, tested, and shared in order to be useful, all these factors mirror the ways academics think and work. Students framed questions, gathered data, interpreted facts, came up with theories of education, and applied all that knowledge to a specific, observable phenomenon—liberal arts education, as it was being accomplished on the students themselves. The virtual classroom proved almost ideal for such an endeavor.

Learning in Virtual Space Privileges the Learner, Rather Than the Teacher

If for no other reason, learners are privileged by the numbers: Far more learners than teachers occupy that virtual space. Because the classroom is a written classroom, and almost all of the writing is generated by the learners, they naturally take a larger role in the learning experience, whether or not they challenge the authority of the teacher. Teachers who try to "ride herd" on all that writing will find themselves too exhausted from the reading to do the sheer quantity of writing that they would need to produce in order to micromanage the class. Consider the figures presented in Tables 3.1 and 3.2.

Ten students produced 266 responses. Ten students produced almost 240,000 characters—about 48,000 words. Although these were the most active participants (and note that neither list includes even one of the teachers), the group totaled 60 students and 5 teachers, and the ASCII file for the 5-week project runs to 1.1 megabytes. No teacher can keep up with that volume of activity, that amount of writing.

Instead, teachers use assignments or structure exchanges in order to set directions, much as the manager in a corporation might do, and the learners take those directions and negotiate among themselves, interpreting the assignments, delegating the tasks, and setting their own deadlines so that they can meet their obligations to each other and to their instructors. As Selfe and Cooper (1990) pointed out, this use of technology creates a real difference, drawing "on the revolutionary potential of computer technology to create non-traditional forums that allow students the opportunity to reexamine the authoritarian values of the classroom, to resist their socialization into a narrowly conceived form of academic discourse, to learn from the clash of discourses, to learn through engaging in discourse" (p. 867). In short, the learners take a larger share of the responsibility for learning when they have to manage their own and each other's tasks than they do when the teacher retains that level of responsibility.

Learners also forge spaces for themselves, so that they meet each others' needs. Consider, for example, the following exchanges (the students' names have been changed to protect their anonymity):

Oct14/93 13:10
9:10) Marian Durst: cont.: I never wrote much about things that don't interest me. The last few . raphs were answered by me only because I

Table 3.1. Top 10 Contributors in Class by Number of Responses.

Student	Number of Responses	Number of Characters
Female Student 1	22	19,191
Male Student 1	22	13,222
Female Student 2	23	6,865
Male Student 2	23	18,648
Female Student 3	24	19,663
Male Student 3	27	14,924
Female Student 4	27	22,905
Female Student 5	29	34,507
Female Student 6	34	21,898
Female Student 7	35	34,897
Total	266	206,720

Table 3.2. Top 10 Participants in Class by Total Characters.

Student	Number of Responses	Number of Characters
Male Student 1	17	19,710
Female Student 1	22	19,719
Male Student 2	21	20,666
Female Student 2	20	20,804
Female Student 3	22	21,750
Female Student 4	34	21,898
Male Student 3	20	22,325
Female Student 5	27	22,905
Female Student 6	29	34,507
Female Student 7	35	34,897
Total	247	239,181

was told to answer questions for my prof. Now I would like to get more personal about myself and inform you of what topics I usually take a stand on. I was raised here in America. I enjoy being with people. I was raised by two typical Filipino parents who still live by the traditions of the Philippines. The way they TRIED to raise me didn't work. I was ordered, not asked to stay home all the time, not associate with anyone else except for "my own kind," study constantly, be nice to everyone who they said was okay for me to be companions with, and do everything that they told me to do even if it was against my morals or whatever you want to call it. Right now my parents are telling me who I should date and who I will not date. They're trying to prohibit me from seeing Jack O'Reilly (a guy that I am dating). They say that they're only looking out for my future. I don't think so! I understand that they don't want me to be with a person who has no ambition, but they want me to get back together with my ex-boyfriend Joseph. He had no direction what so ever. Jack has direction, but I think the reason my parents don't want me to be with him is because he is an Afro-American. Actually, I know that that is the reason why.

- - - - -

Oct14/93 15:15
9:13) Sharon Otterman: Hi Marian. I'm Sharon from Ohio State and I'd like to respond to your essay. I know how it feels when parents don't understand who you are and what you value as important to you. It seems like prejudice will be an issue never full resolved, but it can be—by our generation. I had dated an Afro-American in high school also and my parents, whom I love dearly, forbid it. He was a really wonderful person whom had many qualities that I had never seen in anyone, however, they were blinded by the color of his skin. It seems as if you know what you want and your parents are unwilling to accept that. Well, they are your parents and you must respect their wishes; however, you also must do what makes you happy. Is this boyfriend someone you are willing to sacrifice many fights and hardships with them over? I know that I was a "chicken" and took the easy way out—I stopped seeing him. However, I now realize that I am becoming an adult and many of the choices I make now will be choices I live with for the rest of my life. I'd like to hear more about your situation and your feelings on the matter. So, please respond soon and I will continue to respond. THANKS and talk to you soon!

- - - - -

Oct18/93 17:10
9:17) Sally Park: Hi, Marian. I'm Sally from U of M. I know exactly how it feels when your parents don't understand you, especailly, Asian parents. My parents never understand me well enough, either. They always try to control my social life too. If I ever date a guy with a kid or a Black man, they would never speak to me. But like you, I don't really care what they think either. I'm glad I'm here, thousands of miles away from home, so that I don't need to argue with my parents every day. But my parents call me almost every day anyway. They are about as strict as your parents, I guess. Well, I don't know what to say except that I wish you good luck with your boyfriend and parents and all.

These responses followed the posting of literacy autobiographies in Week 1, and the posts demonstrate the degree to which the students have taken control of this space and directed it toward their own agendas. They are still writing, and they are writing about complex, real-world problems. But for now, they are sharing perceptions about race and racism, information about cultural differences, personal experiences, and personal advice. Later, they returned to the assigned task, but the very fact that they were able to bring this discussion into class represents a marked difference from the way discussions progress in onsite classrooms, as opposed to online ones. Thus, the virtual classroom enables an expansion of agendas, a stretching of the kinds of problems, questions, and issues students bring into the classroom. In addition, the virtual classroom allows students to have a large influence on the directions a discussion takes, without interfering with the class's goals (they did, after all, get back to the project, and this group's essay was particularly successful).

In another case, a different kind of interaction further demonstrates the flexibility of the online learning environment:

Oct21/93 15:01
16:14) Don Atlas: Hello Nan and Ellie. I am back to talk about our school and liberal education. I am supposed to find out about your schools also, and compare. Ohio State, in my opinion, is a liberal school to the extreme. Of course it would seem that way to someone just out of high school right? Ohio State offers many courses, but I think it goes even further with groups, clubs, organizations etc. I think it, the university, being liberal, sets up a good environment for all kinds of students. I'll have to talk to both of you about it in more depth later...bye.

Oct26/93 13:01
16:16) Nan O'Hara: What's going on. Nothing much here. We had a panel discussion the other day with a repre. ative from the faculty, a graduate student, and someone else. I was late so I don't know who the other person was. My teacher, Mrs. Smith just told me. The last person was an administrator. Larry the administrator didn't say much of anything other than he didn't think that UIC did offer a very liberal education. He said that no matter whaty field of study a person decided to go into, the basic classes would already be picked out for you. I didn't particularly care for his outlook on education here at UIC. He did stress that there are many programs, clubs, and various organizations here to help UIC students overcome barriers to acheive academic excellence.

Oct27/93 15:58
16:18) Ellie: Hi, guys! I found my quote about liberal art education from LSA magazine, which was published in my school, U of M. In March of 1993, my school Dean, Goldenberg gave the fourth in the

Presidential Lecture Series, a set of lectures focusing on academic values. The article in this magazine was a condensed version of her lecture. In this writing, she says what is new and different about the climate for higher education today is first, public attitudes. Not as much public support is there compare to the past, she said. A second significant difference is the challenge we are setting for ourselves. We don't educate only the privileged anymore. Thirdly, is the future that young adults will face as citizens. She said it's this last difference—the future facing our young people—that convinces her most about the special role that research universities have to play in undergraduate education. She also stresses that the goals of a liberal arts education extend beyond content to the development of students' abilities to communicate effectively, to think critically, to understand diverse perspectives, and to solve problems. In the past, people have focused so heavily on content that attention to skills and abilities [As is long overdue. his concern drives much of our thinking about undergraduate education in LS&A. These are what she had said in her lecture about education. I'll continue tonight, or later. I have a class to go to now. Bye.

Oct28/93 12:53
16:19) Nan O'Hara: UIC sounds much like your school. I want to know more about general things. Do you guys party all of the time or is your school boring? I have my own fun but my time is very well planned out. If I get off schedule everything is messed up. Based on the discussion that we had, I think that I might stay in school a little longer to learn about more things. My school is so culturely diverse. UIC has much to offer people of different cultures. I haven't even been to all the restaurants here yet let alone the different art fairs and things that are usually going on within the school. I think that UIC has a large advantage over other schools because it is located in such a big city. Their are so many places to go and so many things to do. I never get bored and always manage to stay busy. I like to go to the theater, concerts, and various activities going on around the city. I'm usually in the house during the week working on a paper or the like for school. The crime here is pretty bad and is getting worse. Drugs have pretty much taken over the communities but I haven't seen anyone or smelled anyone that smelled like them here yet. Well maybe its because I haven't been here that long. I hope you both don't mind that I am talking about this but I have nothing to do. Besides this is fun. I want to know more about you guys. Do you all like to party? Have you joined a fraternity or a sorority? What is your everyday life like?

Nov02/93 15:57
16:27) Don Atlas: Ellie, you wrote that you thought that liberal education is more than just improving communication abilities and understanding diverse perspectives. What else is there, in your opin-

ion? I am not dissagreeing with you, I am just interested in that point and you did not quite finish it. Nan, I belive that a degree is not something that guarantees a job, I don't belive it is supposed to, instead it makes getting a job easier. Think about how hard it would be for your mother to get a job if she never went to school. I think it would be close to impossible, I am confident that there are many people who want and need your mother...The only trick is to get connected to this/these persons. On the issue of a liberal education, it -WILL- get you a job much faster than a fixed education. The reason is because everything is always changing, change is more comfortable for a liberal mind than a narrow one. Another point is that a person with a liberal education will be hired first because they are much more useful. They can do a number of different tasks rather than only one or two. The last point I would like to make is that it gives the person options. One can decide what tasks or job he or she would enjoy more, thus being happy. Happiness leads to success.....

First, this selection—just a small segment from Week 3—highlights the ways students can intermingle agendas, personas, and voices. Given the reason to develop a variety of tools, students will do so. The virtual classroom presents the opportunity to work and to communicate from the heart, so to speak, in one's own person(ality). Oddly, moving the class into virtual space, where team members were separated by time and space, allowed for a greater variety of kinds of writing and certainly a wider range of voices than we observe in the papers from a traditional writing class.

In addition, we also see in this passage the extent to which students constructed the classroom and directed the activities. They took charge. Ellie's first entry brings Nan back to the assignment and focuses the group on the task at hand. Dan makes an attempt to negotiate common ground. In essence, these exchanges begin the process of analyzing the information these students have gathered. They are beginning to make sense of their observations, to work toward what they will write in their final, formal essays. Most important, the students are in charge. There is not a teacher in sight.

The Task-Oriented Nature of the Virtual Classroom Creates an Egalitarian Space for Collaboration

We all know to what extent virtual spaces—e-mail lists, MOOspace, electronic bulletin boards, and so forth—are male-dominated. Even an academic list like Megabyte University (MBU-L) can be dominated by males and high-status participants, although in other settings, such as a writing classroom, the same gender imbalances may not appear (Hawisher & Moran, 1993). The surveys all suggest that the virtual world is unfriendly to women. However, statistics from the class this chapter describes sug-

gest that a virtual classroom is different from the kind of electronic space
to which these surveys speak.

Consider, by contrast with Tables 3.1 and 3.2, Tables 3.3 and 3.4
showing the usage statistics from the online version of the Ninth
Computers and Writing (C&W) Conference (the first C&W to go online),
which was also "held" in Confer. Table 3.3 lists the top 10 participants in
that online conference, by the number of responses each participant posted:

Table 3.3. Top 10 Participants in CW93:FORUM, by Number of Responses.

	Responses (Count)	Length (Characters)
Elizabeth Sommers	47	25,232
Wayne Butler	56	36,641
Jeff Galin	63	49,376
Bill Condon	74	21,767
Nick Carbone	90	70,134
Fred Kemp	100	59,532
Jeff Finlay	104	45,887
Eric Crump	117	58,601
Russ Hunt	152	76,806
Michael Day	166	77,356
Total # of Responses	969	

This top 10 is almost exclusively male, as is the one in Table 3.4, which
lists the top 10 participants by how many characters they entered into the
conference.

The difference between the male domination here and the greater
gender balance in the class figures is the orientation to task. Given a project
to complete and a structure within which to work, students of both genders collaborate; given a serious reason to participate online, students of
both genders do so readily and equally. Statistics on number of responses
and overall quantity of response demonstrate that in this task-oriented virtual classroom females' contributions actually outweighed males' contributions slightly. The evidence, both in quantity and quality of participation,
suggests that although males may dominate the more recreational online
contexts, females more than hold their own when mixed groups are
required to accomplished collaborative tasks in virtual space.

Table 3.4. Top 10 Participants in CW93:FORUM, by Total Number of Characters.

	Responses (Count)	Length (Characters)
Tyanna Lambert	41	28,081
Wayne Butler	56	36,641
Mauri Casano	45	42,360
Jeff Finlay	104	45,887
Jeff Galin	63	49,376
Eric Crump	117	58,601
Fred Kemp	100	59,532
Nick Carbone	90	70,134
Russ Hunt	152	76,806
Michael Day	166	77,356
Total # of Characters		544,774

CONCLUSIONS THAT THESE DATA SUPPORT

First, and certainly foremost, this experience was good for the students involved. It excited their imaginations. They were enthusiastic about the idea of it, and they were enthusiastic about the project as it unfolded, as they did the work. The project involved them in actively and collaboratively compiling a set of information that existed nowhere else, and the project invited them to make sense of that information, to give it meaning by interpreting it or by arguing about it. From a curricular standpoint, students engaged in a great deal of higher order thinking as they created some new knowledge. In short, students learned about the topic they were exploring, and because the explorations happened in a written environment, students also learned about writing: about audience, purpose, occasion, invention, research, and so on.

Second, it is possible to do what we did. This conclusion may seem obvious because we clearly did what we did. Still, accomplishing this kind of collaboration represents no small accomplishment. Coordinating the working time for students at institutions with different academic calendars was difficult enough; working out the technical requirements and logistics required exploring new territories. However, this kind of collaboration is even more possible today than in 1993 because advances in technology have created more and easier means for getting students together. MOOs, chat rooms, mail groups, Web-based chat forums such as

GlobalChat, WebForum and HyperNews, all these are becoming easier and more available—and even better tools will be even easier and even more widely available in the coming years. More writing teachers need to accept the challenge that this new medium—new a*gora*, really—presents. We accept that challenge by locating all or some portion of our writing classes in virtual space. We have the tools to make the transformation, however, and that's good news.

Third, despite the optimism of the previous paragraph, computers and teachers will have to advance much further before we actually have virtual classrooms, instead of currently cobbled-together arrangements using often less-than-satisfactory software and hardware. Those who design systems and those who use them must look closely at technology to make the experience of a virtual classroom manageable for students and teachers. The sheer amount of writing in such a space can be a boon, for example, but it can also be overwhelming (Eldred, 1991; Hawisher & Moran, 1993). System designs must accommodate the participants' need to pay close attention to some things and scant attention to others. The whole class simply cannot be actively involved with all the writing that each and every member of the class produces. The tools, then, have to create the virtual classroom equivalent of e-mail's "skim-and-delete" tactic, which helps veteran users make their online lives manageable.

This project, despite solid software and the considerable experience and expertise of the teachers involved in it, experienced many "glitches," as well as many of the same kinds of problems that one finds common in the literature: unequal access, technological difficulties, struggles with interfaces, and so on. These difficulties are fully described in Doerfler and Davis (1998). Outweighing these difficulties, in my judgment, is the fact that the only way to push forward into this new environment is to adapt existing cyberstructures to our purposes, even as we argue for more effective online learning environments. Unless we move writing classes into these environments, no one will have a reason to develop them to suit the needs of writing teachers or student writers. This imperative represents a reverse of a familiar saying: If we come, they will build it. Or, at least, if we don't come, they certainly will not build it. Then, as technology advances and the computer becomes the principal tool for writing and communicating—which, arguably, is already the case—writing classes will become increasingly obsolete.

Finally, we need to build a great deal more experience before we can know in what cases virtual classrooms may be as effective as physical classrooms or provide advantages over physical classrooms. At present, the virtual classroom demands that students carry out most or all their communication in writing; as a result, the virtual classroom promises to increase students' involvement in learning to write and to facilitate active learning. However, the cautions Hawisher and Selfe (1993) raised about electronic writing classes still apply. The technology is not a *good* in and of itself. How much it helps—or hinders—the teaching and learning of writing depends on how thoughtfully we use it, and to what ends. As writing teachers move into the virtual classroom, they must frame their goals carefully and test them fully in order for us to construct the kinds of knowledge that will allow us to choose the best that this emerging technology offers us and to employ it thoughtfully and effectively.

REFERENCES

Doerfler, T., & Davis, R. (1998). Conferencing in the contact zone. In J. Galin & J. Latchaw (Eds.), *The dialogic classroom* (pp. 174-190). Urbana, IL: NCTE.

Eldred, J. (1991). Pedagogy in the computer-networked classroom. *Computers and Composition, 8,* 47-61.

Hawisher, G. (1992). Electronic meetings of the minds: Research, electronic conferences, and composition studies. In G. E. Hawisher & P. LeBlanc (Eds.), *Re-imagining computers and composition: Teaching and research in the virtual age* (pp. 81-101). Portsmouth, NH: Boynton-Cook.

Hawisher, G., & Moran, C. (1993). Electronic mail and the writing instructor. *College English, 55,* 627-643.

Hawisher, G., & Selfe, C. (1993). The rhetoric of technology and the electronic writing class. *College Composition and Communication, 42,* 55-65.

Palmquist, M. (1993). Network-supported interaction in two writing classrooms. *Computers and Composition, 10*(4), 25-58.

Selfe, C., & Cooper, M. (1990). Computer conferences and learning: Authority, resistance, and internally persuasive discourse. *College English, 52,* 847-869.

Selfe, C. L., & Selfe, R. (1995) The politics of the interface: Power and its exercise in electronic contact zones. *College Composition and Communication, 45*(4), 480-504.

Slatin, J. (1994). *Computers and writing: Seeing the future by knowing our past* (A teleconference presented by Ball State University). Boston: Houghton Mifflin.

Spooner, M., & Yancey, K. (1996). Postings on a genre of e-mail. *College Composition and Communication, 47,* 252-278.

Chapter • 4

Teach Us How to Play:
The Role of Play in Technology Education

Gail Matthews-DeNatale

It is often said that "play" is important in maximizing computer-mediated learning. When asked if I "know" a software program, I often respond by saying that "I bought a copy, but I haven't had time to *play* with it yet." In an age of rapidly changing technology, play is becoming an increasingly acceptable way of knowing and learning. Business trainers use computer games of solitaire to help their employees learn mouse-hand-eye coordination; composition instructors take their students online to explore imaginary text-based worlds called MOOs; even peace negotiators used virtual reality to explore boundary resolutions in the former Yugoslavia.

If developing a play relationship with technology is central to becoming adept with computers, then teachers and students probably need to become more reflexive about this process. The experience of composing text on a computer is different from that of penning words by hand—the machine allows us to capture thoughts as they come to us, the nonlinear meanderings of the mind, and then cut and paste our ideas into a more linear and reasoned sequence of prose. Even the term *cut and paste* recalls playful first-grade memories of construction paper scraps and the spicy smell of white paste.

According to Burke (1969b), a process of identification develops between entities that share a common purpose. Identifying, articulating, and toying with the possibilities of that common purpose is central to the art of persuasion– and to the art of teaching (helping novices develop investment in and identification with a given subject). This process of identification can also develop between people and objects of importance: ink-writers develop a love for pen and paper, whereas techno-writers develop a curious kind of relationship with their computers as they both shape words into meaningful prose. Ink-writers often have a favorite pen, color of ink, or a preferred paper stock. Some techno-writers "dress" their machines in screen savers and humorous mouse pads, whereas others go so far as to name their computers.

Whether in ink or in bits, the process of writing involves a great deal of playing with words. But the texture, rhythms, and rules of the techno-writing game are different from that of ink-writing. Some of us are fortunate to forge "friendships" in both sectors, but in an era in which most composition is computer-mediated, exploring the role of play in technology and communication is particularly important for teachers and students of writing.

What is the interrelation between play, learning, communication, and technology? What is the relation between language and play? To what extent is the experience of play inherently individual, and to what extent is it cultural? Can we identify societal patterns or generalizations about play that will help us make meaningful use of play in our classrooms, serving as catalysts for intentional play?

WHAT IS THE RELATION BETWEEN PLAY AND LEARNING?

Anthropologist Gregory Bateson described play as a form of "deutero learning," as a framework for learning to learn. This framework constitutes a forum for communication, an opportunity to consider the *relationship* between things, people, ideas and emotions—an opportunity to make connections between concepts. According to Bateson, play is often misunderstood. People look at the abstractions and imaginary worlds associated with play and mistakenly view them in a literal framework:

> Someone has said that we know that play is important to children because it is in play that we learn role behavior. What I would like to say is that there is an element of truth in that, no doubt, but there seems to be a much more important truth in that it is by play that an individual learns there are sorts and categories of behavior. . . . The child is playing at being an archbishop. I am not interested in the fact that he learns about how to be an archbishop from playing the role; but that he learns that there is such a thing as an archbishop from playing the role. He learns or acquires a new view, partly flexible and partly rigid, which is introduced into life when he realizes that behav-

ior can, in a sense, be set to a logical type or style. It is not the learning of the particular style that you are playing at, but the fact of stylistic flexibility and the fact that choice of style is related to the frame and context of behavior, classified by context in some way. (Schwartzman, 1978, p. 219)

Children at play in make-believe dramas explore categories of relationships, societal roles, and cultural processes. Computers are newcomers to the cast of supporting characters that surround us, and these new characters create openings for the development of relationships between humans and machines (both good and bad). Techno-work and techno-writing are a relatively new realms of behavior—new roles, voices, patterns, relationships, traditions, and communities for us to explore in our play-learning. Techno-play provides a safe but challenging framework for exploring both the possibilities and limitations of the medium.

Organizational researcher Mihaly Csiszentmihalyi contributed greatly to the understanding of the relation between work and play, stating that when a person is playfully invested in work "action follows upon action according to an internal logic that seems to need no conscious intervention by the actor. He experiences it as a unified flowing from one moment to the next" (cited in Dargan & Zeitlin, 1990, p. 31). Csiszentmihalyi (1974) referred to this experiential dimension of play as *flow,* a deep relation characterized by unselfconscious absorption.

Csiszentmihalyi's concept of *flow* is similar to the "deep" play described by anthropologist Clifford Geertz. Geertz (1973) lived in Bali for a number of years and became intrigued by the central role of cockfighting in that culture. He noted that cockfighting

renders ordinary, everyday experience comprehensible by presenting it in terms of acts and objects that have had their practical consequences removed . . . it does what, for other peoples with other temperaments and other conventions, *Lear* and *Crime and Punishment* do; it catches up these themes—death, masculinity, rage, pride, loss, beneficence, chance—and, ordering them into an encompassing structure, presents them in such a way as to throw into relief a particular view of their essential nature. (p. 443)

Geertz distinguished between child's play, in which challenges are modest, and the "deep play" of mature adults that is often extremely challenging and involves an element of adventure, skill, or risk. Consider the gourmet cook, the mountain climber, the gambler, or the home repair aficionado—all these forms of mature play involve finding joy and relaxation in the process of extending one's abilities. For teachers of writing, the challenge is to help students approach the writing process in the spirit of mature play, finding pleasure in the process of "getting there" and extending one's skill.

The frame of play, the context or signals that says "this is play," gives permission to explore and experiment with tough issues. Some sports, such as soccer, help harness the experience and power of aggression, whereas others, such as pole vaulting, explore the fine line between human capacity and limitation. Likewise, make-believe constitutes a space in which we examine facets of our identity, experimenting with both the possible and the improbable. Given the turbulence of adolescence, a time in which the definition of self is extended beyond the confines of immediate family, it is no surprise that youth are drawn to online chat rooms, MUDs, and MOOs in which they explore alternate persona. According to psychologist Sherry Turkle (1995), "At one level, the computer is a tool. It helps us write, keep track of our accounts, and communicate with others. Beyond this, the computer offers us both new models of mind and a new medium on which to project our ideas and fantasies" (p. 9).

"Child's play" may be the opposite of "brain surgery" in our colloquial lexicon, but play is anything but a simple-minded venture. Play is many things at once: a concept, process, form of relationship, state of being, and learning space.

WHAT IS THE RELATION BETWEEN PLAY AND COMMUNICATION?

Play involves exploring concerns that are fundamental to the human condition. The central role of play in language acquisition is no exception. Most people have a profound desire to communicate with others—a longing that is often frustrated by the realities of miscommunication.

Watch any 3-year-old learn how to tell a riddle. Semiotically speaking, riddles are complex routines, involving questions, answers, irony, puns, metaphors, and so on (see McDowell, 1979). The first pattern children discern is that of question $\Rightarrow$ I don't know $\Rightarrow$ answer $\Rightarrow$ laughter. Most children's first attempts at riddling go something like this:

Child: What did the duck say to the other duck?
Adult: I don't know, what did the duck say to the other duck?
Child: Quack! (child bursts into uproarious laughter and adult looks confused)

Fortunately, as the child grows older, he or she becomes more cognizant of the layers of meaning and word play that riddles have to offer. But before the child can tell good riddles, he or she first has to play around with telling bad ones. Likewise, before older students can write well, they need the space and time to pen not-so-perfect prose, developing a playful relationship with words (and imagined audience) that is as deep as it is engrossing. Day and Batson (1995) wrote that "We have to use the imagination to anticipate the expectations of our audience. How to imagine what an audience needs and wants to know? And how to adjust one's style, register, and tone appropriately? In other words, how to shift from what composition specialists call 'writer-based prose' to reader-based prose?" (pp. 25-46).

In Huizinga's (1950) landmark book *Homo Ludens: A Study of the Play Element in Culture,* he stated that both play and language are inherently generative processes, ever-changing streams into which we cast our lines. "We must always bear in mind that the idea as we know it [play] is defined and perhaps limited by the word we use for it. Words and idea are not born of scientific or logical thinking but of creative language, which means of innumerable languages—for this act of 'conception' has taken place over and over again" (p. 28). Viewed within this framework, *play,* an ongoing and iterative process of creation, is both metaphor and synonym for the writing process. Writing is mimetic to the "real" world, yet the words we use and reuse, and the meaning we endow to those words through a magical process of group consensus, constitute filters though which we perceive the world around us.

CASE STUDY: EXPLORING THE POTENTIAL OF PLAY IN AN ONLINE LANGUAGE ARTS CLASSROOM

Convinced that spaces for play are essential in learning new technologies, I wondered if it might be possible to construct an open-ended experience for my students that would engage them in the flow of deep play with computers. As a member of the faculty with the Institute for Educational Transformation (IET) at George Mason University in 1996, I taught the language and culture strand of an innovative masters program in reflective practice for K-12 educators. The 260 teachers enrolled in this program were all full-time employees of public schools. Many of the program participants were veteran teachers, having taught in schools for decades.

I decided to incorporate intentional exploration of the concept of *play* into my teaching, knowing that this strategy might be particularly challenging for my classes. Teachers, as an occupational group, face many workplace obstacles that interfere with their professional development in the area of computer-mediated learning, including but not limited to budget restraints, resource politics, and inadequate unstructured time to keep current with recent advances in technology. Considering these workplace realities, I began with the assumption that the teachers in my classes needed time to discover cyberspace as a "place to play."

In the academic year of 1995-1996, I taught a two-semester course entitled "Emerging Issues in Research: Language Arts." I decided to integrate technology into this course by asking my teacher-students to "play" on the Internet for at least 4 hours, following each session with journal writing about their experiences and thoughts concerning emerging technologies. I offered sessions in how to use Netscape and Internet search engines, but I was concerned that some anxious surfers might have trouble thinking of things to look for, so I also provided sample questions for consideration and URLs in the course bibliography to help reticent teacher-students get started (see Fig. 4.1).

In retrospect, my intent and philosophy were well intentioned, but I was overlooking a fundamental reality: Play is not just a form of engagement, it is also a state or status of relationship. Play experiences are preceded by some form of intrinsic motivation, inclination, or disposition in people. People usually do not choose to "play" with entities that seem cold or hostile to them.

For many people, the Internet constitutes a chaotic jumble that is both threatening and alienating—the last place on earth that they might want to "play." As public school teachers who live and work in a complicated litigious society, many of IET's students are bewildered by computer techno-speak and cyberporn fear-mongering. As my course progressed, I realized there was a difference between the "relationships" that I saw unfolding in the computer lab and the playful interactions that I had anticipated. To understand the dynamics that were taking place in the lab, I needed to learn more about my students' attitudes toward technology.

I began by observing how the people in my class interacted with the lab attendants and with the computers. As I listened, questioned, and watched, I discovered that some of my teacher-students were, in fact, experiencing the kind of play-learning I had envisioned for them. For example, one teacher had a preexisting interest in electric cars. He immediately sought out an electric car site, then eagerly grabbed others from their terminals to show them his "cool" site. He eventually downloaded information that he used to create a unit for his students on alternative energy and transportation. This student was able to transfer the skills and ideas that he learned while at play into other realms of his life, reflecting on the possibilities and translating his learning experiences into action in other domains.

On reflection, I realized that I had not "taught" this teacher how to play: He already had a mature play relationship with technology. His "electronic car" topic further convinced me that, in addition to intuitively playing with computers, he was also the kind of person who gravitated toward emerging technologies.

- *The WWW Virtual Library Games and Recreation Page*
(http://www.cis.ufl.edu/~thoth/library/recreation.html)

- *Games Domain*
(http://wcl-rs.bham.ac.uk/~djh/index.html)

- *Zarf's List of Interactive Games on the Web*
(http://www.cs.cmu.edu/afs/andrew/org/kgb/www/zarf/games.html)

- *An Introduction to MU*s*
(http://www.vuw.ac.nz/who/Jamie.Norrish/mud/mud.html)

- *The World Is Not A Desktop*
(http://www.ubiquitous.com/hypertext/weiser/ACMInteractions2.html)

Questions for Consideration: How are emerging technologies influencing the way that children and adults play? What patterns of relationships are inherent to computer-based play relationships? What kinds of ideas, attitudes, and skills do people learn during computer-based play relationships? What are the implications of these relationships, patterns, ideas, attitudes, and skills for teaching and learning? How is computer-mediated play different from or similar to earlier forms of play?

Fig. 4.1. Sample internet sites relevant to play

The research of Rosen and Weil (1995), as well as that of other psychologists, suggests that about 10% to 15% of the general population are, like the electric car enthusiast, *early* or *eager adopters* of technology, but the rest of the population tends to have resistant or even skeptical relationships with new media. I looked around my classroom and discovered that the numbers reported by Rosen and Weil were about right. I was reaching the *auto-didacts,* about 15% of my teacher-students, but the rest were not acting like people at play. They seemed lost, anxious, and at times even resentful.

In reflecting on my own past experience with computer-mediated communication (CMC), I found myself resisting Rosen and Weil's categories. Despite the usefulness of their schema, the neat categories of early adopter, resistant, and skeptic did not seem to work for me. For example, I loathe server-based e-mail programs like Pine. As a dyslexic, I find this writing environment to be unforgiving and the machinations that are necessary to compose off-line needlessly complicated. I resisted e-mail for years, despite the fact that in the early 1990s I worked with several K-12 programs that were entirely e-mail based. Finally, with the advent of user-friendly programs like Eudora, I found an interface that works for me and with me.

At the 1996 summer Epiphany Institute in Richmond, I heard a personal experience narrative that was diametrically opposed to my personal story about e-mail. One of the institute participants told an extremely moving story about how she became involved with e-mail. She was undergoing chemotherapy for cancer and had a compromised immune system. Unable to leave the house or even receive visitors because they might expose her to viruses that her body was not equipped to fight, she became increasingly lonely and depressed. It was at this point that she discovered e-mail. Soon she was writing to all her friends and asking them to send her messages. Her online community played a crucial role in her recuperation. In comparing my story with hers, I wondered if we each have to articulate our interests and needs before we can make a genuine connection between play, learning, and technology.

I have always been fascinated by the role that art plays in everyday life. My work with vernacular culture has entailed countless hours of interviewing people about their cultural traditions and life stories: artists, immigrants, workers, educators, and so on. With dozens of boxes filled with documentary videos and photographs, one of my ongoing frustrations is the extent to which conventional print media strip away the most interesting aspects of lived experience: the sights, sounds, gestures, smells, not to mention the multilayered meanings of the images and events that surround us. It is for this reason that I am a multimedia "early adopter." The Web is like a dream come true—designing a new site is an intensely creative and rewarding process for me in which I often loose track of time, forgetting to eat or sleep. In composing Web sites, I experience the flow and invigoration of deep, mature play.

If Rosen and Weil had observed me trying to use Unix-based e-mail, they would have seen a resistor. But if they peeked in on me while hard at work on a Web site, they would see an eager adopter. It stood to reason that if my relationship with technology defied monolithic labels, perhaps the same could be said of my students.

I decided to sit in the back of the lab and watch where and how my teacher-students used the computers. I wanted to get a handle on the types of relationships that my seemingly resistant students were developing with the technology. As mentioned before, the so-called early adopters seemed to have what I would characterize as a "play" relationship with the Web: zooming all over the world in a spirit of adventure to find interesting sites.

But other class members seemed to be developing different types of relationships with the Web. In addition to those at play, I noticed four other kinds of interactions:

- *Fearful:* Those who had a fearful relationship tended to team with other class members and have their teammates serve as "mouse masters." When fearful students finally did take charge of the mouse, they tended to seek out sites that would reinforce their preexisting beliefs instead of visiting pages that might their expand horizons and challenge their assumptions. In short, people who were fearful sought out that which they feared (i.e., pornography).
- *Adversarial:* People who had a preexisting belief that the Internet is "full of hype" and not really a "viable educational tool" tended to dwell on commercial sites. They also tended to focus on the dehumanizing aspects of the Web, noting that it could never "replace" face-to-face communication (although I had not once suggested that it should).
- *Superficial:* Some beginning surfers tended to "graze," clicking along the surfaces of preliminary home pages. Because the initial pages of any multilayered Web site are usually limited to indices of subpages, these people did not encounter much in the way of content.
- *Obedient:* A number of people had difficulty believing that I *wanted* them to roam freely, following up on their own interests. These people kept on asking me what they *should* be "looking for." Some even printed out examples of sites they had visited, bringing them to me and asking if they had done it "right." These users tended to gravitate toward "educational" sites like ERIC instead of exploring sites that might offer primary documents that could contribute to learning in a generative way.

The challenge of teaching phobic students is not a new experience for writing teachers. In addition to computers, writing is another domain that many people approach with tremendous anxiety. We even have a term for this kind of phobia: *writer's block*. The preceding list could just as easily describe the range of problematic relationships that people develop with the writing process.

Rosen, Sears, and Weil (1993) stated that "experience alone does not cure computer phobia . . . regardless of how you label the phenomenon, there is a large group of people who experience mild to severe discomfort with computers and other forms of computerized technology" (p. 28). Observing my classes further reinforced this notion that experience does not necessarily lead to reduced anxiety. I decided that the experiential dimension of my course needed some refinement: Simply asking my students to "play" with technology was not going to work for most of the members of my class. But I was also puzzled about what to do. I did not want to retreat into a directed learning environment that would cheat these professional teachers out of an opportunity to find a unique direction, build autonomy, and make their own meaning. Clearly, I had a teaching responsibility to more than just the students who would have "played" without the help of my class. If experience alone is not enough to change a person's relationship with technology, what could I do to could I help the resisters and skeptics in my class develop healthy, curious, and challenging play relationships with technology?

I decided that I needed to develop a framework that would help each person develop his or her own play relationship with technology, a situation into which students could enter and explore. I shared my thoughts with a fellow faculty member, who responded somewhat angrily, "When people tell me to 'play' with technology, it makes me feel resentful. Can't they see that this isn't 'play' for me? My idea of play does not involve sitting in front of a computer and feeling intimidated!"

This faculty response made me wonder if things were even more complicated than they appeared. This was not simply an issue of categorizing or labeling my students as resistors and skeptics and it was not about simply telling students "it's okay to play." Perhaps each person has a slightly different conceptualization of play? If students gain deeper insight into their intrinsic conceptualizations of play, might they then be able to build their own individualized play relationships with technology? Would these relationships develop into the mature play of techno-writing?

INTENTIONAL PLAY: CYBER-RESCUE

My first inclination was to design a Web-based scavenger hunt, but this seemed superficial and too directed. A scavenger hunt would have reinforced the "obedient" relationship that some of my students exhibited toward the Web, the idea that there is a specific set of "right" answers. I wanted their learning experience to be constructivist. What I needed to do was establish a frame for play, to create a context, setting, or environment in which a network of "cues" signified the affective relationship that I hoped would develop between the user and the technology.

The answers to this dilemma emerged during lunch with one of my colleagues, Ann Sevcik. She told me a story about a time when she became lost while trying to find her way to a meeting in a location she had never been before. Stopping repeatedly to ask directions, she suddenly realized that she was experiencing a sense of adventure, exploring new sights and sounds while meeting interesting strangers along the way. In mulling my ideas over with Ann, I realized that what my students needed was an interesting or compelling purpose for their exploratory Web-based play.

In developing Cyber-Rescue, I enlisted the help of Edie Coleman, one of the teacher-students enrolled in my course. Edie is a past master at writing hilarious e-mail messages and her ability to pen textual impersonations of IET faculty voices is unsurpassed. Together we created Cyber-Rescue, a Web-based adventure game.

At the beginning of the Cyber-Rescue session, my teacher-students divided up into teams of three and were asked to read and discuss an article by Duckworth (1975) entitled "The Virtue of Not Knowing." In this article, Duckworth recounts the story of a talented elementary school student who discovered that his sense of self as "knower" (and attendant assumptions) interfered with his ability to puzzle through problems posed during an in-class experiential learning exercise. Other classmates who did not think of themselves as experts in the area of knowing made more rapid progress in exploring the possibilities and responding to the exercise's open-ended questions. Reading this short article helped create a frame through which the unknown aspects of the class' impending computer-based play could be viewed as a form of learning and as a way of knowing. The teams were then asked to go to the computer lab and check their e-mail.

Each team member received a message stating that "mail" was waiting for them at MIT media lab's *Electronic Postcard* site (http://post-cards.www.media.mit.edu/postcards/). Traveling to this site, each team of teachers received a different message from a well-known faculty member conveying a sad tale of woe, a dilemma that the professor had fallen into while visiting or working in another country.

For example, Sharon Gerow, a member of our faculty who teaches qualitative research, is deeply religious and widely known by students for her interest in the spiritual dimension of human existence. Some teams received this message from Sharon:

Dear School-Based Master's Students,
   I am trekking in Nepal, researching the spirituality of the people in this country. It has been a truly rich and rewarding experience. Unfortunately, today as we hiked up to a village located high in the Himalayas, our sherpa guide became ill with altitude sickness and he had to turn back. Needless to say, as a dedicated teacher-researcher, I forged on! Luckily, I've found a temple in the village that has direct Internet access. I can't correspond with each of you individually through email because of the long distance rates, but I could use your help in finding Web-related resources about the area that would help make my stay more comfortable and enlightening. I'll check the newsgroup "gmu.course.iet710" at 3:00 your time to see what you've found for me.

By the way—if you could, please check in at IET, because I suspect my wicked evil twin may have been released and could be imper-
sonating me!

I'm having a moving experience, wish you were here—

Sharon

Messages from other faculty members conveyed tales of becoming lost
while participating in an extended tour of Africa, shipwrecked off the
coast of Newfoundland, and caught in Israeli crossfire. All asked for help
and explained that they would check in on the newsgroup later that day.
As I reviewed the team newsgroup responses, I noticed that all posts
seemed consonant with the spirit of play. One team responded to Sharon's
plight with the following message:

Greetings bold traveler!! We are here to assist you through your trek.
We have kept in mind all the "things" that are important to you during your expedition: spirituality, enlightenment, comfort, and a
healthy Sherpa guide. For your comfort we have found some Sherpa
Boots for your tired trekking tootsies. For some trekking adventure to
enhance your trip we have found some trip packages. We made sure
they had return airfare, because we would like to see you again!
<http://www.highadv.com/TreksHAT/besteverest.html>   &
<http://www.sportiva.com/sportiva/trek.html>
   In the interest of a Sherpa guide, we have found a sherpa guide
expedition for you to try:
<http://www.ourworld.comuserve.com/homepages/armand_ver-
vavaeck>. In case you are
abandoned we have found your contact to the United States of
America through the embassy in Nepal: <gopher://gopher.stolaf.
edu:70/00/Internet%20Resources/us-State-Department-Travel-Aa>.
   In case you lose your passport or decide to get a visa, here is your
connection:
<http://www.lonelyplanet.com.au/letters/indsc/nep_pc.htm>.
   For your protection from crime and theft and your daily travel
advisory call: <http://www.pomo.nbn.com/people/stevetwt/nepal/trad-
vis.Nepal.htm>.
   Monks are terrific to enhance your spirituality here's how to contact them:
<http://houston.chron.com/content/interactive/voyager/mandala/live/q
uestion.html> Happy Trails

   As I perused additional team responses I saw further evidence that
the teachers were suspending disbelief, entering into the play frame, and
experiencing a blurring of the boundaries between real life and the play

world. This blurring is another phenomenon that is associated with the flow of deep play:

> S.J's [one of the team members] sister works for the Mountain Institute in West Virginia. They do expeditions to Nepal and Tibet. They have an office over there so you might want to go see them.

Some posts were elaborate, attaching graphics files to illustrate their newsgroup messages and initiating conversations with the faculty, even though the teams knew intellectually that the dilemma and journey were not real. This post to faculty member Ann Sevcik arrived complete with a portrait of a woman in Zimbabwe:

> Boy! Have you had a trying day. The artwork we found in Africa was breathtaking! Among the many splendid pieces of art, this was the one that kept us dancing online, all the way to Zimbabwe. Some of the other sites you may find intriguing and helpful as you continue your journey are:
> http://www.tiac.net/users/smurungu/indigenous.html "Indigenous Peoples of Zimbabwe,"
> http:www.twi.tudelft.nl/Local/Shona Sculpture/Chapungu.html "Chapungu Village,"
> http://www.sas.upenn.edu/African-Studies/Country_Specific/ Zimbabwe.htm1 "Zimbabwe Page,"
> http:www.tiac.net/users/smurungu/shona_religion.html#NDEBELE "Shona Religion and Beliefs."
> Ann, We hope you enjoyed your online experience. See you when you get back. Don't forget the souvenirs. E-mail to let us know if your trip was a success. It was so nice to hear from you. We wish we were there with you. We can just imagine what a wonderful trip you are having. We can just hear the sounds of the electric drums. Did you see Nelson Mandela? He recently published an autobiography entitled *Long Walk To Freedom.* . . . Have fun! See you at the African American Art Museum in Washington, DC!

Many of the previously cited newsgroup entries were composed by teachers who had, previous to this session, been extremely circumspect about using computers and the Web. Cyber-Rescue had apparently opened up new possibilities for their relationship with technology, but without reflection it seemed unlikely that this experience would transfer into a changed relationship with the medium or into action in other domains. Specialists in experiential learning note that the actual event or action is only one small part of a larger learning cycle that includes the following phases: action, reflection, generalizing, and transfer (see Ewert, 1989; Schoel, Prouty, & Radcliffe, 1988). Mindful of this learning cycle, I knew that I needed to provide a space for teams to reflect on the larger meaning of their play experiences.

I designed a series of sections for reflective writing in the newsgroup, beginning each section with a provocative and open-ended question:

- What virtue do you see in "not knowing"?
- What is the relation between play and "not knowing"?
- What are the implications of play for learning communities?
- What are the implications of play for technology education?
- What are the implications of play for collaborative writing communities?

The newsgroup responses to these questions helped me understand the epistemological meaning that the teams had made of their experience:

> Play is a "not knowing" situation by its nature. For some reason we don't feel threatened as much by not knowing in play. Play is for the activity not for the end result. Some people are involved heavily in being the winner—are these people unable to deal with not knowing? Can they actually play?

> It's okay not to be right. There's some risk in the adventure but it heightens the senses. The "not knowing" builds a camaraderie among the participants.

> It is through play that you determine what you don't know, but with play, you are not under pressure to find out anything in particular. Play is discovering the unknown.

> It focuses more on the process than on the answer. Not knowing allows the learner to discover what he does not know at his own pace and in his own manner. Learners follow their own individual thinking process rather than a sequence that has been preprogrammed by someone else.

> As far as children being better able to use computer technology—I think it has to do with the ability of children to back up and punt. I have seen adults get frustrated when they hit the wrong button, or when an answer is just out of reach. Yet, it seems to me that children are able to say "oh well" and try a different tack. I think adults are afraid of something they feel is impossible to understand and children accept it for what it is.

At the end of the day I asked each teacher-student to jot down some reflections on paper. Many of these writings focused on the day's lesson design and helped me understand the pedagogical meaning that individual teachers had made of their lab experience:

> I can only liken today to a set of firecrackers with a long fuse. All day long the spark climbed up that fuse and then suddenly at 3:30 [the time when they were posting reflections to the newsgroup], the firecrackers started going off as I made connections, one after another. It was a powerful experience and a worthwhile day.

> The time we spent on the computer was most helpful. Today was the first time that I have really felt like something was going to work out and I would leave with a feeling of accomplishment. This tells you something about how I have felt about earlier [computer] experiences.

> It was a fun exercise and gave us some direction on how to use the Net as a means for research rather than as a toy for uses such as surfing.

> It felt good to have something positive happen to me with the computer. I haven't enjoyed the Web thus far. But the dilemmas were fun!! . . . I got a taste of success. I think I'll do another set of hours and see what happens.

> The computer search was fun for me and for my partners. We enjoyed trying to solve Sharon's problem. We were thinking of it as a game and then we suddenly realized that the information that we were pulling up was real. It was like the whole thing was "fixed," but really everything we pulled up wasn't. What a neat way to learn something.

These reflections have helped me revise and restage Cyber-Rescue in other settings and for other pedagogical goals. I have adapted Cyber-Rescue for use as a precursor to discussions about Internet-based research and assessing the value of resources found on the Web. I have also used it, in conjunction with Turkle's (1995) *Life on the Screen* and Bantock's (1996) *The Venetian's Wife* (a novella whose story unfolds in a sequence of e-mail messages and diary fragments), as a means for exploring the concepts of avatar, identity, voice, storytelling, and narrative.

Burke (1969a) likened rhetoric and writing to a continuous drama, a "pentact" of act, agent, agency, scene, and purpose. In essence, Cyber-Rescue is play-acting, participatory drama into which students enter as supporting characters in a high adventure drama that unfolds through the written word, adjourning afterward to a newsgroup for post-theater discussion.

REFLECTIONS

In the time that has intervened since I first developed Cyber-Rescue, I have thought about the exercise often, working my own way through the experiential cycle of action, reflection, generalization, and transfer in hopes of deriving a set of general principles for teachers who want to engage skeptical students in computer-mediated play learning. My thoughts are still inconclusive, but it seems that all of the following concepts were operational in Cyber-Rescue:

- *Fantasy/Imagination:* Cyber-Rescue was powerful because it created a world somewhere in between imagination and reality. In this class, the teacher-students had an experience that was real-not-real. This liminality created an opportunity for reconsidering their relationship with technology.
- *Adequate Time:* "Deep play" relationships take time to develop. Mine was a day-long session, which will not be an option for many teachers. Teachers who want to try this exercise with their own students should try to allow at least several hours for teams to make the transition from preexisting skepticism to a genuine engagement with the material and the technology.
- *Social Dimension:* Technology auto-didacts know how to develop their own internal relationships, dialogue, and direction, but other types of learners need to experience technology in a social context as something that is done with and for others. Resistance often stems not from the lack of a relationship with technology, but instead from a preexisting relationship that is adversarial. For this reason, resistors need an opportunity to experience technology in a social setting in which their negative thoughts can be simultaneously validated as "normal," yet also playfully questioned and challenged.
- *Caring and Responsibility:* The experience should relate to someone or something about which the students care. This sets up a context in which students become motivated by their intrinsic desire to help out a friend, colleague, or professor. In a large class, this means that teachers will need to learn about the lives and interests of their students. At times, the students themselves may want to construct learning spaces out of their own narratives and the knowledge base that they bring to class with them from their home communities.
- *Not Knowing:* Students need to experience the fluidity, ambiguity, nonlinearity, and poly-vocality of hypertext environ-

ments, but they also need to be provided with a framework for understanding that there is no "right" answer.

- *Working Through the Cycle of Experiential Learning:* Although most of us acknowledge the need for processing experiential activities, the reflection, generalization, and transfer phases of this learning cycle are usually given short shrift. Classes need to devote as much time to making meaning of their experience as they do to engaging in the primary "activity." The meaning-making phases of this type of learning are opportunities for students to change their patterns of relationship with technology and with one another.

There will always be students who are auto-didacts. There will always be adventurous early adopters. There will also always be students who know how to learn through play and who can find their own motivation for learning about new technologies. But the challenge for educators is to create contexts in which heterogeneous groups of students can find their "hook," a unique set of motivating factors that will compel them to construct a ludic relationship with the medium that is intellectually challenging. Learning to learn, learning to use computers, and learning to write all go hand-in-hand with learning to play.

ACKNOWLEDGMENTS

I would like to thank Ann Sevcik, Sharon Gerow, and Edie Coleman of the Institute for Educational Transformation, George Mason University, for their assistance in developing the Cyber-Rescue activity. Thanks also to Doug DeNatale, Pam LePage-Lees, Susan-Marie Harrington, Michael Day, and Becky Rickly for reading and responding to earlier drafts of this chapter, and to the Epiphany project for its support.

REFERENCES

Bantock, N. (1996). *The venetian's wife: A strangely sensual tale of a renaissance explorer, a computer, and a metamorphosis.* San Francisco, CA: Chronicle Books.

Burke, K. (1969a). *A grammar of motives.* Berkeley: University of California Press.

Burke, K. (1969b). *A rhetoric of motives.* Berkeley: University of California Press.

Csiszentmihalyi, M. (1974). *Flow studies of enjoyment* (PHS Grant Report). Chicago: University of Chicago Press.

Dargan, A., & Zeitlin, S. (1990). *City play.* New Brunswick, NJ: Rutgers University Press.

Day, M., & Batson, T. (1995). The network-based writing classroom: The ENFI idea. In M. Collins and Z. Berge (Eds.), *Computer mediated communication and the online writing classroom, Vol. 2: Higher education* (pp. 25-46). Cresskill NJ: Hampton Press.

Duckworth, E. (1975). The virtue of not knowing. *National Elementary Principal, 54*(4), 63-66.

Ewert, A. (1989). *Outdoor adventure pursuits: Foundations, models, and theories.* Columbus, OH: Publishing Horizons.

Geertz, C. (1973). Deep play: Notes on a balinese cockfight. *The interpretation of cultures* (pp. 412-453). New York: Basic Books

Huizinga, J. (1950). *Homo ludens: A study of the play element in culture.* Boston: Beacon Press.

McDowell, J. (1979). *Children's riddling: The interrogative ludic routine in child cognition and sociability.* Bloomington: Indiana University Press.

Rosen, L., Sears, D., & Weil, M. (1993). Treating technophobia: A longitudinal evaluation of the computerphobia reduction program. *Computers in Human Behavior, 9, 28.*

Rosen, L., & Weil, M. (1995). Computer availability, computer experience, and technophobia among public school teachers. *Computers in Human Behavior, 6, 9-31.*

Schoel, J., Prouty, D., & Radcliffe, P. (1988). *Islands of healing: A guide to adventure based counseling.* Hamilton, MA: Project Adventure.

Schwartzman, H. (1978). *Transformations: The anthropology of children's play.* New York: Plenum Press.

Turkle. S. (1995). *Life on the screen: Identity in the age of the internet.* New York: Simon & Schuster.

Chapter • 5

Indiscipline:
Obscenity and Vandalism
in Cyberclassrooms

Sharon Cogdill

Much of what happens in a computer classroom is wonderful, but sometimes teachers are faced with situations in which students use instructional computers to test boundaries, strike out angrily or seductively at the closest adult target, or leave sometimes violent or sexualized graffiti for teachers or each other to read. If students strike out angrily, they often do it when teachers are not supervising, or when the teacher's attention, momentarily, is elsewhere. Such behavior, like any acting out in a traditional classroom, can be uncomfortable, partly because teachers don't want to read or see what these students leave, partly because teachers are not completely sure how important it is or what it means to the student, and partly because teachers are not sure who else is looking. Obscene behavior—that which is profoundly, shockingly offensive—is not a regular occurrence in online classrooms, but it happens often enough that it is worth discussing. Only through discussion and reflection can both the theoretical framework and practical policies be developed that will allow teachers to respond to obscenity in a caring way.

Networked computers make surveillance easy. It is easier for teachers, if they are paying attention, to observe their students as they work. And it is easier for people outside classrooms to see what teachers and students are doing. When teaching with networked computers, teachers cannot always be sure a closed door will prevent others from observ-

ing them, unannounced and without permission—and some unethical people cannot resist that temptation.[1] Of course, any extreme behavior that
leads the teacher or the school to call in the police will bring media attention, snatching control of the situation right out of teachers' hands. Such
horror stories can indeed satisfy some critics that computers create problems that threaten civilized discourse if not society.

Such situations result not only from ethical lapses, but also from
changes in the boundaries of the classroom. Because of these changes, as
well as media interest in computers, and the skepticism of colleagues or
supervisors, teachers who use computers in English classes can find it difficult to talk about the obscenity that inevitably shows up in computer-
mediated classrooms. What is more, the stakes can be so high that it is
hard to avoid demonizing offensive behavior or the students themselves.
However, in order to explore the complex issues that such behavior raises,
I propose that teachers resist the temptation to think of offensive language
or behavior in electronic environments as some form of sociopathology. I
propose instead that such language and behavior be viewed as instances of
young people talking among themselves, experimenting with the power of
language to threaten and the power of the Internet to broadcast or
attempting (however clumsily) irony. More to the point, I propose that
such behavior be viewed through the lens provided by Foucault (1979), in
his work with *indiscipline*—which Foucault says "puts itself forward as a
right" against government and technology and surveillance that seem (or
are) oppressive (p. 245). A person who teaches in or manages a small electronic classroom can find it very difficult to tell what is truly pathological
or illegal from what is not. For all these reasons, especially the uncomfortable ones, it is essential we talk openly about online obscenity.

If we're honest with each other, and tell the horror stories and
really know what can happen, we won't repeat the mistakes of the past. I
was able to avoid some mistakes because another teacher had made them
for me and—most importantly—had told me about them. Teachers need
to learn from each other so that their mistakes add up to something, and
so that they are not alone when facing particularly ugly obscenity, or
when they think through their own mistakes in dealing with it. Open discussion is a way of making our learning evidence of growth and intellectual courage and ability, even though some people might call it evidence of
lack of control (on the part of the teacher) or lawlessness (on the part of
the students) or inherent subversiveness (on the part of the Internet itself).

All of the usual caveats apply. I am an English teacher who has
used computers in my teaching for over a decade, who has managed vari-

---

[1]For example, in a small university in the Minnesota State University system,
instructional television was piped into the dean's office, despite the faculty contract that required faculty be notified that they were observed while teaching.

ous departmental computer labs, who uses computers for my own writing and communication, even with my own parents. I am a teacher—I am not a lawyer, not a member of the police department or FBI, not an administrator. I am also not a parent, constitutional specialist, or psychologist. All of these people can be stakeholders in the conflict if a student uses school computers to be offensive, but their stakes are not the same as teachers and their ways of looking at an offense are not the same. Teachers have responsibilities for their own continued effectiveness and commitment to their profession, which include their own and their families' safety as well as security and ease of mind. Teachers have responsibilities for their students, both as a group and individually, as well as, sometimes, the malefactors themselves. We have responsibilities toward all our students' education, which means that not all mistakes are the end of the world and not all crimes should lead to prison. Unless outside intervention is requested, the last word in the classrooms should be the teachers' and their students'. It is sufficient to be the teacher, to be an English teacher. The teacher's expertise is the expertise needed in order to confront these difficult issues.

Some people who have faced eruptive and aggressive behavior from their students on computers can take a kind of arcane joy in discussing the worst of their experiences. People listening can get a similar kind of joy, the "there-but-for-the-grace-of-God" *frisson* gotten from horror novels or slasher movies. But people on the outside, like the president of my university, do not get that same kind of pleasure out of this telling. Neither do the parents of students. Neither, perhaps, do teachers thinking about introducing computers into the program for the first time. These people want to keep the schools "clean," as one administrator put it to me, to keep them and the young people "safe." Some of these people want all the computer programs loaded onto the server, out of the students' control or access, so that absolutely everything possible is controlled and predictable. They want the students not to be able to *write* on the system—a situation, I believe, that calls graffiti out of students and encourages that indiscipline that "puts itself forward as a right." So, for those people who think about containing damage instead of subverting containment, I will try to categorize it. It can be shocking to see it in print, but let's get it on the table so we can look at it.

Here are some incidents of obscenity that have occurred in classrooms:

- Students leaving (sometimes hundreds of) messages on the screen telling the reader which sexual position to assume and what sexual acts to perform.
- Students sending threatening e-mail to a faculty member, another student, or the president of the United States.

- Students sending anonymous e-mail that threatens to kill or torture the recipient.
- Students deliberately broadcasting sexist or racist jokes.
- Students speculating about the teacher's sex life in a class newsgroup or listserv, making graphic reference to the student's own sexual practices.
- Students sitting in an open university lab, looking at large images on the screen that objectify parts of women's or children's bodies that other students walking past cannot miss, and then leaving them there, so one of the lab workers has to deal with it personally, or leaving dozens of bookmarks to sites with lots of sexual content in a Web browser on public machines.
- Students leaving offensive screen savers on machines in public computer labs.
- Students organizing an Internet discussion group for the dissemination of jokes about African-American women.
- Students broadcasting details of a woman's sexual assault or a teacher's homosexuality.
- Students publishing, in a Usenet newsgroup, stories of the sexual torture of a woman whose name, which belongs to a classmate, makes an apparently irresistible sexual pun.[2]
- Students posting long messages to White supremacist Usenet newsgroups, with the name of the school prominently displayed, offering local harassments as political actions.
- Students jamming up the printer with lists of swear words.
- Students contacting any currently active users who might be female, assuming they will be willing to have virtual or arrange to have actual sex; or searching the Web for images of women with long hair, posting their URLs to something like "Chicks of the Web," and writing to them graphic descriptions of their wishes.
- Students spending their time during the class meeting that introduces the World Wide Web finding, examining, and sharing the addresses of Playboy or Penthouse or sites with graphics depicting oral sex or bondage or sex with chickens or whatever they can find.

---

[2]The details of this case, which led to a federal lawsuit against University of Michigan student Jake Baker, are documented in the Massachusetts Institute of Technology Student Association for Freedom of Expression Archive, located at http://www.mit.edu:8001/activities/safe/safe/cases/umich-baker-story/summary.html.

- Students stalking another student with harassing, unwelcome e-mail.
- Students appropriating another student's identity and writing from it.

As this list suggests, one of the hardest things about discussing obscenity on the Net is its variety. For my purposes, *obscenity* is not what is considered obscenity by people in the legal professions, for whom the term has been reasonably clearly defined.[3] Rather, obscenity in a classroom context is all the offensive writing (and occasionally offensive drawing) that students can do with computers. In some respects, the actual definition is not that important, because if a student does something that any observer *considers* obscene, the teacher will have to deal with it, whether he or she agrees that it is actually obscene. Some of the obscene things students can do are legal, however offensive they may be to some people. Others, however, are federal offenses, and most fall somewhere in between. Some raise questions of free speech, which may not be a guaranteed right in school, but which is an important issue for many teachers.[4] Some raise questions about the psychological status of the offender, and some raise large questions about the expectations in our culture for how people should act with regard to people who are different from them—different race, class, gender, sexual orientation, degree of ability or disability, and so on. Whether teachers find some particular behavior obscene or offensive, if others do, teachers will be dealing with it.

A striking example of this occurred at a community college in a conservative western city where an English teacher was using synchronous electronic discussion software in a class.[5] One day, two young men got into an argument that escalated into a flame war. The next day, each showed up on campus with a loaded gun. Very angry, the president of the college called the teacher into his office and said that "this" was the result of bringing computers into the classroom. It is obvious to me, however, that computers did not do "this," but that some other factor(s) did. I can see why anybody would want to understand the young men's behavior. But it is crucial to think critically about the nature and causes of what we label *obscene,* just as it is crucial that we think critically about whether computers are relevant to the case.

---

[3]People in the legal professions distinguish *obscenity,* which is illegal, from *offensive language* or *behavior,* which is not. And everybody recognizes that *pornography,* for example, is actually impossible to define in any functional way.

[4]As a number of court cases have recently shown, free speech is not guaranteed in public schools, and it is not something people in a university can count on, either, regardless of what they think.

[5]This story was reported to me at the 1994 Computers and Writing conference in Columbia, Missouri.

To think that obscenity somehow comes from computers just because the computer is used as the means of creation or transmission is to mistake the instrument for the agent: to think the computer did something that in fact a student did. It is like blaming the telephone if terrorists use it to plan an attack or blaming xerography for duplicated instructions for building a bomb. It might be worth examining the special characteristics brought to the offense by the instrument—the special efficiency in broadcasting via the Internet or the special compelling power of instructions as they appear on a monitor, for example—to get a better understanding of the form of this particular offense or the strength of that particular reaction, but in general, the computer is no explanation of the offense.

What really caused this incident? And what questions should we be asking about such situations? Is the real question something like, "What is the effect of bringing computers into the classroom?" Is it something like, "What effect does electronic discourse have on the social inhibitions of adolescent males?" Or is it something like, "What are the causes of human aggression?" It is easy to see the value of a solid answer to these questions, especially that last one, but in the case of classroom obscenity, seeking this kind of reason for offensive behavior is tracking a red herring. Regardless of the causes, the teacher in that western city had to deal not only with two volatile young men with guns, but also with an angry, scared, and possibly incoherent president and other administrators. And if, imagining the worst case, somebody had been shot, the media would have been present, and "computers" would have been on the evening news.

But the offense in this situation was not using networked computers or synchronous communications software in an English class. Nor was the offense arguing in class or getting into a flame war with classmates. Nor was the offense failing to stop the flame war in class. The offense was bringing a loaded gun onto campus, and I expect that the right people at that college knew very well how to handle that kind of problem, assuming they could have stopped to identify it as the problem.

It can be very difficult to think clearly about obscenity in an electronic classroom. Theory can help identify what the real offense is, or even if there is a real offense. We need some kind of framework for situating the unfolding event, especially if people disagree about nature of the offense or its malignity, or if we begin to have reason to doubt the perspectives of people involved, including our own. Theory can also help us put off coming to an inappropriately easy resolution, especially if that resolution oversimplifies or scapegoats or if it encourages us to react unconsciously, thoughtlessly.

In particular, Foucault suggests that where technology, education, and coercion or punishment come together, and students feel powerless and controlled, they will react not merely against the authority of the teacher or the technology but also against the general, *monitoring* authority that Foucault calls "the Prince." The Prince is Machiavelli's Prince; it is also the government, and it is also teachers, even if in their own eyes they are as manipulated by the technology as their students. To students, the face of the Prince can look like the monitor of a computer. An electronic cowboy or cowgirl feels that it is his or her right to undermine the discipline of the classroom if it looks like the discipline of the Prince. This dogged, systematic subversion of the Prince's authority is Foucault's indiscipline. Although students see teachers allied with the Prince in their roles as teachers, as learners, teachers too look at those monitors and see the Prince, see surveillance, see technological "discipline."

Foucault's is not the only valuable theory for analyzing obscenity and indiscipline in the classroom. Because there can be a high level of emotionalism around educational technology, especially when there are problems with that technology, some people find theories of personality helpful. Also valuable are theories of educational or psychological development, legal theories, sociological theories of community and culture, theories of language and linguistic behavior, theories of gender, pseudonymity, and anonymity, and performance theory. A grounding in theory can help us know when we are looking at something that has the imminent potential to offend, hurt, silence, or coerce people who don't have the power or know how to get themselves out of the situation they don't like. Once we have determined if there is potential for harm, then we need to ask exactly what the real offense is and whether "computers" have anything to do with it.

I said that to blame computers for people's misbehavior is to mistake the instrument for the agent, but it is not true that computers are vacuums devoid of values, culturally neutral, empty screens people project onto. In fact, technology is the vector for certain organized value systems, and sometimes those values are the real target of the obscenity, especially when those values are intensified by the teaching situation or the personal style of the teacher. Words like *execute, kill, crash,* and *bomb* are metaphors that reflect some of the militaristic origins of computing, networked computers, and wide-area networks (see, e.g., Bernhardt, 1993). Selfe and Selfe (1994) explored the capitalistic orientation of the Macintosh interface. With its (presumably clean) desktop, its trash can, ticking watch, and folders and files, the Macintosh, like Windows, reveals a capitalistic orientation, despite its counter-culture and "friendly" image. Other scholars have pointed out the bias that presupposes male experience as the norm (see Cherny & Weise, 1996). All these ways of looking at the values carried by computers and computer environments, including Foucault's association of generalized governmental control with the Prince and his insight about the increasing surveillance networked computers make possible, provide ample motivations for people to subvert that hierarchy. The pressure to subvert is especially great for people who exist in hierarchical relationships within structures defined by military, capitalistic, gender, and social discipline. It is, as Foucault points out, these people for whom indiscipline seems to be a right. We can see their work in obscenity left as electronic graffiti in public electronic spaces.

Something about a lab of networked computers, where students are by and large working alone, even if they are in a room full of people or in a class supervised by a teacher, something about that unsupervised time with that blank screen suggests to some students that they should be able to say and do things they normally would never do in class, face to face with the teacher and the other students. Theory tells us that students say and do these offensive things sometimes because they have ideas about how they have been treated or situated by authority, technology, class, gender—and because it gives them an opportunity to take power in a situation in which they have consistently been powerless. They can speak, take verbal action, without associating that action with their bodies or their voices or even, sometimes, their identities. They can subvert the discipline, the conditioning, that the machines impose.[6] In a way, when students are leaving electronic graffiti, they may be acting lightheartedly or casually, although not insincerely; teachers who feel responsible for the "level" of discourse in an electronic space, however, may not be able to read or remove that graffiti lightheartedly or casually.

One of the interesting aspects of the way people interact with student-created obscenity is how deeply they are affected, how much energy and attention the experience takes, how much time is spent processing what happened, and what needs to be done. Listed on the page as they are, my examples of student misbehavior may seem simple and contained, but that sense of them arises because I have encapsulated them here. In life, they eat up time, energy, intelligence, and trust, seemingly endlessly. For example, here's the real story behind the offense of using the efficiencies of electronic dissemination to broadcast details of a woman's sexual assault and a teacher's homosexuality. I'll call the student Adam.

A teacher in a new networked high school English department lab wasn't sure he "liked" computers, and he didn't know much about them,

---

[6]One reason people distinguish between *education* and *training* is the mechanical and mechanistic nature of training. A deeper level of learning than training takes place, however, on computers. When we internalize how to use the machine without making a lot of mistakes that cause it to crash and without getting ourselves hopelessly frustrated, we have actually been conditioned by the machine and by its makers. Inasmuch as the inhumanistic qualities of Skinnerian conditioning are, precisely, mechanical, it is not wrong or ridiculous to be indisciplined to a machine.

but when the new lab was installed in the journalism room, he said he was willing to give it a try. Adam, a 16-year-old student (whose parents were completely absorbed in their own personal World War III) heard from town gossip that his teacher was homosexual. Logged on under his own user ID and password, Adam began to create hundreds of files whose only purpose was the file name: eight-character hints of what Adam imagined could be done to a homosexual man. The teacher did not challenge the student, and knowledge of what was happening and even the practice spread among other students. For several weeks, the teacher did not address the problem with the boy, the other students, the department chair, or any of his colleagues. One day in class, Adam sent 200 pages of sniggering, aggressive, appalling file and directory names to the laser printer. When the first pages came out of the printer, the teacher turned the printer off. At the bell he dismissed the class.

When it came time for the students in the next period to print, their teacher realized that they couldn't because the printer was turned off, and she turned it back on. One hundred and ninety-some pages came out of the printer, pages apparently targeting the previous hour's teacher. This teacher immediately took the problem to the chair of the English department. In turn, she talked to Adam, who would not admit what he had done; then she talked to the boy's mother, who refused to accept any of her suggestions for getting him out of the teacher's class or punishing him. The chair had no policy in place to refer to or use, and the English department faculty took part in no systematic, organized discussion, partly to protect the gay teacher from talk.

The boy returned to the class, having gotten off scot free. His next target was another teacher whom he had heard was raped, but he may have chosen her for no other reason than because he knew the user ID and password of a boy in her class, his former best friend, a boy whom he had reason to fear would soon be his stepbrother. Like the gay teacher, this teacher also was not comfortable with the technology and knew how to perform only the most basic operations. She did not challenge her own student, so she did not learn that Adam, not her student, was guilty of this insurrection. She did not defend herself or ask for help. In a way, as with the first teacher, it became her secret—not the students'. Once again, another teacher more confident with the technology accidentally found out and put the problem in the hands of people who would confront it.

This whole sequence of events took an entire semester out of those people's lives, time they spent repeatedly going over what had happened, what was happening, what could or would happen. The phenomenal amount of time the faculty spent processing Adam's lists of ugly words was part of what it takes to handle an experience of student-created obscenity like this, and an index of how difficult it can be to work with language whose offensiveness increases the longer it persists. With the benefits of hindsight and being a consultant in this school, I can say without reservation that it is immoral to blame the teachers for their own victimization, especially to others who might use their mistakes against them. But we must be able to speak honestly about ways in which everybody contributed to the intensity of this experience. Here are some conclusions we can draw (from a long and safe distance):

- The department chair needed a policy in place. The department needed a policy in place. The school needed a policy in place. There are rules about student behavior in chairs, around books, in the cafeteria. There need to be rules about students on school computers.
- The boy needed to know that logical consequences would follow from his actions, and he needed for them actually to follow.
- The other students needed to be addressed as well because they knew what was going on and some contributed to it. Even though one faculty member knew about it, then two, then the chair, and then four, the students were in fact unsupervised: Their thinking all occurred without the benefit of adults framing the situation into a safer, more understandable, and thus more educational form.
- The teachers who were willing to experiment with the technology without knowing a lot about it needed support from the institution, perhaps even a mentor who would directly ask about difficult situations she had the experience to expect would come up. This is a place where the consultants (especially me) could have done better. My care not to be a PhD bull in a public-school china shop prevented me from asking revealing questions that would have made the problem an open, practical issue.
- The teachers who had been targeted by the student needed to be more open about the attacks on them, and the members of the department needed to know how to rally around their attacked colleagues without violating their private lives or opening old wounds or endangering their careers.
- The school counselor needed to know enough about writing and electronic classrooms to be able to help manage the psychological aspects of the situation once he was called in.

Here, in a nutshell, is the real crux: This was not an inherently alien situation to these teachers. If the boy had stood up in class and begun shouting or even speaking these things, what would he have been doing? What would his teachers have done? What would everybody have thought? I think these two teachers were so acutely conscious that a computer was involved that they were paralyzed by knowledge of what they did not know, as if their inability to control a computer meant that they did not know how to handle this kind of behavior. For Adam, perhaps, the computer gave him a way to write graffiti not in his own hand, not (to his way of thinking) in any way traceable to him. The fact that he could leave his lists of file and directory names in a place that only somebody with authority could find—this fact meant that he was writing on their bodies, insofar as their bodies were monitoring him. For the teachers, I think, it felt as if the technology conspired with their oppressors to threaten them and hurt them again. The homophobia and violence against women in the culture found a new voice in the technology in their classrooms, and that technology made the voice of the teenager, which sometimes speaks from a perspective wildly uncomfortable with difference and divergence from peer norms, powerful. The technology in Adam's high school made the powerful Prince take on the values and social opinions of a teenager (for a powerful telling of an analogous story, see Regan, 1993).

But the kinds of threats and injury those teachers experienced can happen without the computers, and those kinds of threats and injuries, however nasty, teachers already know how to handle. Any teacher would be horrified or outraged if a student began shouting the things this boy wrote. Little time would be needed to decide what to do, and more would be done than attempt to ignore it, even if teachers are gay or have been raped and are afraid of exposure. Any teacher would be horrified and outraged if two students showed up on campus with loaded guns, but they would not conclude that violence resulted from bringing books into the classroom.

The next most important conclusion to draw is that the high school English department chair needed a policy in place that she could slap down on the table in front of the boy's mother, that would get him out of the class and off the class computers and under supervision. In this case, the boy needed help getting his feet back on the ground emotionally and help working on the quality of his contributions to his community. A policy could have directed the department chair to get a counselor involved if she felt that a specialist in students' emotional lives would be useful. The sanctions against him needed to escalate as he continued to offend, within a clearly articulated hierarchy. A policy could have set the original sanction and articulated its escalation. It is clear that his behavior was unacceptable all along, but fairness requires that he be told explicitly what the consequences of that sort of behavior would be and what the consequences of its continuance would be. Furthermore, the other students needed to know about that policy (and perhaps even have agreed to abide by it), so that teachers addressing the general citizenship and "netizenship" questions with them would have a concrete place to begin. One way to dilute students' sense that the technology directs authority and discipline at them, which would lead some to resist that discipline, is to illustrate for them that they, too, have power and authority, that they too contribute to the intellectual life of the electronic world. *Netizenship,* that is, contributing to an electronic community productively, is available to anybody online, regardless of their age or their status in school.

In fact, one reasonable way to handle this extreme—and, fortunately, rare—situation would be to engage the students in a project of *writing* a policy, right then, if not for their school or department or lab, then at least for their class. This kind of writing assignment does not waste class time or misdirect course resources. It is an excellent exercise in argument, logic, clarity, and audience, not to mention an example of the ways action in the world can take the form of writing and the ways writing is social.

Writing a policy would be one reasonably productive way of addressing what happened and what netizenship is about with the other students, of course, but much of what was happening in this particular case was really personal to the boy. The social issues around homosexuality would be very difficult to work with in the classes described here because in the community in which this whole slow-motion crisis took place, homosexual teachers are not universally accepted and the teacher's sexual orientation would, for some citizens, routinely be considered a concern for the community at large. Some parents would probably have demanded he be fired on that basis alone. Although I personally believe that the students should be confronted with their homophobia, I understand with sadness the reluctance of that gay teacher, as well as the chair and the English department faculty, to address it publicly, just as I understand their reluctance to put their colleague who had been raped in the position of having to discuss her assault in a professional setting.

It is easy enough to say there should be a policy, but the practical aspects of writing good policies or dealing with ones written by the wrong stakeholders are quite difficult. That is, it is impossible to write something that anticipates or prevents all problems. In fact, the teachers in Adam's school actually already had the most important defense against offensive behavior: They were willing to experiment with their teaching and with new technologies; they were willing to see what happens and deal with problems as they arise. And the teachers in that English department— especially the two who were willing to be disadvantaged by introducing unfamiliar and in some ways alienating networked computers in their classes—deserve respect for their courage.

Looking again at my list of student-created acts of indiscipline, and trying to be sane about this incendiary subject, I notice some patterns of mistakes that were made, and what could have been done in a better, less harried world. From past mistakes, perhaps some principles for handling similar problems more successfully can be found.

A fundamental principle is that some problems cannot be prevented, either by policy or technology. Some students will figure out how to send anonymous e-mail, particularly in settings where it is easy to do. I get e-mail from "Bill Clinton" every April, reminding me to pay my taxes. Because of my technical expertise, I can tell which computer the message was sent from, but I think that there is no point in spending any time at all tracking down humorists like this unless we have a record somehow of which student used which machine at the time stamped on the e-mail message. Even then, it is not worth it for teachers to track down offenders unless, for pedagogical reasons, they want students to think about the potential seriousness of this kind of practical joke, as, for example, in a situation in which the offense stops being a "computer crime" and crosses the line into "real" crime.

A very unhappy student sent several anonymous e-mail messages to a German faculty member I know. The anonymous e-mail swore at him, called him a Nazi, and threatened to kill him. After the third such message, it occurred to us that the messages were intended for a different person on campus and that the charge of Nazi was unrelated to my friend's heritage. Once we deduced that the e-mail was addressed to the wrong person, it was easy to guess from the content of the messages who the real target probably was. Another group of messages from the same writer went to the university Web team, probably because the link on a university Web page seems to send e-mail to the university itself. Although these messages were received by the university Web team, clearly they were aimed at the same person, threatening to cut off his genitals and put his head on a pike "for the campus to jeer at."

As shocking and convincing as this threatening e-mail was to my friend as well as to the members of the Web team and to the target himself, even the most draconian solutions—which deny students access to e-mail or the Internet except under highly controlled conditions—cannot actually guarantee that it will not happen again. No amount of technology, legislation, or campus rules can completely prevent anonymous e-mail or guarantee that the name of an e-mailer will not be laundered. What is more, the loss to the students—in experience with electronic rhetorical situations, with writing e-mail or Web pages or MOO dialogue—far outweighs the little gained with an attempt to *prevent* all such errors. This problem cannot be prevented. It can and should be handled pedagogically, but it cannot be prevented, no matter how strict teachers are. So what should teachers do? Teach to it, talk about it in class, and put it on the table so students understand it. Threatening anonymous e-mail can actually be a federal offense, and students need to know that once the FBI gets involved, the resources available to solve the mystery make the chances of catching them much, much better and the scope of the punishment much, much greater. There is almost no chance, once the FBI gets called in, that anybody will be able to argue that, because the institution is educational, an attempt should be made to educate rather than merely punish the offender.

Offensive language in an electronic classroom environment is so common that probably all teachers experienced in using these kinds of software actually expect and prepare for it. I suppose that, technically, such offensiveness could be prevented with sufficiently vigorous legislation and surveillance, but such an attempt to control student discourse so absolutely and so a priori strikes me as pedagogically untenable and, actually, suspect. For one thing, the instructions would have to be so clear about exactly what kinds of language would not be acceptable that no student experimenting with boundaries or effects would make any mistakes at all—unlikely, in my opinion, at least with my instructions and my students. And I think I would rather not have students prevented from making mistakes if it means that they are not experimenting at all. In a nutshell, people who teach students using electronic tools, like computer-mediated communication, need to be teachers who can let students try new things, who can help students turn mistakes into productive and educational experiences.

As a result of using networked computers in my classes, I am much less worried now about what used to strike me as inappropriate discourse for the classroom. For example, one of my classes decided to relieve end-of-term writing-deadline stress by posting dirty jokes to the class listserv. According to the unarticulated rules of the contest, not only did the jokes need to have sexual content but they also needed to be sexist (with both genders apparently equally under attack). Although, personally, I would rather my students did not bring jokes like this into what seems to me to be classroom discourse, the question of whether I am dealing with offensive language really depends on how bothered I am by it and how bothered any of my students are, not on whether dirty sexist jokes are or are not acceptable on the face of it. One way to handle it would be for me to tell the jokesters to stop because the jokes are dirty and sexist and thus probably inappropriate for academic discourse. This would stop the jokes and (re)establish my control over the list and the language of the classroom. Another way to handle the sexist-dirty-joke contest would be to use some kind of classroom assessment technique, like asking them in class to write anonymously for a minute or two, answering a question like "Have you been offended by the contents of messages on the class list?" or "Have you been reluctant to read or post to the list because of the jokes being told recently?" and then deciding what to do about the jokes based on that (for a full discussion of classroom assessment techniques, see Angelo & Cross, 1993). Another approach would be to wait and see what the students would do, which is what I did. I talked to everybody whom I thought might be offended or silenced by the jokes, to see how they felt and to be sure they saw themselves as able to speak or able to delete the messages unread. It has been my experience that once a student crosses some line and goes too far, almost everyone else feels the transgression and almost everyone pulls back, which is exactly what my students did. They read the messages that were coming at them, and they stopped telling the jokes. If students do not feel the transgression and do not back off, then I think I have a slightly different problem from the one I had: It's one thing for them not to have the rhetorical sophistication to *predict* what the line is. It's another for them not to be able to sense it when they step over it.

At heart here, of course, is a sense of the ownership of the discourse in a classroom. Just as I am not the only decision maker in the class and not the only person with autonomy, I am not the only owner of classroom discourse. Students own the discourse as much as I do, although in a different way; they are decision makers with autonomy, or at least they should be. My attitude here is closely related to the attitude that associates student mistakes with their having taken risks, rather than with moral depravity, emotional immaturity, socialized weakness or excess testosterone, or any other sweeping social put-down. This attitude places much of the control for the conduct of a class in the hands of the students and is suspicious of top-down control, especially of discourse. This attitude lets a certain amount of offensive language slide by, so long as nobody is getting hurt or silenced.

Beyond these pedagogical concerns, one way to look at the differences between my reactions to the sexist, dirty jokes and my students' desire to tell them is to think about my professionalization as a teacher. Never much of a prude, I was probably at least as offensive as they are when I was a teenager, but over the years I have come to see the classroom as one of the most important sites of my professional work. My standards for my own behavior have gone up, and I am less and less accepting of slack days or time-wasting exercises, and more and more respectful of my students' stabs at going beyond what they know is safe. This is all to the good, and it's raised the level of my own discourse in the classroom. But my students have not professionalized around my classroom the same way I have, as they should not. It is my center, not theirs, and they have the right to their own centers.

One final example of offensive language that cannot really be prevented is hard to describe because it is so technical, based in cyberspace, and because the distance between the technology and its emotional impact is so great, mostly because there is no analog for it in real life. In a MOO or other synchronous communication environment in which people can create objects, a reasonably talented student will eventually figure out how to make it look like somebody else is writing what the student, in fact, has written. An object that does this is called a "voodoo doll," and when a doll is activated, other people in the MOO room will read that you are willingly taking part in an action, no matter what you actually type or how strongly you protest. In the situation described in Dibbell's (1993) "A Rape in Cyberspace," the people attacked in this way by Mr. Bungle in the room on LambdaMOO found themselves engaged in self-mutilation and virtual sex with him against their wills and saw responses that he had written for them printing to their screens.

The violent and sexual content of what the voodoo doll wrote to the screen, however, is only part of the problem. People who have high levels of electronic literacy are accustomed to seeing some of their unspoken thoughts written out on the screen, but only when they are doing the writing. To see what purports to be and what looks like your thoughts printed to the MOO screen but to read things you haven't thought or don't want to see broadcast is very disturbing, more disturbing than can be expressed to someone who doesn't have exactly this kind of experience. For my personal use on a MOO, I created an object, called BloodPressure, that was intended to do what many well-written MOO gestures do: put into written language some aspect of mood or mind that might in real life be expressed by body language. I wrote it at first so that if someone typed "raise bloodpressure," then everybody in the room would see "Your skin begins to tingle" and then "There's a singing in your ears" and then "Your hair begins to lift off your scalp" and then "It feels like rage" and then "BANG! You pop a cork." When I put it in a room and let somebody try it, however, it wasn't funny. At first, I thought it wasn't funny because the end is so macabre, so I rewrote it to have a happy ending: after "Your hair begins to lift off your scalp," everybody would see "You think of Percival's garden . . ." and then "Your hair gently settles back down" and then "Whew!" and then "You almost popped a cork!" But the humor still wasn't working.

It took me a day to realize that what was so chilling was everybody in the room reading a narration they had not written that nonetheless purported to describe their own internal state. I have a reasonably developed sense of rhetorical nuance, especially compared, say, to the general population of undergraduates, who will do worse. There are strong sanctions among the MOOers I know not to use voodoo dolls or to appropriate others' language or consciousness, but no such sanction would have worked on me because I never intended to do anything bad, to create a voodoo doll or to colonize the others in the room. Once it was done and I sensed that there was something wrong, I had to think about it for a while to see the problem. I had to make the mistake before I could see that it was wrong. Everyone who is witty or ironic in electronic discourse sooner or later makes a mistake in tone, the perfect control of which is arguably the most difficult thing to manage in the electronic world. Trying to be funny or witty—the intention—is not a federal offense, and neither is the effect in this case. Used offensively, of course, a mistake like the one I ended up making is close to a capital offense in many electronic communities. In any event, such a mistake can't be prevented by a priori policies; the solution to a student's doing it by accident, as I did, should replicate my experience. The student would need a chance to figure out exactly what's wrong with writing a voodoo doll, with help if necessary, and then have the chance to fix it. Such a solution gives students responsibility for their own language and behavior, it gives them ownership in the class, and it rewards risk-taking learning by making mistakes educational rather than actionable.

We must realize, however, that almost none of the student-created offensiveness I described at the outset of this chapter can be prevented by policy or legislation or sanctions, although some of them, perhaps, can be regarded as evidence that students are taking risks in their learning. In any event, a teacher is neither helpless in the face of such problems nor required to accept every thing students try. First, a great deal depends on how much playful, experimental, informal, student ownership of the classroom discourse the teacher wishes to foster. As I said, I am able to handle a great deal more playfulness than I used to. Furthermore, I don't read the class listserv or the MOO the same way I read papers turned in to me for a grade, even though students' participation in electronic discussion in the class is at least as important to me as their reading, paper-writing, or participation in face-to-face discussion. In part, letting them talk to each other freely, electronically, makes me less the center and clearinghouse for the discourse, which means I read it differently than I read formal papers and "listen" differently than I listen in class. I read it, at least to some degree, as them talking to each other. In their course evaluations, my students are clear that the reduction in the intensity of my gaze at their language and performance frees them to say things more provisionally or to be more risqué or to be more encouraging with each other. They feel more able to think creatively and brainstorm effectively on the list and the MOO than they do in class. From my perspective, they experiment more with intellectual positions and rhetorical stances. They try things out, something I want them to do, even though I don't always love the effects of a particular experiment or admire the heavy way they wield their new-found sense of irony or critical distance.

And it does happen, of course, that I occasionally become dissatisfied with the level of their discourse, the nature or the kind of things they are saying, or their treatment of me or one or more of their number. At that point, I have the right and responsibility to do something about it—to say that I am unhappy with the language or the level of thought, to say what I would like to see happen differently and why. In the MOO I can (and do) draw attention to their avoidance of the difficulties of someone's argument, and I can (and do) directly address language I don't like. But it is not clear to me that the teacher really always has to do something about this kind of behavior—unless someone, particularly a student, is uncomfortable with it or silenced by it. What's more, it is not clear to me that comfort is always the best environment for learning. Within some limits, people decide to change, to learn, when they are uncomfortable. They look at their discourse when it stops working or when somebody else's discourse makes communication difficult. Without some dissonance, people are not challenged to examine their preconceptions or received ideas. When the comfort generally available in an accepting, decentered classroom gets removed, then the community has to find a way to look at what has happened, at what effect language can have, and that uncomfortable moment is a teachable moment.

When we examine a medium of discussion that is much less dominated by our own voices, we see what students sound like and talk about when we don't dominate. I was much less happy "listening" in on peer-oriented discourse in the beginning than I am now. I am less bothered by the phatic (community-building) discourse now, less bothered by the informal, hilarious, disrespectful language. The personality of the class itself, as in so many other things, makes an important difference as well.

A very large, lower division class, where my general level of interaction with the students is so much less intense, can get out of control or be deadening (or deadened) much more easily than a small, upper division writing class can. In a large class of younger, less-experienced students, where their levels of general literacy are being challenged, one student or a small group of students can silence the others, who will wait for the teacher to come in and discipline the miscreants rather than confronting them themselves. It can be very effective to bring in a print copy of the offending writing, show it to the class, and ask them to think through what about it is inappropriate for classroom discourse. I did this more in my first days online than I do now, because I have come to see it as very aggressive and directive on my part, partly because offensive language actually looks worse in print than it does on the screen.

Printing up the sexist, dirty jokes on the class listserv and bringing them to class as a handout would have been another strategy for getting my students to stop the contest, but public attention like this will pinpoint the individual students whose postings are the ones we end up scrutinizing and holding to the standards of print, especially classroom print. Scapegoating individual students when a group has participated is not fair, and it is too heavy handed unless the problem needs to stop immediately. Printing up a log of a troubling MOO discussion is similarly effective, although perhaps less (apparently) controlling, because the individual postings will be short enough that it will be easier not to scapegoat one or two students.

The best strategy, of course, is to get the students to pause and read their discourse as discourse, as responses to rhetorical and social situations, to read it not only for what it says but also for how it says. Printing it out for them can be a very aggressive way to get them to pause and look at the discourse itself, and in my experience, printed-up electronic discourse, especially printing up offensive discourse, looks punitive to them. Most of the time, nobody needs punishment if they have time to think about their language, to reflect on disturbing classroom discourse, to situate the writing rhetorically. That is, instead of thinking of themselves as good or bad boys and girls, or teachers as good or bad cops, teachers need to help students try to think about their discourse rhetorically. I would like them to ask questions like "What kinds of writing does this situation call for?" "What kinds of audience do we have?" "What are the implications of the teacher's different level of power?" "What are the implications of silencing some of the members of the class?" and "What are the forms that power and authority can take in discourse?" This kind of discussion shifts the thinking from pleasing the teacher or calculating how to be a good boy or girl to something much more intellectually satisfying, like "what would be an effective strategy for making my case" or "what is the best language to use in order to do what I want to do?"

Perhaps another reason I am less troubled by seemingly unacceptable student discourse is that I do not have students do much general discussing any more, and this raises the quality of student discourse. My classes' most successful MOOs are tightly focused on getting work done. When students are on task, in my experience, as a whole they spend very little time socializing and kidding around, which reduces the chance for some kinds of offensive behavior or language. In one of my classes in particular, even though they met in 3-hour blocks and normally would have been much more relaxed about how much time they had to get the work done, the MOO focused them and increased their concentration. A young, creative teacher I know divided her students into groups and had them brainstorm ideas for papers on the MOO (Amundson, personal communication, 1997). Then she took the MOO logs in and asked the entire class to identify what they liked best about the different discussions. The mild but overt competition that arose between the groups improved the quality of the online discussions noticeably—because they were purposeful and, once the competition began, specifically directed toward convincing and impressing a particular audience. Another teacher I know, using Daedalus InterChange, asks his students to read the logs looking for three statements made by other students that they like and that they can use, properly attributed, in their writing (Kemp, 1997). Because students want to be taken seriously and quoted, they work in the InterChange sessions on writing substantial pieces or making substantial statements, not competing for the most shocking position or getting distracted by irrelevancies.

To be honest, I must say that a colleague of mine has seen students who wanted to get work done get into a flame war with students who didn't. Even though insisting on productive and efficient electronic communication can help students avoid some kinds of disruptive behavior, having them on task is no guarantee they won't be offensive (this particular flame war included some pretty angry and explicit language). Something about the privacy people feel when they are looking into a monitor, something about the absence of the person addressed, something about the apparent lack of affect on a computer leads almost everybody to overstate their feelings. It is almost as if writing on a screen is enough closer to thinking than speaking that we say what we would normally keep to ourselves and put into language, seductively exciting language, what we would normally moderate.

What is more, experience does not protect me from unpleasant electronic classes. Some problems I have yet to figure out or be able to forestall or teach through. Despite how much I love electronic discourse and electronic teaching, I still have sessions I actually hate. One situation I cannot seem to head off before it gets out of control is one where MOO, listserv, and newsgroup discussions are dominated by one student or a very small group of students. Handling this problem of a dominating student is difficult for teachers who would rather not just shut difficult students down. So the first thing to ask is, "Is this problem a feature of 'the computer' or not?" Usually not, in my experience, although the form the domination takes can be unique to networked electronic environments. A student who dominates face-to-face class discussion is not always the student who dominates electronic discussion, but there can be a terrible consistency to people's real-life and online personalities. Domination can take the form of frequent, lengthy postings that people feel coerced into reading. It can take the form of flaming. It can take the form of argumentativeness and an incendiary conversational style.

In my experience, however, teachers are more likely to feel coerced into reading every word of every posting than their students, who don't feel responsible for reading everything written by every student in the class. I have run assessments on this, and most of my students do not read carefully—and many do not read at all—postings that are too long, hard to read, elevated in tone, or intimidating. So, for example, unless one or more of the students engage the offender in a flame war, or unless teachers decide to confront the offender themselves, students handle long, pompous, obscurely written postings in a way that can be particularly powerful—with indifference.

When students dominate an electronic class discussion by intimidating, insulting, or patronizing other students into silence, it is important for teachers to address the problem—which may be the dominating student, but the problem may also be the silenced ones. My own teaching style leads me to run an assessment, to ask my students for anonymous notes or for e-mail answering some questions that get at the nature of their silence. The effect of this kind of action is threefold. First, the silence itself becomes something that is identified and acknowledged and at least capable of being openly discussed, honoring, of course, its right to exist. Second, I find out some things about the atmosphere of the class as a whole, and I can better judge how important it is for me to intervene; sometimes it is less important than it had seemed to me from the outside. Finally, the fact that I asked at all seems to reopen lines of communication that may have gone down, at the very least reminding students troubled by what is happening in the electronic space that I am willing to listen to them as well as to the dominator.

Other forms of domination can take the form of aggressive, inappropriate, offensive or obscene language. In this case, it is not so much the voice that dominates as it is the agenda. Worse, ultimately, however, than too many words, offensive or not, can be silence itself. For example, I had a student whose reading and writing skills were not good enough for him to be able to keep up in an in-class MOO of upper division English majors. By his gender, size, and general obliviousness he was accustomed to dominating one-on-one discussions, and by his general liveliness and uncritical confidence in his own opinions he was accustomed to dominating class discussions, especially those run by women. Foolishly, although understandably, I was not suspicious of his reticence on the MOO, and I failed to take action (although in hindsight, it is obvious that, silenced, he was a stick of dynamite waiting to go off). By the time he was ready to speak, he was explosive. Everything he wrote was sexualized and coyly seductive, rudely dismissive, or aggressive. Most of the other students were so angry with him that they would not speak to him, and he was contemptuous and defensive to them, both online and in class.

Doing my best not to make the same mistakes twice, I now systematically make sure students who have been reticent or silent are able to be part of the conversation by asking the group via assessments, or individuals via e-mail or paging or direct questions, if they are okay. I talk to them about learning styles and how some people are reflective, working best when they have time to think, and how I always respect people who take the time to think. I keep checking on them if they continue not to take active part, but otherwise I leave them alone. Coercing a student—into silence or into speaking—even gentle coercion, "for their own good," creates the situation Foucault describes, in which students need to take power, a situation that when articulated may look aggressive, offensive, or obscene. Ever since I began this open conversation with students who do not contribute much about the nature of the discourse as they experience it, none of those sticks of dynamite has actually exploded.

Beyond making observations like these, it is impossible to draw real conclusions about obscenity in an electronic, computer-mediated, computer-enhanced, or computer-intensive classroom. For one thing, the topic itself is coherent only in the fact that, in every one of these cases, somebody will be offended. Other than that, in some ways, my examples do not describe a coherent or organized system; except for the fact that there was an offense, some of my examples are completely unrelated to the others. For another, many of the problems teachers have with obscenity on computers in the classroom really do not have anything to do with computers. The problem may have more to do with the student's family or textbook or brain. In different cases, it is not the student, and the problem has something to do with the school or the teacher or the culture. And in more cases yet, it is not the teacher, it is power and domination and the disenfranchisement of young people. And it's impossible, really, to come to a place where problems and ideas and discussion stops, or where it should stop. In fact, stopping discussion is the last thing I want. I want people to take up this here's-what-happened-in-my-class baton and pass it on, so some collective knowledge, collective skills, and collective solutions can develop.

Some solutions will come from technology. Parents, for example, will buy software that prevents children from finding explicit sexual material on the Web, even if it means that innocent or even useful sites are also blocked. Some parents will even get their children's schools to buy the same kind of software. Some solutions will come from legislation that will, for example, rewrite what free speech is, revising what was thought in the age of print. But the best solutions will come from us, from teachers, from English and rhetoric teachers, who will let students experiment and try different kinds of language and adopt different rhetorical approaches. Teachers will know how to turn the failed experiments and attempts into lessons and opportunities for thought and reflection and growth. Teachers will handle the eruptive language one incident at a time, talking to each other, narrating what they did right and what they did wrong, learning how to distinguish the important revolution from the unimportant indiscipline. Teachers can look kindly and not be threatened; they can cut the students slack; they can teach students and their colleagues how to tolerate students really writing to other students as well as to them. They can recognize that somebody who reads obscenity or threats day after day can become sensitized to it and become fearful or cynical. Teachers can ask the origin of the misbehavior, testing themselves for stereotypical thinking about, for example, ageism ("all adolescents are rebellious"), sexism ("boys will be boys"), pathologizing ("all flaming is repressed rage"). Teachers will learn not to react to every online explosion but to notice when language really offends. Instead of thinking first of punishment, teachers will make these situations teachable, warm with respect for others' autonomy and responsibility for their discourse.

REFERENCES

Angelo, T. A., & Cross, K. P. (1993). *Classroom assessment techniques: A handbook for college teachers* (2nd ed.). San Francisco: Jossey-Bass.

Bernhardt, S. (1993). The shape of texts to come. *College Composition and Communication, 44*(2), 151-175.

Cherney, L., & Weise, E. R. (Eds.). (1996). *Wired women: Gender and new realities in cyberspace.* Seattle, WA: Seal Press.

Dibbell, J. (1993, December 23). A rape in cyberspace or how an evil clown, a Haitian trickster spirit, two wizards, and a cast of dozens turned a database into a society. *The Village Voice,* pp. 36-42. Rpt. online in a number of places. One such site is <http://www.panix.com/~julian/writing/bungle.html> (1 May 1997).

Foucault, M. (1979). *Discipline and punish: The birth of the prison* (A. Sheridan, Trans.). New York: Vintage Books.

Kemp, F. (1997, April). Reported in a conference session, *Great Plains Alliance for Computers and Writing, first annual conference.* South Dakota School of Mines and Technology, Rapid City.

Regan, A. (1993). "Type normal like the rest of us": Writing, power, and homophobia in the networked composition classroom." *Computers and Composition, 10*(4), 11-23.

Selfe, C. L., & Selfe, R. J. (1994). The politics of the interface: Power and its exercise in electronic contact zones. *College Composition and Communication, 45,* 480-503.

Chapter • 6

"Why Should I Use the Web?"
Four Drawbacks and Four Benefits to Using the World Wide Web as a Pedagogical Tool for Writing Classes

Steven D. Krause

In December 1993, my Bowling Green State University (BGSU) colleague John Clark and I were working on the finishing touches of a presentation proposal for the November 1994 National Council of Teachers of English Conference in Orlando, Florida. Titled "Gopher is No Longer Just a Rodent," our proposal said we would describe how teachers of writing could use "cutting-edge" Internet technologies like Gopher as a means of connecting to various educational resources and as a pedagogical tool in the writing classroom. We both had heard of and seen the World Wide Web before we put together our proposal, but frankly, neither one of us thought much of it. Although it seemed like an idea with some potential and the graphics were pretty neat, there did not seem to be much information available that would be of much use to teachers—certainly not as much as the huge variety of documents accessible via Gopher. So we closed our proposal with a couple sentences that suggested we might talk about some other resources besides Gopher, if we had time.

By the time the conference rolled around almost 1 year later, the World Wide Web was rapidly becoming the fastest growing and most used resource on the Internet (besides e-mail). I found myself spending an inordinate amount of time "surfing" the increasing number of "pages" that covered almost every conceivable topic, and before long, I learned how to create my own home page. As John and I were putting the finishing touches on our Gopher presentation, I was developing a Web page for the class I was teaching. And by the time we were actually speaking in Orlando, I think it became clear that the closing portion of our presentation on the future applicability of the World Wide Web—one of those "other" resources—was ultimately the most useful for our audience.

I begin this chapter with this anecdote for two reasons. First, I think my experience is an example of the unnerving speed of Internet technology and how it can radically alter our pedagogical practices. I revised a draft of this chapter in 1997 (for a book that won't be widely available until 2000), which, in "Internet time," is two or three generations away. In short, much of what I am suggesting here about using the World Wide Web as a teaching tool will inevitably be dated, passé, and only somewhat useful by the time someone actually reads it. I have tried to minimize this by concentrating on broad themes and on the drawbacks and benefits I believe will always be a part of the Web, but the risk of becoming irrelevant is the price I pay for trying to predict a very unpredictable future.

Second, the usefulness of the Web (or any other Internet resource, for that matter) as a teaching tool depends on the ability of teachers to get access to the right hardware and software, their ability to devote time to facing a continually challenging learning curve, and teachers' and their students' willingness to try new things. In other words, teachers' own answer to the question I explore in this chapter, "Why should I use the Web?" has as much to do with their own evolving relationships to the technology as it does with the technology itself.

My goal here then is to provide a brief and generalized reflection on my own experiences and observations on what I see as the major drawbacks and benefits to using the Web as a teaching tool. This is by no means intended to be complete or to offer any detail on how individuals actually can develop their own Web pages. (At the end of this chapter, I include an appendix that lists several excellent online and in-print resources for getting started with Web publishing.) Nor am I arguing that these are the *only* drawbacks and benefits to the Web as a teaching tool; rather, I am focusing on what I have experienced and observed so that the benefits and drawbacks can be considered.

After an introductory example and definition of the Web, I begin on a cautionary note by discussing what I see as the four drawbacks of the Web as a pedagogical tool: The Web is extremely time consuming, HTML can be intimidating, the Web's advanced features require high-end (and expensive) computer equipment, and there are a number of "access" issues limiting students and teachers. Then I discuss the four major benefits of this pedagogical tool: The Web makes the distribution of course materials easy, it provides excellent opportunities for student research, it is a unique and "real" publishing opportunity for students and teachers, and it is an excellent facilitator of collaboration between teachers and students, regardless of institution. Needless to say, the borders between these drawbacks and benefits are not as clear-cut as this organizational strategy might imply. Many teachers and students might not view the Web's pedagogical benefits as significant given their inabilities to overcome the drawbacks of the Web. Conversely, many students and teachers interested in pursuing the advantages of the Web in writing classrooms might view the drawbacks I discuss here as minor setbacks at best. In other words, I think it is important to keep in mind that my categorization of these four drawbacks and benefits are not meant to be seen as "absolutes." I think the significance of these (and other) drawbacks and benefits will vary tremendously depending on the reader's own context.

WHAT IS THE WORLD WIDE WEB, ANYWAY?

Perhaps the best way to begin is to offer a definition and example. Briefly put, the World Wide Web is a dynamic global network (part of the larger Internet network) that supports hypertextual, interactive, and graphically intense documents commonly referred to as pages or home pages. Based on programming concepts that date back to the 1960s and brought online in its current form at CERN (the European Particle Physics Laboratory) in 1992, the Web community has grown quickly from a few scientists sharing technical reports with each other to a vast and international network of millions of users reading and writing documents on every subject imaginable.

Increasingly more individuals are setting up their own Web documents or pages through educational institutions and online services, and it is becoming increasingly common to see ads for a wide range of consumer goods accompanied by Web page addresses or URLs in the small print. Several software developers have created and fueled this interest by developing easy-to-use programs called Web browsers that allow users to take full advantage of the Web's hypertextual features. Currently, the most popular of these browsers is Netscape, although there are several other similar programs available and more becoming available all the time.[1]

---

[1] As I revised this chapter in 1998, Microsoft's MS Explorer, has surpassed Netscape as the most popular Web browser in the U.S. market. But my original point remains the same: Neither Netscape nor Explorer is the same thing as the World Wide Web; rather, Netscape is but one of many software packages you can use to browse the World Wide Web.

Figure 6.1 is a good example of what I mean by all this. This is a screen image of what my current home page looks like when viewed with the browser Netscape on a Macintosh computer. (Netscape, like most other Web browsers, is also available for MS Windows, Unix, and other computer environments.) As can be seen, this electronic page is a "graphically intense" example (the animated graphic, the layout, etc.) and it contains a number of hypertextual links. For example, if a user clicked on the highlighted word "Teaching," he or she would be taken to another Web page that is a list of some of the courses I have taught. If you were to click on one of the highlighted class titles on that page, he or she would be taken to yet another Web page I created that might include a course description, a syllabus, and examples of student work. It is also possible to create hypertextual links to other types of computer files. For example, with an advanced Web browser like Netscape running on an advanced Macintosh or Intel-based computer, users can also potentially access sound clips, "real time" (i.e., "live") radio-quality audio, and even short digitized video clips.

As a Web page author, I can create links to whatever pages on the Web that I want. For example, if a user were to click on the highlighted word "Links," he or she would be taken to just that: another Web page that is a list of links I have put together from all over the world—links to the Department of Education, the *Chronicle of Higher Education,* universities in Europe, databases on movies, electronically published magazines and journals, other people's home pages, and so on. In other words, everything on the Web is potentially connected to everything else, and everything on the Web is potentially accessible to everyone and anyone who wants to look at it.

What's even more fascinating is that the vast majority of these functions and links are possible through a relatively simple set of scripting commands that make up HTML. Although HTML presents some challenges to new users, it is not a complex computer language per se; rather, it is a series of commands that are placed within a normal, ASCII-text file (plain, unformatted text that can be created on any word processor) that is accessible via the Internet. In other words, creating Web pages is considerably less complicated than "programming" a computer or creating a software package from scratch. In fact, it is the relative simplicity of HTML that has made the great proliferation of Web pages possible in the first place.

The Web is obviously useful for advertising products and electronically publishing everything from *Time Magazine* to a list of my favorite recipes. The Web is also a lot of fun to "surf," to point and click on the underlined, highlighted text and follow the links to the next (frequently silly) page. But how can this possibly be of any use in a writing classroom?

Steven D. Krause

Links

Teaching

CV

Diss

Bio

Unofficial Page

Department of English / Eastern Michigan University / Ypsilanti, MI

Figure 6.1. Krause's homepage:
http://www.online.emich.edu/~skrause

At first I thought the answer to this question was simple—it wasn't. But as I learned more about some of the more useful (i.e., pedagogical) Web pages and about how to create my own Web pages, I gradually realized there were lots of ways to integrate the Web into my teaching.

As my primary example for discussing the drawbacks and benefits of teaching with the Web, I refer to a Web page I set us for a section of a course I taught as a graduate student at BGSU in 1995 called "Great Ideas." This interdisciplinary humanities course examines and problematizes some of the major ideas of Western civilization.[2] Other than the fact that students were required to use the class Web pages and a class e-mail listserv as key resources for participating in class discussion and writing

---

[2] At BGSU, this class satisfied a variety of general education requirements and was for most students a sophomore-level class. There was some standardization about the curriculum between different sections of the course, but I taught it primarily as I would an advanced first-year writing course or an intermediate writing course. The Great Ideas program textbook, which was developed by three faculty members in BGSU's English department, quite consciously integrating writing into the learning process. It is similar in structure and intent to first-year writing textbooks that emphasize the teaching of writing across the disciplines, and my understanding is this type of curriculum is used at many schools as a core course in a writing across the curriculum program.

activities, my section of Great Ideas was not dramatically different than any other offered that semester. My class was not taught in a computer lab, nor was there any presumed expertise with computers or the Internet. As is often the case with Web spaces, this page no longer exists; however, I think the discussion that follows here is an adequate to exemplify my points.

"WHY SHOULDN'T I USE THE WEB?" FOUR DRAWBACKS TO TEACHING WITH THE WEB

I think it becomes abundantly clear in this chapter that I am very much an advocate for using the Web as a teaching tool. I certainly hope to continue using Web pages and similar Internet resources in my teaching, and I think the Web can be of great use in virtually any writing course. However, there are more than a few challenges and drawbacks to using the Web as a teaching tool that teachers should carefully consider in developing their own Web pages. I certainly do not want to make the claim that these are the only potential drawbacks to using the Web as a teaching tool, but generally speaking, I think there are four basic problems that teachers interested in incorporating Web pages into their classes need to consider: First, it is extremely time consuming; second, HTML can be difficult and intimidating; third, the hardware can be expensive; and finally, many access questions still remain.

Time Consuming

I think the most significant challenge that teachers who want to incorporate Web activities into their classrooms have to consider before they get started is that the Web is extremely time consuming in a variety of ways. Although the Web (like virtually every other technological advancement in the information age) increases capacity for accomplishing certain tasks (such as gathering information or publishing documents that can reach a wide audience), this increased capacity does not necessarily save time for teachers. For example, while distributing class information for my Great Ideas class via the Web was advantageous (as I discuss later), it probably would have been easier for me to stick with the traditional system of passing out paper copies of materials. Although I think it was beneficial to my students and myself to offer them the chance to publish some of their class writings, it clearly took more time than the alternative—not publishing the material at all.

Researching with the Web is also a frequently frustrating and time-consuming activity. There are a wide variety of very effective and continually improving keyword search devices currently available that can make locating Web pages on particular topics relatively easy. But because there is no standardized lexicon for searches (as there is with the Library of Congress system, for example), some keywords may not return all the desired results. Searching with the words "Gulf War" may leave out Web pages that use the words "Operation Desert Storm" instead. Keyword searches can also be slowed by heavy Internet traffic—quite literally, because too many people on the Net are searching for too many things at any one point and time, searches frequently are not processed initially. In other words, although the keyword search devices on the Web work in more or less the same way as the search devices common in most college or university libraries, the library's system is (hopefully) much more efficient.

Dealing with students' all-too-frequent fears and resistances to computer technology can also be time consuming. While all of my Great Ideas students eventually recognized that retrieving information from the class Web page was quite easy to do, I initially had to personally accompany a handful of my students to one of the computer labs on campus and walk them through every step of the process. This was a teaching opportunity that I was more than willing and able to share with my students, but it did involve a few additional hours in an already crowded schedule.

In short, although there are many benefits to using the Web as a teaching tool in the writing classroom, "efficiency" is definitely not one of them. Although some advances in efficiency result from increased capabilities, I argue that it is not a given that increasing our capabilities to do different things (which is what the Web is all about) result in efficiency. I think teachers who want to incorporate Web-related activities into their classes should recognize that the Web is an example of a time consuming technology instead of time-saving one, and they should plan initially to spend a great deal more preparation time to get Web pages up and running, to conduct research, and to work closely with students struggling with the technology. I also think that teachers should make every effort to ensure that deans, principals, and other supervisors recognize this limitation as well.

HTML

Currently, one of the reasons why the Web is so time consuming is HTML, the relatively simple system of codes placed in simple text documents that make Web pages work. I say "relatively simple" because HTML is by no means as difficult to master as traditional computer languages. Still, it can be challenging. For example, Figure 6.2 shows the text version of my home page complete with HTML coding or "tags."

```
<HTML>
<HEAD>
  <TITLE>Krause's Homepage</TITLE>
  <X-CLARIS-WINDOW TOP=90 BOTTOM=600 LEFT=12 RIGHT=542>
  <X-CLARIS-TAGVIEW MODE=minimal>
</HEAD>
<BODY BGCOLOR="#FFFFFF" LINK="#009900" ALINK="#FFFF00" VLINK="#FF0000">
<P> </P>

<P><TABLE BORDER=0 CELLPADDING=2 WIDTH="100%">
  <TR>
    <TD VALIGN=top WIDTH="50%">
      <P><A HREF="mailto:skrause@online.emich.edu"><FONT SIZE="+3">Steven
      D. Krause</FONT></A>

      <HR ALIGN=left>

      </P>

      <P><A HREF="Links.html"><FONT SIZE="+1"><TT>Links</TT></FONT></A></P>

      <P><A HREF="http://www.online.emich.edu/~skrause/teaching"><FONT
SIZE="+1"><TT>Teaching</TT></FONT></A></P>

      <P><A HREF="http://www.online.emich.edu/~skrause/CV"><FONT
SIZE="+1"><TT>CV</TT></FONT></A></P>

      <P><A HREF="http://www.emunix.emich.edu/~krause/Diss"><FONT
SIZE="+1"><TT>Diss</TT></FONT></A></P>

      <P><A HREF="me.html"><FONT SIZE="+1"><TT>Bio</TT></FONT></A></P>

      <P><A HREF="http://www.geocities.com/Athens/Delphi/9046/Steve"><FONT
SIZE="+1"><TT>Unofficial
      Page</TT></FONT></A></P>
    </TD>
    <TD VALIGN=top WIDTH="50%">
      <P> <IMG SRC="Elocutor.gif" WIDTH=277 HEIGHT=307 ALIGN=bottom
naturalsizeflag=3></P>
    </TD>
  </TR>
</TABLE>
</P>

<CENTER><I>Department of English / Eastern Michigan University /
Ypsilanti, MI</I></CENTER>
</BODY>
</HTML>
```

Figure 6.2. Source code for my home page

To the uninitiated, this appears to look something like a normal text document with a bunch of odd characters and phrases inserted. Closer study reveals that the vast majority of these odd characters and phrases are inserted between the "less than" and "greater than" signs, as in "<hr>" or "<A HREF="http://www.online.emich.edu/~skrause/teaching">". Web browsing programs (like Netscape) recognize these codes between the "less than" and "greater than" signs and act accordingly—inserting a horizontal line for "<hr>" or a link to another document called "teaching.html" for "<A HREF="http://www.online.emich.edu/~skrause/teaching">".

For those not familiar with computer programming (and I would include myself in this group), HTML presents two general frustrations. First, a lot of the commands are not easy to remember or fully understand. Although a "Headline Font" command might make a certain amount of sense (<H1> produces large headline font, <H2> produces headline font a size smaller, and so forth), most commands do not. Second, HTML is extremely unforgiving. Like all computer programming, the smallest mistake in coding—a misplaced space, a forgotten ">" or a different number or letter—can make the Web page unreadable, and can also be difficult for the Web page author to detect. (In the appendix of this chapter, I list several user-friendly sources I recommend for learning HTML.)

Fortunately, an increasing number of software products are currently available that make authoring Web pages much easier. Some simple software packages (such as WebWeaver or RTF/HTML) are "shareware" or "freeware" applications available at various sites on the Internet. The more advanced, user-friendly applications (such as Quarterdeck WebAuthor, Adobe PageMill, SoftQuad HotMetal Pro, and InContext Spider) are widely available from $50 to $200. Furthermore, new versions of popular word processing software (Microsoft Word and WordPerfect are two current examples) have built-in HTML conversion capabilities. In other words, although HTML will present challenges to Web page authors into the foreseeable future, a wide variety of software promises to ease these difficulties substantially.

Hardware and Software

Another current challenge to using the Web in the teaching of writing is the necessary computer hardware and software. Web browsers like Netscape function best on relatively high-end computers (Macintoshes with 8MB of RAM or better; 486, Windows-driven PCs with 8MB of RAM or better) that are connected to an Internet server via an Ethernet, Novell, or similar network connection. This level of connectivity is hardly universal. For example, when I taught Great Ideas at BGSU there were a number of computer labs on campus that had these capabilities, and some faculty members in some buildings also had Ethernet connections on the computers in their offices. However, the building that housed the English Department in 1995-1996 was not connected to the rest of the campus' computer networks via Ethernet, and many faculty members were still using computers that were too old and underpowered to take advantage of the Web's graphic features. And of course, most of the teachers of writing at BGSU—graduate students, adjuncts, and full-time instructors—do not have easy access to computers at all.

This of course does not make developing Web pages impossible; it simply makes it more challenging. For example, although I did not have the necessary equipment to develop Web pages located conveniently in my office at BGSU, I did have access to the necessary hardware and software in the on-campus computer labs. It is also possible to make connections to the Web with less sophisticated equipment and software (such as the text-only Web browser called Lynx), and "point-to-point protocol" modem connections make it possible to use Netscape from a computer connected to the Internet via telephone.

Like the challenges of working with HTML, this is a problem that will eventually be solved for most writing teachers by the inevitable upgrades in hardware and software, along with upgrades in networking facilities. Increasingly, students and faculty alike are demanding and receiving the necessary upgrades in hardware and software, in part because computers (like most high-tech appliances) tend to break or wear-out and are often easier to replace with updated equipment than to repair, and also in part because current software packages frequently will not work on older computers (Windows 95 and Netscape are both very typical examples). I also think it is fair to say that networking facilities are being upgraded at many colleges. Most (if not all) buildings on campus at BGSU have been connected to the larger campus network as I revised this chapter, and new buildings on campus are being wired to the network before anyone moves in. I suspect that this is the case for many other educational institutions as well. Nonetheless, the current hardware in many English teachers' offices—especially the limited and out-of-date hardware that is all too common in many English departments—and the complete absence of hardware from the majority of writing teachers' offices presents an obvious barrier that teachers must successfully address in order to teach with the Web.

Access

Finally, the abilities of teachers and students to get the necessary access to both publish and read documents on the Web remains difficult and could potentially get worse. As I already discussed, simply getting access to a computer that is connected to the Internet and capable of browsing the Web can be challenging for both writing teachers and students. The access necessary for publishing Web documents is even more scarce. For a college or university to make Web space available to members of the academic community takes a lot of resources in the form of additional staff members, special software packages, and "servers," the computers dedicated to serving Web pages to requesting users, or "clients." The more access an institution provides, the higher the cost (which is one reason why many institutions have yet to let undergraduates publish Web pages).

Making Web publishing accessible to one and all also presents some potentially sticky legal questions that institutions will have to answer before they are able to provide easy access to students. What sort of materials can and cannot be published on university-sponsored Web pages, and how does an institution decide? What if a member of the academic community decides to publish an essay photocopied from *Harper's* magazine? Who is liable for the copyright infringement? What if someone publishes a controversial work of art or, even more extreme, a work of child pornography? How can large academic institutions that might have tens of thousands of Web pages produced by students, faculty, and staff possibly enforce any of the publication rules they devise?

But beyond these relatively local concerns of access are the larger, more abstract challenges of the Web presented by commercial interests. Although educators may see the Web as an excellent place to publish a wide variety of academic materials and to conduct research on every topic imaginable, the business community sees the Web as an excellent place to sell corn chips, deodorant, and automobile tires. How long will these competing and frequently mutually exclusive goals be allowed to flourish in the same virtual space? After all, television was originally thought of as a medium that served the "public's interests," yet other than local community interests broadcasting and some public television, it is difficult to find examples of "public service" on television nowadays. And other than quirky public access channels provided by many cable systems, there are no individual or amateur efforts allowed on television.

I hope that these warnings appear alarmist and extreme in the near (and difficult to predict) future, but it seems to me that the millions of Web publishers and users worldwide who see this medium as truly unique and empowering need to constantly remind themselves that this "open-access" system could potentially be closed. I think teachers who are willing and able to overcome the other challenges I addressed in this section (time constraints, challenges of HTML, and cost of hardware and software) need to also remain vigilant regarding the many and evolving questions of access.

"WHY SHOULD I USE THE WEB?" FOUR PEDAGOGICAL ADVANTAGES

Although the disadvantages I just discussed are significant, I still think that the Web is an extremely useful resource for humanities teachers at the vast majority of educational institutions. Simply put, I think the benefits justify the time and effort required to overcome the drawbacks.

What are the pedagogical advantages to the Web? Again, I certainly would not want to claim that these are the Web's only pedagogical advantages, but basically, I think the pedagogical benefits and uses of this technology fall into four broad categories: First, as the distribution point for class materials; second, as starting points for research; third, as opportunities for student publishing; and finally, as a facilitator of opportunities for collaboration among students and teachers.

Distribution

As I discussed earlier, my most complete and successful use of the Web in teaching to date took place in my section of Great Ideas at BGSU. Instead of distributing traditional "paper copies" of course policies and syllabi on the first day of class, I distributed instructions on how to get to the Great Ideas home page. My students' first assignment for the class was to find these materials, print them out if they wanted, and bring them to class. Although there were a few students who needed some more personal help from me to get them started (a time-consuming drawback that I discussed earlier), this method of distribution was beneficial to both my students and myself. On a purely logistical level, using the Web to distribute materials was extremely convenient because I was able to avoid the departmental bureaucracy of photocopying or mimeographing materials, and because there was no such thing as a "lost" assignment or one that was "missed" by an absent student. Once I uploaded the files, the materials were just there, and they were available as long as I wanted them to be available.

But beyond mere logistics, I think distributing course materials with the Web created a different class atmosphere of proactive responsibility. Literally, students did not have everything simply handed to them—rather, they had to take the initiative to find the materials for the class themselves. In fact, when students asked questions about the course syllabus or policies, I routinely provided a brief answer followed by the phrase, "Be sure to check out the class home page for more details." The Web was thus established as a vital resource that the students needed to access in order to understand the day-to-day operations of the class. Although I don't think this act alone single-handedly taught my students the benefits of the Web, I do think it was a good first step.

Research Starting Points

Besides being a useful resource for teachers to distribute class materials, the Web is also an excellent place for students and teachers to begin their research. As I discussed previously, there are a number of keyword search devices (commonly referred to as search engines) and indexes useful for conducting Web-based research. The Net Search option on Netscape is probably the most commonly used of these devices, but there are a variety of other popular services as well (I've listed some of the most common search engines and large Web indexes in the Appendix). Not unlike the computer search tools available in most university libraries, the user enters a keyword and is provided a list of links to Web pages that include that word.

In fact, that's how I initially compiled the list of resources I made available to my Great Ideas students. The "great" (not necessarily "good," but "important") ideas we examined in my section of Great Ideas included classical Greek humanism, religion, democracy, Marxism, feminism, and postmodernism. For each of these general topics, I initially provided a few links that students used to get started on their writing projects and presentations. As the semester went along, students also let me know about URLs to Web pages they had found on their own that I added to the list of research links on the class Web page. So ultimately, the list of links that served as our "starting points" for research in the class was itself a collaborative project between myself and my students.

Some topics proved to be much more "researchable" on the Web than others. For example, during the spring of 1995, there were a lot more resources on religions of all sorts on the Web than there were on the ancient Greeks. But the absence of resources was also interesting and important to consider. I think the lack of materials on topics suggested in some sense the different priorities of these "great ideas" in contemporary culture (at least contemporary Internet culture), and it provided some ideas to students about what original material could potentially be added to the Web. Yet another Web page on religions of the world probably would duplicate a lot of previous efforts, whereas a Web page on Plato's Symposium would probably constitute a more unique contribution. Although these conditions are rapidly changing, I think this represented a valuable lesson to my students on how the definition of what information is "important" shifts in different environments.

Few of my students were ever fully satisfied with their Web research efforts. They were frequently disappointed at the absence of detailed information on the topic they were researching and they often wondered about the accuracy of the information available on the Web (which also raised some valuable questions about the "accuracy" of information they find in print as well). Still, I think using the Web as a research tool was ultimately very beneficial. It provided students with excellent starting points for researching their writing projects that more often than not helped and enriched their "traditional" library research. Furthermore, it proved to be a space for collaboration between me and my students, a project that I think would be useful in almost any writing class.

Student Publishing

Besides its uses as a means of distributing class information and as a starting point for research, the Web is an excellent way to publish student writing and to put students in direct contact with large and "real" audiences. I think it is a widely accepted premise among writing teachers that the act of writing is a social process that changes dramatically depending on the demands of different rhetorical situations and audiences—that is, there is no "right" way to write anything. The "five-paragraph theme" may be useful for some academic situations and audiences, but it is certainly not a "universal" or transcendent methodology that is always appropriate regardless of purpose, audience, or situation. The challenge of the traditional writing class (where students write essays to and for teachers) is how to move beyond these perceived universal forms. Many teachers construct assignments that ask students to address hypothetical audiences they should keep in mind when writing, and some teachers and students have great success in going out into the community to find "real" writing projects (e.g., newspaper articles, brochures, advertising materials, technical manuals, etc.) on which students can work as part of their graded coursework. But in my experience, these efforts frequently have mixed results. Although I believe we should ask students to write for an audience other than their teachers and I think we should construct writing assignments that ask students to carefully consider specific audiences, contexts, and purposes, I think students often go through a complicated process of second and third guessing, trying to figure out what audience the teacher has in mind in the first place. And although "real-world" writing projects can be very successful, they are often logistically difficult or impossible to coordinate. In other words, even in the hands of innovative teachers, I don't think the structures and demands of the traditional (and static) college writing classroom facilitates a pedagogy that sees writing as a complicated, socially governed, and contextually dynamic process.

Although I don't think student Web publishing is a definitive solution to these challenges, I do think Web publishing holds great promise for better realizing a dynamic and socially governed writing pedagogy in traditional educational institutions. Realistically, the primary audience for most student Web page texts is of course still the teacher and the other students in the particular class. However, the possibility for a wider audience is created with web publishing because the student-created web page is no longer a "paper" exchanged only between an individual student and an individual teacher; rather, a student-created web page is a "published" document accessible to the entire Web community. Although merely creating a document on the Web does not guarantee an interested audience, it is possible (and likely) that other Web users (e.g., college or high school students at other schools) conducting a keyword search on a topic discussed in my section of Great Ideas will come across one of the essays or Web Pages my students wrote and published as part of the requirements of my class. In short, student publishing on the Web is just as "real" as other publishing on the Web, and (unlike traditional "papers") it demands that student writers be conscious of a larger, beyond-the-classroom-and-teacher audience.

Although I think student Web publishing is a good idea, there seem to be two significant "risks" teachers should consider carefully. First, plagiarism potentially becomes much easier if the hypothetical student is indeed able to find a Web page from a student at another school that closely meets his or her needs. This is not a reason why students should not be publishing their work on the Web. Restricting access and discouraging a multitude of voices from making their thoughts, beliefs, and research available on the Web because of the potential of misuse is just as illogical and silly as restricting student access to the millions of texts in a university library. Because teachers do not typically see it as their responsibility to "police" their students' access to conventional print texts in order to prevent the possibility of plagiarism, I do not think teachers should feel the need to control access to electronic texts. Still, it seems to me that teachers should be aware of the possibilities of plagiarism via the Web and should construct their assignments to discourage this (e.g., very class-specific assignments, collaborative work, writing projects that include rough drafts and self-reflexive meta-essays as part of the assignment, etc.)

Second, students might not be as eager to publish their work on the Web as might be assumed. I certainly made this mistake with my students. As I already mentioned in this chapter, undergraduates at BGSU typically did not have access to the proper computer accounts for creating their own Web pages when I taught my section of Great Ideas. To overcome this access problem, I offered to help any student who was interested in publishing his or her writing project as part of the class Web page in my own computer account. All they needed to do was provide me with a disk copy of their writing project, or, for those interested in learning more about HTML and developing a full-blown Web page, a disk that contained the HTML scripting and appropriate support files (i.e., graphics, sounds, etc.). This was a completely voluntary activity, although one I strongly encouraged. Still, despite my semester-long support and efforts, only five students published their conventional writing projects (allowing me to simply convert their traditional text essays into HTML), and only one student created his own Web page. There are a number of possible explanations for this lack of interest that I hope to consider at a later date, but beyond the facts that publishing on the Web was a completely voluntary act (i.e., it had no influence on their grade) and my experiences here are potentially an isolated case, it seems to me that most of my students were intimidated not only by the initial complexities of HTML but also by the great power of the Web. Their experiences with the Web showed them that an essay published there really could be potentially read by a "real" and "interested" audience outside of our class, and I think that potential frightened and discouraged them. Several students told me point-blank that despite the fact that they had opportunities to share rough drafts with their colleagues in peer-critique sessions and I provided a variety of opportunities and suggestions for revision, they simply did not think their writing was "good enough" to be published on the Web.

Having said all this, I still think making student writing accessible to a real audience outside of the classroom is one of the great potential advantages of the Web as a teaching tool. Granted, there are concerns regarding plagiarism that need to be considered, and student Web publishing efforts should probably "count" for something and need to be gently encouraged throughout the semester. However, I think the teacher who recognizes and is able to negotiate the challenges of student Web publishing will help students recognize the presence of audiences beyond the teacher and the classroom, thus opening up exciting new possibilities about what it means to be a "writer" in a "writing class."

Collaboration

Finally, I think the Web offers writing students and teachers excellent opportunities for collaboration on a variety of levels. I have already suggested that a class Web page could be used by teachers and students as part of an on-going collaborative project. Teachers and students could work together not only to develop a list of helpful links related to class activities (as was the case with my Great Ideas class), but they could also collaborate on developing the virtual space of the class home page itself (e.g., collaborating on decisions regarding layout, what should be included or excluded, etc.). Students could also work with each other on publishing Web documents, which would likely ease the anxieties individual students might have about writing for the Web, and it would probably make it easier to negotiate the complexities of HTML.

Class Web pages can also become collaborative tools in the sense that they are readily available to other teachers and students involved in similar classes. For example, while I created the Great Ideas home page with my particular section in mind, a variety of other teachers of other sections of Great Ideas at BGSU regularly recommend to their students that they visit and use this Web page. This sort of Web- and Internet-based collaboration between sections within the same program can certainly be taken much further. At the University of Michigan's English Composition Board, Rebecca Rickly's and Wayne Butler's sections collaborated on their sections of a course titled "Writing for the Information Superhighway." Rickly and Butler coordinated their individual sections so that the students participated together in an on-going e-mail discussion and on collaborative Web pages, where they presented class readings, syllabi, assignments, announcements, and student "Webfolios" of writing done during the term. (The Web pages for this course are no longer available, but a similar curriculum is described in Condon & Butler, 1997.)

In an e-mail message to me about the "Information Superhighway" collaboration, Rickly pointed out that this project (like all collaborative projects) involved some difficulties. For example, because Rickly's role was based in developing and maintaining the collaborative Web page while Butler was more involved with the collaborative e-mail discussions, students initially perceived Butler as more "involved" in the course. To address this perception, Rickly wrote that she "started to post more messages to the [collaborative mailing] list during the second half [of the term], and I think students were satisfied. They thought they were doing so much work, I think they felt angry that one of the teachers wasn't pulling his/her fair share." Overall however, Rickly found the collaboration satisfying for both her, Butler, and their students. Both teachers seemed to have learned a great deal about their own pedagogies by working with each other, and Rickly said that the students were able to rise to the challenges of keeping up with the readings, the electronic mail, writing for the Web, and producing some excellent Web pages and writings.

Besides these "active" collaborative exercises, I think the Web can also be an excellent source for what I would call "passive" collaboration—the subtle tips and suggestions we all seek out from colleagues in both formal and casual settings to better our own teaching practices. There are a series of Web resources (such as the "World Lecture Hall" shown in Figure 6.3 and those listed in the appendix of this chapter) that are currently available that seem to me to be excellent resources along these lines. Teachers and students can use resources like the World Lecture Hall as a grand and ever-changing collection of ideas about readings, writing assignments, student publishing, Web page layout, links to other resources, and more. I have learned a lot about how I can better incorporate the Web into my teaching by not only visiting the Web pages of other writing classes, but also by examining Web pages for students in

http://www.utexas.edu/world/lecture/

Search World Lecture Hall: *(Accepts AND, OR, NOT, and *)*

_____ || Submit | Clear

The World Lecture Hall (WLH) contains links to pages created by faculty worldwide who are using the Web to deliver class materials. For translating course URLs from or into English, Spanish, French, German, or Portuguese, try a translation service. See also distance education courses offered by The University of Texas System.

Here's a form to add your materials (and a form to update materials and send comments, too). For recent additions to the WLH, see What's New (23 November 98). And thanks to those who have contributed to our commendations page.

A	Accounting	African (American) Studies	Agriculture
	Anatomy	Anthropology / Archaeology	Architecture / Building
	Art and Art History	Astronomy	
B	Biochemistry	Biology and Botany	Biomedical Engineering
	Biotechnology	Business Administration	
C-D	Chemical Engineering	Chemistry	Civil/Industrial Engineering
	Classics	Communication	Communication Sciences and Disorders
	Computer Science	Cultural Studies	Distance Learning Institutions
E-F	Earth Science	Economics	Education
	Electrical / Computer Engr.	Engineering	English / Writing / Rhetoric
	Environmental Science	Finance	French
G	Geography	Germanic Studies	
H-K	Health (Public) / Nutrition	History	Humanities
	Journalism	Kinesiology	
L	Languages	Law	Library and Information Science
	Linguistics		
M	Management	Management Information Systems	Marketing
	Mathematics	Mechanical Engineering	Medicine
	Mexican-American Studies	Microbiology	Middle Eastern Studies
	Music		
N-O	Neuroscience	Nursing	Other
P-R	Petroleum and Geosystems Engineering	Pharmacy	Philosophy
	Physics	Political Science	Psychology
	Public Affairs	Religious Studies	Russian / East European Studies
S	Science and Technology	Social Work	Sociology
	Spanish and Portuguese	Statistics	
T-Z	Telecommunications	Theatre and Dance	Veterinary Medicine
	Women's Studies	Zoology	

World Lecture Hall | U. S. Universities | U. S. Community Colleges | K-12+

23 November 98
Copyright *ACITS* at *UT Austin*
Send *comments* to *World Lecture Hall.*

Figure 6.3. The World Lecture Hall:
http://www.utexas/edu/world/lecture

other humanities and science courses as well. These indirect collaborative activities are easily facilitated on the Web, where connections to colleagues teaching and learning all over the world are only a few links away.

CONCLUSIONS

I have tried to refrain from any direct answers to the question I offer in the title of this chapter and have instead tried to describe a variety of the disadvantages and advantages of the Web any writing teacher who is considering incorporating the Web into their pedagogies needs to consider. Although I clearly think the advantages of using the Web as a teaching tool far outweigh the difficulties and challenges, teachers should consider this and other online technologies carefully. As the fine print on most television commercials points out, "your results may vary," and the mere presence of a new and exciting technology does not justify its use in the classroom. And as a myriad of other pedagogical and technical "advances" have taught us over the years, quick and unexamined adaptation of any new teaching tool—whether it is online or not—doesn't work very well.

Of course, these risks should not keep anyone from trying, and, for some, adopting. Incorporating the Web into my own teaching has been a great challenge, and, as I tried to emphasize here, the Web's rapid rate of change makes predicting any future uses of it (in the classroom or otherwise) volatile at best. But at this stage, the question I have to ask myself is not "Why use the Web?" but "Why shouldn't I use the Web?"

APPENDIX: A VERY BRIEF LIST OF WEB RESOURCES

This information is changing all the time of course, but the following is a list of online and offline resources that can get those new to the Web started. The best, most current, and most inexpensive resources about the Web are available on the Web itself. However, because books are easier to read, are frequently more convenient, and dramatically more permanent than Web pages, I have included some of those resources in my list as well.

About HTML

Books

Aronson, L. (1995). *HTML 3 manual of style* . Emeryville, CA: Ziff-Davis Press.
December, J., & Ginsburg, M. (1995). *HTML and CGI unleashed.* Indianapolis: Sams.net Publishing.
Graham, I. S. (1995). *The HTML sourcebook.* New York: Wiley.
Taylor, D. (1995). *Macworld's creating cool web pages with HTML.* Foster City, CA: IDG Books.

Online

A Beginner's Guide to HTML. Document about HTML published by NCSA. (http://www.ncsa.uiuc.edu/demoweb/html-primer.html)
HTML Quick Reference. A handy "cheat-sheet" on HTML. (http://kuhttp.cc.ukans.edu/lynx_help/HTML_quick.html)
Crash Course on Writing Documents for the Web. A short and clear set of instructions written to help the people in the *PC Week* Labs. (http://www.zdnet.com/pcweek/earmonn/crash_course.html)
OneWorld/SingNet WWW & HTML Developer's Jumpstation. Links to lots of documents on HTML. (http://oneworld.wa.com/htmldev/devpage/dev-page.html)
Virtual Computer Library at the University of Texas—Austin. A very large and useful collection of resources on computers, the Internet, and the Web. (http://www.utexas.edu/computer/vcl For information specifically on HTML, go tohttp://www.utexas.edu/computer/vcl/www.html)

Web Indexes and Search Engines

Books

Breeding, M. (Ed.). (1996). *The world wide web yellow pages* (1996 edition). Foster City, CA: IDG Books.
File, D., & Yang, J. (1995). *Yahoo! Unplugged: Your discovery guide to the web*. Foster City, CA: IDG Books.

Online

Netscape's "Info-Seek"/Net Search Page. This is the URL you go to if you simply click the "Net Search" button in Netscape. (http://www.utexas.edu/world/lecture/)
WebCrawler. A keyword search device. (http://webcrawler.com/)
World Wide Web Worm. A keyword search device.(http://guano.cs.colorado.edu/wwww/)
Lycos. A combination search device and catalogue of Web resources. (http://lycos.cs.cmu.edu/)
The Whole Internet Catalog Home Page. Just what the title says! (http://gnn.com/wic/wics/index.html)
Yahoo. Probably the most popular and complete Web index currently available. (http:www.yahoo.com)

Education and Humanities Resources

The Chronicle of Higher Education. (http://chronicle.merit.edu/)
The U.S. Department of Education. (http://www.ed.gov/)
American Universities with WWW Pages. (http://www.clas.ufl.edu/CLAS/american-universities.html)
The World Lecture Hall. (http://www.utexas.edu/world/lecture/)
The English Server. A very large humanities database run by students, faculty, and staff of the English Department at Carnegie Mellon. (http://english-www.hss.cmu.edu/)
The Voice of the Shuttle. An excellent humanities database from the University of California—Santa Barbara. (http://humanitas.ucsb.edu/)
EdWeb Home Page, an excellent resource for elementary and secondary schools. (http://k12.cnidr.org:90/)

Rhetoric and Writing Resources Online

The Alliance for Computers and Writing Homepage. An excellent
resource for any writing teacher. (http://english.ttu.edu/acw/)
Writer's Resources on the Web. A highly eclectic collection of pages.
(http://www.interlog.com/~ohi/www/writesource.html)
Purdue University's Online Writing Lab. One of the first and the best, this
Web page includes links to many other online writing lab environ-
ments. (http://owl.trc.purdue.edu/)
A List of Dictionaries. Many English and other language dictionaries are
available here. (http://math-www.uni-paderborn.de/HTML/
Dictionaries.html)

REFERENCES

Condon, W., & Butler, W. (1997). *Writing the information
superhighway.* Boston: Allyn & Bacon.

PART • II

FOCUS ON COMMUNITY

This section focuses on reports of successful pedagogies in the online classroom. Interestingly, many of these chapters revolve around the creation of a participatory community in the composition classroom. In "Composition, Collaborations, and Computer-Mediated Conferencing," Bowen recalls how she incorporated VAX Notes, a computer-mediated conferencing system in her first-year composition and literature courses. She found that this medium offered a flexible environment that encouraged engagement with ideas from texts and from students. She recounts the difficulty of moving beyond question-and-response type interaction to a more lively class discussion, noting that both she and the students had to take risks to make these conferences more productive. Bowen's experience with VAX Notes allowed students to listen and respond to one another more thoughtfully.

In "Improving Classroom Culture: Using Electronic Dialogue to Face Difference," Gay describes her struggle to engage a variety of voices in the budding classroom community by using computer-mediated communication (CMC). By including a series of challenging readings that students first had to consider and then respond to, she was able to elicit a series of inclusive, critical discussions online. She notes that engaging all the voices in a classroom community discussion is a "complicated, messy, and sometimes uncomfortable process, even for an experienced writing teacher." She warns of the dangers of electronic communication gone awry, and outlines some valuable advice for new teachers in technological environments.

Craig, Harris, and Smith relate their experiences teaching collaboratively online in "Fostering Diversity in the Writing Classroom: Using Wide-Area Networks to Promote Inter-Racial Dialogue." Connecting students from a rural Pennsylvania university and a West Virginia community college to George Washington University via e-mail, the authors were able to increase students' cultural awareness and challenge some commonly held misconceptions using a common ground of reading, a common syllabus, frequent and volatile e-mail discussion list correspondence and four MOO meetings. Interestingly, although the two predominately White classes in West Virginia and Pennsylvania were made self-aware of some of their cultural misconceptions, it was the student body at George Washington that benefited the most in the realm of improved writing and literacy.

Because technology is becoming a force to be reckoned with in U.S. society, in "Writing a Narrative: MOOs and e-journals," Watts and Taniguchi emphasize the need for teachers to learn to successfully integrate technology into their teaching philosophy, examining critically how their teaching style might be enhanced by using various forms of technology, and how teachers might then master the tools they need. Using their Rainbow Advantage program as an example, these authors describe how they used MOOs and electronic e-mail journals to "engage freshmen in their own education" emphasizing communication, cooperative learning, and community participation. With some insightful student examples, Watts and Taniguchi portray a learning community that extended beyond the classroom walls. But they don't stop there. They use these specific examples to point out possible problems as well, urging instructors to "take responsibility" for the tools they use, integrating them wisely and thoughtfully into their emerging practice.

Hanson details the effects of CMC on both rhetoric and literature in "Advanced Composition On-line: Pedagogical Intersections of Composition and Literature." Locating her practices in theory, Hanson describes how she integrated CMC in discussions both in her own class and between sister classes, and outlines the resulting dialogue. She summarizes basic observations about her experience using CMC for several years, then evaluates this practice in what she describes as microcosm of the academic community. This thoughtful piece nicely integrates theory and practice, situating them both in the CMC-assisted classroom.

Finally, in "Effective Teaching in the On-line Classroom: Thoughts and Recommendations," Barber draws on ethnographic studies of writing teachers making the transition from traditional to online classrooms. He notes that such a transition can be traumatic, but that with preparation, planning, and a rethinking of pedagogy, teachers can make this a successful transition. This chapter outlines computer theory and pedagogy and includes specific representations of actual electronic dialogue in his classes. The thoughts and recommendations section of this chapter should be made required reading for new teachers in an electronic setting.

Chapter • 7

Composition, Collaborations, and Computer-Mediated Conferencing

Betsy A. Bowen

28.17
CPAPENBROCK   12-DEC-1993
I have a lot to say about positive reinforcement and comments to other students' comments. I agree with E. Curry when she says positive reinforcement is needed in the classroom to succeed. Positive reinforcement helps in any situation but especially in education. Studies have suggested that . . .

I was fascinated by the discussion that AHo, Emi, and Brande were having about good role models here at Fairfield. B. Nichols said that only two out of her five profs. knew her name but that she had friends [at other schools] who were in classes of about 300. . . . Emi asked, "Should teachers go out of their way to meet each student's needs or is it the student who should meet the teacher's requirements?"

This excerpt from a student's message is part of the correspondence that students and I wrote using VAX Notes, a computer-mediated conferencing system. For 2 years, I have used VAX Notes with first-year students in composition and literature courses. Although I have learned that computer-mediated conferencing is occasionally time consuming and frustrating, I have also found that, at its best, it encourages students to engage with ideas from texts and from one another in exciting and unexpected ways.

INSTRUCTIONAL PROBLEM

Like many writing teachers, I wanted to provide students with opportunities for informal but substantive writing and to introduce them to the collaborative process that underlies much academic work. Students at this small, Jesuit liberal arts school were, in general, relatively skilled writers but, like first-year students at many universities, were reluctant or not well prepared to read and write critically. These students, I believed, would benefit from writing informally about complex ideas and exchanging their writing with other students. Such writing would, I hoped, nourish their intellectual development in the course and enrich their longer, more formal papers.

The need for more and broader opportunities for writing has been frequently articulated. More than two decades ago, Britton, Burgess, Martin, McLea, and Rosen (1975) observed that students were too often expected to write for a narrow purpose—to demonstrate what they have learned—for a single audience—the teacher. Such writing, while important, is unrepresentative of the writing that students will be expected to do outside of school and discourages students from recognizing the role of writing in developing thinking. More recently, social constructionists such as Bruffee (1984) have drawn attention to the processes by which knowledge is established and maintained within disciplines, a process often likened to conversation. Few first-year students, however, view the creation and development of ideas as a dynamic process.

Literature on computer-mediated conferences suggested that electronic conferences might provide opportunities for substantive, informal writing and sustained discussion of ideas. Years of work by Levin and his associates (see, e.g., Levin, Riel, Boruta, & Rowe, 1984; Riel, 1990) had revealed the attractions of long-distance exchanges in the social and natural sciences. Other researchers had identified the promise of computer-mediated conferencing within classes rather than across continents. Although Hawisher and Selfe (1991) carefully noted the dangers of uncritical use of electronic conferences in teaching, they nonetheless maintained that such conferences, used astutely, can "help teachers create new and engaging forums for learning" (p. 62). Similarly, Hawisher and Moran (1993) argued that e-mail and networks can "make collaboration easier by dissolving the temporal and spatial boundaries of the conventional classroom" (p. 633). More recently, Duin and Hansen (1994) examined the social context for writing on computer networks. At Carnegie Mellon University, Hartman and colleagues (1991) found that "network technology and collaborative writing tools support student efforts to become better writers by providing opportunities for practice and for receiving feedback from and audience that includes both teacher and classmates" (p. 104).

These accounts made me optimistic that computer-mediated conferencing on the university's VAX Notes system might enhance students'
abilities to read critically and write reflectively. Even so, I worried, fearing
alternately that this online discussion would be redundant, merely a perfunctory rehashing of ideas already discussed in class, or that the dialog
on VAX Notes would be so animated that it would drain all the energy
from our in-class discussions. Although the latter possibility might have
been exciting evidence of the usefulness of VAX Notes, it would not, I
felt, have made for a satisfying writing class, or at least not one that I was
comfortable teaching. The best use of VAX Notes, I thought, would be to
extend, rather than replace, class discussions while providing opportunities different from those offered in class.

DESCRIPTION OF VAX NOTES

The VAX Notes system is similar to many computer-mediated conferencing systems designed to support asynchronous conferences. VAX Notes
allows participants to write notes that other participants in the conference
can read and respond to at their convenience, using any computer—on or
off campus—that can connect to the university mainframe. Although correspondence in the conference is "public"—that is, available to any member of the conference—it is not available to other computer users outside
the course. As Hartman et al. (1991) noted, asynchronous computer-
mediated communication offers several benefits: It is convenient because
participants do not have to be in the same place at the same time; it mini-
mizes cues about social status of participants; and it can enable participants reach a wider audience than they ordinarily would in the classroom.

Two features of VAX Notes distinguish it from some other computer-mediated conferencing systems. First, all messages posted to the
VAX Notes system must be identified as either a *note*—that is, a new
topic in the discussion—or a *reply*—a response to a previous note. Any
participant in the conference can initiate a new topic in the discussion.
The conference is thus organized by participants into a set of numbered
topics, each identified by the author's name and a title, followed by a set
of replies. Feenberg and Bellman (1990) observed that the "item-reply
interface" enables users to create a series of subconferences on topics
within the larger conference. A section of the directory from one of the
conferences illustrates this organization.

Topic	Author	Date	Replies	Title
9	BOWEN	23-OCT-1993	18	Ecology & responsibility
10	BOWEN	2- NOV-1993	25	Competing defs. of feminism
11	KDAMBROSIO	5- NOV-1993	18	Conway's adult childhood
12	KFEENEY	5- NOV-1993	3	effect of land on JKC
13	BNICKELS	5- NOV-1993	10	JKC's relationship with mother
14	PGLASS	6- NOV-1993	6	bush ethos
15	KJURCZAK	8- NOV-1993	11	Athletics and Education
16	KMENNUTI	8- NOV-1993	3	college athletics/opinion

Second, VAX Notes displays the author's user ID (first initial and last name) with each message. Communication, therefore is neither anonymous nor conducted with pseudonyms as has been the case in some studies of computer-mediated conferencing (see, e.g., Cooper & Selfe, 1990; Hawisher & Selfe, 1992).

The program offers some attractive features for writers. At any time, participants can print out selected entries or the entire transcript of the conference. With a bit more difficulty, participants can also split the screen, displaying a message to which they are responding at the top and their response at the bottom. Because the conferencing system is relatively easy to use, students were able to learn the basics of VAX Notes in a single class period. They learned more advanced techniques—such as splitting the screen or saving a reply without posting it to the conference—as the semester continued.

OBSERVATIONS

I decided to use VAX Notes because the technology seemed likely to further goals I had for composition courses. I hoped that corresponding on VAX Notes would help students focus more deeply on issues raised in the texts or in class discussion, extend that discussion beyond the classroom, and engage in speculative writing that the more formal papers in the course too often seemed to inhibit. Britton et al. (1975) called such writing "thinking aloud on paper" and described it as "writing addressed to a limited public audience assumed to share much of the writer's context" (p. 89). Such writing, he argued, is the matrix from which other forms of writing develop.

For 2 years, I have used VAX Notes in first-year composition courses and, less extensively, a literature course. In the composition courses, VAX Notes was introduced as an adjunct to class discussion and a replacement for conventional short written homework assignments.

Students were expected to log on to the conference at least twice a week, read some of the new messages, and write a message of their own. Messages in the conference were expected to be related in some way to the readings for the course or to issues raised in class discussion. (Readings in the course included a series of autobiographies that focused on the writer's education, as well as articles on public policy issues related to education.) Students knew that I would be one of the participants in the conference. They also knew that their work in the conference would be evaluated as part of their homework grade for the course, although initially neither they nor I really understood what it meant to evaluate contributions to an electronic conference.

Hartman et al. (1991) offered a sensible caution to teachers who are about to introduce new technology of any kind into the classroom. They point out that "realizing a technological innovation is a complex problem-solving process in which teachers and their students must reason about the potential of the new technology in order to create practices that meet classroom goals" (p. 82). In adapting VAX Notes to my classroom—and my classroom to VAX Notes—my students and I had to develop new ways of working that would capitalize on the technology. We did so, with varying degrees of success.

VAX Notes was most successful when the conference involved students from two sections of the same course. In that conference, students were forced to rely on written communication alone to convey their ideas. They could not assume that their audience could refer to class discussion to "fill in the blanks" in their messages. Instead, their messages had to stand alone as autonomous texts. As a result, the communication in the conference was never a surrogate for, or replay of, class discussion. It offered students an unusual chance to participate in an exchange of ideas, rooted in common readings, with people whom they had not met.

The VAX Notes conferences were not, however, always successful, particularly in the literature course. Sometimes discussion lagged and messages seemed perfunctory. At those times, students referred only infrequently to other students' messages and only superficially to the readings in the course. Yet there were enough substantive and lively exchanges to encourage me to persist in adapting this technology to the writing classroom.

The remainder of the chapter examines three features of the conferences: the writing that students produced, the place of evaluation in computer-mediated conferences, and the role of the moderator. The chapter concludes with a brief discussion of problems I encountered in using computer-mediated conferencing.

Students' Writing on VAX Notes

What I wanted to achieve with VAX Notes was the online equivalent of lively class discussion, not a series of isolated questions and responses. At the start, however, it was difficult to move beyond a truncated version of the pattern of question-answer-evaluation that Mehan (1979) and others have identified as typical in classroom exchanges. In the beginning of the first semester in which we used VAX Notes, neither the students nor I knew how to use the conferencing system effectively. Instead, we treated the conference as we had treated conventional homework assignments: I asked questions; they wrote answers. Even more disappointingly, the answers suggested that students had written without ever reading the entries of other students in the conference. We clearly had not yet figured out how to take advantage of the "public" nature of computer-mediated conferencing.

It was ultimately a note from a student that articulated the problem clearly and convinced me to talk to the two classes about it. (All excerpts from the conference are reproduced as participants wrote them and with the permission of participants.) This student wrote:

> OCT 31, 1993
> Dr. Bowen
> I've been having a difficult time with the VAX Notes. It seems that people do not fully understand the idea behind these notes. I think that people are only reading your initial questions and writing an answer to it, rather than reading the comments of the other students and writing on all of the positions presented. . . . Without ideas to feed off of, this program is pointless. There is no interaction between the students at this point (which, I believe, was your intention).
> Please explain to the en11 sections that the idea of VAX Notes is to respond to everyone's ideas, not just yours. (Shouldn't VAX Notes be more like a class discussion and less like a short-answer question?) Thank you.
>
> brande/k

At the next class meeting I spoke to students in each section of the course about the differences I saw between "pen-and-paper" assignments and discussion in a computer-mediated conference. Students and I both began to take more risks. I developed more open-ended questions, especially ones that picked up unresolved issues from class discussion. Students began to read and refer to other students' messages and, eventually, to initiate new topics of their own. Occasionally I commented in the conference or in class on messages that seemed to advance the conversation in especially productive ways. (Such commenting is not without risk; see the discussion on evaluation.)

The VAX Notes conference gave me the opportunity to reflect on class discussion and synthesize students' comments in a way that was difficult to manage during lively discussions in class. Often, in the press of class discussion, it is difficult to handle adequately students' comments—especially on controversial or sensitive subjects. Not surprisingly, one of the topics that generated the most heated discussion in the conference was feminism. While reading Jill Ker Conway's account of growing up in Australia in the 1940s, *The Road From Coorain* (1990), students disagreed sharply on whether to consider Conway a feminist. I knew that I had not handled one section's discussion of this issue well; in the VAX Notes conference, I had a chance to clarify my comments:

10.0
BBOWEN   2-NOV-1993

Well, it seems clear after yesterday's class (Section K) that there's more to be said about the issue of feminism. Two comments interested me most in that discussion: Ren's claim that "All women—and many men—are feminists because they want a better, more equitable situation for women." (Is that a fair paraphrase, Ren?) The other was Siobhan's reply that, "No, unfortunately—many women don't want to improve their situation."

Ren's comment struck me because it was such a broad and generous definition of feminism. It suggests that one might be a feminist even without claiming to be one or even regarding yourself as one. Ren's definition suggests too that it's actions, not philosophical or political commitment, that matters.

Siobhan's comments also struck me. They suggested that you feel, Siobhan, that many women (& presumably men) feel that the status quo is just fine and that they don't recognize (or that they even resist) attempts to change the present conditions. Underlying your comments is the sense that the status quo is not yet equitable, even if it's considerably better than it was in Conway's day. . . .

The conference gave students a similar chance to clarify positions that they had taken in class or test their understanding of other students' comments. A week after my note on feminism, Siobhan returned to the topic, in response to a student in the other section of the course who had replied to my note:

10.20
SDOOLING   9-NOV-1993

BNickels,
My comments in class must have been misunderstood because I did
not say "many women are oblivious to the situation." Ren had said
she thought every woman had some degree of feminism, and I
explained I didn't think that was really true. I believe there are some
(not many!) women would don't want to be considered equal to men.
. . . That's all I said. I NEVER said "many" women are oblivious to
existing conditions between men and women. I only meant that I feel
there are SOME men and women who are oblivious to inequalities
that exist between the sexes and who, even if they were aware,
wouldn't want to change anything. It's too bad my comment was misunderstood. I hope I cleared it up.

P.S.—You referred to me as "he." I'm a she.

    As the postscript to Siobhan's message makes clear, many of the
students in the conference that semester had not met one another. The
conference was composed of students from the two sections of the first-
year composition course that I taught. Because they used the same syllabus and read the same works, they were able to correspond with one
another despite never having spoken face to face.
    Hawisher and Selfe (1992) pointed out that more information is
needed about "how participants build community over the network and
how the ties of community manifest themselves in face-to-face encounters
outside of the network and in the classroom itself" (p. 27). Student experience in this joint conference leads me to some preliminary observations.
Although the students were in different sections of the same course, they
discussed issues they had in common with apparent ease. Students routinely responded to others whom they did not know. (These messages
were easy to identify because, in them, writers addressed their correspon-
dent by his or her "user ID" rather than first name.)
    Moreover, students' correspondence in the conference occasional-
ly led them to continue the discussion outside of the conference. One student wrote the following invitation to a student in the other section of the
course, whom she had come to know through the conference:

34.19
KOCONNOR   13-DEC-1993
Emi, Unfortunately racism, I believe, will always be confusing to people. . . . My last paper was on "political correctness" or should I say
"equality with sensitivity." Since writing this paper I have thought

about racism and prejudices and freedoms alot recently. I would really like talking to you further about this topic and sharing my paper with your because I feel this topic deserves more attention.

At this moment, and a few others, the VAX Notes conference helped students find pleasure and real companionship in learning. Using it, they were able to establish a temporary community of ideas that transcended the individual conference

At other points in the semester, correspondence in the conference became heated. Twenty-five students in the two sections, for instance, wrote in response to my message on competing definitions of feminism; 27 replied to a message on a related topic, the differences between gender roles in Conway's Australia and the United States in the 1990s. No other topic in the conference elicited anything near that response.

Strangely, however, these topics received little attention in class, perhaps because it was difficult for students to take positions they feared differed from their peers' or that they assumed differed from mine. Although they knew I was a participant in the VAX Notes conference, they seemed to consider me a less significant one there than I was in class. Such an interpretation would be consistent with what others such as Eldred (1990) noted about computer-mediated conferences. Cooper and Selfe (1990) maintained that one advantage of computer-mediated conferences is that it attenuates the teacher's influence. Because many of the social cues of the classroom are eliminated, they argued, these conferences allow students to "experiment with and confront discourse in a less threatening context, one in which the teacher's authority to privilege or forbid discourse is not so absolute, and what matters is ideas, not personalities" (p. 866).

Students also attempted to test or correct their understanding of other students' notes in the conference. One began a reply, "I'm not sure I know what you mean by your first sentence. However, I am interpreting it correctly, I believe that you are asking . . ." (39.2, 1993). Sometimes, perhaps because they were reluctant to disagree openly, students attempted to minimize or even mask disagreement. One wrote, for instance, "I agree with Chris completely but he seems to be ignoring one aspect. . . ." Only in the most heated discussion were disagreements overt, although generally—if not always—polite. Such notes began, "Chris, I am not sure I agree with you on this issue . . ." (19.4) and "MKoroghlian, I still disagree with you. I think . . ." (10.21).

The students' restraint may seem surprising, in light of the frequent discussions of "flaming" in literature on electronic networks (see, e.g., Hawisher & Moran, 1993). The context, however, reduced the likelihood of vituperative exchanges. The VAX Notes system clearly displayed the author's name with each message; no messages were anonymous. Furthermore, students knew that I was a participant in the conference and that their work in the conference constituted part of their semester grade. Finally, the character and small size of this university meant that hostility is rare or at least covert. The social sanctions for violating the norms are high. Because of this self-restraint, the conferences probably sacrificed some of the candor and intensity that Cooper and Selfe (1990), for instance, noted in the conferences they observed.

At the same time, the comparatively restrained tone may have made the conferences more inviting to less self-assured students. The computer-mediated conference seemed to encourage some students, at least, to speculate on complexities or ambiguities in ways that they less often did in class discussion or papers. In class discussion, students seldom had the leisure to pursue a point fully; they felt constrained, it seemed, to "share the floor." In their papers, many students seemed to reduce the complexity of their thinking. In this respect they are typical of beginning college students. As Hayes, Flower, Schriver, Stratman, and Carey (1987) observed, less skilled writers frequently reduce the complexity of a writing task by simplifying the task, the data, or their perceptions of the audience's needs. More skilled writers frequently increase it.

In the VAX Notes conference, however, several students were better able to weigh competing ideas than in either class discussion or more formal papers. For instance, in response to a comment by Richard Rodriquez that his autobiography *Hunger of Memory* (1983) offered only a "very selective and partial view" of his life, one student wrote:

6.5
CDENKOVICH   4-NOV-1994
I must say I am experiencing ambivalent and conflicting opinions. Although I want to say that a writing should tell an entire story in an impartial way, I know that I would never take my own advice. It is really impossible to tell a story to someone without being partial unless that story has no relation or effect in regards to the speaker. And obviously since this work Hunger of Memory is an autobiography there is no way for Rodriguez to speak of his life in a detached manner. . . .

Several students who spoke infrequently in class were, somewhat surprisingly, among the most active and thoughtful participants in the conferences. This observation is consistent with what Hartman et al. (1991) found in their carefully controlled study of communication in networked and non-networked composition classes. They hypothesized that "less able or poorer performing students [would] be the primary beneficiaries of increased opportunities for communication." Network tools may provide these students with "communication opportunities that they may not have in the regular classroom because of efforts to maintain self-esteem, shyness, or slower reaction time" (p. 50). Having found this hypothesis supported, Hartman et al. concluded that "the availability of electronic communication, in a sense, allowed a more equitable distribution of attention" (p. 82) than is generally found in the classroom. Such a finding is significant because it suggests that, when appropriately used, computer-mediated conferencing and related technology can expand students' opportunities in the classroom. Although my students did not have as rich or accommodating a technological environment in which to work, their response to electronic communication, in this respect, seems similar to that observed by Hartman and colleagues.

To different degrees each semester, students gradually took over more of the responsibility for introducing new topics into the conference. Sometimes they asked participants in the conference to help them consider issues which that wanted to write about in their papers. At other times, students quoted from the conference transcript in their papers. After reading Mike Rose's book, *Lives on the Boundary* (1989), one student wrote:

41.0
ECURRY   7-DEC-1993
Fellow Classmates:
I'm having a problem coming up with an argument for my paper. I would like to write about the influence of his teachers on [Mike Rose]. I believe that the book suggest that their is alot of potential out their in the remedial classes that is being hindered or ignored due to the teachers apathy. However, I believe that the parents of the students have even more of an influence on the students. Can we blame teachers for all the problems, or can we place some of the blame on parents?

Fourteen students replied in the next week, responding both to the original question and to other students' comments. Together, they questioned the writer's premises, pointed out evidence in the text, and offered their own experience to support their claims. Although it is impossible to be certain that this exchange helped the writer develop a stronger argument than she would have on her own, it is encouraging that she sees other students as useful resources for ideas.

Sometimes students introduced topics into the conference that connected their experience outside of class to the readings. After racist graffiti appeared on campus, one wrote the following:

19.0
RJELINEK   9-NOV-1993
Recently I got into a discussion with some friends about racism. They
were speaking of how racism is so prevalent in society today. They
claimed that even the most fair person may be racist and not know it.
In the spirit of Richard Rodriguez and Lorene Cary, I was prompted
to analyze this further. I asked them. . . .

In 3 days, 17 replies followed this message. The length and complexity of the exchange indicate that the topic tapped a deep concern for
students. As the discussion moved away from the original incident that had
prompted it to larger questions about race and social policy, it became—
not surprisingly—particularly animated. Several students challenged what
they saw as Ron's reactionary position; others agreed with him, offering
anecdotes from their own experience to bolster their positions.

During the exchange, Ron himself took on the role of moderator,
returning to the discussion several times to comment on the replies his
note had prompted. Two of his replies illustrate his skill as ad hoc moderator. In each reply, he begins by quoting from or paraphrasing the other
student's earlier message in order to identify a point of agreement. Having
established that bridge to his audience, he goes on to challenge some part
of the writer's position.

19.13   11-NOV-1993
I agree, Jill. We should, as you say, all have rights as Americans . . .
[but] the fact that we give special rights to people of color in issues
such as affirmative action and quotas, draws more attention to skin
color rather than away from it . . .

19.14   11-NOV-1993
Kara, I understand your desire to "stop the hate." I feel, though, that
we are not being compassionate as others think we may be as long as
we support . . . welfare and affirmative action . . .

His skill as moderator helped students produce a discussion that was vigorous but not rancorous.

I learned that I could not predict the topics that would attract students' interest and lead to lively exchanges. Sometimes, students posted
topics that seemed to me to be trite or already exhausted in class discussion, only to find that these topics captivated other students' interest. For
instance, after we had discussed Jill Ker Conway's relationship with her
family extensively—and, I thought, exhaustively—in class, AnneMarie
posted the following note in the conference:

21.0   11-NOV-1993
How did the family affect JKC's life? In what ways did Conway benefit from her relationship with her parents. And what were the costs of
the relationship?

Instead of being ignored or treated perfunctorily, that note generated the
most enthusiastic response of any topic that year. The series of replies
began: "GOOD QUESTION AnneMarie! The family definitely . . ."
(21.1) and "AnneMarie, I really liked this question. I agree that . . ."
(21.2). Although computer-mediated conferences may not, as Hawisher
and Selfe (1992) pointed out, tap what Robert Brooke called the "underlife" in the classroom, they may at least reveal and give voice to students'
otherwise unexpressed excitement about ideas.

Evaluation

As Eldred (1990) pointed out, "our classroom dilemmas do not disappear
with a computer network; they change" (p. 54). Evaluation is perpetually
vexing for writing teachers and becomes even more so as we adapt new
technology that upsets the equilibrium in the classroom. Teachers using
electronic conferences need to determine, first, whether evaluation of students' contributions to the conference is appropriate and, second, what
form that evaluation should take.
    Strong arguments have been offered against evaluating students'
work on computer-mediated conferences. Hawisher and Selfe (1991), for
instance, argued that such evaluation works against the potential of electronic networks to "provide room for positive activities—for learning, for
the resistant discourse characteristic of students thinking across the grain
of convention, for marginalized students' voices" (pp. 63-64). Drawing on
Foucault's analysis of punishment in society, they contended that when
teachers select examples of students' writing in the conference for praise
or criticism, "they are employing electronic conferences to discipline, to
shape the conversations and academic discourse of their students" (p. 63).
    Although their argument is appealing, it is not the only perspec-
tive on this issue. I knew that I was using the VAX Notes conferences to
advance specific goals in the course—to enrich students' reflections on the
texts and to enhance their ability to collaborate in learning. For that reason, I evaluated students' participation in the conference twice each
semester. I checked first that students had met the minimum criterion for
the task—writing at least twice a week in the conference. (Most did, each
semester.) Then I looked at the degree to which their responses grappled
with complex ideas from the texts or from other students' messages, and
the frequency with which students introduced new topics into the confer-

ence. Early in the conference I commented in class on examples that seemed especially rich or thoughtful.

Role of the Moderator

In her discussion of the role of the moderator in computer-mediated conferences, McCreary (1990) commented:

> The moderator is like the lead player in a jazz ensemble. Participants do not know in advance what roles they will play in relation to the others; they begin the ensemble in pursuit of a theme; but how that pursuit will progress, the contributions to be made by each member, and how it is to be resolved to a satisfactory conclusion remain to be discovered. It is the moderator who organizes and leads each participant to create an ensemble. (p. 121)

McCreary's analogy is appealing. It suggests the fluid character of computer-mediated conferences, at once goal-directed and unpredictable. The analogy does not, however, answer questions that teachers are likely to have: Should the conference be moderated and, if so, by whom? What does effective moderating look like? What conditions encourage students to assume the role of moderator? Should the moderator intervene if disputes arise online or if the conference seems unproductive?

Two kinds of computer-mediated conferences predominate outside of the classroom: well-defined groups, usually in business or academia, which share a clear task or interest; and loosely defined groups, often with fluid membership, which are brought together only by a shared interest in a topic. In the former, the moderator often assumes considerable control and has special responsibilities in helping the group manage its task. In the latter, there may be no moderator at all or only an occasional one.

In education, however, the appropriate role for the moderator seems much less clear. The "task" is often less tangible than those in other forms of computer-mediated conferences and may be defined differently by students and teachers. Unlike participants in many computer-mediated conferences, who are separated from one another by long distances, participants in a conference such as this one can communicate, perhaps even more easily, in other ways. Furthermore, students may be required to participate, regardless of the value they see in the conference. As a result, the moderator—whether teacher or student—may need to function in special ways.

In the literature on computer-mediated conferences in education, the arguments about moderating conferences parallel those about evaluating conference participation. Several researchers point out the constraining effect that a teacher as moderator may have on the conference. Cooper and Selfe (1990), for instance, discussed the extent to which students in one unmoderated conference "assumed control over the discussion in the conference." These students felt that the conference was "their place, and . . . they knew best about what to do in it" (p. 857).

Eldred (1991), however, argued that productive exchanges in conferences "[do] not emerge automatically" (p. 56). Rather, they are assisted by intervention from a skillful moderator. Such a moderator, she contended, can help lessen the frequency of both "flames" and highly introspective, writer-based messages, both of which reduce the effectiveness of the conference. She pointed out that students can learn to serve as moderators and, in that process, learn a great deal about synthesis. The exchange on racism, described earlier, illustrates that some students can indeed take on the role of moderator spontaneously. Others may need encouragement or instruction to do so.

Problems in Computer-Mediated Conferences

If success in the conference can be measured by students' rate of participation, then the conferences in the writing courses were far more successful than that in the literature course. To a large degree, that difference reflects the different requirements in the two courses. In the literature course, participation in the VAX Notes conference had been voluntary; in the composition courses, participation was required. In the literature course, the conference in this course served mainly to convey information—about assignments or additional readings—rather than a vehicle for discussion. Not surprisingly, few students logged on. With so few participants, discussion in the conference was enervated. Because I could not count on students in the course having read messages in the conference, I began to summarize information from the conference in class. The conference became redundant, then defunct.

In retrospect, it is easy to see why problems arose. My own expectations for the conference were uncertain. I failed to give students a clear sense that the conference was something that I took seriously and that I believed would contribute significantly to their learning. Feenberg and Bellman (1990) claimed that "unless computer communication is built into the course formally, as an interactive method to facilitate close discussion of topics," students will not use it (p. 91).

I suspect that the fundamental cause of the difficulties in the literature conference was that I had not thought as seriously about the teaching of literature as I had about the teaching of composition. Consequently, I had a less clear idea of the purposes computer-mediated conferences might serve in the course. Such an interpretation would be consistent with the observations of Hartman et al. (1991) who found that success in using network technology increased as overall teaching experience increased.

CONCLUSION

Like most other educational technology, VAX Notes offers both potential benefits and clear costs. Using a computer-mediated conference demands patience and effort, from both teachers and students, and offers no guarantee of success. Nevertheless, when used with what Hawisher and Selfe (1991) called "necessary scrutiny and careful planning" (p. 55), it can assist in the important work in the classroom of teaching students to write thoughtfully and take one another's ideas seriously.

REFERENCES

Britton, J., Burgess, T., Martin, N., McLeod, A., & Rosen, H. (1975). *The development of writing abilities*. London: MacMillan.

Bruffee, K. (1984). Collaborative learning and the "conversation of mankind." *College English, 46*, 645-652.

Conway, J. K. (1990). *The road from Coorain*. New York: Vintage.

Cooper, M., & Selfe, C. (1990). Computer conferences and learning: Authority, resistance, and internally persuasive discourse. *College English, 52*(8), 847-869.

Duin, A. H., & Hansen, C. (1994). Overview: Reading and writing on computer networks as social construction and social interaction. In C. Selfe & S. Hilligloss (Eds.), *Literacy and computers: The complications of teaching and learning with technology* (pp. 89-112). New York: MLA.

Eldred, J. M. (1990). Pedagogy in the computer-networked classroom. *Computers and Composition, 8*(2), 47-61.

Feenberg, A., & Bellman, B. (1990). Social factor research in computer-mediated communications. In L. Harasim (Ed.), *Online education: Perspectives on a new environment*. New York: Praeger.

Hartman, K., Neuwirth, C., Kiesler, S., Sproull, L., Cochran, C., Palmquist, M., & Zubrow, D. (1991). Patterns of social interaction and learning to write: Some effects of networked technologies. *Written Communication, 8*(1), 79-113.

Hawisher, G., & Moran, C. (1993). Electronic mail and the writing instructor. *College English, 55*(6), 627-643.

Hawisher, G. E., & Selfe, C. L. (1991). The rhetoric of technology and the electronic writing class. *College Composition and Communication, 42*(1), 55-65.

Hawisher, G. E., & Selfe, C. L. (1992). Voices in college classrooms: The dynamics of electronic discussion. *The Quarterly of the National Writing Project, 14*(3), 24-28.

Hayes, J. R., Flower, L., Schriver, K. A., Stratman, J., & Carey, L. (1987). Cognitive processes in revision. In S. Rosenberg (Ed.), *Advances in applied psycholinguistics* (pp. 176-240). Cambridge, UK: Cambridge University Press.

Levin, J., Riel, M., Boruta, M., & Rowe, R. (1984). Muktuk meets Jacuzzi: Computer networks and elementary schools. In S. Freedman (Ed.), *The acquisition of written language* (pp. 160-171). New York: Ablex.

McCreary, E. (1990). Three behavioral models for computer-mediated communications. In L. Harasim (Ed.), *Online education: Perspectives on a new environment.* New York: Praeger.

Mehan, H. (1979). *Learning lessons: Social organization in the classroom.* Cambridge, MA: Harvard University Press.

Riel, M. (1990, January/February). Building a new foundation of global communities. *Writing Notebook,* 35-37.

Rodriquez, R. (1983). *Hunger of memory: The education of Richard Rodriquez.* New York: Bantam.

Rose, M. (1989). *Lives on the boundary.* New York: Penguin.

Chapter • 8

Improving Classroom Culture: Using Electronic Dialogue to Face Difference

Pamela Gay

> Listen to the . . . voices. Listen to the silences, the unasked questions, the blanks . . .
> —Adrienne Rich (1979, p. 243)

> To engage in dialogue is one of the simplest ways we can begin as . . . critical thinkers to cross boundaries, the barriers that may or may not be erected by race, gender, class, professional standing, and a host of other differences.
> —bell hooks (1994, p. 130)

In a computer-networked discussion, unlike in most face-to-face classroom discussions, everyone can participate. Egalitarianism is a frequently cited advantage (Bump, 1990). The political potential is obvious. Computer networks "provide forums for students heretofore excluded, marginalized, or silenced in the traditional classroom" (Wahlstrom, 1994, p. 173). Free from the gaze of the teacher and many sets of eyes, students tend to be more honest, especially when pseudonyms are used (Peterson, 1989).[1] Computer-networked discussion de-faces (or levels) difference. A

---

[1]Research reports I read in 1990 when I first started using computer-networked discussion made this claim. For 5 years I mostly used pseudonyms. However, in an advanced composition class (Spring 1997), I found that students using their given

participant's gender, size, shape, age, color and accent are unknown. As a student in one of Lester Faigley's (1990) classes put it, "The computer has only one color" and one printface (p. 307). The teacher can prompt a discussion and be a participant but cannot monitor or control it. Participants do not have to wait their turn to speak. Anyone can jump into the dialogue any time; technically, everyone can speak at once.

At the 1990 Conference on College Composition and Communication, Gail Hawisher pointed out that online conversations could be used to "help mask cues so we won't know who said what." "So we don't have to face each other," I wrote in my conference notes. There was also talk at the Computers and Writing (C&W) conference that year about raising seats or lowering computers so that students working in computer clusters could face each other while writing online using pseudonyms.[2] But this is not the kind of facing that I am talking about here. I wanted to move from masking cues "so we won't know who said what" to unmasking and facing each other and learning *who* said what.

When I first began using synchronous electronic dialogue in 1990, I used networked discussion for "free talking," a kind of warm-up for further writing students would do on their own. I treated these discussions much as I did conventional classroom discussions. We did not look back on them; except for a scroll-through, they more or less disappeared. One of the advantages of a networked discussion, however, is that you can look back and read transcripts of whole-class or small-group discussions. I wanted to take full advantage of this technology.

Who is speaking or writing? What is the (sociocultural-historical) location of the speaker-writer? As Mohanty (1989-1990) said, "The point is not simply that one should have a voice; the more crucial question concerns the sort of voice one comes to have as a result of one's location—both as an individual and as part of collectives" (p. 208). In her critical

---

names were just as honest. The next term (Fall 1997), a student reported that she did not really say what she wanted to in a discussion because her real name was being used. The key variable, as always, is the learning context. In the Spring 1997 class, we had worked collaboratively in many other ways, including the development of this innovative, Internet-based course linked with the University of Auckland, New Zealand, and a "safe" environment was well established before we began having networked discussions. In the Fall 1997 class, we had our first networked discussion before a sense of collaboration and trust had been developed. Students weren't sure yet if it was okay to "open up."

[2]In a computer-networked discussion in which I was a participant (pre-conference workshop, Computers and Writing Conference, El Paso, 1995), we were "talking" about our understanding of "community" when someone got up from behind a computer cluster across the room and walked over to someone at a computer next to me. She had guessed the writer behind the pseudonym and really wanted to talk face to face.

study of learning to teach, Britzman (1991) described what she called "a critical voice"—an engaged voice—as being "concerned not just with representing the voices of oneself and others, but with narrating, considering, and evaluating them" (p. 13). How can we engage (the voices that represent) difference? How can we reposition ourselves to see from another perspective or other (multi) perspectives? How can we learn to occupy the subject position of the other?

I am struggling to engage voices brought into the classroom community through various forms of computer-mediated communication (CMC). I offer one sample of a modest beginning of one exploration.

SCREEN-BASED TEXTS: ONE EXPLORATION

For a discussion prompt in one computer-networked discussion, I gave basic writing students a news article about the controversy surrounding the use of Native American names by professional sports teams and the behavior of some Atlanta Braves' fans who wore chicken feathers, painted their faces, and waved rubber tomahawks (Wilkerson, 1992). This class was working on a larger ethnic identification writing project (Gay, 1995). Students clicked away steadily for 30 minutes. I asked them to read the entire transcript for the next class, either on disk if they copied it or a hard copy I placed on reserve in the library.

The following is an excerpt from a transcript of the electronic discussion. Notice the play at the start of the conference and then how several students address the controversial issue.

Moonset:	Hello, This is Moonset. I am here with my tomahawk! Watch out!!!!!
Tonto:	Injuns! Pull the wagons up in a circle. (We get better reception that way.)
Minnie haha:	Hee Haw!
Captain John Smith:	I agree that sports teams should change their names because it is not a trivial thang.
navaho night:	I'd be mad if someone decided to call a team the blackskins. That is just an outright blatant stereotype.
Bish Bash:	The only reason the sports teams don't want to change their names is partly because of tradition but mostly due to MONEY.
Minnie haha:	If you were at the Braves game sitting among these feathered fans, how would you respond?
Chief Talking Bull:	Some Indians might not mind the name. Some might even be proud.

Sun Rise:	Write back moonset.
Chief Talking Bull:	I've been to the southwest and I've met indians out there. They are treated realy [sic] badly, like pests. I don't blame them for being bitter.
Minnie haha:	Hey, remember when Mariott had ethnic themes in the dining halls and they put up pictures of Chinese coolies and the Asian American Student Union said that it was racist? And Marriot said they were trying to be nice. They didn't know. The Braves fans probably didn't know that chicken feathers were sacred. If you don't understand, are you racist?
Dawakuli:	WHY WOULD YOU BE UPSET if a team called themselves the blackskins?
Mets:	People watch out.
Chief Talking Bull:	If someone thought it was funny to imitate my ancestors, I'd be mad to [sic].
navaho night:	I stated why I would be upset. Read the whole message.
Moonset:	I think that people should have respect for the Indian names, and should not use them in a trivial way because Indian traditions are deeply rooted in Indian society and it hurts their pride.
Captain John Smith:	Gimme a break, navaho night. Indeed, minnie haha.

While Sun Rise and Mets are still warming up ("Write back moonset"; "People watch out"), some others are engaged in a serious discussion. Navaho night and Dawakuli are having their own conversation about the issue, and clearly navaho night is irritated by Dawakuli's query. Captain John Smith quickly addresses the tension ("Gimme a break, navaho night") and joins the main discussion, applauding minnie haha's remarks. There is a lot going on in this brief space; what perhaps looks like a casual discussion is quite intense.

For the next networked discussion I used as a prompt this passage:

Minnie haha:	Hey, remember when Mariott had ethnic themes in the dining halls and they put up pictures of Chinese coolies and the Asian American Student Union said that it was racist? And Marriot said they were trying to be nice. They didn't know. The Braves fans probably didn't know that chicken feathers were sacred. *If you don't understand, are you racist?*

Students again clicked away for another 20 minutes. Then I interrupted with this question: "Is anyone here racist?" Students stopped clicking keys and looked around the room. I asked them to write a sentence beginning with "I am not racist because . . ." Again, I asked them to read the transcript for the next class. (Most students wrote some variation of this statement: "I believe people should be treated equally no matter what their skin color or race.") In addition to the transcript, I asked them to read an essay by Yamato (1990) in which she talked about covert as well as overt racism.

During the next class, I asked students again to address the question: "If you don't understand, are you racist?" They responded this time informed by their reading of Yamato's essay as well as much discussion among their peers. I interrupted after a few minutes with this prompt: "What would Yamato say and do you agree with her?" I directed students to read the transcript of the discussion for the next class where we would meet face to face.

In the conventional classroom we had a lively whole-class discussion as students worked toward positioning themselves on this issue. Students tried to "get right" what they thought Yamato would say. They argued for their own viewpoints to be heard and understood. They interrupted each other. One White male was still angry with an African-American female who earlier in the course had used "we" in an essay she had written about African Americans. He had told her he didn't like her use of "we" because he (a White male) was not included. A Caribbean woman had told him she did not like his use of "we" because it did not include her. This tension was in this community as well as other tensions. On campus, the president of the Student Association (SA) had been accused of being racist and not allowing students of color to be represented or even heard in a meeting that was supposed to be open. A student protest received national attention. Everyone was talking about racism and everyone had a point of view about what had happened and what should happen on campus.

After our face-to-face discussion, we returned to the networked classroom to try to clarify and support various positions. I interrupted with another prompt: "What in your background and experience led you to this viewpoint?" (Who is speaking or writing?). Hooks (1994) warned teachers that they must "teach students how to listen, how to hear one another" (pp. 149-150). I paired up the students so they could interview each other and more easily move beyond information gathering toward understanding each other's subject position.

For the next session, I asked them to tell the class their dialogue partner's viewpoint and to say something about the speaker-writer's location or context. More discussion followed. Writers clarified, explained, argued. Listeners talked about what they heard and they raised questions. We worked toward understanding by trying to step inside someone else's shoes or do what I call "really listening."

The work I have described here is a small step beyond acknowledgment of difference to engagement. I am an experienced teacher whose research interest is pedagogy. I am always reflecting on my practice. I read current literature in composition theory and pedagogy and participate in national conferences and write essays about my pedagogical projects. I have been working with computer-networked discussion for many years and have carefully thought about uses of CMC for practicing theory. How can CMC help me create a polylogic classroom? How can I co-author the classroom community with my students? How can we write our time together?

It is difficult to find ways to include multiple voices (hooks, 1990). CMC makes inclusion look easy. However, the challenge comes in using our voices to face difference, including the difference of status between teacher and students, and other differences as well (class, race, etc.). Including voices beyond a surface "coming to voice"—engaging all the voices in a classroom community discussion—is a complicated, messy, and sometimes uncomfortable process, even for an experienced writing teacher. Adding previously silenced voices to classroom conversation, as the following tale dramatically demonstrates, is not as easy as adding technology and can be explosive, silencing everyone, including the teacher.

BEHIND THE SCENES: A CAUTIONARY TALE

A new teaching assistant (TA), whom I call Sally, attended a workshop I conducted to introduce interested TAs to the computer-networked classroom I had set up on my campus. It was a hands-on workshop. After summarizing the advantages of a networked discussion, I asked the TAs to role-play, using the transcript from a student discussion based on the "Indignant Indians" prompt I cited earlier. Afterward, they commented on how students seemed to be getting into the discussion in a way that does not happen so easily in a conventional classroom. Most new TAs report difficulty in getting students to engage in discussion, and computer-networked discussion can appear to be a simple solution to this problem. In fact, after the workshop, Sally decided that an electronic discussion might be just what her class needed. No one actually said anything, she told me, but the class just was not working.

A few days later I learned from Sally that her students had taken over the network and trashed her "on screen." After initially responding to a question she posed, they took advantage of this sudden freedom:

They broke the silence, uncovered the hidden, and "claimed and used classroom space for their own purposes" (Faigley, 1992, p. 197). One dared to speak and then another joined in and then another until everyone, at least it seemed to Sally, was attacking her. Although "the teacher may wonder, at times, what her charges would really say about her if they could speak their minds" (Rothstein, 1993, p. 94), Sally was devastated. Her students remarked on the Whiteness of her skin, the color and style of her hair (a blonde curly bob), her mannerisms, and the way she conducted the class. One student even took her first name as a pseudonym. Alarmed, Sally looked around. Who was speaking? Who said what? She stopped scrolling, not quite believing what had happened. She did not dare look around at the faceless faces nor did she attempt to break in. Students quickly left when the class time was up. Sally stayed behind her computer terminal. Due to some glitch, the discussion was not saved, but she vividly recalled what she had read.

Most of Sally's students had been admitted to the university through the Educational Opportunity Program (EOP) and had just participated in a strong summer program based on critical pedagogy and the work of Paulo Freire. These mostly non-White students from New York City had been used to a de-centered classroom and sharing authority, including participation in curriculum development as well as evaluation. They were taught to question and be active rather than passive learners.

The summer EOP program is staffed by experienced TAs who work collaboratively before and during the program. They receive a modest stipend for their pre-program work. Not only do they read relevant articles in composition theory and critical pedagogy but they also work on curriculum together. Sally's students had just worked with a TA who had won a teaching award. They felt prepared to move beyond basic writing (BW), and they did not want to be separated from other incoming students in the fall. Nevertheless, urged by their writing teacher and EOP counselors and appeased somewhat by their placement in the most advanced BW course, they enrolled and waited.

When an experienced TA resigned just before fall term, Sally was asked to teach this BW course. Although she had no teaching experience and was reluctant, especially with no time to prepare, she felt obliged to help out the department. Sally was White and had been raised in a small, Upstate New York town with only four Blacks in her graduating class. She was unprepared, even theoretically, to teach composition, especially in a multicultural classroom.

Sally used an already chosen rhetoric reader that focused on argument and included essays on a variety of controversial issues. She planned to use the reading and class discussion to prompt student writing. Her plan seemed workable, especially because several other TAs were using this text and they would be in staff meetings together. Sally, however, could not get class discussion going and felt a hostile silence building. She confessed that she did not bring this problem up in staff meetings because she believed the other TAs were not having problems, and she kept thinking the next class would be better.

Sally's students became increasingly frustrated and impatient when the course was not nearly as challenging as the one they had taken during the summer and they did not embrace a similar participatory pedagogy. Some of the students talked with EOP counselors, but no one felt comfortable speaking in class about the problem, which they realized was not entirely their teacher's fault. They were beginning to feel trapped, powerless, and angry about the system that put them and their TA in this position.

Sally wanted to forget what had happened and just get through the rest of the term. She had never intended to teach, and now she certainly did not ever want to teach. "I can't help it if I'm White," she said, "And one student wouldn't even look at me during her conference. She wouldn't acknowledge me. And her writing's not very good. She needs help. I'm good at responding to student writing. I told the student we had to talk, and she said, 'You mean we have to have *another* conference?' and stormed out of my office."

Sally did not know how to handle the predicament she was in and asked me for help. She did not want to confront the class at the moment, nor did she want to return to the computer-networked classroom. I proposed that we work together, at least for a few classes, on a new project on ethnic identification (Gay, 1995). Sally liked this plan and was obviously relieved.

When I entered the classroom, Sally was writing on the blackboard the names of some speakers who were coming to campus and whom she thought would be of special interest to these students. The students were seated in desk-like chairs that had derailed from the traditional rows. No one looked at the blackboard until Sally spoke, and then no one noted the information but me. Sally introduced me, and I explained that she had invited me to come in and help start off this project I had designed.

We began by asking students to write about how they identified themselves ethnically. I suggested we move the chairs into a circle so we could face each other when speaking. Sally and I hoped that she could talk about her identification as White at some point and lead naturally into a discussion of what happened in the networked classroom. My goal was to accomplish something like the polylogue Sally was trying to create with CMC but couldn't.

Everyone was engaged in conversation with a neighbor when one student interrupted: "Do White students have to do this?" Everyone stopped talking. I looked across the circle. "Because they should," a young African-American woman stated openly. "Why are we the oppressed always writing about our oppression? *They* are the ones who need this. We know. We want to do something else." "Yes," someone else said.[3] Then other voices entered, but we weren't on a computer network where turn-taking does not apply. Everyone tried to speak at once. No one could be understood in this babble of voices. In effect, all were silenced. In this moment, I certainly missed the advantage of synchronous CMC, which would allow multiple comments to be sent at once and printed on the screen.

Sally's students wanted to know why they had to take this course. I tried to explain how they could benefit, get help with their writing, that—"The White man always says, 'This will benefit you. This is good for you,'" said the woman-who-interrupted, pointing at me, the accused. "[C]olonizing tendencies always exist, . . ." explained compositionists Knoblauch and Brannon (1993), "whenever those with power set out to 'do something for' those without it" (p. 12). Spivak (1990), a postcolonial critic, sees this benevolent gesture—the First World helping the Third World to develop—as imperialistic: "What's wrong with you? You're getting all these benefits from the U.S. educational system. You've been given an educational opportunity." The tension in this class was being let out, and I "took the heat" while Sally tried to recover herself.

For the next class, I asked students to write their responses to this classroom scene and to write about what they wanted to do, and I told them that they could not make any personal attacks. After listening to the voices of her students one by one in the next class, Sally regained her strength and returned to class on her own with a proposal that the next writing project be a collaborative investigation of the history of basic writing at this institution and elsewhere. How were students placed in BW courses? What about TA preparation? Why weren't there any TAs from underrepresented groups teaching? The students voted in favor of the project and to select three students to read their final essays to the class and invited guests, including some English Department administrators. [4]

---

[3]In retrospect, I think this complaint is legitimate, and I no longer use or recommend this project for EOP students who participate in our summer enrichment program. However, I used a variation of this project (Fall 1997) with a group of upper level students from Binghamton and the Czech Republic in a linked course. We shared writing and reading about cultural identity through our linked course pages on the Internet, e-mail correspondence and asynchronous discussion as well as "real-time" discussion, using Internet Relay Chat (IRC).

[4]Although much of the research could have been done on the Internet, Sally's use of computers prior to the networked discussion was limited to word processing. She left the means of research up to the students. An English Department committee was formed to discuss the ongoing problems of TA assignments and profes-

What can we learn from this tale? It is certainly a dramatic reminder of the importance of teacher preparation and in particular the preparation of TAs who barely have institutional authority. As Webster (1989) pointed out, the practice of having graduate students teach composition courses without having had any teaching experience "and, in some cases without any desire to teach" is widespread. "Not only is the situation not seen as ridiculous," she added, "it is seen as normal."

If Sally had been more confident as a result of preparation and experience, she could have turned the silent power struggles into productive engagement.[5] Students could have aired their concerns during a computer-networked discussion. Sally could have read a transcript of the discussion and responded. They could have worked together on the problem rather than making Sally the target. The process of engaging all the voices, including her own, however, would not have been easy, not as easy as "just adding" technology. That is really the message behind this cautionary tale.

If a teacher-centered class is not going well and that teacher is inexperienced with barely any institutional authority and no earned authority and students are suddenly let loose in a student-centered networked discussion, then the result could be devastating, as in Sally's case. However, if a class is teacher-centered, but the teacher is moving more and more toward a student-centered pedagogy and the class is going reasonably well, then trying out a computer-assisted discussion could turn out to be more than a fun and games one-class stand. Such an experience could even help the teacher imagine ways of making the conventional classroom more dialogic.

A group of high school teachers I introduced to electronic dialogue, for example, remarked about how "hearing" all the voices in a discussion motivated them to want to talk and listen more. How could they get discussion to take off like this in a conventional classroom setting? I suggested they try the Bard Method of asking students to write a response

---

sional development as well as the department's relationship with EOP. A plan to link some writing courses with introductory courses in other disciplines, following the model of the Binghamton Enrichment (summer) Program (BEP) directed by Steve Duarte, has been implemented. More emphasis is being placed on developing writers across the curriculum.

[5]Newly liberated students can certainly get out of hand. Mayers (1996) reported that a networked discussion in one of his classes degenerated into "a rather disturbing display of name-calling and accusations." How did he handle this classroom scene? Smartly, I'd say. He didn't reprimand them for their behavior, but he did hold them responsible. He asked the class to read a transcript of this discussion for the next class and then "discuss why the discussion proceeded the way it did and who should be considered responsible for the potentially dangerous turns the conversation took" (p. 150). But Mayers is an experienced and confident teacher who has been working with networked discussions for some time, and his pedagogy is student centered.

to a passage of a text and then pass their writing to the person on their left for response and then go back and forth a couple of times, finally sharing some conversations with the whole class.[6] The teachers began to talk about various ways of getting students more engaged in face-to-face class discussion and also about working on a proposal to network computers in their resource center.

(IN)CONCLUSION

What follows is a too tidy conclusion to a monologue that cannot do justice to the complicated political issues I raised.

CMC makes it possible for all students to voice themselves and hear difference in ways not possible in a conventional classroom setting, but it takes more than CMC—it takes good theory in practice, or else the polylogue is ignored or stifling. In a computer-networked discussion, students can more freely voice their differences and also "hear" multiple voices, enabling them to see a wider angle of perspective. This wide-angle vision, however, could result in just surface acknowledgment or peripheral inclusion. A multicentric perspective requires learning to occupy the subject position of the other. Productive use of CMC can help teachers develop a new pedagogy of voice, a pedagogy that not only encourages students to voice (acknowledge) difference but also to face (engage) difference. This work is challenging and ongoing.

Engagement is not tidy. Nor is this conclusion. I wonder if teachers and students can bear the discomfort truly letting all the voices out or in may bring to our lives in the classroom community. This conclusion, however, is hopeful. If difference is viewed as struggle, and respect and understanding as goals in a participatory democracy, then the struggle, however uncomfortable, is worthwhile.

REFERENCES

Britzman, D. (1991). *Practice makes practice.* Albany: State University of New York Press.

Bump, J. (1990). Radical changes in class discussion using networked computers. *Computers and the Humanities, 24,* 49-65.

---

[6]This method is frequently used at workshops held at the Bard Institute of Writing and Thinking at Annandale-on-Hudson in New York State.

Faigley, L. (1990). Subverting the electronic workbook: Teaching writing using networked computers. In D. Daiker & M. Morenberg (Eds.), *The writing teacher as researcher: Essays in the theory and practice of class-based research* (pp. 290-311). Portsmouth, NH: Boynton/Cook, Heinemann.

Faigley, L. (1992). *Fragments of rationality: Postmodernity and the subject of composition.* Pittsburgh: University of Pittsburgh Press.

Gay, P. (1995). *Developing writers: A dialogic approach.* Belmont, CA: Wadsworth.

hooks, b. (1990). *Yearning: Race, gender, and cultural politics.* Albany: State University of New York Press.

hooks, b. (1994). *Teaching to transgress.* New York: Routledge.

Knoblauch, C., & Brannon, L. (1993). *Critical teaching and the idea of literacy.* Portsmouth, NH: Boynton/Cook.

Mayers, T. (1996). From page to screen (and back): Portfolios, Daedalus, and the "transitional classroom." *Computers and Composition, 13,* 147-154.

Mohanty, C. T. (1989-1990). On race and voice: Challenges for liberal education in the 1990s. *Cultural Critique, 16,* 179-208.

Peterson, N. L. (1989). The sounds of silence: Listening for difference in the computer-networked collaborative writing classroom. In T. W. Batson (Ed.), *Proposal abstracts from the 5th computers and writing conference.* Washington, DC: Gallaudet University.

Rich, A. (1979). *Taking women students seriously. On lies, secrets and silence* (pp. 237-245). New York: Norton.

Rothstein, S. W. (1993). *The voice of the other: Language as illusion in the formation of the self.* Westport, CT & London: Praeger.

Spivak, G. (1990). *The post-colonial critic* (S. Harasym, Ed.). New York: Routledge.

Yamato, G. (1990). Something about the subject makes it hard to name. In G. Anzaldua (Ed.), *Making face, making soul* (pp. 20-24). San Francisco: Aunt Lute.

Wahlstrom, B. J. (1994). Communication and technology: Defining a feminist presence in research and practice. In C. L. Selfe & S. Hilligoss (Eds.), *Literacy and computers: The complications of teaching and learning with technology* (pp. 171-185). New York: MLA.

Webster, J. (1989, Spring). Composition teachers: No experience necessary? *ADE Bulletin,* 41-42.

Wilkerson, I. (1992, January 26). Indignant indians seeking changes. *The New York Times,* p. A14.

Chapter • 9

Fostering Diversity in the Writing Classroom: Using Wide-Area Networks to Promote Interracial Dialogue

Leslie D. Harris
Robert Smith
Terry Craig

> At the root of the American Negro problem is the necessity of the American white man to find a way of living with the Negro in order to be able to live with himself. . . . In this long battle, a battle by no means finished, the unforeseeable effects of which will be felt by many future generations, the white man's motive was the protection of his identity; the black man was motivated by the need to establish an identity. . . . It remains for him [the "black man"] to fashion out of his experience that which will give him sustenance, and a voice.
> —Baldwin (1984, pp. 172-173)

In "Stranger in the Village"—the essay from which the epigraph is taken—Baldwin describes his experience of spending a summer and two winters in a small Swiss village, amid people who had never before seen a Black man. His presence in the village was at first astounding, for the villagers had to readjust their worldview and come to terms with the realization that non-White cultures exist, with people very different from themselves. The children's cries of "Neger! Neger!" (p. 161) in the street, the villagers' tendency to touch his hair or his skin out of amazement at his difference, and their proud professions of their custom "of 'buying'

159

African natives for the purpose of converting them to Christianity" (p. 163) revealed in many ways the villagers' cultural naiveté, as they struggled to come to terms with what Baldwin calls his "human weight and complexity" (p.161)—that is, his existence and his rights as a fellow human being.

Although Baldwin describes that Swiss village at length in his essay, he uses the village to make a more significant commentary on U.S. society and its struggle to acknowledge the "human weight and complexity" of the African Americans who were forcibly brought to American shores. As Baldwin puts it, "the question of his [the African American's] humanity, and of his rights therefore as a human being, became a burning one for several generations of Americans" (p. 170). The legacy of slavery in the United States makes that question particularly pressing for African Americans; however, it has relevance to other ethnic groups as well. If, as the *Declaration of Independence* claims, "all men [and women] are created equal," and if they are "endowed by their Creator with certain unalienable Rights," then those rights should apply equally to people of color, regardless of their ethnicity. As Baldwin perspicaciously revealed, the presence of non-White people in a predominantly White culture forces a conflict between an ideology of equal rights and opportunities for all and a reality of discrimination that denies or limits those rights for the non-White.

Despite the hegemonic ideology of the United States as a "melting pot," in which racial distinctions become "irrelevant," we live in a multiethnic society, composed of people with disparate backgrounds.[1] However, this racial and ethnic diversity tends to distribute itself unevenly by region and by state, a *de facto* segregation that is exacerbated by class differences as well. These factors give rise to enclaves that are almost as homogeneous as the Swiss village Baldwin described. For example, according to estimates by the U.S. Bureau of the Census, 20.6% of the nation's 1997 Hispanic population were resident in Texas, whereas only 2.2% of that population lived in the northeastern states of Maine, New Hampshire, Vermont, Massachusetts, Rhode Island, and Connecticut combined (U.S. Bureau of the Census, 1998, p. 34). Similarly, although the nation in 1997 was 12.1% African American, the state of Georgia was 28.4% African American, whereas Wyoming, South Dakota, and Montana were only 0.8%, 0.7%, and 0.3% African American, respectively (U.S. Bureau of the Census, 1998. p. 34). U.S. universities replicate that uneven distribution by race. According to *The Chronicle of Higher*

---

[1]According to the 1998 *Statistical Abstract of the United States*, the U.S. population in 1997 was 12.1% Black, 0.7% American Indian, Eskimo, or Aleut, 3.5% Asian or Pacific Islander, and 11% Hispanic (U.S. Bureau of the Census, 1998, p. 19).

Education (1998), 49% of California college students in 1998 were minority group members, whereas only 4% of Maine's college students were non-White.

If teachers are to help students learn how to communicate with people from diverse backgrounds both within the United States and internationally and if students are to understand the "human weight and complexity" of people very different from themselves, it is necessary for teachers to enhance the diversity of their own classrooms. Teachers can use the resources of the Internet to foster this diversity by connecting their students with students across the country and even across the world. As students exchange ideas and opinions with this diverse peer group, they can begin a process of productive dialogue, in which majority students can become aware of their own stereotypes and presuppositions, and students of color can—in Baldwin's words—"fashion out of [their] experience that which will give [them] sustenance, and a voice" (p. 173). Within virtual space, some of the limitations of physical space can be overcome, facilitating an interracial dialogue that is much more difficult to achieve in America's predominantly segregated classrooms.

For two of the authors of this chapter, and for many others teaching at predominantly White campuses, the Swiss village that Baldwin described still remains an American reality. We teach students who come from racially homogeneous backgrounds, students who have had extremely limited contact with members of other ethnic groups. For example, Susquehanna University (SU) is located in rural Pennsylvania, in Snyder county, which is 99% White. The student population at SU (with 1,492 total students) is 95% White. Instructors most frequently teach classes that arc 100% White. In six semesters of teaching first-year composition, for example, Leslie Harris had only one non-White student among approximately 90 students in those classes. The New Martinsville campus of West Virginia Northern Community College (WVNCC) is also located in a rural area. Its 491 current students are 100% White. In the last six semesters of teaching first-year composition, Terry Craig has had only 2 students of color among 300 students.

Students enrolling at both SU and WVNCC-New Martinsville come primarily from small communities. When we taught our collaborative composition class in Spring 1995, 100% of the students in the SU and WVNCC classes were White. Fifty-three percent of those SU students reported coming from rural backgrounds, 35% were from suburban backgrounds, and only 12% came from larger cities. In the WVNCC class, 100% of the students reported coming from rural backgrounds. Of those students, 55% came from all-White high schools; the average reported percentage of minority students in their high schools for the full WVNCC class was 1%.

Despite their extraordinary lack of experience with people of color and with cultures different from their own, both the SU and WVNCC students showed a surprising lack of awareness of their own cultural isolation. On an initial Likert-style questionnaire administered at the beginning of the semester, students were asked to respond (using a 1-5 scale, with 1 representing *strong disagreement,* 3 representing *neutrality,* and 5 representing *strong agreement*) to several statements related to the subject of race. One such statement was: "I have frequent personal contact with people from other ethnic groups (for example, many times a week)." Despite their 99% White high schools and their 100% White campus, the WVNCC students only slightly disagreed with that claim, responding on average 2.55 (just on the disagreement side of neutrality). Despite living in a community that is 99% white and attending a school that is 95% White, the SU students responded slightly above neutral, with an average response of 3.09. To the question, "I interact comfortably with people from other ethnic groups," the WVNCC students recorded agreement, with an average score of 3.82. The SU students also agreed with that claim, responding on average 4.15. Similarly, to the statement, "I understand my own ethnic background and how it differs from the ethnic backgrounds of other racial groups," the WVNCC students agreed with the claim, with an average response of 3.91. The SU students also agreed with the claim, responding at an average level of 3.71. These responses are summarized in Figure 9.1.

The students' higher than expected responses reflect two phenomena: the "better-than-average effect" (Alicke, Klotz, Breitenbecher, Yurak, & Vredenburg, 1995, p. 804) and the "availability" heuristic (Tversky & Kahneman, 1974, p. 1127). Despite their racially homogeneous environments and their cultural isolation, the WVNCC and SU students (and people in general, according to the "better-than-average effect") want to believe themselves to be above average in positive qualities, and especially socially desirable qualities. The three claims were expressed as positive comments—ones the students would like to and therefore would believe true unless they possessed very specific counterevidence (which they lack, since their environments have been so homogeneous). The "availability" heuristic reinforces this phenomenon, especially for the second and third statements. If students have had few experiences interacting with people of color, then they will also have few experiences of uncomfortable interactions or of cultural misunderstandings. They will thus tend to agree with the claim, because counterexamples are not available to them.[2]

In order to increase our students' cultural awareness and to challenge some of their misconceptions, we planned our composition courses

---

[2]This analysis relies upon conversations with M. L. Klotz, Susquehanna University.

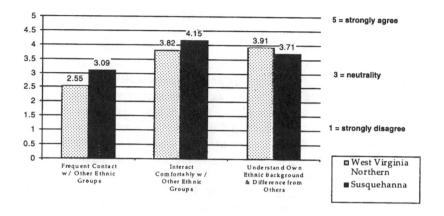

Figure 9.1. Sample WVNCC and SU responses: Race-related questionnaire (to see an online version of the full questionnaire, see the following URL: http://www.du.org/places/du/cc/racesurv.html)

around the theme of families across cultures. Drawing our readings from the anthology *Rereading America: Cultural Contexts for Critical Thinking and Writing* (Colombo, Cullen, & Lisle, 1992), along with Baldwin's *Notes of a Native Son* (1984), Sandra Cisneros' *Woman Hollering Creek and Other Stories* (1991), Harvey Fierstein's film *The Torch Song Trilogy* (Bogart, 1989), and Amy Tan's *The Joy Luck Club* (1989), we explored family and cultural identities of mainstream, African American, Hispanic, Native American, homosexual, and Asian American communities. In addition, we paired each of our classes with another composition class at George Washington University (GWU), a larger urban campus (approximately 6,000 undergraduates, and 15,000 graduate and undergraduate students) with a much more diverse student population: 6% African American, 3% Hispanic, 6% Asian, and 10% other ethnic minorities, for a total of 25% non-White students. Each of the GWU classes (one paired with SU and one paired with WVNCC) had 33% students of color. We shared syllabi for the course, establishing a common ground of readings among the students.[3] Four times during the semester, the two pairs of classes (WVNCC-GWU and Susquehanna-GWU) convened on Diversity University MOO to discuss their shared readings, meeting first in a virtual auditorium.[4] Modeling our discussion strategy after the "Tuesday Cafe" meetings of the Netoric Project run by Tari Fanderclai and Greg Siering, we first showed a series of virtual slides to the students, announcing the topic of the day and explaining how the discussion would run.[5] Students (who were divided into groups of five or six, with members from the two paired classes in each group) then dispersed into smaller discussion rooms, each containing a blackboard with specific discussion questions.[6] Students read the blackboard and discussed the topic, with one student responsible for leading discussion (and keeping it on track), and a second student summarizing the discussion to the class as a whole. Through this process, the students engaged in the MOO equivalent of small, face-to-face group discussions, but within a text-based online environment. They composed their ideas at the keyboard, learning to express those ideas as clearly as possible to a synchronously present audience.

The following unedited excerpt from an actual MOO discussion gives a sense of the synchronous writing environment:

---

[3]A sample syllabus from this class (for Leslie Harris' version of the class) is available online at the following URL: http://www.du.org/places/du/cc/en1008sl.html.

[4]MOO is an environment for synchronous computer-mediated communication (CMC) among people with access to the Internet. Those who connect to a MOO (using telnet or a telnet-like "client" program) land in a virtual room, whose description gives the room "concrete" existence within the virtual environment. Here, for example, is the description of our virtual auditorium space on Diversity University (DU) MOO:

> Laragrove Auditorium
> A large spacious room, with rows of padded chairs, each with its own swing-up arm on which to rest books. There is a multimedia computer station in the front, connected to a back-lit projection screen. A soft light on the lectern glows amidst the darkness.

People who connect to DU MOO (by telnetting to the computer that serves as the MOO host) can converse in real time with anyone else who has also connected to DU and who has moved his or her player self (the character name he or she adopts on that MOO) to the same virtual room. The computer mediates the conversation, echoing the utterances made in that room to the screen of everyone currently "in" the room.

[5]For a more extensive discussion of the "Tuesday Cafe," see Cogdill (1996). See also Greg Siering's Web page concerning The Netoric Project, sponsor of the Tuesday Cafes: http://bsuvc.bsu.edu/~00gjsiering/netoric/netoric.html.

[6]Here is a sample discussion question, placed on a virtual blackboard in one of our virtual small-discussion rooms on DU MOO. The command "read

Raoul-GW says,   "I feel that with some cultures, they tend to "celebrate" in order to separate themselves. Feedback?"

Christine-GW says,   "When it comes down to it, we all the same things inside, and that means we share more common things than we are different."

Christine-GW says,   "I have to agree with Raoul"

Leipzig-SU says,   "I agree with Raoul too."

Carol-GW says,   "raoul, you are correct in your feelings, I think that some cultures are afraid that if they don't separate themselves, they will lose their culture""

Cheryl-SU says,   "i think that some cultures do celebrate but not to intentionally separate themselves. they are just proud of their heritage.""

Christine-GW says,   "When they celebrate their culture, all of them flock togehter, and push out the other people, only strengthening their group"

Suzanna-SU says,   "maybe people think that they need to prove there culture"

Carol-GW says,   "exactly""

(Group 2, GWU-SU, 27 February 1995)

We see in this early MOO session (the second of the semester) an active exchange of ideas, with all six of the students in the group contributing to the discussion. Raoul's "Feedback?" represents a direct address to his audience, calling for a response to his ideas. Students are eager to agree with one another, and they respond very specifically to their peers' comments. However, the students do not identify themselves in terms of their own racial heritages. Instead, they talk about "some cultures" and "they"—distancing themselves at this point from any personal acknowledgment of difference.

Chalkboard" is what the students would type in the room in order to see the discussion questions for their group:

read Chalkboard
When talking about African-American families, is it crucial to talk
about race (that is, about their being African-American)?
Is there some "universal ground" that transcends questions of race
or makes such questions irrelevant?
To what extent is Baldwin's family history influenced by his racial
background? To what extent is the Huxtable family life influenced
by their racial background? To what extent is that history/family life
independent of their race?

These MOO sessions were complemented by an online, collaborative journal, to which the students sent their group summaries and to which they contributed throughout the semester. The journal created a continual asynchronous connection between the paired classes, with students linked in a collective group by an electronic discussion list (or listserv). As students realized while they were writing, messages sent to the class "journal" were read by all members of the paired classes (as well as by the two instructors for each pairing). In order to foster a continuing dialogue, each student was responsible for posting one discussion question to the journal during the semester, along with a minimum response rate of one journal entry per week.

As a result of the MOO sessions and the class journal, we hoped to create a writing community between the paired classes and a site of frequent inter- and intracommunity dialogue. The journal allowed the students to discuss the course readings with a group of peers, some of whom were very different from themselves, and the MOO sessions provided a synchronous audience who could provide immediate responses to the students' assertions. In addition, by pairing our rural, ethnically homogeneous classes with more diverse students from an urban campus, we reinforced the multicultural focus of our class syllabus. Students from very different socioeconomic and regional backgrounds worked together as a writing community, exploring their similarities and negotiating their differences while reading and discussing not only representations of families across cultures, but also their own differing responses to those shared readings.

By the conclusion of the course, we found that students in all four classes had certainly developed a greater awareness of the complexities of audience and adjusted both their modes of address and methods of argument accordingly. However, to our surprise, and contrary to our initial expectations, we discovered that the most obvious and significant rhetorical changes occurred not in the SU and WVNCC classes, but in the writing of the minority students at GWU. Increasingly frustrated by the startling naiveté of their predominantly White audience, the GWU students were able (in Baldwin's words) "to fashion out of [their] experience that which will give them sustenance, and a voice," discussing with authoritative power their unique perspective as students of color living in a predominantly White America.

Although the cyberspace environment thus proved immensely liberating for minority expression, the often startling rhetorical fireworks served paradoxically to intimidate and in part to silence the students at the paired schools, who faced a ferocious dismantling (and occasional dismissal) of their opinions. Although the initial naiveté of the SU and WVNCC students regarding the lives (and anger) of others was continually and seriously challenged, the worst stereotype of all—the image of the aggressive, angry minority—may perhaps have been subtly (and quite unintentionally) reinforced. As a result, our "communities" were not always sites conducive to *dialogue* per se, but to an exchange of divergent views that unsettled but did not fundamentally alter the students' tenaciously held long-standing beliefs.

INITIAL NAIVETÉ

The initial cultural naiveté of the SU and WVNCC students appeared not only in their beginning-of-semester surveys (as described earlier), but also in their early journal entries. For example, in an early SU entry, one student described an experiment aired on the *Oprah Winfrey* show, in which African-American men used cosmetics to appear White, then asked for directions on street corners and received frequent responses, went into stores and received assistance from store clerks, walked past security guards in "important" buildings who paid no notice, and so on. When the men removed their disguises and performed the same actions as African Americans, motorists refused to stop or to provide directions, clerks in stores ignored them, and security guards stopped and questioned them. Many of the SU students expressed surprise at what is a common experience for people of color. For example, one SU student commented:

> I felt that Sherrie brought up a good point with her question about racism. I was surprised by the way the Black men were treated differently when they took on a White appearance. It just bothers me the way that we deal with this situation today. Everyone keeps on bragging about the big strides we have been making in the racism department of society today. The Black man may have made a name for himself over the years, but he still can't get the monkey off his back. . . . It just isn't fair to the Black man who is being turned away because this is supposed to be the land of freedom and opportunity. (Geoff-SU 19 February 1995)

Although well-meaning, this entry reveals the student's cultural naiveté. His discussion of "the Black man" is vague and overgeneralized, and his colloquialism "he still can't get the monkey off his back" is potentially offensive. Even though he has been made aware of the unequal opportunities for people of color, he still accepts the mainstream ideology that "this is supposed to be the land of freedom and opportunity." Another SU student (who mentioned in a journal entry that she has a close female friend and a brother-in-law who are African American) complained about her fellow students' stereotypical reactions to the film *Boyz 'n the Hood:* "This is one of the reasons why I don't like to go to such a 'White' school. I'm sick of the stereotypes and the attitudes of the students. It really makes me think that some people are just to[o] ignorant sometimes" (Vanessa-SU 15 February 1995).

Like their counterparts at SU, most students at the WVNCC-New Martinsville campus have had little or no opportunity to meet students of different ethnic or cultural backgrounds from their own, and they therefore feel incapable of thinking about or commenting on African American or Asian American literature. In the classroom, these students are speaking only to others like themselves, and so stereotypical attitudes tend to be reinforced rather than challenged. According to the students, they don't want to be prejudiced; they simply have no way to counter what their parents have told them, because few of them have ever met an African American. As one student said during a past semester, "I don't want to be prejudiced, but I don't know what I'd say or do if I ever met a Black person. I know I will, one day, and I'm afraid I'll say something wrong."

The students' initial timed writing sample revealed this lack of awareness of ethnic groups other than their own. The students were asked to write an essay in response to the following set of questions:

> How would you define a "typical" American family? How is that family different from other possible family structures: for example, those of ethnic groups different from the mainstream? According to your definition, is your family typical? Why or why not?

These essays were anonymous; students attached an identification number to them rather than a name. Most of the WVNCC students described a typical family as one that mirrored their own—parents or stepparents, children, house, car, pets. But most of them essentially ignored the question about "ethnic groups different from the mainstream." Most had nothing to say about the question because they had no experience with or understanding of the subject. Similarly, the majority of SU students defined the typical family in highly traditional terms: married parents, children, pets, all living in a "nice house" (as one student put it), although the students acknowledged the wide divergence from that model in contemporary U.S. society. Those who mentioned other ethnic groups tended to do so in vague, idealistic, or stereotypical terms. For example, one SU student stated: "There is no reason to believe that because of someone's color their family life will be any different. All families should be give[n] the right to learn, love, and grow together, if not then society is wrong and being prejudice. . . ." Another SU student referred briefly to Muslim fundamentalists in Indian society in potentially correct but overgeneralized terms: "Ethnic groups in India say that a woman has to stay at home and when she does leave the house she has to be totally covered." A WVNCC student who described himself as having traveled extensively and "seen other cultures" presented this view of U.S. family life:

> I believe that today, cultural backgrounds play a small role in deter-mining the structure of the American family. . . . America has really become the melting pot in which cultural characteristics are not uni-fied but exchanged.

Like his counterparts at SU, this WVNCC student relies uncriti-cally on the illusion of the happy melting pot, hoping to minimize the importance of cultural difference and racism in a family's life experience.

CONTACT WITH DIFFERENCE

Once the WVNCC students moved to the computer lab to compose their initial entries for the online journal, they quickly discovered their own naiveté. Acutely aware of the fact that their audience would include stu-dents of other ethnic backgrounds, particularly African Americans, they wondered how properly to address those students. One WVNCC student asked the instructor to read her post before she sent it because "I like everybody and I don't want anybody to think I'm prejudiced but I'm afraid I'll say the wrong thing." Another student sat staring at his key-board and his screen, typing, reading, editing, staring. Finally he called the instructor over and asked, "Should I say 'Black' or 'African American'? I don't want to offend anybody and I don't know which term is preferred." Yet another student wondered whether or not to capitalize "Black" because, of course, he didn't want to offend anyone.

Like the inhabitants in Baldwin's Swiss village, the SU students tended to forge ahead blindly, unconsciously revealing their prejudices. For example, one SU student disputed the conclusions of the *Oprah* episode, which argued that African Americans are treated unfairly in this country. She argued:

> I don't think skin color is why people would not help those in ques-tion. When I saw it, the Blacks disguised as Whites were dressed very nicely and very polite in asking for directions. When they asked as Blacks, however, they were dressed more "bummy" and weren't near-ly as polite. . . . They approached people completely differently as Blacks. (Linda-SU 19 February 1995)

The student makes a valid point, in that class also plays a significant role in how we respond to passers-by. However, race is still crucially important, and the student's attempt to deny the role race played reveals a desire to maintain the illusion of racial equality in this country—a desire that is common among SU students. Like the "monkey" comment of her fellow SU student, this claim about the "bummy" appearance and lack of politeness indicate her unchallenged acceptance of mainstream standards of dress and speech, as well as a lack of awareness of the potential offensiveness of her comments.

In racially homogeneous environments, students lack the experience and knowledge to challenge such stereotypical opinions, especially when the views reinforce their own ingrained beliefs. Instructors can try to provide opposing viewpoints, but students resist having an authoritative voice imposed on them. When their peers at a more ethnically diverse campus challenged their stereotypical opinions and responded with anger to their naively racist remarks, however, the students were forced to support and perhaps even to reconsider their beliefs. That process of challenging naive ignorance and internalized racism served to energize the writing of the minority students in the District of Columbia. The GWU students now had the opportunity to address directly an anonymous and amorphous White audience whose assertions about racial matters often revealed a limited knowledge of, and slight acquaintance with, the everyday realities of U.S. minority life. Early in the semester, one White student sounded this cautionary note: "Just keep in mind that e-mail has made us all colorless." But in fact the e-mail journal did not make the GWU correspondents colorless at all. On the contrary, students frequently announced their own ethnicity as a preliminary to speaking authoritatively about their own different experience.

For example, when one Asian American student objected to an ongoing discussion's continual focus on Black-White relations, he did so by introducing the evidence of his unique personal perspective, the authority of his experience:

> I, myself, am neither Caucasian nor African American, but a minority nonetheless. I am not only a "neutral observer," having watched both groups feud between each other, but I am also a victim of this existing racism. No one can say that I am biased because I have felt the pain and anger of being stereotyped as an inferior to the majority, the majority being everyone else. Many times, I have even been referred to as "the stranger, the intruder, the minority," because I am from a different race. My friends of African-American descent say that I cannot relate to the anger which they have for the White man because I am not a "true minority." Little do they know, that the pain that I feel is not only caused by the White majority, but also from the members of

all the different cultural groups which exist in America. (Shimo-GWU,
18 February 1995)

Later in the semester, a student from the Middle East used the
same strategy to reveal that the basis of her empathy with the anger of
U.S. minorities is her own subjective experience of a phenomenon that
afflicts them, the pervasive racial stereotyping by the U.S. media:

> Being an Iranian I know that most people I meet immediately assume
> that I am a fanatical muslim living in a male dominated family etc.
> They may have gotten this view from movies like *Not Without My
> Daughter* or simply by the images conveyed in the media. This is
> understandable yet very frustrating. I always feel that I have to justify
> myself and tell people what I'm really about. Well—this frustration is
> felt by many minority groups in this country. This frustration leads to
> anger and hence racial tension. . . . (Rahim-GWU, 6 March 1995)

In these entries, the students convey with powerful honesty the
pain they feel at being ostracized and stereotyped. Rahim's comment
about stereotypes concerning Muslims provides an opposing voice to the
earlier SU student's comment about "Ethnic groups in India" requiring
women to cover themselves in public—an observation derived (perhaps)
from valid information, but overgeneralized based on stereotypical views
of Muslim women.

Often, GWU students proved adept at introducing the authority
of personal experience into a specific journal thread in a usefully informa-
tive way, often as a corrective. This was especially evident in our discussion of Tan's (1989) *The Joy Luck Club*. When White students focused on
what seemed, from their perspective, to be dysfunctional (and sadly unaf-
fectionate) mother-daughter relationships in the novel, Asian American
students quickly corrected some obvious misconceptions:

> to address sarah's question, i must say that you're probably reading
> into the story all wrong. i am a first generation american direct from
> vietnam. vietnamese tradition is exactly the same as those of the chi-
> nese considering that the chinese have always held and influence on
> us. i can totally relate to the stories—the traditions, the food, the cul-
> ture, and even the relationships between the parents and the children.
> it isn't that the families are distant or that the mothers are "nagging"
> that is not true. i know, orientals are louder, but that's the culture. i
> guess in the american culture, women have achieved so much more in
> the sense of independence and education—that's why we tend to judge
> other cultures by our own standards. oriental families are very close,

very extended. the thing is they do not show too much affection in the way we deem affection to be because the measure of love is manifest in how much respect we give to our parents. shame is the worst form of disrespect a child can give to his parents, because your family name is all you have. (Hoang-GWU, 29 March 1995)

Another student of Asian descent discovers that her unique cultural location permits her not merely a possible correction of others' misreading, but also a subtle critique of what she sees as a pervasive stereotyping within Tan's novel itself:

I am part Asian, although my mother is not the one who passed that culture down to me. However my Grandmother is Chinese, and she is not anything like the mothers in the The Joy Luck Club. I also have a close friend who is chinese. Her and her family were all born in China. I don't see her mother at all like the mothers in the story. In fact she is a lot like my own mother. . . . I really liked *The Joy Luck Club*. It was a cute story, but it did edge on a stereotype about Asian mothers. The asian culture has a lot of superstitions and unique cultural beliefs, and they do affect many parts of their lives. This is what I picked up about their culture from this book, not a nagging, overprotective mother-daughter relationship. (Cat-GWU, 29 March 1995).

This critical positioning is unavailable to most of her peers, giving Cat and Hoang the opportunity to establish their own authoritative voices within the larger group. Such a proclamation of their ethnicity provides strong examples of what Romano (1993) called the "public ownership of personal difference," which she considers "essential to egalitarianism" in the classroom (p. 24).

The initial declaration of racial identity as a grounding for the authority of personal experience became a notable rhetorical strategy, perfectly suited for supporting impassioned argument online. For example, in response to a discussion thread monopolized by perhaps naive assertions that "some day" racial harmony would become a reality, a student responded:

i'm not quite certain that the goal that blacks and whites will one day live together in harmony will never be attained. what i know about racial equality and inequality is what i have myself experienced. when i came to washington from hawai'i, i had no idea what to expect. i had never endured racism myself, because hawai'i is truly a melting pot of all races and cultures. when i got to dc however, i experienced my first bout with racism in a restaurant. it hurt. (Hoang-GWU, 17 February 1995)

Similarly, in response to claims by a number of White students that an obsession with racial heritage may detract from the larger goal of having pride in America, a Black peer angrily responded as follows:

> Can you not have pride in America and keep ties with your heritage. . . . Forgetting about your heritage is just like giving up who you are. You might believe that America is apple pie, baseball, mustangs . . . stuff like that. But to me all that is Bullshit. I would believe that if every time I stepped foot out my door I didn't have to worry about if I was going to be able to step foot back in my door. Or if I didn't have to worry about if I am going to be accused of something because of the color of my skin. Or have someone follow me in a store to see if I am going to steal something because they think I can't afford it. I would like it if more people would look at the person I have become instead of the person they think I just to be. . . . Never Will I give up my heritage because that is what is responsible for the person I am today. I have come a long way I had to bust my ass to get where I am today and I will never forget. You are never suppose to forget where you came from. I came from Africa to America from the projects in SE to the TownHouses of NorthWest and I am going to keep going until I feel i have accomplished everything I could have. My motivation does not come from America it come from my heritage. (Devon-GWU, 25 March 1995)

The very next day, the same student chose to narrate another personal story that provided a haunting reminder that Baldwin's remote Swiss village is still relevant to contemporary U.S. society:

> It would be great I think for all individuals to be subjected to different ethnic groups so that the understanding and the communicating process can start early. . . . I worked in a day-care here in NW and the girl who was five was scared of me because she had never seen a Black person before. (It shocked me since they caught the bus to get to the day-care) But it is like that sometime. . . . We need to stop hanging with own so often and go mingle with others. . . . (Devon-GWU, 26 March 1995)

Unfortunately, we do tend to "hang . . . with own" too often, and the homogeneity of our classes can prevent our students from interacting with others unlike them, leading to the ignorance and fear that Devon powerfully described.

What "mingling with others" in the realm of cyberspace did for the minority students was to facilitate the release of a powerful and often angry voice rarely heard, or at least seriously muted, during in-class discussion. Often, minority students in the classroom face pressure to be what hooks (1994) calls "native informants" (p. 44)—that is, *de facto* representatives of their ethnic groups—an untenable and unfair burden that, inevitably, either muffles their expressiveness or reinforces their alienation and tokenization in the classroom.[7] However, freed from the pressing obligation to embody diversity by the disembodiment afforded them by cyberspace, and temporarily liberated from the cruel somatic exposure of the classroom, minority students seemed to feel far more assured and confident in responding to expressions of covert racism by their peers.

Consequently, we find Black students responding forthrightly to vaguely condescending assertions about African-American culture —the kind that often go unchallenged in class discussion. For example, in response to one White student's praising of the movie *Boyz 'n the Hood* for its realistic portrayal of life in the inner city, one young black woman, actually a resident of southeast Washington, DC, coolly observed:

> This part is to Bill. Why are you so infatuated with the movie *Boyz in the Hood*? I found it to be particularly stereotypical and quite upsetting, to say the least. I mean, I see where you're coming from when you say that it shows how diverse our society is, but is that really the reason why you loved this movie so much? I imagine that there's more to this than you're telling us. (Tarneisha-GWU, 23 February 1995)

Although enigmatic, Tarneisha's remarks subtly suggest that Bill enjoys the movie *Boyz 'n the Hood* because it reinforces his stereotypical attitudes of African Americans: prone to violence, frequently unemployed, living in single-parent families.

Realizing that asynchronous communication afforded more time to develop a coherent argument for a position unpopular with their White peers (and therefore easily dismissed by them in an internal classroom debate), Black students were also more willing to assume controversial stances in cyberspace. For example, a few African-American students argued, again on the basis of their own personal experience, that same-race adoption was in the best interests of Black children. One Black student asserted the following:

---

[7]Hooks (1994) described the phenomenon at length:

> Despite the focus on diversity, our desires for inclusion, many professors still teach in classrooms that are predominantly white. Often a spirit of tokenism prevails in those settings. . . . Often, if there is one lone person of color in the classroom she or he is objectified by others and forced to assume the role of "native informant." For example, a novel is read by a Korean-American author. White students turn to the one student from a Korean background to explain what they do not understand. This places an unfair responsibility onto that student. (pp. 43-44)

I do feel that every effort should be made to find adoptive parents for kids within their race. I say this because this could be a very cruel and unjust country for minorities and I honestly don't feel that a White couple could genuinely understand their struggle, give them pointers on how to cope with ignorance and hostility, due to their colored skin. Yes, they may be loving, caring and good providers but it takes a bit more than that to raise a child of color in this day and age. (Tarneisha-GWU, 4 April 1995)

Her entry produced a plethora of negative reactions, including accusations of reverse racism. However, she found strong peer support in a powerful restatement of the terms of her argument by a fellow African American in the class:

Now I have read about these wonderful stories where Whites adopt Blacks and Koreans and everyone lives happily ever after. That is great, I too have a Black friend and he was adopted by a White family. I still believe that a positive Black father is the best possible father for a Black child! One of the things that many Blacks in the inner city suffer from is lack of positive Black role models. Lacking a positive role these Blacks are ill equipped to face a society that is not exactly minority friendly. A Black parent can better prepare a child to deal with a racist society than a parent that has not had to deal with racism. (Houston-GWU, 13 April 1995).

Once again, the student is arguing that direct experience of racism is crucially important to understanding what it feels like to be a minority in this country. He relies on his own unique experience to establish his authoritative voice, carving his own powerful space in the community discourse.

The students' willingness to assume more controversial positions than they might in the classroom (where their own race often paradoxically serves to silence or muffle their responses) and their newfound freedom to vehemently attack White opposition evidenced the liberatory potential of the medium.[8] Indeed, GWU students' remarks on their anonymous exit surveys about the success of the journal support this observation.

---

[8]Many authors in the computers and writing field have commented on the increased and more "egalitarian" student participation that occurs with CMC. For example, Faigley (1990) argued that "Instead of being tools of repression in the skills-and-drills curriculum, computers joined in a network can be a means of liberation, particularly for those students who are often marginalized in American classrooms" (p. 291). In a later work, Faigley (1992) stated that "several of the women [in his class using InterChange, a program for synchronous CMC over a LAN] agreed that they never would have talked so much if the class had depended exclusively on oral discussion" (p. 181). Hawisher (1992) described the findings of Selfe and her col-

Although one student noted that "the journals served as a great open forum for discussion [producing] many interesting exchanges on the journal and I felt this was beneficial to our MOO sessions and classroom discussion," another was more specific about what was especially beneficial, noting that the journal "was an excellent forum in which to state *ideas that for one reason or another could not be stated in class*" (italics added). Indeed, the students themselves observed that "a lot of people who say very little in class had a *real voice* in the e-mail journal" (italics added) and that "*Some of us had more nerve* when we didn't have to say things to people's faces" (italics added).

In fact, this emboldening effect of the cyberspace medium was more generally true of all minority speakers. Hispanic students at GWU were also quick to respond to examples of what of they suspected was latent racism. For example, when an SU student asserted (again in reaction to the Oprah episode), "Maybe people should be willing to help no matter what the color or appearance, but when the appearance is like that, can you blame them?" (Linda-SU, 19 February 1995), one GWU student pointedly responded: "I do not like the 'maybe'. You are implying that it is acceptable to treat someone differently because of their color or appearance. 'Maybe' you didn't mean to put the word 'color' in there, so I will just give the benefit of the doubt (because if it is there on purpose I will give you hell, so please get back to me on that one)" (Maria-GWU, 24 February 1995). That strong reaction anticipates the ferociousness of this later response to an "immigration" thread, specifically to a Susquehanna student's message that again relied on stereotypical information about illegal aliens:

> I am writing in response to [Paul-SU's] entry about keeping out those "disease spreading and hazardous" illegal aliens from out of these United States of America. I must agree, those people can really be very dangerous. Those pregnant five foot tall women and the little old ladies and little kids which they tote with them over the border are just simply intimidating. . . . And why the xenophobia, Paul? Judging from the sound of your surname, it's obvious that your own forefathers originated from a different country. You think they were haz-

---

leagues, who "found that three foreign-born students participated significantly more in the electronic conference than in face-to-face discussions" (p. 97). Zuboff (1984) described a similar effect in a business setting. Employees who used a synchronous and asynchronous electronic conferencing system called DIALOG "felt less inhibited with the conferencing system than in direct interaction because of the absence of any palpable sense of the people they addressed. . . . These factors also contributed to a general sense that the conferencing medium made it easy to disagree with, confront, or take exception to others' opinions" (p. 370). For an important corrective to this generally accepted "egalitarianism narrative," see Romano (1993).

ardous and brought illegal diseases, too, perhaps? The main difference between those immigrants and these present day ones is just the fact that these guys are mostly Mexicans and those of earlier years, European. That and the fact that laws were much laxer back then than they are today, concerning immigration. Don't you feel that those same opportunities which were given to your ancestors should be given to these people? That's only what's fair, y'know? Just check out the many contributions which immigrants have brought this country: money, power, and more power. Those German immigrants alone gave the United States [the ability] to blow up the whole world, through the creation of the atom bomb. And what about those hazardous Cuban aliens in Miami? All they've done is deposited many millions of dollars to Florida's state treasury. I say give these people a fair and equal chance to prove themselves. One should not be judged when one's own potential has not yet been achieved. (Raoul-GWU, 4 April 1995)

Certainly, the fact that our classroom discussions coincided with news of the ongoing California debate concerning Proposition 187 and illegal immigration further energized Hispanic students who found the uncomprehending White audience of their peers a simulacrum of the larger community.

Further evidence that the GWU students from minority backgrounds found the medium liberating appears in their frequently expressed bewilderment that their peers at the other schools were, in fact, purposely inexpressive: In particular, they were frequently incensed by any suggestion that euphemism was conducive to racial harmony. The sarcastic bitterness of Raoul's response to Paul just above is perhaps best understood in the context of this earlier entry:

I'm responding to [Aaron's] entry about using euphemisms to hide one's racism or to merely use to the right words to hide rascist remarks. This DOES NOT solve anything. Just because something is said in a nicer way, it doesn't mean that the malice that is intended is not there anymore. From what I understood in your message, it's okay to be rascist so long as you do not use crude or vulgar words. In effect, would you approve of comments such as "Minorities' mental abilities are hindered by a chromosomal aberration in the 22nd chromosome" as opposed to "Minorities are stupid"? This is actually how most rascist organizations operate. They subtly use just the right words and employ propaganda to spread out their messages. (Raoul-GWU, 8 March 1995)

The student who advocated same-race adoption also seemed suspicious of the latent racism of her peers:

You know, I don't understand how some people can sit there and say
that if someone censors their thoughts before actually saying them is
"a step in the right direction" CRAP!! If I had to double think what I
was going to say, that'll show me that I have a problem. I shouldn't
have to be worried that I'll offend someone by how I feel. If you are
rethinking your opinions and thoughts on, say racism and racial slurs,
then that's a clue to you about your own prejudices. YOU HAVE A
PROBLEM! That can be positive, I guess, if you look at it as understanding yourself better, but excuse me, there's nothing good about
having to censor yourself because you're afraid that your prejudices
may spill out and offend somebody. Check yourselves! (Tarneisha-
GWU, 8 March 1995).

Tarneisha-GWU's angry remarks challenged her paired SU students'
naive assumptions that everyone can get along, as long as we're "nice" to
one another. In order to promote true racial understanding, students need
to examine their stereotypical presuppositions, she suggests, and the open
dialogue of the e-mail forum promoted such honest exchange.

Interestingly, as the semester progressed, the suspicion of the
minority students that their White peers' responses were not always "honest" extended beyond the e-mail journal and became a more general questioning of the course structure and, by implication, of the honesty of the
professors who devised it. In short, the students asked the professors to
"check [them]selves." One Hispanic student queried:

Why are hispanics the forgotten minority? We concentrated on
Blacks for a month and half. Then we spend a week and a half on
Hispanics. . . . We hardly scratched the surface when talking about
the Hispanic culture. Moving right along to the next minority. But
why? Why did we breeze through the Hispanic culture? For the Black
culture we read several different selections from different authors.
For the Hispanic culture we only read one book. I feel that we should
have read different selections from different authors with different
nationalities. Latin Americans tend to be lumped together into one
group. The different cultures are not acknowledged by non-Hispanic
Americans. They simply assume all Hispanics are alike and they
relate hispanics with Mexicans. Just like the people who set up our
syllabus. . . . I'd like people's thoughts on Hispanics in the media.
Actually it's more like: What Hispanics in the media? There are
Hispanic TV channels and radio stations in most major cities and
their surrounding area. These are all in Spanish. Why is it that
Hispanics have felt the need to set up their own stations and channels? Is it because of the language? Or is it that the mainstream
media refuses to acknowledge their culture? I'm just asking, not necessarily implying anything. (Maria-GWU, 12 March 1995).

Despite her final disclaimer, this student *is* implying something—an implicit criticism of the course that she would never feel comfortable expressing to a teacher within the classroom setting or even in the security of a one-on-one conference. Her comments about the media and about the course itself make the same crucial claim: that "mainstream culture"—including the academic culture that created this course—excludes Hispanics from the majority discourse.

The interclass debates became striking intraclass arguments as well, especially between the different minority groups who comprised the GWU classes. Once again, the cyberspace medium allowed a powerful openness of exchange, fostering disputes to which the majority White audience often bore mute (and somewhat stunned) witness. Particularly memorable in this context was the use of racial identification as strategy by a Hispanic and a Black student in a furious exchange. The Hispanic student observed the following:

> What else must the White man *do* to make up for mistakes in the past? Mistakes which his ancestors, not he, created many generations ago. I mean, nowadays, everything that goes wrong with the Black community is blamed on the White man: Black children score lower on their test scores because White men conspire to have their kin be better and smarter; or some Black families are on welfare because that is the white man's way of keeping their power in check. . . . I suppose that if I *were* White, I would be seriously chided for making these statements, but you know what??? I'm *not* White. I wasn't even born in this country. I feel that my views come about as a result of being a neutral observer. I feel for and pity the Black people for all that was done to them, but after observing and hearing about some of their behaviors for ten years now, I somewhat feel that it might be they, themselves, who are causing their own problems and present set-backs. (Raoul-GWU, 23 February 1995)

Strongly offended, the African-American student produced the following dramatic rejoinder:

> I was once told that to remain silent when you don't agree with what is being said, is to silently support that cause. For fear of everyone on line believing that silence on behalf of GW students means we are all in accordance with remarks made by Mr. Gonzalez, I am truly compelled to respond. . . . I was very pleased that you (Mr. Gonzalez) made it known that you were not White. This just proved that, racism and the ability to express oneself in an unclear and unintelligent manner knows no color barriers and transcends all racial and cultural boundaries. Something made you believe that because you are not White, your com-

ments would not bring you any "chiding," by the time you read my response you will think differently. . . . I would like to state some facts, unlike anything that I read in your response. 1) November, 1994, Francis L. Lawrence, President, Rutgers University; while arguing that standardized tests such as the S.A.T. may be unfair to minorities said, "Do we have to set standards in the future so we don't admit anybody with the national test? Or do we deal with a disadvantaged population that doesn't have the genetic, hereditary background to have a higher average." 2) September, 1994, AT&T magazine "Focus," in an advertisement to promote world wide services, had people representing every continent except for Africa which was represented by a monkey using a telephone to depict Africans. 3) February 13, 1995, The Washington Post, releases a survey on racial and ethnic biases in the federal court system in the District. In a city that is 66% Black, only two of eleven federal appeals judges are Black, and the rest are White. . . 4) February 22, 1995, The Washington Post, According to 1990 census data, college, educated Black men on average earned 76% of what there White counterparts earned. . . . Stories like these are commonplace in the U.S. The proof is right in front of our faces. In the final analysis, the truth of the matter is that racism is so imbedded in our social infrastructure that only through a consorted, conscious effort, can the hegemonic forces that constitute the conditions of racism be dismantled. . . . I speak from a lifetime of experience in a system that is as racist as it was in the 60's. The only difference is that racists are much more covert today than in the past. Make no mistakes, I am not asking anyone for anything, nothing is owed is to me. . . . As far as your "pity and your feeling for the Black people" as you so eloquently put it, save it for yourself. Pity and feeling for an unjust system is not going to change a thing. I pity those who think that they are so well informed and really are not. . . . The fact that you attempt to prove that you are not racist in the end of your response, has little validity when the majority of your response is oozing racism out of its every pore. . . . (Houston-GWU, 28 February 1995)

This response is extraordinary—both for its eloquence and its powerful rhetoric. Houston argues strongly that racism is an inherent part of U.S. society—hidden, perhaps, but still perniciously present. He cites very specific anecdotal and statistical evidence, relying on his own knowledge and on extensive and clearly presented research. Although the SU students were mere observers to this exchange, the point about the September 1994 AT&T Focus magazine's use of monkeys to depict Africans recalls Geoff-SU's earlier comment about the "Black man" not being able to "get the monkey off his back"—showing once again the subtle but undeniable presence of racist attitudes.

Interestingly, the strategy of personal revelation, and in particular the success of ethnic identification, led to its eventual imitation, as a technique of almost defensive confessionalism, by other GWU students. For example, one student interjected: "Don't get me wrong, racial prejudice is unfortunately abundant, and although I am a White male, I am a minority being Jewish. With the new rise of neo-Nazis in America (Michigan Militia and the Oklahoma bombing) I too feel the pressure of prejudice" (David-GWU, 26 April 1995). More striking, however, is the following example of personal experience by a White female student. This narration is not only revealing in its newfound identification with the other, but also because it serves as a means of bridging the gap between her early life and her new urban experiences and serves as an engagement of her predominantly White peers at the other school. Her recent experiences have been challenging to her beliefs, and so might their beliefs be similarly challenged in a new environment appears to be her metamessage:

> Well, I grew up in a small, predominately "White" suburb in Mass. I never knew what it felt like to be a minority. But last week I found myself in that very situation. I was on the metro, I looked up to see what stop we were at and it hit me I was the only person with light skin on this car. A strange feeling came over me . . . it wasn't fear or anything like that, it was a weird feeling that I didn't belong. This made me realize a concept I had supported but never really knew what it was. It is horrible to feel like you don't belong. No one on that car made me feel like they didn't think I should be there (in fact I don't think anyone one else even noticed me, or at even cared that I didn't "look like everyone else.") But this made me imagine how I would feel if this was played up on. Like if people were always making a big deal that they were different, or that because they were different they belonged on a different level. (Beth-GWU, 29 March 1995)

This rethinking of an earlier position we also found duplicated in the peer classes in end-of-semester surveys.

INCREASING AWARENESS: WVNCC AND SU STUDENTS

As we observed earlier, despite the powerful, liberatory discussions that often developed between the students in the paired classes, no miracles were worked as a result of these ongoing debates. Students from the White rural communities were not suddenly enlightened, nor were their attitudes concerning issues of diversity significantly transformed. Indeed, at times they seemed merely sullenly polite, shocked into inexpressiveness by the vehemence of their peers' reactions to comments they still found innocuous and inoffensive. As one WVNCC student stated, in discussing his objections to interracial dating, "I have no problem with everybody getting along in society. But getting along is where I draw the line. I have alot to say on this subject, but I don't think this is the place to speak my mind" (Kevin-WVNCC, 7 April 1995). Despite that growing unwillingness to engage their GWU peers in a potentially painful dialogue, most SU and WVNCC students also admitted that they had become more aware of others as a result of talking with and writing for the GW audience, and that issues that had once seemed clear-cut had now acquired a new, troubling complexity. A displacement had clearly taken place, and many of the students admitted as much in end-of-semester writing samples and surveys.

Responding in their final essays to the same questions about "typical" U.S. families that they addressed at the beginning of the course, some students came up with markedly different answers. On the first day of class, one WVNCC student wrote in fairly vague terms about the changing family:

> The typical American family is rapidly changing into many shapes and forms. This may not fit the definition of typical but these family forms are being more and more accepted by society. For instance, a single mother working and raising children has become very common in the United States. Other family forms are also arising such as, homosexual couples wanting to adopt children and start a family unit. Over all the typical American family usually suffers many hardships.

On the last day of class she wrote the following:

> Some of the different family structure that are working their way into the mainstream are created by a single parent, unmarried couples, interracial couples, and many different ethnic backgrounds. All of these nontypical or nontraditional families have suffered some sort of discrimination at one time or another. Single parents were discriminated against because they were thought to be poor, neglectful, and usually a woman. Unmarried couples were probably most easily excepted but still thought to be unstable when it comes to issues such as adoption. Interracial couples discrimination is just a stem from the discrimination of different ethnic backgrounds but are becoming more accepted. Discrimination of different ethnic background has come from the narrow-mindedness of many who are afraid of people they don't understand and are unwilling to learn to understand. Furthermore it would seem that certain ethnic backgrounds are easier accepted than others. For instance, Native Indians, who are natives to the country, and Blacks, who have been here a very long time and have helped built this nation, have been discriminated against probably more than any other ethnic background.

We can see from her later writing sample how much she has learned from the community discourse: Discrimination is present in this country, narrow-mindedness does exist (and derives from fear and the unwillingness to learn), Native Americans and African Americans in particular face strong discrimination. Another initial response by a WVNCC student made no mention at all of ethnic families. By the end of the semester, the same student had adjusted her thinking:

> Mainstream culture stigmatizes the lifestyles it cannot understand. Homosexual or interracial marriages are ostracized because they are not like the traditional family. People cannot comprehend how these couples could love each other as much as a heterosexual couple of the same race could. They might think these couples are just creating a rebellion that can be stopped. Other cultures might embrace this new lifestyle where we wouldn't.

The discussions with her multiethnic peers reinforced the course readings, broadening her understanding not only of the diversity of family structures in this country, but also of the discrimination that such alternative families face.

Some SU students also acknowledged that their classroom experiences influenced their beliefs. One student claimed on the final writing sample:

> After completing this class, I believe that my view of the "typical" American family has changed somewhat. This class has opened my mind to the fact that there are many different family structures, possessing qualities, good and bad, which make them unique. Because there are so many variations on the family structure in today's society, I feel that there really isn't a "typical" American family. . . .

Others maintained their original ideas, although they were at least able to recognize when their comments were stereotypical. The student who made the early generalization about Indian ethnic groups at the beginning of the semester observed the following:

> Another type of ethnic family, that does not meet the "typical" standard, is the Hispanic family. This is stereotypical to my knowledge, but I believed that it should be discussed. This family stereotypically contains a father, mother, and many children. The part about many children is stereotypical. Not every Hispanic family contains an overabundance of children.

This comment reveals the pertinence of Maria-GWU's critique of the course structure. One or two Hispanic voices (and one Hispanic text) are insufficient to counteract pervasive stereotyping, even if the students become aware of their own limitations.

Despite these limitations, end-of-semester essay portfolio letters did suggest an increasing cultural awareness on the part of students. For example, one WVNCC student commented:

> I enjoyed discussing different cultures and customs with the students at George Washington because their class had more students of different backgrounds than my class at West Virginia Northern Community College. The MOO sessions allowed me to hear from those who have the firsthand experiences of the different cultures.

Another student discussed the benefits and challenges of this kind of dialogue:

> I felt this class and the discussion list were very interesting. By being able to converse with the students from GW we were also able to get differing cultural views. Sometimes the discussions got heated and feelings may have been hurt but this can be an intricate part of learning.

One SU student wrote:

> This is another reason that I felt that the journals were an overall success, because all the fighting that occurred was actually helping to achieve the purpose of challenging one's long-standing ideas and beliefs.

Of the MOO sessions, one SU student wrote: "I liked the MOO sessions, because it combined everyone's ideas, and showed all the varied opinions." A GWU student commented:

> Overall, I felt that the MOO discussions were very interesting. They gave you a chance to express your feelings about a topic and to see what others felt. It was a time when you could be completely honest, because it was over a computer, which was more comfortable than face to face. I learned a lot during these sessions on other people's ideas & opinions. It was a good cultural experience & I feel that I have grown as a person because of it.

One WVNCC student who objected strongly in an early posting to interracial relationships wrote:

> I thought that communicating with different cultures was quite refreshing. I learned a good deal about what other people think, and also led me to reconsider what I think. My opinions haven't changed, but I am definitely more considerate of others' opinions.

Such a comment is revelatory. Over th̄ course of one semester, teachers cannot expect to change stereotypical views that have been reinforced throughout the students' lives. They can hope only to reveal to students their own naiveté and their own need for greater open-mindedness: that they must come down from their homogeneous villages and experience the diversity of cultures in this country—and in the world.

REFERENCES

Alicke, M. D., Klotz, M. L., Breitenbecher, D. L., Yurak, T. J., & Vredenbruth, D. S. (1995). Personal contact, individuation, and the better-than-average-effect. *Journal of Personality and Social Psychology, 68*(5), 804-825.

Baldwin, J. (1984). *Stranger in the village. Notes of a native son.* Boston: Beacon Press.

Bogart, P. (Director). (1989). *The torch song trilogy.* Burbank, CA: Columbia TriStar Home Video.

The Chronicle of Higher Education: Almanac (1988). *45*(1).

Cisneros, S. (1991). *Woman hollering creek and other stories.* New York: Vintage Books.

Cogdill, S. (1996). @Go Tuesday. *Kairos, 1*(2). On-line. http://english.ttu.edu/kairos/1.2/3.html

Colombo, G., Cullen, R., & Lisle, B. (Eds.). (1992). *Rereading America: Cultural contexts for critical thinking and writing* (2nd ed.). Boston: Bedford Books of St. Martin's Press.

Faigley, L. (1990). Subverting the electronic workbook: Teaching writing using networked computers. In D. A. Daiker & M. Morenberg (Eds.), *The writing teacher as researcher: Essays in the theory and practice of class-based research* (pp. 290-311). Portsmouth NH: Boynton/Cook.

Faigley, L. (1992). *Fragments of rationality: Postmodernity and the subject of composition.* Pittsburgh: University of Pittsburgh Press.

Hawisher, G. E. (1992). Electronic meetings of the minds: Research, electronic conferences, and composition studies. In G. E. Hawisher & P.

LeBlanc (Eds.), *Reimagining computers and composition* (pp. 81-101). Portsmouth NH: Boynton-Cook.

hooks, b. (1994). *Teaching to transgress: Education as the practise of freedom.* New York: Routledge.

Romano, S. (1993). The egalitarianism narrative: Whose story? Which yardstick? *Computers and Composition, 15*(3), 5-28.

Tan, A. (1989). *The joy luck club.* New York: Ivy Books.

Tversky, A., & Kahneman, D. (1974). Judgment under uncertainty: Heuristics and biases. *Science, 185,* 1124-1131.

U.S. Bureau of the Census. (1998). *Statistical Abstract of the United States: 1998* (118th ed.). Washington, DC: U.S. Government Printing Office.

Zuboff, S. (1984). *In the age of the smart machine: The future of work and power.* New York: Basic Books.

Chapter • 10

Writing a Narrative: MOOs and E-Journals

Margit Watts
Megumi Taniguchi

OVERVIEW

Computer technology is a part of U.S. society that students will no doubt deal with directly or indirectly for the rest of their lives. Technology, however, is but a tool, and has no intrinsic value, except that which is given to it. Thus, it is up to teachers to master their tools and use them to good advantage. The issues with which teachers must ultimately concern themselves have little to do with computers, networks, modems, baud rates, Webs, or for that matter, blackboards, videos, and pencils. It has everything to do with whether students learn or not and is the area in which teachers must invest their energies. Many of today's students come to college often flat, devoid of passion, aimless, and uninterested. Learning has not been a pleasant, challenging, or important part of their lives. They attend college for numerous reasons—as an alternative to working, as a means to fulfill parental expectations, as a chance to make it to the big time through an athletic scholarship, or as a way to follow the misguided notion that somehow a college degree will guarantee a better job and life.

For teachers, quite simply, one of the best uses of technology is for them to make connections with students in order to open lines of communication on both figurative and literal planes, and to afford them opportunities to reflect about themselves as well as the rest of the world.

Postman (1995), Sizer (1992), Goodlad (1994), and others called for educational reforms that will create a seamless educational experience for students K-16. These educators focus on creating environments that encourage students to take ownership of their learning, that foster connections across curricula and with the community, and that offer students opportunities to relate new ideas back to personal experiences. Creating true contexts for learning only happens when teachers can take the "text" of the learning and add it to the "text" of personal experience to make meaning.

To provide avenues that foster this integration of texts, learning environments must be created that develop the self. Discovery of the self never occurs in a vacuum; it occurs as a response to—or reflection and synthesis of—interactions with other people and ideas. Access to the human conversation is of greatest importance to this endeavor. Constructivists are correct in emphasizing that it is the activity of the mind that translates input (information) into knowledge, and that this construction of knowledge is a social phenomena. Individuals make sense of the world by integrating new experiences and knowledge into what they have previously come to understand. They either interpret new ideas in such a way that they conform to present rules, or they generate a new set of rules that help them to integrate and order their worlds. Computer-mediated communication (CMC) offers students the chance to discover, reflect on new information, have discussions with others, revise their thinking, and make meaning of ideas.

Brady (1989) suggested that the traditional view of how curricula is created is that it is "derive(d) from the needs of learners, the problems of society, the content of academic disciplines" (p. 3). That may be true, and that may also explain why teachers have lost the "engagement" of so many students: Their realities have not been deemed crucial to the development of educational experiences. And yet, it is their realities that will help them to synthesize new information, analyze new problems, and integrate it to make meaning that will serve them in their lives. Postman (1995) called for a new overall "narrative" to guide the decision-making process in the educational realm. Here, we argue for a personal narrative that will guide students to become lifelong learners.

So for us, technology provides platforms on which students can find these personal narratives. In the Rainbow Advantage Program (RAP), the integrated learning community for first-year students in which we both teach and administrate, we have chosen e-mail journals (e-journals) and the text-driven MOO environment as our platforms for communication. One of our guiding principles is to help students use writing to make meaning out of the knowledge that they will be faced with throughout college and life. Although some of our students are familiar with computer technology, many have limited experience and e-mail and the MOO become new territories for exploration. Many students initially fear these environments, yet take to them quickly and soon end up knowing more than we could ever teach them. These environments provide different modes of communication, allowing students to distance themselves from the disappointing writing experiences of the past and develop a new sense of confidence in working with technology, and by extension, writing and thinking.

We consciously selected these kinds of technology because they enable students to see writing in a social context and encourage communication and participation in communities. Ultimately, these very basic vehicles may be the most conducive to learning. Studies have repeatedly shown that when students write for an audience, they do some of their best writing and thinking: Writing e-journals, participating in conversations and discussions on the MOO, and posting messages for groups are all writing endeavors that require an audience. Metaphorically and literally, e-journals and MOO discussions start important dialogue between students and instructors.

RAINBOW ADVANTAGE PROGRAM

Six years ago the University of Hawai'i at Manoa implemented a program to try to meet the challenge of engaging freshmen in their own education. RAP is a tightly woven learning community based on the coordinated studies model. It operates within the larger framework of the arts and sciences core curriculum, and purposefully restructures it to offer a supportive academic environment that promotes a sense of community. Students are actively engaged and encouraged to be full participants in the educational process. Therefore, they are not simply required to be onlookers or receptacles for information; they are challenged to view learning as a developmental process that builds connections. The focus of RAP is on collaborative learning strategies, cooperative learning, and bridging connections between their learning activities and the community.

Providing a small college atmosphere within the larger university framework, RAP students take up to 15 of their 24 full-time credits together in their first year. Emphasis is placed on communication, critical thinking, and research skills. These skills are developed within the core courses as well as in a year-long foundation course that serves as the center for synthesis, analysis, enhancement, and presentation of the learned skills. The concept of a global classroom guides the philosophy behind, and activities within, this learning community and students are urged to make connections on local as well as global levels in order to fuse academics with the "real world."

RAP students are connected to these communities in three ways: (a) they have corporate and community leaders as mentors who often offer experiences outside of the classroom, (b) they must fulfill a program requirement to spend at least 2 hours a week in a community service project, and (c) they participate in an international project called Collaboratory. This project links together RAP students with K-12 students, library resource people, and museum personnel for purposes of creating exhibits, both real and virtual. Teams of students work on Walden3 so the hub of activity is found both in the classroom and on Walden3 MOO (an interactive virtual community), a space where students, museum staff, and others participate in an interactive text-based community.

The purpose of Collaboratory, the project imbedded within RAP, is to encourage discovery and to guide students in the creation of their own narratives. It is a project designed to help students explore their own learning styles as well as their interests; it is a project designed to help them understand who they are in the wider global community in which they must learn to live and for which they must assume responsibility. Much of the activity within the process of these discoveries is writing based. Students communicate with each other, with their linked teams, museum personnel, faculty and other students from around the country in text-based environments such as e-mail and our MOO. It is within these frameworks that they begin to reflect, make meaning, and begin to understand the process of the construction of knowledge.

MOO ENVIRONMENTS

MOO is an acronym for MUD, object-oriented, and MUD is an acronym for multi-user dungeon or multi-user dimension. A MOO is a species of MUD, the single-user adventure games that surfaced in the 1970s. Although MUDs often are portrayed as sheer entertainment for computer-literate college students, MOOs are communication-based environments that are favored by academics who see these environments at their best as potentially alternative teaching and learning venues. MOOs can become highly specialized conferencing systems, virtual universities with classroom equipment specially programmed for use, or text-based communities in which people can socialize, discuss issues, and share their work. MOOs provide the ability for synchronous and asynchronous communication as well as distance education and are also a medium in which the user can subscribe to lists, post messages, send mail, and participate in a wide variety of educational projects. Classes can be logged (recorded for later use) and made available for those who missed class.

What gives MOOs an advantage over chat modes is the actual environment they provide. For instance, Dr. Watts has a "study" on the pond that includes Persian rugs, a white ginger garden (not possible to grow these indoors in the real world!), a koa wood desk, violets in vases, and a rainbow hologram on the wall (through which her staff can move to access their own offices). Ms. Taniguchi has a penchant for pigs and thus has created an exit from her office to Meg's Debate Pen (a virtual pigpen in which she holds conversations with her students). Classrooms can also be equipped with various tools such as bulletin boards, blackboards, overheads, and notes. Private offices in which to meet students can be created as well. These virtual spaces tend to make the participants feel more grounded in a shared reality, even if the reality is text based. The social aspect of the MOO emulates to face-to-face classrooms very closely as well. MOO environments utilize text-based body language; a participant can emote: smile, laugh, groan, hand objects to others, shake hands, giggle, fall on the floor, drink a cup of coffee, and more. These activities tend to humanize the virtual space.

After a while, many people feel very comfortable in this virtual environment and their text flows naturally and easily. MOO environments also offer a safe place for discovery for many socially withdrawn students. Many become experts on the MOO after logging endless hours, constructing vast empires and conversing with anyone and everyone who frequents the virtual community; these students freely express themselves, discover who they are in reflection of how others see them, and can begin to make meaning of their lives. Often students who are quite shy and uncomfortable in classroom settings find themselves accepted easily within this virtual environment. They try out their ideas, concerns, insights on the other students in this relatively benign environment and soon find they are merely a part of the larger group, learning, discovering, exploring. This translates to their face-to-face encounters in a very positive manner as we find they open up, become more talkative, are less shy about working in groups, and generally find themselves comfortable members of the learning community.

There is movement toward a seamless integration of the MOO and the World Wide Web. Many programmers, both at Xerox PARC and across the country on the various MOOs, have developed MOO/Web interfaces that are still a bit slow and buggy, but will soon emerge as smooth transitional programs. When that is accomplished, students will no doubt be even more inclined to become members of MOO communities, because MOOs will serve as gathering places from which they access the web and its myriad collections of information. Students can presently access articles and books and textual information from the Web. As Cooper (1995) noted, servers soon will be interconnected and a single virtual environment may be supported opening up dramatic new potential for collaborative exploration of the new frontier of cyberspace. In other words, with the advent of new programs to make the links between MOOs and between MOOs and the Web seamless, cyberspace can indeed become a web of interconnected villages.

Walden3 MOO is a multiuser academic environment serving the students at the University of Hawai'i, high school students enrolled in the electronic school in Hawai'i, and other teachers, students, and museum staff around the country who participate in Collaboratory. It is a text-based environment that is enhanced by ASCII art to provide a visual sense of place and direction. Walden3 supports a number of educational endeavors and is housed at the Maui High Performance Computing Center. It is a virtual environment in progress that has been up on the Internet for 6 years and is now poised to become the electronic environment for teachers and students for the Department of Education in Hawai'i as well as to teachers and students from around the world. The name Walden3 reflects the notion that a community in cyberspace can be, in Oldenberg's (1997) terms, a "third place" for us. Future plans include completion of links to the Web and the development of a strong culture committed to community service as well as fostering connections with the rest of the world.

As a text-based environment, it affords students the opportunity for conversations across the world. To date, Walden3 has been used for numerous educational projects. Students from the University of Alberta have gathered to discuss their philosophy courses, compile notes about their class, post ideas, take quizzes, or meet with their professor. Another group of students from Alberta has developed a network of information for their freshman year experience, while yet another meets to discuss legal problems. Chemistry students from the University of Hawai'i at Hilo have developed labs, experiments and presentations on the MOO. These will be shared with other interested students from around the country. And, of course, RAP students have used Walden3 for discussions, lectures, office hours, and the sharing of their museum exhibits.

We seek to offer our students in RAP help in developing a personal narrative, give them the freedom and encouragement to write, and foster the sort of safe academic environment that will engage them in their learning. For these purposes, Walden3 has been used, as of yet, sparingly. Students, however, have used this virtual environment in numerous ways.

1. Students are given a character on the MOO. This offers them the possibility to describe themselves to others.

A MOO is an environment that is constructive by its very nature. It is up to the people who log in and inhabit this virtual space to create both their own description and that of the space in which they congregate.

One of the most enriching experiences on MOOs is the ability to create a virtual self for others. Finding one's narrative is all about understanding yourself in the context of the world around you, and thus, creating your "self" on the MOO is a textual activity and has proven to be quite illuminating. In fact, we find that students are more likely to expose sides of themselves that are not apparent in their day-to-day personalities. Like the e-journal environment, the MOO environment encourages freedom of expression.

2. Bringing together museum staff, librarians, faculty, and students offers resources in a new manner.

RAP students gather on Walden3 to discuss their classwork, projects, and community service involvement. A librarian is integrated into the RAP learning community, he often holds virtual office hours wherein he can be accessed for help with the variety of projects in which the students are involved. Museum personnel who are involved in the year-end exhibits also contribute to the online discussion when they are able. Even more importantly, the RAP students enjoy the opportunity to connect with other students (locations vary semester by semester).

3. Having students learn how to navigate the MOO increases their comfort with technology.

It is clear that students today will be negotiating the 21st century through a variety of technological means. Therefore, an integral part of the RAP program is to encourage students to become comfortable with technology on different levels. We have workshops for them that teach them the basics of e-mail, navigation of MOO environments, and a study of the electronic library environment and tie them all together in a way that allows students to see these avenues as resources. In this, we have been very fortunate to have our librarian, Randy Hensley, be an integral component of the teaching team. But even beyond viewing technology as a tool for resources and information gathering, we hope our students view the new technologies as methods of connecting with the rest of the world.

4. Interactions on the MOO can be as rich (sometimes more so) as real life conversations and the text-based environment encourages the honing of writing skills.

A conversation on a MOO is in text; students must communicate in written form. Although their expression is somewhere between conversational and formal written style, they are able to utilize this venue as a place to toss around ideas, get instant feedback, and revise their ideas as part of the discourse.

All in all, time spent in MOO environments offer students text-based experiences that enhance communication skills, conversations rich with meaning, alternative learning sites, and places for discovery of self and the other.

E-MAIL JOURNALS (E-JOURNALS)

E-journals are used extensively in RAP. Students are required to write e-journals in at least one course each semester. An e-journal is basically an individual journal sent by a student to a teacher via e-mail. Although we require students to comment on readings and class sessions, they are also able to write freely about topics that interest them. E-journals have definite advantages over their written counterparts. We continue to support the use of e-journals based on five theoretical premises.

E-Journals Often Are the Most Important Way by Which Students and Teachers Communicate

Despite all our best efforts as educators, it is probably safe to assess that much of the time spent in the classroom is spent communicating at—rather than with—students. Class sessions are, all too often, a session guided by the advice and wisdom of the instructor. To engage students more actively in education, educators must offer them an opportunity to be heard; the very nature of e-mail encourages dialogue. Although it can be time consuming, we have found it essential to respond to all e-journals for two reasons: e-journals allow us to establish a supplementary sense of rapport with the students and also can give us insight into their content-based ideas that are often shared or brought up in class. Once students receive responses to their ideas, thoughts, and feelings, their writing is informed by the fact that they are engaged in a process. As one student noted, "Sometimes I'm glad I can write to whoever it is I'm writing to so I can express my thoughts and stuff. It's good to write out how you feel and get some kind of feedback."

Feedback is important in any type of communication. It is even more essential in cases that the student needs validation as a writer. We often forget that students tend to feel intimidated by professors, and that they are surprised to discover that their professors are human too. This realization can be important in allowing them to find their own voices.

At the end of the semester, students assess journals they have written and answer the question: "What did you learn by doing e-mail journals?" One student simply wrote, "I learned to communicate with the teacher." This student realized that the teacher was someone with whom he could communicate—and that, by extension, learning would be a kind of conversation in which the construction of knowledge can emerge. Although we may see communication as an open conduit between student and teacher, the student is more apt to see it as a selective channel, in which communication with the teacher is not something to be taken for granted. The meta-message imbedded in this simple statement is powerful: Teachers should encourage students to communicate with them so that students will learn how valuable their voices truly are.

E-Mail Gives Students a Voice

Because many students view phone calls and office visits to professors as the domain of those who are a little too eager to make a good impression on the instructor, they often feel it necessary to have a legitimate reason to see the professor. This is why many students would rather take their chances and sneak in a quick question as the instructor is gathering up materials and leaving class. Indeed, e-mail is less intimidating than individual face-to-face encounters on many levels. One researcher pointed out that in the business world, "electronic mail blasts aside typical corporate hierarchies because the messages are undifferentiated—there is no fancy letterhead or secretary to place a call and ask the person called to hold for president so-and-so . . ." (Perry, 1992, p. 28). Students who might feel uncomfortable dropping in on the professor are more likely to drop her or him a short e-mail. Both teachers and students have discovered that "electronic mail is not as intrusive as a phone call. It does not interrupt the recipient, and for the sender, takes less time since he or she need not run through the social amenities" (Perry, 1992, p. 25). E-mail also can equalize participation for students who have phobias about speaking in class and gives students a voice that they otherwise may not use: "E-mail can be excellent for people who have difficulty or hesitation expressing themselves in the more public setting of the classroom" (Lowry, Koneman, & Osman-Jouchoux, 1994, p. 23).

Spinuzzi (1994) mentioned the fact that e-mail messages are "purely delivery" and that each piece becomes a "speech" itself (p. 215). Thus, students who are fearful of being cut off will not have to leave thoughts half expressed or incomplete. They are able to hold the floor as long as they wish without being interrupted. We have found through our own experiences that not only do students appear more comfortable expressing personal ideas, posing questions, and pondering material, but they seem to write more often in a less restricted style, are less intimidated by faculty members, and welcome the 24-hour access afforded through e-mail. Because we respond to all e-journals, they are able to test out ideas and have uncertainties clarified.

Our program is based on creating a supportive learning environment for students, and part of that involves accessibility of faculty. Many instructors double as program staff. Thus, students who drop by our main offices can expect to bump into many of their instructors. We definitely support face-to-face contact, but also see the need for alternative modes of communication. In our classes, communication via computer supplements, not supplants, face-to-face communication. Thus, we support Myers' (1995) call to "view the computer as a learning tool which enhances, not replaces, teaching or direct communication" (p. 667) because we feel education ultimately must have human meaning invested in it.

Any discussion of the use of computer technology to improve communication in education evokes the unwarranted fear that students will become more comfortable with a computer screen than a human image. However, we, and others like Hartman et al. (1995), have found the opposite to be true: Critics of the use of electronic communication tools in education worry that highly valued aspects of the teacher-student relationship will be eliminated. They fear in particular that face-to-face interaction will decrease as more "impersonal" modes of interaction, such as networked communication, increase. This was not the case in our study. We found that using network communication tools to support collaborative learning and writing did not replace traditional forms of communication with teachers, but in fact, total teacher-student communication about writing increased (Hartman et al.).

Thus, e-mail offers a valuable opportunity to reach students and to show them that teachers truly want to communicate with them by opening various channels. Students quickly see e-mail as a means to communicate with other students, family, and friends. Many times, once students discover communication through e-mail, they are more likely to participate in class as well. Recognizing students who have pertinent points to make and asking for further clarification often is the simple incentive needed in order to see the value of their contributions in class.

E-Journals Provide/Force Teachers to Truly Listen to Students

Hawisher and Moran (1993) noted that "E-mail in dissolving boundaries of time and space, breaks down some of the barriers that have long been established between students and professors" (p. 635.) This is not a feature of e-mail that should be taken lightly; we have found that students are brutally honest in e-mail messages and journals. Many instructors have proposed the use of short writing exercises ("What confused you in this class?") at the end of class as an evaluation tool to find out what they need to cover. E-mail provides a similar forum, but it provides some time and space so that students are not anonymous and can reflect on and analyze class content. Although e-journals are sent with the students' e-mail addresses, students will quickly admit their confusion and raise questions about what they are doing in class. In that regard, e-mail is one of the best sources of instant feedback. In e-journals, even the shyest students are willing to ask questions to clarify confusing issues. They are also more apt to give their interpretations of class events, question the purpose of an assignment or the rationale behind a requirement, and even object to the teacher's handling of the class. Students also clarify their classroom behavior, provide their own perspectives on the content and class dynamics, and often allow us helpful views into the way they perceive themselves in the context of the class. One student, for example, wrote:

> We tend[ed] to analyze books, plays and poetry rather than learn about writing and how to write. All we ever did [in high school] was learn about others' writing and their techniques. This is why I don't ever say much in class. It's not that I'm not interested it's just that I don't know the work that well and I'm trying to take in everything that you say. . .

Later, in the same e-mail, the student commented:

> People in our class are very overpowering and egotistical. . . . So if we do ever say anything intelligent and they don't agree with it then we just get cut for it anyway. So to me it's not worth saying anything. The teacher disliked the classroom dynamics in this class; however, she didn't do anything because students in this class had seemed to be comfortable speaking and working with each other.

When another student echoed this writer's sentiments, she confirmed the dissonance that was affecting the classroom environment. This e-journal was important in two ways: It gave the teacher a better understanding of why the student, who had otherwise seemed concerned about her work and had valuable opinions in class, seemed so reticent and strangely reserved, and gave the teacher an honest and enlightening assessment of the classroom environment in hopes of improvement.

E-mail journals often help teachers understand why students perceive the assignments the way they do. Teachers are able to see a more complete (or shared) picture and can think about how to expand the students' contexts. For example, one student wrote, "I haven't written too many papers that needed a thesis statement, so I think that was another reason for not doing [my paper]. I am very familiar though with writing papers that are comparison and contrast papers that need to be backed up with facts, evidence, or quotes. That is mainly what I have to do, yes?" This journal offered the teacher a valuable chance to respond and remind the student that she could always feel free to contact the teacher to ask questions. On her next essay, the student did in fact call on the phone to ask a question. Many teachers are experiencing this dynamic. "I felt this technology was an opportunity for authentic reading and writing, was more personalized, and could be used to clarify assignments and lectures as well as empower students to gain control of their learning" (Myers, 1995, p. 666).

E-journals can be used to gauge how well students are understanding the content, as well as provide insight into their lives. As educators it is important to keep in mind the students who are served. If educators are not sure where the students are coming from, they have no hope of showing them any other optional directions. Or, put another way, if teachers do not understand the narratives students are currently living, they can never hope to reach their students. The student who is a first-generation college student and the student who is expected to play pro football obviously have different goals and dreams. In class, one can address the highly relevant issues that students cover well in their journals. Students do recognize their own comments and it is powerful to them to have others acknowledge their ideas.

Cynics may say that this is simply "feel good therapy," but dismissing it easily misses the point. Students are not a static group and their contexts change as do the contexts of educators. It is easy, and more comfortable for educators to stay isolated, separating themselves and mass producing their product for the students than to connect and develop a product together through interaction, development, and design. Drawing on their comments shows an understanding of where the students' thinking lies. Many teachers have forgotten what it is like to be students. They get e-journals about speeding tickets, roommate problems, efforts to find jobs, car accidents, and dorm food. In RAP, even though we deal exclusively with freshmen every year, we find ourselves repeatedly surprised to find homesickness, culture shock, and struggles to balance the new demands of college with newfound freedom.

Students ask all kinds of questions, ranging from "What do you do when there's just too much? How do you handle the situation?" to "Is there a time when I can come into your office and talk to you about revisions on the last essay on comparing similarities and differences?" to "Do guys have a big ego that if you ask them to dance, you're in love with them? I hope not!" Comments about students' personal lives may seem superfluous for many teachers. But these comments are essential clues that may help teachers better reach students. Students often volunteer information in e-mails that teachers would never hear about otherwise. One student, who suddenly started to act especially difficult and rebellious in class, sent an e-journal that started off:

> In the next couple of weeks if I start acting like more of an ASS than I already do in class, it is because my parents are divorcing and my dad is leaving. . . . I don't know how I will react (much less) how I will deal with it. I'll try to hide it, I know.

Although the student did not receive any special treatment, the instructor was able to be supportive and ask questions that indicated to the student that someone cared that work was completed. The student could have easily been written off as a trouble maker. Instead, the small amount of concern expressed may have helped to prevent this student from dropping out of school that semester. Teachers need to give students every opportunity to learn.

One of our students shocked us by sending long e-journals that helped us to better understand why she never was able to become fully invested in anything we did in classes:

> Things that have happened from the past still haunt me. I cannot forget the things that happened because it was never solved. I always wanted to run away because it was so scary and made my life into something I thought . . . would never happen. . . . Someone really close hurt me really deep . . . and that in turn has made my life change . . .

Educators may not be able to exorcise the demons of their students' pasts, but in the simple act of sharing their feelings, students often alleviate the burdens they carry. "I just want to say thanks for listening to my problems when you read my journals. You actually are someone (who) doesn't think that I am insane or very disturbed." Journal entries that are timely and seem to capture students' sentiments well often unexpectedly serve as evaluation ballots. They really are much more meaningful than most traditional forms of evaluation in the sense that they can have an immediate impact on and improve teaching throughout the semester rather than at mid-semester or at the end of the semester, the two traditional evaluation periods.

Hawisher and Moran (1993), who have written on e-mail's use in composition warned, "E-mail increases the teacher's accessibility and can therefore bring additional telework for writing teachers. Once our campuses are wired and networked, we will have to learn how to manage class use of e-mail" (p. 637). Indeed, one student wrote in amazement, "Do you actually read every single journal entry, I mean everything, then write back? It seems like you do, but I (would) find it tiring." However time consuming they might be, reading and responding to journals is time well spent. We view the time we spend responding to e-journals as class preparation time; it really gives us a much clearer idea of what we want to cover in class. The 30 minutes we spend responding to e-mail journals each week help us to make each class session an enriching one that has been guided by the students' comments.

E-Journals Provide Opportunities for Supplemental Teaching to Occur Outside the Classroom Because They Extend Time and Accessibility to Both Students and Teachers

E-mail is available 24 hours a day. This extension of availability is not only useful, but is sometimes powerful. For example, two students who had difficulty revising their work and were afraid to make errors asked if they could revise over e-mail over the weekend. They sent re-envisioned paragraphs that showed that they were striving to discover the meaning that was relevant to them. They received quick initial reactions to their new versions and a promise of a more complete response later. Printouts with comments were returned at the next class meeting. The instructor felt that these students learned more over the course of that weekend than they did the rest of the semester combined because they were free from anxiety, had time to work on their writing, revise and get feedback, and were happy with the communication exchange that occurred. They acquired a sense of confidence and ownership through their initiative. As Lowry et al. (1994) pointed out, "E-mail is self-paced and, therefore, gives people an opportunity to reflect on their contributions" (p. 23). Many teachers are coming to realize the advantage of the 24-hour access students have through e-mail and appreciate the open access it gives students.

E-Journals Combine All the Best Attributes of E-Mail, Journals, Free Writing, and True Brainstorming

There are three reasons why e-journals are able to synthesize and capitalize on the best elements of e-mail, journals, free writing, and brainstorming. These reasons have to do with unmediated thought, ungrammatical writing, and nonlinear thinking.

Unmediated Thought. Journals are often primarily meant to be vehicles through which students explore unmediated thought and creativity. Interestingly enough, however, their unmediated thoughts seem to encourage reflection and analysis. As mentioned earlier, e-mail gives students the opportunity to prepare what is in essence a written speech and enables students to focus on ideas and not audience. Journals have long been heralded as excellent tools for increasing students' writing and critical thinking skills. Fulwiler (1987, 1991), among others, documented and classified the various modes in which journals can stimulate and develop students' thoughts: observations, questions, speculation, self-awareness, digression, synthesis, revision, and information. Although they have been honored as a valuable form to stimulate creativity and despite repeated attempts to prevent it, some educators constantly relegate journals to the status of low stakes writing, or writing that is preparation to the writing itself, but not considered significant. This is ironic because writing that is of personal significance may ultimately have more of an impact on students. In e-journals, students are not given limiting prompts; they are given a blank computer screen to fill. Because no direct topics are provided, they are forced to find their own meaning. Students emerge as creative thinkers as this method provides an open mike for written expression. In one class, journals are required to be at least 50 lines per week. Although students initially balk at the number of lines, they eventually become so comfortable that they go over the required number because they are in the midst of expressing an important thought. In response to this requirement, one student perceptively noted: "These journals become personal only because they have to be long. There isn't much to write about when you try to stay superficial. It is like trying to have a surface conversation with someone quite often. After a while your conversations get deep."

Another student wrote a journal based on a set of readings that she felt were redundant. An interesting dynamic unfolded. In the journal, she expressed the idea that although the examples found in the reading were true, the articles were overstated. Then, she evaluated the merit of each article, and objected to certain statements, agreeing with others. Her frustration was evident. Ironically, what the student did not realize was how much she had gotten out of the articles and how much she had taught herself. She was involved and—despite her best efforts not to be—engaged in the content and her own ideas about it.

In addition to the positive impact on students' writing and thinking, the conversations that unfold in e-journals allow teachers valuable opportunities to point out important points of their own. Teachers can also benefit from e-journals. In clarifying and articulating their ideas, they become better teachers and are forced to elucidate some of the principles of their own teaching methods that may have become hazy or unconscious in their own minds.

Ungrammatical Writing. Journals offer students the opportunity to not concern themselves with grammar. E-mail can be ungrammatical in many respects. Many people follow the Fulwiler method that suggests that students should freely express themselves in journals, disregarding grammar rules. However, this is difficult for most students because for years they have been trained to be vigilant of their grammar problems. Knowing that a teacher will be reading their work puts them on the alert. Indeed, it is somewhat hypocritical of teachers to be encouraging students to write journals without attention to rules. Yet, the e-mail environment with its newness and seeming lack of conventions is a perfect environment in which to hone their skills.

Tillyer (1993) used e-mail to facilitate e-mail correspondence with English as a second language students. What he found was that "there is little regard for grammar, spelling, or other conventions in E-mail—only meaning. The rudimentary editors and immediacy of the communication of E-mail virtually rules these conventions out" (p. 69). We feel that when students notice that teachers cannot put those awful grammatical marks on the screen, they happily disregard subject-verb agreement and are able to simply write. We attempt to enforce their comfort with free writing by deliberately typing to them all in lower case letters.

The July 1994 issue of Time magazine included a short article entitled, "Bards of the Internet: If E-mail Represents the Renaissance of Prose, Why is so Much of It so Awful?" This article discusses the awful prose demonstrated in e-mail: "it can be very bad indeed: sloppy, meandering, puerile, ungrammatical, poorly spelled, badly structured and at times virtually content free" (Elmer-Dewitt, p. 66). This same article also discusses how "Brock Meeks, a Washington-based reporter who covers the online culture for Communications Daily" has observed that "There are a bunch of hacker kids out there who can string a sentence together better than their blue-blooded peers simply because they log on all the time and write, write, write" (p. 67). Ironically, on many levels, the relaxed atmosphere of the MOO and of e-mails are comforting ones for students that allows them to get valuable practice in writing. Both atmospheres give shy students a chance to voice their ideas and give expressive students a more dialogue-oriented type of writing to ease into.

Nonlinear Thinking. As Fulwiler (1991) pointed out, journals can be used to encourage many forms of creative nonlinear thinking through forms such as free writing and brainstorming. E-mail, by its very nature, also can encourage free writing because "users tend to type in their thoughts in the order the thoughts occur to them, rather than arranging the thoughts in any particular order" (Spinuzzi, 1994, p. 215). Spinuzzi also noted that "E-text messages also tend to be serial, organized chronologically rather than in the more structured patterns that we expect from writing" (p. 215). The wording of this description is revealing. E-mail, like free writing, disrupts commonly held "patterns" (while possibly creating others) and e-mail, like brainstorming, also discourages or withholds judgment ("what we expect"). In addition, because e-mail journals are typed, they can potentially benefit students. Many students can type faster than they can write, so e-mail can be helpful for students who find writing a frustratingly slow means of recording ideas. Students who cannot type may find more active incentive in typing e-mail or MOO messages rather than simply transcribing their final drafts.

Many students have taken journal writing into various forms. One of the more fascinating developments we discovered was that several students unconsciously turned their journal entries into concise, well-written, and powerful debates or commentaries. What was surprising about this was that these particular students consistently had difficulties organizing their essays and they wrote the essays in a markedly stilted and formulaic style with overstated arguments. Their journals, in stark contrast, actually were more well-developed than their essays. These students said they felt comfortable, relaxed, and in control while they were writing the journals. When it was suggested that perhaps the label *essay* was making them tighten up, one of the students started to experiment more, and was able to incorporate some of the elements of his journals into his essays.

E-mail is an indirect way of getting students to truly brainstorm. Facing a blank sheet of paper is intimidating, and staring at a blank computer screen would seem to be no less intimidating, yet students often find it easier to compose because in the conversational format of the e-mail journal, they often are driven to ask questions and then answer them. In the following example, the student talks out his own problem and in doing so, finds his answers. The subject matter, in this case, is irrelevant, but the following comments scattered in the journal attest to the fact that the student is testing out his writing ability as well as his ability to create meaning.

> I'm having a really rough time with my final paper. I have no idea where to start and what to talk about. . . . I tried to make a list . . . here's what i can explain . . . wait a minute. could i use this as a thesis or something? . . . how does that sound? . . . so what else can i write about? . . . well, from what i notice . . . another thing i notice is . . .

This thinking-through process encouraged by the format of an e-mail journal was thus an important part of the student's process of composing his essay. He was able to brainstorm, come up with a thesis, and even ideas for several supporting paragraphs.

Like MOOs, e-journals facilitate text-based learning. Although MOOs are creative spaces because they allow purposeful building of communities and parameters of learning, e-journals are creative in the absence of these things. As a platforms for writing and thinking, e-journals can encourage productive communication, allow students to express their opinions, remind teachers to make use of the valuable feedback students provide, and extend the time and place of learning.

CONCLUDING THOUGHTS

Postman (1995) pointed out, "A new technology does not merely add something, it changes everything" (p. 192). Technology is not inherently good or bad, useful or useless, engaging or distracting. Some educators feel that the keyboard is the remedy for all difficulties that will unleash students' fingers that will in turn open a channel to the contents of their minds. Others complain that students should not be limited by such distracting, cold, and inconvenient mechanical environments. We must take responsibility for the tools we invent and acknowledge that we can control them. Barlow (1995) suggested that "When we behold some new species of technology, we should ask ourselves one question: does it connect or does it separate? And since every powerful technology will probably do a lot of both, we should ask which of these properties is naturally dominant" (p. 142). And once we decide the usefulness of the tool, we need to know when to log in and when to log out (when to and when not to integrate it into our pedagogy).

Technology affords teachers many opportunities to supplement and enrich the teaching they already do. It offers students new ways to be creative, bold, and innovative, charting for themselves that new frontier as they build the necessary skills to become productive members of their local communities and the emerging global village. The students in the RAP are given the tools and encouraged to do the discovery through text. We hope to help them find that narrative, that guiding personal vision that will carry them through their lives as informed citizens, with a spirit of inquiry and an openness to new ideas.

The possibilities are endless, exciting, and often overwhelming. But we must begin at the simplest level. This student has articulated it well:

> This week I had my first experiences with electronic mail and they were wonderful. I called my immediate family (all of which have their own addresses) on Friday to give them my address, and on Tuesday morning when I checked my account I had seven messages waiting! My sister had passed my address out to several of our mutual friends,

so they all "dropped me a line" as did my mother and father. What a tremendous way to feel connected. Its amazing that I can type a letter on this small island in the middle of the Pacific and it can travel digitally through the phone lines to its destination. . . . Now I know how Alexander Graham Bell must have felt! There is something about typing my thoughts and feelings that I can't get over the phone. I am less inhibited when I am composing a letter I think because I do not have to predict the immediate response of my coparty to my statements. I am more willing to speak (or type) my mind, because once I send my letter, there is no retracting it. This is one example to me that not all technology is detrimental to society; however, I do not think it should be used to replace actually "touching" that someone.[1]

Communication. Simple, yet the most complex of platforms. A place for us to begin.

REFERENCES

Barlow, J. (1995, December). It's a poor workman who blames his tools. *Wired* (special edition), 120-124.

Brady, M. (1989). *What's worth teaching?* Albany: State University of New York Press.

Cooper, W. (1995). Walden Pond MOO. *Computing and Network Services, 8*(2), 6-8.

Elmer-Dewitt, P. (1994, July 4). Bards of the internet: If e-mail represents the renaissance of prose, why is so much of it so awful? *Time,* pp. 66-67.

Fulwiler, T. (1987). *The journal book.* Portsmouth: Boynton.

Fulwiler, T. (1991). *College writing: A personal approach to academic writing.* Portsmouth: Boynton.

Goodlad, J. (1994). *Educational renewal: Better teachers, better schools.* San Francisco: Jossey-Bass.

Hartman, K., Neuwirth, C., Kiesler, S., Sproull, L., Cochran C., Palmquist, M., & Zubrow, D. (1995). Patterns of social interaction and learning to write: Some effects of network technologies. In Z. L. Berge (Ed.), *Computer mediated communications and the online classroom* (pp. 47-78). Cresskill, NJ: Hampton Press.

Hawisher, G., & Moran, C. (1993). Electronic mail and the writing instructor. *College English, 5,* 627-643.

---

[1]Angela Knowles asked to be acknowledged publicly for this quote as she feels so strongly about the value of electronic communication. It has changed her life in many ways.

Lowry, M., Koneman, P., & Osman-Jouchoux, R. (1994). Electronic discussion groups: Using e-mails as an instructional strategy. *Techtrends, 3*(2), 22-24.

Myers, E. L. (1995). Open to suggestion: Using e-mail with developmental college students. *Journal of Reading, 38,* 666-667.

Oldenberg, R. (1997). *The great good place.* New York: Marlowe.

Perry, T. S. (1992). E-mail at work. *IEEE Spectrum, 29*(10), 24-28.

Postman, N. (1995). *The end of education.* New York: Alfred A. Knopf.

Sizer, T. R. (1992). *Horace's school.* New York: Houghton Mifflin.

Spinnuzi, C. (1994). A different kind of forum: Rethinking rhetorical strategies for electronic text media. *IEEE Transactions on Professional Communications, 37,* 213- 217.

Tillyer, D. A. (1993). World peace and natural writing through e-mail. *Collegiate Microcomputer, 11*(2), 67-69.

Chapter • 11

Advanced Composition Online: Pedagogical Intersections of Composition and Literature

Linda K. Hanson

When Winterowd (1987) observed that over the last century, "literary studies were purified to theory and rhetoric was purified of theory—with lugubrious consequences for the humanities" (p. 257), he not only pointed to the overarching significant problem of English as a discipline and the extent of its impact, but he also implied potential for solution in the current multiplicity of theoretical perspectives. In forging the cross-disciplinary profession of composition and rhetoric, we have learned to value the many voices articulating those different perspectives, many of them shared with literary studies. The Modern Language Association's 1982 recommendation to broaden the definition of literature and to improve existing relations between literature and writing validated divergent voices within literary studies as well. Such riches provide unparalleled opportunity, as we move into the 21st century, to transform the dynamics of classrooms and actively engage each student in making meaning. In most English departments, the first course that purports to teach English majors how to write about literature provides the richest set of conflicts and the greatest potential for successfully integrating composition and literature.

THEORETICAL CONTRIBUTIONS TO AN INTEGRATED PEDAGOGICAL MODEL

Pragmatic concerns for the consequences of separating composition from literature, practice from theory, have prompted theorists, practitioners, and historians alike to redress that imbalance, in part by recognizing the legitimate breadth of the realm of inquiry. Even Miller (1983) advocated a unified pedagogy for composition and literature, and recent attempts to fuse the two are yielding some refreshing theoretical frameworks (Clifford & Schilb, 1985; Knoblauch, 1985; Phelps, 1991). Integration efforts abound: Composition and literary scholars share a large body of work, including diverse social philosophers (e.g., Bakhtin, 1982, 1986; Derrida, 1978; Foucault, 1970), rhetoricians (e.g., Booth, 1961, 1974; Burke, 1931/1953, 1963; Ong, 1982; Winterowd, 1986), subjective or transactional literary critics (e.g., Bleich, 1975, 1978; Fish, 1980; Iser, 1974, 1980; Rosenblatt, 1978, 1938/1983), deconstructionists (e.g., de Man, 1971, 1985) and semioticians (Eco, 1979, 1984). "The gap has been bridged," as Winterowd (1987) noted, but he lamented that "traffic apparently flows in only one direction" (p. 265). North (1987) pushed the implications of that effort by compositionists even further:

> It has become increasingly fashionable to try to make connections between literary studies and Composition. Toward a general goal of maintaining a unified English, such a trend seems all to the good. But for the purposes of Compositions's growing power as a field, a knowledge-making society, the terms of such a rapprochement—*how* the gap gets bridged—matters a great deal. (p. 119)

Ultimately, each teacher must bridge that gap. But classroom practices are hard to change. An educator's pedagogical habits reflect his or her own learning experiences and the teaching models he or she learned to value. Even given the theoretical framework to locate literature and composition in the same classroom, then, a teacher's pedagogical habits can often interfere with effective implementation.

Pattison (1982) and Freire (1970) remind us that education in English functions within a sociopolitical framework—a framework that particularly in this country has tended to support a subject-based curriculum to match the "discipline models" of science and math. The discipline model for English, comprising separate subjects of literature, language, and composition to be mastered, continues to flourish despite the pedagogical acceptance in composition of a "growth model" that recognizes the individual student as an active participant in his or her learning.

Harris (1991) suggested that the conflict between the "growth model" that has become associated with composition and the discipline model associated with literature is a conflict between teaching and research, between meeting the needs and expectations of students and the public versus those of other scholars. I suggest that more fundamental differences separate the two models, differences in their concepts of knowledge and language. The pedagogy, theory, and historical practice associated with each area—composition and literature—rest on conflicting epistemological assumptions. The view of knowledge as communally constructed through a participatory process is at odds with an elite, hierarchical view of knowledge as received wisdom reserved for a few. Recent debates about "political correctness," the "dead white guys" canon, and Hirsch's (1987) cultural literacy are logical outgrowths of the clash between the two epistemologies.

Ehninger (1972) provides the theoretical vantage point from which this schism seems bridgeable: He defines *rhetoric* as "that discipline which studies all of the ways in which men may influence each other's thinking and behavior through the strategic use of symbols" (p. 8). Ehninger focuses on epistemology as the key to differing perceptions of rhetoric and concludes that the "notion that rhetoric is something added to discourse is gradually giving way to the quite different assumption that rhetoric not only is inherent in all human communication, but that it also informs and conditions every aspect of thought and behavior: that man himself is inevitably and inescapably a rhetorical animal" (pp. 8-10). Such an assumption is inclusive, encompassing rhetoricians whose formalist emphasis is derived from classical rhetoric (Britton, 1978; Christensen, 1978; Corbett, 1971; D'Angelo, 1975; Kinneavy, 1971; Young, Becker, & Pike, 1970) as well as those who focus on the epistemic and social vitalism of rhetoric (Bereiter, 1980; Berlin, 1984, 1987; Berthoff, 1981, 1984; Coles, 1974, 1980; de Beaugrande, 1982, 1984; Emig, 1983; Gardner, 1982; Murray, 1987; North, 1987).

Similarly, it can encompass the rich diversity of literary theory that has emerged since Rosenblatt, in 1938 in the context of the New Criticism, spoke against the solitary authority of the text and for its social context, suggesting a transactional epistemic understanding of how we read and create texts. Other voices have contributed to that conversation: Rosenblatt cited A. C. Bradley whose "dynamic process of reading," based on the distinctions he drew between the text and the experience of drama, modeled a reader-response theory that recognized the ambiguities and contextual cues involved in making meaning. Richards and Ogden (1923/1938) provided additional scaffolding for her view, arguing in 1923 in *The Meaning of Meaning* that meaning is contextual, that it does not inhere in words but depends on interpretation. In his 1931 *Counter-Statement,* Burke (1931/1953) first argued that literature should be considered a branch of rhetoric because, like other texts, it seeks to affect the reader through language. Bakhtin (1986) extended these positions. In "The Problem of Speech Genres," he treated literature as but one set of discourse genres, all of which imply social interaction and the attendant contextual complexities of intention, interpretation, immediate social context, and historical circumstance. His theory of language locates meaning in dialogue, whether between author and reader or speakers and listeners. Booth (1961), too, argued in *The Rhetoric of Fiction* that all literature is discourse addressed to a reader. He locates meaning in the rhetorical relationships among reader, writer, text, and context, emphasizing further that as readers we bear ethical responsibilities to the text, the author, society, and ourselves to engage in the dialogues through which we make meaning. Berthoff (1981) contributed one more essential piece to the theoretical underpinnings for an integrated pedagogy. Acknowledging her indebtedness to Richards (1936; Richards & Ogden, 1938), in *The Making of Meaning,* Berthoff (1981) identified reading and writing as processes mutually supportive of the construction of meaning.

Together, Bradley, Richards, Burke, Rosenblatt, Booth, Berthoff, Bakhtin, and Berlin provide a persistent confirmation of the transactional epistemology necessary for us to renew the dialectical relationship between *poetics,* the study of interpreting texts, and *rhetoric,* the study of creating texts. The crucial test of such an integrated pedagogy comes, of course, in the classroom. This chapter focuses on the pedagogical model used in an advanced composition course that serves as prerequisite to our core literature courses, a course, in short, where our majors and minors are expected to learn how to write about—and read—literature.

THE COURSE

ENG 230, Advanced Composition and Creative Writing, is required as a prerequisite to our literature classes. The Ball State University Catalogue states that the goal of the course is to provide "Instruction in critical writing about literature beyond that provided for the general student, including the study of techniques of literary research, criticism, and documentation. Instruction in creative writing, particularly fiction and poetry." The corollary is that students must learn the methods and language of the discipline and traditional literary genres as well as specific forms within those genres; they must prepare to participate in an "interpretive community." In its narrowest sense, this goal has prompted both teacher and student to focus on producing the formal, critical, usually "New Critical," analysis of a literary text that has traditionally been privileged by professors teaching upper division literature classes. In its broadest sense, however, the goal prompts an integrated pedagogy built on concepts of process and community essential to making meaning.

The last piece of the catalogue description, creative writing, may seem out of place. Expediency years ago prompted a curriculum committee to include creative writing in ENG 230 to meet state teaching requirements—an action I view as serendipitous because that component was the catalyst that enabled me to see the disparate requirements as a coherent course. Students struggling with their own characters or metaphors or rhythms must look at literature from the inside, a perspective missing from the formal critical analyses typically required in upper division literature classes. To make the components of the course cohere for my students, I added one more component as a tool: a computer network. Networking the class both literally and figuratively reinforces the opportunity the course offers both students and teacher—to view literature from both inside and outside, as writers, readers, creators, responders, participants, observers.

DEVELOPING AN INTEGRATED PEDAGOGY

Our integrated pedagogy is hard won, even for those of us who developed it. And not every teacher assigned to our Advanced Composition class is willing to embrace it. Historically, Advanced Composition was taught by the literature faculty to prepare majors and minors to write about the literature they would be reading; composition faculty were confined to the general studies writing courses or, exacerbating the split in composition between practice and theory, to the graduate courses in composition and rhetoric. As composition faculty gained stature in the department, however, we gained staffing control over all the writing courses in the department. As a first step, we sought faculty who had feet in both composition and literature to teach the Advanced Composition course. The course bewildered or frustrated many because the pedagogical habits they brought to it—from either the literature classroom or the composition classroom, sometimes from both in uneasy juxtaposition—did not enable them or their students to meet the expectations of the course.

The primary difference between the pedagogical approaches brought from writing classrooms and those most often used in literature classrooms can best be articulated through models. In the traditional model most familiar to the literary scholar, the model Freire (1970) labeled the "banking method" of teaching, the student is a passive vessel to be filled by the teacher. Knowledge is revealed by the teacher, implying that classroom exposure to course material is sufficient—and necessary—for learning. What the student does outside of class is subordinate, simply fixing the revealed wisdom in his or her mind. For courses defined by their subject matter—Shakespeare's tragedies, Victorian nonfiction prose, Jazz

Age fiction—the assumption is that course content is (or can be) clearly defined, the teacher knows it, and his or her task is to "cover" it all for the student, primarily through lectures. "Objective" tests, library research papers, reports, or annotated bibliographies typically comprise the favored discursive rhetorical forms. A course like the Advanced Composition class that is not inherently defined by subject matter, however, poses special problems for a teacher who has no models except the presentational or "banking method" from which to choose. A teacher might import subject matter—literature, model essays, grammar—or look to an alternate model.

The most effective alternate mode of instruction Hillocks (1986) labels environmental: The student is an active participant in his or her learning, working in collaboration with other students and the teacher. In such a model, the teacher makes it possible for students to learn by exposing them to possibilities; providing access to information and other resources; structuring problems to work, issues to grapple with, mysteries to solve; and offering guidance, encouragement, and constructive criticism. The epistemology at work is subjective, focusing on a procedural mode of inquiry, on "how people claim to know" rather than on what they know (North's distinctions), and the privileged rhetorical forms would likely be presentational—writers' journals or logs, observations, interviews, records of writing group discussions—each one honoring the writer's authority. Computer networks can mirror the environmental mode, and the ancient guilds and the apprenticeship models still in place in science education provide parallels for this mode of instruction. Computer technology, too, can support the active learning model in any discipline by expanding opportunities for modeling the social construction of knowledge. Most frequently in English departments, however, as Kemp (chap. 13, this volume) points out, computers are linked with composition, putting even greater distance between the pedagogical approaches that differently trained literature and writing faculty bring to a classroom (for studies focusing on writing pedagogy in networked classrooms, see Barker & Kemp, 1991; Batson, 1989; Bump, 1990; Flores, 1991; Forman, 1990; George, 1990; Madden, 1989; Selfe, 1991). Only over time as graduate students and junior faculty see a genuine shift in the attitudes of senior faculty toward both composition and literature, in the ways educators value their professional endeavors, will those pedagogical differences be resolved.

Pedagogical choices are tied to perceptions of the relations among power, authority, and knowledge (Foucault's 1970 problematizing of the power-knowledge dynamic). Although composition has gained recognition as a discipline replete with history, theory, and research methodologies (albeit appropriated from related fields of inquiry), as North (1987) pointed out, that process has discredited practice as knowledge, maintaining the status quo for the vast majority of writing faculty, subordinate both to literature faculty and, now, to composition faculty pursuing systematic research and scholarship—North's two types of formal inquiry. Phelps (1991) points out just how difficult—perhaps impossible—resolving pedagogical differences might be. Even among educators in composition, differences abound, sometimes labeled as distinctions between rhetoric and composition, sometimes as tensions between composition theory and practice.

> We cannot effectively change the psychology and politics of teachers' relationships to theory (as North recognizes) without confronting this underlying failure to conceptualize a strong role for practitioners, as thinkers, in a field that set out to reform teaching by grounding it in theoretical knowledge. The refusal of practitioners to submit to that purpose challenges fundamentally the tacit understandings that govern most composition studies (and perhaps the academy at large): the view of theory as applying without mediation by human judgment; the assumption that activity and experience are uncritical, non-epistemic; the hierarchies that prize formal knowledge over practical wisdom, knowing over acting, research over teaching or learning, writing over talk. Seen this way, the current tensions between theory and practice, and their inarticulateness to one another, are not accidental, occasional, or temporary obstacles to progress. Rather, they provide essential clues to the nature of the field. (p. 864)

In composition classrooms, students find themselves at the interstice between academic study and communal participation. Social, aesthetic, and ethical values may be safely distanced from the personal when a text is being studied; but the same issues of value challenge students—and faculty members—when they must commit themselves to words in print. Teaching grammatical and rhetorical forms, teaching to models, teaching processes, teaching plot, character, theme, figurative language—each can successfully permit avoidance of engagement with either writing or reading tasks. As Elbow (1990) noted in *What is English?* "writing is the creating or constructing of meaning, not the transmission of meaning already worked out; . . . indeed, . . . the construction of meaning tends to be a social enterprise as much as if not more than an individual one" (pp. 134-135).

Rich (1979) observed, simply, that "writing is renaming" (p. 43). Renaming may be naming again, repeating, to make the sound and thereby the word itself one's own; it may be rehearsing, to learn word and context; or renaming may mean naming anew, seeing with another perspective, "revisioning" what has been seen before. The recursiveness contained in Rich's simple statement suggests the varied active and reflective roles we play as participants in a community of scholars. Yet we tend to forget that, for our students, writing tasks in literature classes can be more than formal critical essays or essay examinations. Diversifying both writing and reading experiences can not only expand students' learning opportunities but also allow reader-writer relationships with the literary text to move naturally to the fore as student readers themselves participate as writers in a limited discourse community.

Simply diversifying the assignments on a syllabus, however, is insufficient. Educators must transform the metaphors by which they conceive their classrooms, rename the learning experience they wish for their students. Sketches in one of my students' journals brought home to me the contradictory metaphors that govern the pedagogical approaches developed to teach writing and those most often used in literature classrooms. In trying to explain the qualitative differences between our class and another literature class he was taking, Scott sketched the dynamics he had observed in the two rooms, labeling ours a "conversation" and the other a "ladder" (see Fig. 11.1).

The hierarchical ladder ostensibly offers each student the opportunity to compete with others climbing toward the exclusionary goals of authority, knowledge, and value. Because competition is the mode of progression, those above will impart as little information and climbing technique to those below them as is possible, the determiner being the amount that maintains their superiority. In the classroom, authority resides visually and procedurally with the teacher standing or otherwise elevated above the students in the front of the room, and knowledge is dispensed in measured amounts by the teacher to each student, most often in lecture format. The occasional "discussion" rarely moves beyond a question-answer format because discussion presupposes mutual acceptance of each participant as qualified discussant, not an authority-novice relationship in which an answer must be judged "right" or "wrong."

Communal conversation, however, is inclusive. The mode of progression into full participation is cooperation, with those who are knowledgeable sharing their expertise with those who are not, shaping and refining their own knowledge in the sharing. In the classroom, authority is decentered, each writer or speaker taking authority and responsibility for his or her texts and learning. The apprenticeship model in the sciences, or the internship model springing up in higher education across the nation, acknowledges the impact of inclusion on one's motivation to learn. Writing groups formed by aspiring writers through the centuries outside the academy, practices spread by participants in the Breadloaf School and the National Writing Project, and the concepts contained, for example, in Elbow and Belanoff's (1995) *A Community of Writers* all recognize that students can and do learn from inside a discipline.

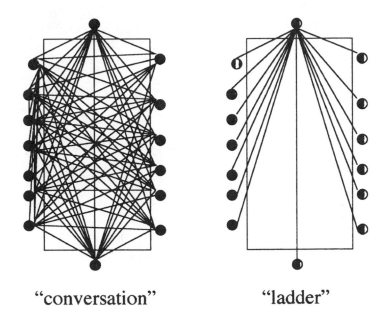

"conversation"   "ladder"

Figure 11.1. Classroom dynamics

Taking the communal conversation model from a writing classroom into a literature classroom, however, requires calling also on concepts of discourse community and on Fish's (1980) concept of an "interpretive community," concepts already familiar to literary scholars. Members of a discourse community know and abide by implicit rules of language use; in an academic discourse community, those rules include the expectations that members use appropriate terminology, that they write in the "privileged" forms accepted by major journals, that they follow accepted procedures for research and reporting research. Fish's "interpretive community" similarly depends on shared implicit assumptions and expectations for the interpretation of literature. Neither community, however, is static; its members continually redefine or rename it as they work within it, some intuitively, some consciously examining the functioning of the community itself. Those dimensions enhance the understanding of the communal conversation model as it can function in a literature classroom or a hybrid course like our ENG 230, Advanced Composition and Creative Writing.

In the communal conversation model, the single classroom community may be viewed as nested in progressively larger communities, from a course, to a department, to the entire national and international discipline community (see Fig. 11.2). Having worked with the communal con-

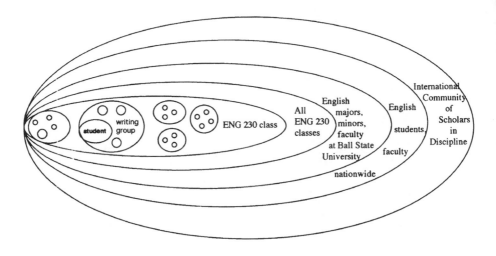

Figure 11.2. Communal conversation model

versation model in my writing classrooms, facilitated by both synchronous and asynchronous conversations on various computer networks over the years, and having introduced my British literature survey class to both synchronous and asynchronous discussion using Daedalus InterChange with markedly positive results, I saw in ENG 230, one of our first two courses required of English majors, an unique opportunity to introduce our students to the multiple dimensions of the roles they will be playing in the academic discipline they have chosen to enter.

METHODOLOGY AND COURSE CONTENT

The classroom community seeks to model the larger scholarly community in building a sense of common purpose and in developing an awareness of writing as interaction with a particular audience. Centered in a networked computer environment running Daedalus software, our model for writing and communicating recognizes both the solitary and the social dimensions of writing and reading, providing for both personal response and expression and for progressively more public statement. Daedalus software integrates a basic word processor with writing assistance in the form of heuristics and revision prompts; bulletin board programs for posting class assignments, turning in assignments, and "publishing" final drafts; an e-mail program that provides for asynchronous communication; and InterChange, which provides for synchronous discussion within small groups or among all members of the class. Students may write in a private environment using only the word processor and perhaps the writing prompts, then share a draft with another student through e-mail, turn the next draft in to class files for their writing group's response, and finally submit the completed version for the entire class to read.

To model more fully the larger scholarly community, a colleague and I have each assigned our students to respond over the network with blind reviews to three papers belonging to students in the other class. In turn, then, each student receives three blind reviews of the paper he or she submitted. When circumstances fit, I have also had students submit their work as proposals for presentation at undergraduate or professional conferences. They do not get detailed feedback on their proposals, but they do begin to understand the stakes and dynamics involved in making their writing public, in actively participating in the larger disciplinary community.

The writing tasks also recognize the necessary range of private to public forms in which we all engage. To bring students into the conversation, to include them in our scholarly community, we must allow them to know that we explore ideas in many forms before we draft, revise, and edit them into the articles we read in professional journals. Accordingly, my students build a portfolio of writings during the term to include journals, creative writing, and critical papers on literature (see the syllabus in Appendix A). The reading-and-writing journals they share with me in whole or in part, as they choose; as the syllabus states, their task in the journal is to examine self-consciously the dimensions and intersections of the two roles as they play them during the semester:

> Linking your roles as writer and reader is the literature we will be reading this term. Literature itself is a dialogue between writer and reader. You will be participating in that dialogue from various angles—as reader of poetry, drama, and fiction, as writer of poetry, drama, and fiction, as reader communicating your reading experience to others in both formal and informal writing. Your initial responses to your reading should appear in your journal. Possible responses range from emotional to intellectual, from subjective to objective, from creative diversion to focused analysis.

The creative writing tasks include one to two poems, one dramatic scene, and one short story, each to be shared and reviewed for completeness and negotiated criteria but not evaluated for a grade. One student's reflections in a journal entry reveal that the combination of writings and reading have produced the desired effect. By writing a poem, by seeing literature from the inside, the student has become aware of the interplay between her roles as reader and writer:

> I do feel that writing my own poem gave me a better appreciation for the poetry we have read. It is very easy to think of poetry as being simple, and easy to create, because of the shortness of length as compared to a novel perhaps. While some poetry may be relatively short as compared to other literary works, the general populace sells it way too short. The more I read of GOOD poetry, the more I appreciate what goes into its creation. (Mary)

The critical papers include one devoted to each of three genres (poetry, drama, fiction), one additional paper of choice, and a research/revision paper—one of the critical papers expanded and revised as the student places his or her statements into the context of the on-going scholarly conversation. Specific topics emerge from the student's responses to the reading and are negotiated and clarified through discussion with me, with members of the student's writing group, and frequently with the entire class. Much of that discussion is written, either in the student's journal or in InterChange sessions or on e-mail, so that by the time the student begins to compose, she has rehearsed ideas and has a record not only of her thinking but of responses she will have to answer as she develops her thoughts about the issue. I very deliberately encourage students to find their own issues and questions because every critical perspective, elevated to theory or not, has emerged from such grappling with text, context, expectations, and negotiations with other readers.

It is crucial that activity in the course link the portfolio and the literature, the writing and the reading, and that it link all of us in the interpretive community. Students and teacher (sometimes including students and teachers from other sections) read and respond to the literature and share and respond to one another's ideas and texts in progressively more public forms. Before students read any published criticism of the literature we are reading, we consciously collaborate in the meaning-making continuum of reading, inquiry, and reflection that lies behind published work. Very early in the course we analyze transcripts of two InterChange sessions, one on the question "What is poetry?" and the second on the first poems or short story we read.

Each term, students meet in the computer classroom on the second day of class and are introduced to the Daedalus software, primarily to InterChange. For 30 minutes they wrestle with a definition of *poetry*—in a word, a metaphor, examples (composed on the spot or created from memory), favorites, experiences. They all "talk," developing respect for names and ideas on the screen rather than for physical attributes as they "meet" their classmates fully for the first time. Although students' names appear with their comments, they begin that class as essentially anonymous. The experience startles many, as these journal entries reveal:

> We know people will respond to the ideas themselves and not to the person who offered them. Even though comments are signed, composing written rather than spoken thoughts seems easier to many students. This way we can express our thoughts without having to worry about people looking at us or hearing a stutter. (Mary)

> It really made me happy to know that you noticed my poems on the computer. . . . Poetry is very personal, don't you think? I like people to read my stories, but I was really nervous when I typed in my poems. It was like exposing the very center of my being. (Emily)

The transcript from that first day allows me to demonstrate that the students are knowledgeable, that they can enter the conversation in the parlors of our discipline. Each student has a voice in the collaborative response. The computer classroom serves as the site of public, communal discourse, and each person has contributions to be taken seriously. We engage in recursive thinking as we compare students' responses in the transcript—some aesthetic, some formal, some procedural—to those proposed by poets and scholars, and then I encourage students to continue to explore and refine their own inquiry in their journals, perhaps to bring to the public forum again at a later time. Emily took me seriously:

> I know we're not familiar with each other yet, but I intend to get personal in this journal. I'm going to tell you things you'd probably just as soon not know; but if I'm going to examine my roles as reader and writer, my responses will require that you know my frame of reference. Please, . . . comment on any remark I make. I want to use this journal to supplement my classroom participation. (Emily)

The second transcript provides further opportunity to privilege each learner. It demonstrates in microcosm the intellectual conversations academics and other scholars carry on face to face at conferences, in journals, and through books. Because the students are the primary participants in the conversation, they tend to respond unself-consciously, to take risks; in doing so, they increase their own authority and control over the text under discussion as well as over their own texts, and they demonstrate incipient critical perspectives that once again can be compared to approaches taken by published scholars. One InterChange session we analyzed was conducted in five subconferences, one for each writing group. Students had read five poems in advance and were to explore their responses for potential topics for critical essays. In the 50-minute period, they averaged more than 10 comments each (201 for 18 students), demonstrating a significant variety of approaches—historical, biographical or social criticism, psychological or archetypal criticism, new criticism, reader-response or feminist criticism.

For some students, the viability of multiple perspectives is bewildering. A nontraditional student reacted to the in-class analysis of our second transcript this way:

> Before I begin my thoughts on this weeks [sic] poetry, I would like to comment on the approach this class is taking, if I may. Back in the "olden days" when I first attended the university you learned ONE thing, in my experience, but you learned it fast or you were lost. This thing that you learned was that in the literature and composition classes if you were to succeed you must live, breathe, and interpret as your instructor did. I have received good grades on papers that were verbatim copies of class notes while my more creative and braver classmates received lesser grades for probably what were better works. I always felt as if I was somehow selling out when I did this, but the bottom line was the grade. So it was with much disbelief that I listened to an instructor tell me to find my interpretation of the work. Being no fool I listened carefully to all information she bestowed on the class. I knew eventually she would casually drop her opinion during the lecture and I would be there to catch it. Session after session I waited. No views were forthcoming. Could she have been serious about using our own views? Something akin to panic filled my very soul. MY interpretations could only be wrong! I didn't know what they were talking about. At times I was certain even THEY didn't know what they were talking about. My views were always so simplistic. I saw a red dog biting a small child. My instructor saw the Communist Party oppressing the weak. Good grief! . . .
> I thought back on all the years of complaining . . . .
> At 18 years of age I was full of opinions and no one wanted them. Now I find myself 34 years of age and I have no opinions. Where did I lose them along the way? (Mary)

Mary also felt ill at ease in the InterChange conversation that joined two sections. The other class had had different preparation and different discussions than we had, and she was unprepared.

> We had our interchange on the Zenith today and discussed "Ode." After reading some of the comments by the other class, I was afraid to enter anything of my own. I thought maybe we had read different "Ode"s. The rest of my group was as baffled as I was which is small consolation. I think the other instructor told his class what to write just

to make us look like idiots; either that or someone was having some fun with us. I truly found some of those students' remarks as hard to decipher as the poem itself. Maybe I am in the wrong major. (Mary)

It did not take Mary long to recover her confidence, however, and 3 years later she attributed her refocused career goals, her high scores on the LSAT, and her admission to law school to her learning experience in this class. Renaming the classroom experience, providing her a different model in which taking responsibility for her learning meant participation and collaboration rather than emulation or regurgitation, enabled her to participate fully in other academic conversations as well.

Kirsten approached InterChange sessions with less trepidation than Mary, benefitting even when she had not prepared her reading. Her journal too reveals a level of comfort and trust in the classroom community:

I love that InterChange on the computer. I'm not just saying that because it's "like" a blow-off day—because, even through all of the "nonsense" talk, I actually learn some things. Using that system is like a release—I love it! I hadn't read Antigone when I was supposed to— so, I paid attention to what the class was saying about the drama through interchange—even the things that were supposed to be humorous. Then when I read the drama—I started fitting in what people said in the play. Actually, it made for smooth and interesting reading. (Kirsten)

Writing groups of four persons comprise the basic units for collaboration within the classroom. Students are placed in groups based on dissimilarities of writing style preferences, determined by a brief questionnaire that correlates to the Myers-Briggs Type Inventory. The groups generally serve all term as reading and responding groups as well, providing for subconversations in InterChange sessions. When I worked with a sister class, however, a "blind" review prompted the class as a whole to bond as a single community consciously distinct from the other ENG 230 class. The student who received the review posted e-mail to our entire class:

I received a critique from an anonymous student (whoever it was used the initials XYZ) and it really bugs me. What I had submitted for peer responding was a VERY rough outline of what I PLANNED to focus on in my essay. This joker proceeded to systematically rip my ideas apart. I wonder if anyone else received similar responses? Anyway, the main reason it bugs me is because I would never tear someone's work up in this manner. Of my four responses, this one was the only overtly negative one. And, just because you don't agree with someone's interpretation, that doesn't give you the right to undermine their ability. (Jason)

A flurry of incredulous e-mail and then outraged oral discussion followed, all contained within our class. I opened an InterChange session and asked the class to comment on the incident so we could pass our response to the other class as well. Students elaborated on Jason's attention to community expectations and to ethical behavior within a community, surprised that they had formed such a strong classroom community but also that they were placing themselves within the larger scholarly community by articulating what they perceived as that community's code of professional behavior.

Before the other class met, my colleague and I examined all the reviews to try to determine who the culprit was, and with some certainty he presented the situation to his class for response on InterChange as well. The student we believed to be the culprit delayed entering the conversation until he had seen outraged responses from nearly every student in the class. Then in a brief entry he joined the rest of the class in condemning the behavior, logged out, logged back in as XYZ and offered self-justification for pointing out "empty ideas," logged out, and then logged back in to continue as part of the community. My colleague did talk to the apologetic young man later in private, but the public evidence of community building provided us—and our students—a telling reinforcement for continuing to use and develop our integrated pedagogy. The public and private forums are both necessary, it seems, and both must be integral parts of the pedagogy.

The best evidence that students do take responsibility for their own learning in a classroom that stresses communal construction of meaning lies in their texts. As students become conscious of themselves at the points of intersection between reader and text, writer and text, reader and writer, they test the boundaries of the forms and genres they receive. Wil, for example, wrote his first critical paper in the form of a dialogue in order to give more than one critical perspective on Poe's "Annabel Lee." Danielle wrote a short story, a dramatic monologue entitled "The Woman in the Wallpaper," as response to "The Yellow Wall Paper." Self-conscious narrators emerged in the short stories and dramatic scenes of Wil, Scott, Craig, and Mary as each of them struggled with issues of point of view, audience, and selection. Emily, Craig, and Scott each independently recorded his or her painful and joyous process for writing a poem. And in the most striking example, Scott used InterChange as a metaphor for meta-discourse, creating a fictional InterChange to present social, historical, and deconstructive approaches to Kafka's "The Bucket-Rider" (see Appendix B for his text). On their exams, too, we can expect not just facts, details, and memory, but understanding of the concepts and methods of critical inquiry. To demonstrate their meta-understanding of the discipline, students have been asked on their final, for example, not to analyze Susan Glaspell's "Trifles" from a feminist perspective, but to state the basic principles of feminist criticism

and then explain WHY it could offer an important reading of "Trifles"—
or why social criticism could illuminate Shirley Jackson's "The Lottery," or
archetypal criticism illuminate *Riders to the Sea* or "A Worn Path," or psychological criticism illuminate "Really, Doesn't Crime Pay?" or post-struc-
turalism illuminate *The Gap.*

EVALUATION

With the exception of the student who wanted a product-oriented lecture
class (and his customary A), the student evaluations of this integrated pedagogy have been overwhelmingly positive. One example will suffice, from
a student's first journal entry and his final course evaluation:

> First, [in my past] there has been a scant amount of writing. "As an
> English major, you should . . ." I fail that, absolutely. Those expecta-
> tions, I mean. We should read and write, as English majors, prolifically.
> Ha—I know of rooms in distant lands where concerned chumps of
> turnips are gathering to donate blood for a transfusion for my muse. . . .
> (Scott)

Course Evaluation:

> Presentation of course material: Diverse—usually extremely effective.
> Computer learning threw me at first, with interchanges, contacts, class
> assignments, etc. . . . But something happened mid way in the course—
> It started making more sense. Keep developing the computer section.
> Course requirements: Ideally, we would have written even more with
> the same amount of reading; although, I'm not sure how I would have
> handled the extra load.
> Tests and grading: That no final grades appeared on the first papers
> turned back liberated me from product-dominated thinking about my
> paper and told me that Dr. Hanson aimed to develop me as a writer.
> Additional Comments: She has worked beyond common boundaries
> and expectations to help me grow as a writer/reader. (Deliberately
> signed, Scott)

SUMMARY AND CONCLUSIONS

Figure 11.3 models the circles within which students and teacher and
members of the larger disciplinary community interact during the course
of the term. At the minimum, each student shares journal entries only
with the teacher; poems, dramatic scenes, and short stories are shared

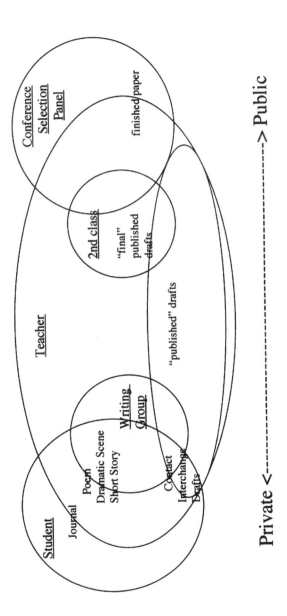

Figure 11.3. Student-community interaction

with the teacher and the student's writing group; drafts of critical papers are first shared with the teacher and the writing group, then "published" on the network and "submitted" for review by other members of the class or by members of a sister class; final "published" drafts or finished papers may then be submitted for a departmental undergraduate conference, for one of the regional undergraduate conferences, or as a few of our students have successfully demonstrated, for a professional conference. Dialogue occurs orally, through e-mail, InterChange, and in scribbled notes, all giving opportunity for students to retain the private, one-on-one interaction when their drafts are tentative but encouraging them to move to progressively more public forums to test their ideas and their own places in the community.

Our integrated pedagogy reinforces community, not hierarchy. In our decentered classroom, the conversation metaphor holds: Each person must listen to know where the conversation is, what the context is, before jumping in. The metaphor plays out in InterChange sessions as well as in the view of research as revision. We value a multiplicity of points of view with the conversation metaphor—in InterChange sessions, in the critical approaches to literature, and in the exploration of our commonalities and differences in reading and writing. As we explore literature, we consider our varying relationships to text and to community—as author (of creative writing and journals), as participant (gives full human response), as observer (describes text as artifact in social or historical context), as critic (incorporates judgment regarding quality), and as analyst (examines text as text, rather than as artifact).

Taking the communal conversation model from a writing classroom, calling on concepts of discourse community and on Fish's (1980) concept of an interpretive community, and electronically networking the classroom community to the larger scholarly community has enabled us to redefine our purpose of writing instruction, broaden concepts of research and critical approaches to text, build awareness of professional communication and publication, and raise questions regarding the nature of academic discourse. The networked classroom community models the larger scholarly community in building a sense of common purpose and in developing an awareness of writing as interaction with a particular audience. Networking the class both literally and figuratively reinforces the opportunity the course offers both students and teacher—to view literature from both inside and outside, as writers, readers, creators, responders, participants, observers. Our Bakhtinian goal is to foster both the centripetal and centrifugal forces that make dialogue and the construction of meaning possible.

APPENDIX A: SYLLABUS

Dr. Linda Hanson
RB 2104 285-8535
00lkhanson@bsu.edu

ENG 230
ADVANCED COMPOSITION AND CREATIVE WRITING

COURSE DESCRIPTION AND RATIONALE
This course provides instruction in critical writing about literature beyond that provided for the general student, including the study of techniques of literary research, criticism, and documentation. Approaching literature from the inside as well as the outside, the course also offers experience in reflective and creative writing, particularly fiction and poetry.

ADVANCED COMPOSITION AND CREATIVE WRITING fulfills the state requirements for English undergraduates in teaching programs. It provides intensive study of and practice in the skills (including computer) necessary to complete the writing requirements in undergraduate and graduate courses, with emphasis on including library research in a major writing project. It also provides study of and practice in the methods and terminology of literary analysis and creative writing. Because English 230 is directly related to the academic discourse all English majors and minors do use, the course develops skills needed for the successful study, discussion, and teaching of literature and creative writing.

REQUIRED TEXTS

Gibaldi, Joseph. *MLA Handbook for Writers of Research Papers*. 4th ed. MLA, 1995.
Landy, Alice S. *Heath Introduction to Literature*. 3rd ed. Lexington, MA: Heath, 1988.
Lynn, Steven. *Texts & Contexts: Writing about Literature with Critical Theory*. Harper Collins, 1994.
Holman, C. Hugh, & William Harmon. *A Handbook to Literature*. 6th ed. Macmillan, 1992.

Collaborative Learning
Much of your activity in the course will involve sharing and responding to each other's ideas and texts. The classroom community will model the larger scholarly community in building a sense of common purpose and in developing an awareness of writing as interaction with a particular audi-

ence. The basic unit for collaboration within the classroom will be the writing group of four or five persons; you will be placed in a group early in the semester.

Computer Environment
We will use a model for writing and communicating that is centered in a computer-based environment; this environment comprises both English Department computer lab/classrooms, the Zenith Lab in RB 282 and the VAX terminal lab in RB 292. See the handout "Computer Guidelines" for details of how we will be using computers in the course.

ATTENDANCE
Your attendance at each class session is necessary, both for your benefit and for the proper functioning of peer groups. Unless you are ill or have a serious emergency, I expect to see you at each meeting. Please inform me about problems that might lead to your missing class. If you are absent two or three times, I will request a conference with you. Good attendance will have a positive effect on borderline grades; poor attendance will jeopardize your success in the course.

PORTFOLIO
During the term you will build a portfolio of writings from which you should also select papers to include in your Major Portfolio. The ENG 230 portfolio should include three critical papers, one research paper, your journal, and creative writings (fiction, poetry, dramatic scene).

WRITING ASSIGNMENTS
1. Three critical papers, one devoted to each of three genres (poetry, drama, fiction); length at least 750 words
2. Either one of the critical papers expanded and revised with research into more substantial form, OR a research paper on a new topic; length at least 2,000 words
3. Creative Writing: two poems, one dramatic scene, one short story. These will be shared and reviewed by me for completeness but will not be given a letter grade
4. Journal Entires: At least 1,000 words per week in entries that reflect your reactions to the readings and discussions and your perceptions of your personal reading and writing processes. These writings will be reviewed regularly for completeness but will not receive letter grades. I will, however, occasionally comment on how I see your reading and writing processes emerging in your journal entries and other writings. PLEASE HAVE YOUR JOURNALS UP TO DATE AND IN CLASS WITH YOU AT LEAST EVERY WEDNESDAY FOR RANDOM REVIEW.

EVALUATION

Course evaluation will be based on your portfolio, midterm and final exams. The course grade will reflect your grades on (in order of relative importance): research/revision essay, elective essay, final exam, genre-based critical essays, midterm exam. But your level of commitment to course processes as demonstrated in your portfolio will also be a factor. In order to be eligible for an A grade, you must show strong effort in fulfilling and exceeding minimum requirements, especially in your journal and creative writings since they will not receive letter grades.

JOURNAL ENTRIES, WEEK ONE

Your journal will highlight your roles as both writer and reader this semester. Part of your task will be to examine self-consciously the dimensions and intersections of the two roles as you play them. To begin that exploration this first week, I ask you to respond in your journal to the following questions about your writing and reading processes. As you make additional discoveries during the term, while working on one of your creative pieces, for example, add those to your journal as well.

What kinds of writing do you do? Everything from lists to novels belongs in the enumeration if it represents writing you do. Considering the audience(s) for whom you write may help you remember or define additional types of writing.

In what environment do you typically write? Is that the same environment in which you would prefer to write? What tools and materials do you use? What about lighting? Sound? Movement? Snacking?

What strategies do you use to write? To generate ideas or raw material for your writing? To organize that material? To refine it? To prepare it for others to read?

What kinds of reading do you do? Everything from the comics to scientific treatises belongs in the enumeration if it represents reading you do. Considering the purposes for which you read may help you remember or define additional types of reading.

In what environment do you typically read? Is that the same environment in which you would prefer to read? What about lighting? Sound? Movement? Snacking? Do you select different environments depending upon what you are reading?

What strategies do you use to read? Are you aware of using different strategies to read for different purposes? Can you articulate the differences?

Linking your roles as writer and reader is the literature we will be reading this term. Serendipitously, the articulated philosophy of the Heath text is that "literature is a dialogue between writer and reader, an art form whose subject is a vision of humanity and the universe" (p. xi). You will be participating in that dialogue from various angles—as reader of poetry, drama, and fiction, as writer of poetry, drama, and fiction, as reader communicating your reading experience to others in both formal and informal writing.

The second type of entry you will be making in your journal will be response to your reading. Your initial responses to the literature should appear in your journal, but your journal may also serve as your "workshop" for testing different perspectives on a poem, a short story, or a play. Possible responses range from emotional to intellectual, from subjective to objective, from creative diversion to focused analysis. As you read poetry over the next few weeks, consider the following questions as guides to get you started writing:

> What particularly struck me in this poem?
> What contributed to its impact?
> How did other aspects of the poem contribute to my response?

> Particular questions you may want to pursue:
> Who is speaking?
> How would you characterize the speaker?
> Of what or whom is he or she speaking?
> How is the object, action, or person being described?
> What is the speaker's attitude toward the object, action, or person?
> Are we led to share those attitudes or to reject them? How?
> What characteristics of this text make it a poem?

Our exploration of different critical perspectives and methods during the term will provide you additional questions to pursue in your journal. Ultimately, your journal should be your richest resource to mine for the more formal and public texts that will communicate your reading experiences to others.

APPENDIX B: STUDENT TEXT

S P

When we focused on "The Guest," we addressed the dual topics of theme and irony with intriguing results. today, we'll focus on Franz Kafka's "The Bucket-Rider" (pp. 305-306). With a similar two-fold emphasis, these questions should give us ample fuel for discussion, initially

How does Kafka's style affect you, the reader, throughout the story?

How would you describe the narrator's position? What is his/her relationship to his/her environment? to the other characters? to the reader?

How do choices made affect relationships? Are there any moral, social, or other human issues involved? What's at stake? How much freedom does each individual experience in making choices?

S P
P.S.—Once again, we will be using pseudonyms.

Wink Electric
Hi gang. I'm on, and I'm talking existentialism. So far I feel all alone. Who's going to join me?

Haven
Do we have to discuss this story? I didn't think it made sense. Anybody want to defect to "The Haircut"?

Colin
Wink, you are all alone. I'm talking nihilism. What's it to you?

Ganbei
i thought this story was like dr. seuss with a hangover still pretty baked, but with a mean streak sky=wide.

Hoka Hey
Kafka employs a deceptively simple, fantastic, and paradoxical style that extensively involves the reader in the adventure despite its absurd nature.

Mr. Superent
you're right, gan bei. "lost forever" is a big switch from "happily ever after."

Wiggs
ganbei, gROOVY.

Wink Electric
Yes to you, Hoka, since the narrator speaks directly to me on a very personal level, I identify strongly with him and feel lost when he vanishes.

Ganbei
and the coal seller's wife was like the grinch or the guy who wouldn't try green eggs and ham. talk about frigid.

Kinky Java
Personally, I was a little distressed by this story.

Lux
I liked this story. I don't really remember it, but at one point it was the best thing I'd ever read.

Shenannigan
a-ganbeister, i don't think she was frigid at all. she was shooing narrator-man away like the ex-lovedog he was.

Guess
Kafka's unfortunate portrayal of the woman perpetuates a negative stereotype model. she bears no resemblance to real women.

Haven
the narrator was servicing the Frau coal-dealer?

Ann B. Davis
he's a real nowhere man, sitting in his nowhere land . . . isn't he a bit like you and me?

Wiggs
Ganbei, that is just nuts.

Colin
Well, if you would read the story more carefully, Miss Guess, I think you would find that Kafka has actually reversed the stereotypical gender roles here. The man has a soft heart and wants to help the narrator. The woman is all business, heartless, and turns the guy out into the cold because he can't pay for her worst coal.

Haven
I'm waaaaaaaaaaiting. is anyone interested in the haircut?

Colin
hey, Ann, footnote that.

Ganbei
no, really, this story is too short, and it has an ugly ending. kind of like turning a can of nestle's quick upside down and opening it directly over your mouth and then trying to swallow as much powder as you can before it all hits the floor, but then you throw up any way so what's the difference?

Shenannigan
Mais oui. why do you think she wouldn't let her husband go up the stairway to see the guy? how do you say . . . ribaldry?

Ganbei
you know, this is sort of like alice-through-the-looking-glass, except the looking glass is warped and cracked—like a funhouse mirror without the fun.

S P
So, ganbei, you seem to be saying that Kafka frames his tale in a form generally reserved for light stories or children's fiction; however, the subject matter seems quite grave. How else does he invert or pervert common perceptions of reality? Hoka Hey mentioned paradox and absurdity. Can anyone elaborate on these assertions or find examples for them?

Mr. Superent
Doesn't Kafka sound like a Lithuanian name for a baby cow?

Zippo
I ould take Kafka's stove in for a Refund. cold air in the winter reminds me of the air system here.

Kinky Java
You make a good point, colin. I see that as a reversal of historically dominant gender roles. women are usually depicted as compassionate and powerless, while men rule like pseudo-machiavellian swine. women listen with their hearts, while men tend to ignore with their heads.

Ganbei
i had an aunt estelle once, and mom would always take me to visit her, even though we all knew that mom didn't like to go there, i didn't like to go there, and aunt estelle didn't want us there. it had 'bad idea' written all over it, but we kept on going to visit her three or four times a year. she lived in minnesota.

S P
Kinky, you've tapped into a significant inversion of expected reality; although, the gender roles you describe seem also stereotypical and unfair. Your basic point is valid, however, as one example of Kafka's overturning properties which people tend to take for granted. What other examples might you draw of a universe which defies being taken for granted?

Haven
Lather, wash, rinse, repeat.

Shenannigan
O I don't no. how bout the beggar in the sky blown away by an apron? (detached sigh)

Hoka Hey
The sensual bombardment of cold strikes me as characteristic of an indifferent universe, harsh, haphazard, numb.

Lux
I think i've met your aunt. is she still alive?

Nnapalm
cold comes out of the stove and fills the room in the opening lines, and (inherent in the ice mountains) it totally swallows the narrator in the final sentence.

Shenannigan
Well, frost burns his voice hollow, and I wouldn't normally expect frost to burn—bite maybe, but not burn.

Wiggs
Ganbei, heavy.

Lux
haven't you heard of freezer burn?

Hoka Hey
had Kafka, or any of his contemporaries?

Mr. Superent
his tears freeze and dim his eyes from cold. man can't see past his suffering.

Colin
Is Mr. Wiggs going to grace us with a sentence longer than six words today?

Wink Electric
The narrator desperately seeks salvation in the forms of the stove, from biblical commandments, from emotional appeals to Frau Coal-Dealer, and seemingly, the sky as well. None of these potential sources come through for him.

Ann B. Davis
sort of like looking for love in all the wrong places

Zippo
boy, y'all are just "laughs on parade" today.

Kinky Java
Anne, good point. there doesn't seem to be any right place to look for love in this story.

Wiggs
Colin, I think if you would read the descriptions of the coal-dealer more carefully, you would find that what moves him is more financial than you originally thought. At no time does he mention giving the coal away. The woman still has an apron, and women have always controlled, whether or not me have been aware of it.

Kinky Java
what about the way he was going to use the biblical commandment against murder? I find his plan exploitative. Is this a knock on religions and charities that send people on guilt trips?

Mr. Superent
I don't see what he's complaining about. At least he gets to take a magic bucket-ride.

Hoka Hey
about the exploitative guilt-trip.

1) he is desperate, and his lack of coal will definitely kill him. if someone has coal, isn't he or she morally obligated to share some of that coal regardless of the charity involved?

2) it would only be exploitation if it worked. obviously there is no compassion in the coal-dealer's wife, nor does the coal-dealer contain enough compassion to override his wife's cruelty. nothing to exploit=no exploitation. she's only in it for the money, and he has no control.

Nnapalm
Supy (mind if i call you supy?), what good is it to fly in a bucket when one is destitute, freezing, and starving?

Wink Electric
I think Kafka traps the audience into a situational irony. The bucket flies, carrying the author horsey-style. This contains a paradox the bucket is harder to propel down the stairs than up, into the air. It openly defies gravity. Most people consider up, sky, and flying as good or, at least, favorable. Here they are bad because they exaggerate the emptiness of the bucket. The splendor of flying is killing the narrator.

Colin
brown wipes off, but grades are forever—eh, hoka?

Kinky Java
i think the bucket ride is also a metaphor for the vanity of human existence and endeavor in the unfamiliar face of an indifferent or even hostile universe.

Nnapalm
Wink, do you mean that the narrator is an icarus figure?

Ganbei
what does that have to do with anything?

Nnapalm
what does anything have to do with anything?

Kinky Java
AHA! now we're getting somewhere.

Mr. Superent
We're getting nowhere, fast. And this technology is only getting us there even faster. Poor old-fashioned Kafka had to rely on an archaic bucket to make him lost forever.

Hoka Hey
She raises her fist in the air in the last paragraph. this is the official gesture of the communist Party, no? Where was Franz Kafka from? Is this a social statement on the shortcomings of a Communist government which neglected its citizens?

Wink Electric
no the narrator is not an icarus figure, because he flies simply to convince the coal-dealer to give him coal. he is not an over-achiever. Ultimately, he flies too high out of rejection.

Ann B. Davis
I like fake bacon.

Shenannigan
You mean sizzelean? or shakespeare?

Lux I think heights are bad for the narrator because they are farther away from the earth and even colder—also because the air is thinner, harder to breathe.

Nnapalm
The narrator is lost in the abstractions of a Higher Mind. He needs substance concrete coal to weight his bucket down. He is becoming less and less significant (and he was painfully insignificant to begin with).

Ganbei
I don't think there is any Higher Mind—at least not an intelligent one in this story. If there is a Mind, I think it's reptilian and probably hibernating.

Hoka Hey
But, Nnapalm, you're right. abstractions not rooted in action tend to dissipate as ineffectually as the narrator did. the old ideal/real dichotomy.

Mr. Superent
The coal dealer can't recognize need—he asks, "Is that a customer I hear?"—he never asks, "Does somebody need help out there?" He only speaks in supply and demand—no credit.

Nnapalm
I think his bucket's inability to resist reiterates its lack of content. he is subject to the winds.

Kinky Java
What do you make of "My bucket has all the virtues of a good steed except powers of resistance."? I can get the rest of the story, but that plot twist has me baffled.

Shenannigan
well, as i'm sure you've all suspected, Franzy was addicted to LSD.

Zippo
The narrator's in one big pickle. this guy has a problem and nothing will help him, even when some things could.

Colin
is that dill or sweet? i hope it's gherkin.

Guess
the narrator is a pussy.

Zippo
I have to agree with you, guess. he keeps talking about pitiless components of his universe, while i find enough self pity in those two pages to make the universe vomit.

Wiggs
dude, sweet.

Hoka Hey
To the extent that he must have coal, or warmth, to live, any person or thing that denies him warmth is his enemy (the stove, the sky, the coal-dealers, the cold itself). this story has multiple antagonists.

Mr. Superent
this story is more economic than we've admitted, so far. notice that when he tells the Coal-dealer's wife that he can pay, but "'not just now,'" the words sound like a knell. he has just sealed his doom. humans could save him, but they won't because he doesn't play monopoly with them. he has to head for the mountains—do not pass go, do not receive $200.00.

Kinky Java
It's only two pages. I'll say it's economical.

Wink Electric
ahh. the plight of existential man. he ends up "disappeared," as it were.

Ganbei
This narrator is nothing more than a greasy water spot on the crystal glass of the universe and the powers which be cascade his sorry buckethead out of there.

Ann B. Davis
down came the rain and washed the spider out.

Hoka Hey
So, while "The Guest" inspired discussion of divided loyalties and the pain of choice, "The Bucket-rider" features no real choice. the abjectly impoverished can only follow survival instincts, their choices dominated by securing essentials. the coal dealers are slaves to their routine, their "trifles."

Colin
Ann, you're slipping, babe. go for coffee.

Nnapalm
now wait a minute. don't you think the coal dealer-schmucks have a moral obligation to help keep that man alive?

Shenannigan
whether they do or not they don't. dig?

Ganbei
So it happened that Franz Kafka deprived an audience of its metaphysical footing. they sprawled down steep, bumpy cliffs riddled with linguistic incongruencies, sharp bluffs of mutant physics, and twisted, shredded, support cables. after their sprawl, they floated up, up into the middle of nothing.

Mr. Superent
And the lizard king rasped, "waiter, there's an amoeba in my soup."

Wiggs
word.

Scott, you've captured the quality of interchange even to the nonsense that may contribute imaginative leaps of insight for others. Simultaneously you've provided a reader insight into the story itself—well done.

REFERENCES

Bakhtin, M. M. (1982). Discourse in the novel. In M. Holquist (Ed.), *The dialogic imagination* (pp. 259-422). Austin: University of Texas Press.

Bakhtin, M. M. (1986). The problem of speech genres. In C. Emerson & M. Holquist (Eds.), *Speech genres and other late essays* (pp. 60-102). Austin: University of Texas Press.

Barker, T. T., & Kemp, F. O. (1991). Network theory: A postmodern pedagogy for the writing classroom. In C. Handa (Ed.), *Computers and society: Teaching composition in the twenty-first century* (pp. 1-27). Upper Montclair, NJ: Boynton/Cook.

Batson, T. (1989). Teaching in networked classrooms. In C. L. Selfe, D. Rodrigues, & W. R. Oates (Eds.), *Computers in English and the language arts: The challenge of teacher education* (pp. 247-255). Urbana, IL: National Council of Teachers of English.

Bereiter, C. (1980). Development in writing. In L. Gregg & E. Steinberg (Eds.), *Cognitive processes in writing* (pp. 73-93). Hillsdale, NJ: Lawrence Erlbaum Associates.

Berlin, J. A. (1984). *Writing instruction in nineteenth-century American colleges*. Carbondale: Southern Illinois University Press.

Berthoff, A. E. (1981). *The making of meaning*. Upper Montclair, NJ: Boynton.

Berthoff, A. E. (Ed.). (1984). *Reclaiming the imagination: Philosophical perspectives for writers and teachers of writing*. Upper Montclair, NJ: Boynton/Cook.

Bleich, D. (1975). *Reading and feelings: An introduction to subjective criticism*. Urbana, IL: National Council of Teachers of English.

Bleich, D. (1978). *Subjective criticism*. Baltimore: Johns Hopkins University Press.

Booth, W. C. (1961). *The rhetoric of fiction*. Chicago: University of Chicago Press.

Booth, W. C. (1974). *Modern dogma and the rhetoric of assent*. Chicago: University of Chicago Press.

Britton, J. (1978). The composing processes and the functions of writing. In C. R. Cooper & L. Odell (Eds.), *Research on composing: Points of departure* (pp. 13-28). Urbana, IL: National Council of Teachers of English.

Bump, J. (1990). Radical changes in class discussion using networked computers. *Computers and the Humanities, 24,* 49-66.

Burke, K. (1953). *Counter-statement*. Los Altos, CA: Hermes Publications. (Original work published 1931)

Burke, K. (1963). *A rhetoric of motives*. Berkeley: University of California Press.

Christensen, F. (1978). *Notes toward a new rhetoric* (2nd ed.). New York: Harper.

Clifford, J., & Schilb, J. (1985). Composition theory and literary theory. In B. W. McClelland & T. R. Donovan (Eds.), *Perspectives on research and scholarship in composition* (pp. 45-67). New York: Modern Language Association.

Coles, W. E., Jr. (1974). *Composing: Writing as a self-creating process.* Upper Montclair, NJ: Boynton/Cook.

Coles, W. E., Jr. (1980). *Composing II: Writing as a self-creating process.* Upper Montclair, NJ: Boynton/Cook.

Corbett, E. P. J. (1971). *Classical rhetoric for the modern student* (2nd ed.). New York: Oxford University Press.

D'Angelo, F. (1975). *A conceptual theory of rhetoric.* Cambridge: Winthrop.

de Beaugrande, R. (1982). Psychology and composition: Past, present, and future. In M. Nystrand (Ed.), *What writers know: The language, processes, and structures of written discourse* (pp. 211-68). New York: Academic Press.

de Beaugrande, R. (1984). *Text production: Toward a science of composition.* Norwood, NJ: Ablex.

de Man, P. (1971). *Blindness and insight.* New York: Oxford University Press.

de Man, P. (1985). *The rhetoric of romanticism.* New York: Columbia University Press.

Derrida, J. (1978). Force and signification. In *Writing and difference* (pp. 3-30). Chicago: University of Chicago Press.

Eco, U. (1979). *Role of the reader: Explorations in the semiotics of texts.* Bloomington: Indiana University Press.

Eco, U. (1984). *Semiotics and the philosophy of language.* Bloomington: Indiana University Press.

Ehninger, D. (Ed.). (1972). *Contemporary rhetoric: A reader's coursebook.* Glenview, IL: Scott.

Elbow, P. (1990). *What is English?* New York: Modern Language Association and National Council of Teachers of English.

Elbow, P., & Belanoff, P. (1995). *A community of writers: A workshop course in writing.* New York: Random House.

Emig, J. (1983). *The web of meaning.* Upper Montclair, NJ: Boynton/Cook.

Fish, S. (1980). *Is there a text in this class? The authority of interpretive communities.* Cambridge: Harvard University Press.

Flores, M. J. (1991). Computer conferencing: Composing a feminist community of writers. In C. Handa (Ed.), *Computers and society: Teaching composition in the twenty-first century.* Upper Montclair, NJ: Boynton/Cook.

Forman, J. (1990). Leadership dynamics of computer-supported writing groups. *Computers and Composition, 7*(2), 35-46.

Foucault, M. (1970). *The order of things: An archaeology of the human sciences.* New York: Pantheon.

Freire, P. (1970). *Pedagogy of the oppressed* (M. B. Ramos, Trans.). New York: Seabury.

Gardner, H. (1982). *Art, mind, and brain: A cognitive approach to creativity.* New York: Basic.

George, E. L. (1990). Taking women professors seriously: Female authority in the computerized classroom. *Computers and Composition, 7* (special issue), 45-52.

Harris, J. (1991). After Dartmouth: Growth and conflict in English. *College English, 53,* 631-646

Hillocks, G., Jr. (1986). *Research on written composition.* Urbana, IL: National Council of Teachers of English.

Hirsch, E. D. (1987). *Cultural literacy.* Boston: Houghton.

Iser, W. (1974). *The implied reader.* Baltimore: Johns Hopkins University Press.

Iser, W. (1980). *The act of reading: A theory of aesthetic response.* Baltimore: Johns Hopkins University Press.

Kinneavy, J. L. (1971). *A theory of discourse.* Englewood Cliffs, NJ: Prentice-Hall.

Knoblauch, C. H. (1985). Modern rhetorical theory and its future directions. In B. W. McClelland & T. R. Donovan (Eds.), *Perspectives on research and scholarship in composition* (pp. 26-44). New York: Modern Language Association.

Madden, F. (1989). Using computers in the literature class. In C. L. Selfe, D. Rodrigues, & W. R. Oates (Eds.), *Computers in English and the language arts: The challenge of teacher education* (pp. 227-240). Urbana, IL: National Council of Teachers of English.

Miller, J. H. (1983). Composition and decomposition: Deconstruction and the teaching of writing. In W. B. Horner (Ed.), *Composition and literature: Bridging the gap* (pp. 38-56). Chicago: University of Chicago Press.

Murray, D. (1987). *Write to learn* (2nd ed.). New York: Holt, Rinehart, and Winston.

North, S. (1987). *The making of knowledge in composition: Portrait of an emerging field.* Upper Montclair, NJ: Boynton/Cook.

Ong, W. J. (1982). *Orality and literacy.* London: Methuen.

Pattison, R. (1982). *On literacy: The politics of the word from Homer to the age of rock.* New York: Oxford University Press.

Phelps, L. W. (1991). Practical wisdom and the geography of knowledge in composition. *College English, 53*(8), 863-885.

Rich, A. (1979). *On lies, secrets, and silence: Selected prose 1966-1978.* New York: Norton.

Richards, I. A. (1936). *Philosophy of rhetoric.* New York: Oxford University Press.

Richards, I. A., & Ogden, C. K. (1938). *The meaning of meaning: A study of the influence of language upon thought and of the science of symbolism.* New York: Harcourt, Brace. (Original work published 1923)

Rosenblatt, L. M. (1978). *The reader, the text, the poem: The transactional theory of the literary work.* Carbondale: Southern Illinois University Press.

Rosenblatt, L. M. (1983). *Literature as exploration.* New York: Modern Language Association. (Original work published 1938)

Selfe, C. L. (1991). Technology in the English classroom: Computers through the lens of feminist theory. In C. Handa (Ed.), *Computers and society: Teaching composition in the twenty-first century* (pp. 118-39). Upper Montclair, NJ: Boynton/Cook.

Winterowd, W. R. (1986). *Composition/rhetoric: A synthesis.* Carbondale: Southern Illinois University Press.

Winterowd, W. R. (1987). The purification of literature and rhetoric. *College English, 49,* 257-273.

Young, R. E., Becker, A. L., & Pike, K. L. (1970). *Rhetoric: Discovery and change.* New York: Harcourt.

Chapter • 12

Effective Teaching in the Online Classroom: Thoughts and Recommendations

John F. Barber

With increased promotion of computer technology like MOOs, local and wide area networks, e-mail, World Wide Web pages, Internet Relay Chat, discussion lists, hypertextual multimedia authoring systems, and commercial network-based collaborative writing/conferencing programs by government agencies, school districts, and individual teachers, much interest exists in "the online classroom" as a site for teaching and learning where multiple individuals can create social presences and realities that are both interactive and collaborative.

Scholars, researchers, and teachers interested specifically in using the online classroom for the teaching of writing point to several potential benefits: creation of social writing spaces or discourse communities that transcend the time, space, and place boundaries of the traditional classroom; new forms of writer-audience interaction; enfranchisement of marginalized voices; and movement of classrooms toward a more learner-centered context.

But, as Anderson Benjamin, Busiel, and Paredes-Holt (1996) rightly pointed out, the current realities of the online classroom do not always match the idealistic promotional hype. Critics[1] argue that access to

---

[1]Postman (1992) traced the movement of technology from supporting cultural traditions to competing with them to, finally, creating a totalitarian order with no use for tradition. Postman examined specific ways in which he saw technology tyrannizing

and utilization of computer technology is far from egalitarian; that writing created in computer-augmented environments is often vapid, and even offensive; that the claimed surmounting of gender and other socioeconomic differences is less than successful; that the loss of traditional contexts associated with teaching and learning (e.g., face-to-face interaction) is disorienting and disturbing for both teachers and students; and that the steep learning curve and extra work required of both teachers and students may offset the productive utilization of computer technology and the learning of course content. As Stoll (1995) said, "The struggle to write is entirely in the head. A computer cannot speed up the process" (p. 140).

Teachers of composition and rhetoric know that effective writers must consider the needs of their audience, as well as the purpose and language of their writing. Berlin (1982) called this a complex and ever-changing relationship between writer, reader, and the use of language to create reality. Although computers may not, as Stoll argued, speed up the writing process, they may facilitate the acquisition and effective utilization of writing processes, as well as promote the potential benefits cited earlier by facilitating a fluid, nonlinear, nonhierarchical context in which writers have a more immediate sense of interaction between writer and reader.

---

human culture. For example, he said that "In automating the operation of political, social, and commercial enterprises, computers may or may not have made them more efficient but they have certainly diverted attention from the question whether or not such enterprises are necessary or how they might be improved" (p. 116).

Following in this vein, Roszak (1986) argued that the driving force behind the so-called information age is a coordinated effort of technicians, bureaucratic managers, corporate elite, the military, and security and surveillance agencies to utilize computer technology and theory to obfuscate, mystify, intimidate, and control others. This "cult of information" operates like any other public cult, using catchphrases and clichés ("the information age/economy/society") to enlist "mindless allegiance and acquiescence" (p. x). One thrust of this mindset is to view computers as better or more proficient than the human brain, capable of surpassing or replacing the human brain through the development and implementation of artificial intelligence. "Accordingly, the powers of reason and imagination are in danger of being diluted with low-grade mechanical counterfeits" (p. xi). This results in a transfer of power to technicians, managers, and owners, the more affluent members of our society, and all promoters of the cult of information. Computer technology thus is diverted or subverted from democratic to subversive or oppressive functions that endanger freedom and survival, as well as the true art of thinking.

Balancing both Roszak and Postman's dark views, Talbot (1995) acknowledged the potential benefit of computer technology as a tool for the improvement of society, but only if we remain critical of both the context and the content of what it produces. "Machines become a threat," Talbott said, "when they embody our limitations without our being fully aware of our limitations" (p. 33).

Driven by this belief, many in the computers and composition arena are asking how they can most effectively make the connection between computer technology and teaching composition. They question how they can effectively and productively utilize the online classroom for teaching, how they can create online classroom contexts that support their pedagogies and curricula. Finally, they wonder how to deal with the changes to pedagogies and curricula wrought by the move into this new space for teaching and learning.

In this chapter, I suggest some answers to these questions by synthesizing my ongoing participant-observer ethnographic studies of university-level writing teachers making the transition from the traditional to the online classroom. In these studies, I watched writing teachers in "an amphibious stage" (Klem & Moran, 1991, p. 132) operating partly in print, partly on screen as they moved between the familiar traditional classroom and the unfamiliar online classroom. The gist of my findings is that although the experience may be unsettling, teachers can successfully make this transition and effectively utilize the online classroom. To do so, however, may require planning, preparation, and practice different or more extensive than what is required for the traditional classroom. In addressing this topic, rather than providing what ethnographer Geertz (1973) called "thick description" (p. 10), I synthesize and summarize some of my research findings and then, using these findings as examples, posit practical thoughts and recommendations that may help teachers become more comfortable and productive in the online classroom.

BASIS FOR ONLINE CLASSROOM STUDIES

Although there is debate concerning the effectiveness of computer technology for improving student writing, many promoters say that the online classroom is a place where discourse and interaction can be continuous and collaborative, affording participants the opportunity to extend and elaborate the oral culture they operate within on a daily basis (Zuboff, 1988); that this electronic dialogue can occur at any time, between multiple readers, and from distant locations, thus affording new models for pedagogy (Hiltz, 1986); that this social interaction in the online classroom can be built on multiple perspectives, and grounded in metaphors powerful enough to capture the essence of our current understanding of technology and "continue to extend our grasp of its potential" (Eldred & Fortune, 1992, p. 68).

Contentions like these have become the basis for the acceptance and utilization of computer-augmented composition, as well as the move toward the online classroom. Rather than a panacea for a variety of pedagogical problems, these and other studies suggest the complexity of issues that emerge for student writers and teachers when the traditional class-room, through the introduction of networked computer technology, becomes the online classroom. This work provides the beginning for understanding both the strengths and limitations of the online classroom as opposed to the potential for its use.

I believe that teachers considering using the online classroom should critically yet creatively examine the implications such a decision holds for their pedagogies and curricula. They should describe more and less productive modes of student uses, as well as teacher-supported peda-gogy. They should explore the different issues that emerge when writing teachers begin to examine the use of the online classroom or engage in a period of serious reconsideration of its use in order to develop broader descriptions of successful and unsuccessful online classroom pedagogical practices.

With these thoughts in mind, I conducted participant-observer ethnographic studies of writing teachers making the transition to the online classroom. One of my study sites is a northeastern state university where 17 students (all successful, practicing writing teachers) use an online classroom for a doctoral seminar investigating the implementation of computer technology into their developing pedagogies and curricula and what potential implications this may hold for the teaching and learn-ing of writing. They are, in essence, learning by doing, and observing them from the standpoint of an insider may provide useful guidelines for others wishing to utilize the online classroom. My choice of research methodolo-gy stems from repeated calls for naturalistic, qualitative, ethnographic forms of research and narrative related to the impact of computer technol-ogy on our pedagogies and curricula and on the social constructivist learn-ing of our students (Curtis & Klem, 1992; Herrmann, 1990; Klem & Moran, 1991; Selfe, 1992). By ethnography, I mean reporting culture, or as Barthes (1972) contended, developing a form of communication that decodes one culture while recoding it for another. This decoding and recoding, according to Van Maanen (1988):

> Rests on the peculiar practice of representing the social reality of oth-ers through the analysis of one's own experience in the world of these others. Ethnography is therefore highly particular and hauntingly per-sonal, yet it serves as the basis for grand comparison and understand-ing within and across a society. (p. ix)

And, as Allwright and Bailey (1991) suggested, this genre of research is characterized "as being a participatory, self-reflective and collaborative approach to research" (p. 44).

What this means is that qualitative ethnographic research can help develop theories grounded in concrete human realities of interaction and meaning by seeking the perspective of the insider. Furthermore, it may also influence the practice of research. For example, Jorgensen (1989) said participant-observation does not set itself against the participants in a study. Instead, where the tendency of a more objectivist quantitative research stance might be to provide a judgmental and evaluative frame for understanding the problems that teachers face in the online classroom by pitting the ethnographer against the participants, participant-observation adopts a more descriptive stance, one that is constructed through the observer's participation in the site or culture of the study. And, although these findings are fundamentally site specific and may not be universally applicable to similar situations (Lincoln & Guba, 1985), they can be used as insights to guide efforts in similar contexts.

INSIGHTS

With these caveats in mind, I offer these insights about the nature of the online classroom based on my studies.

Acceptable Level of Reality and Reliance on Writing

Discourse in the online classroom is conducted primarily through typed text displayed on computer screens. Despite the lack of face-to-face inter-action, participants feel this form of communication has an acceptable level of reality. A precedent for this notion is the use of the telephone. Although we speak and listen at our telephone handsets, we believe our conversations occur somewhere between our phone and that of the person to whom we are talking, and that our telephone conversations are "real" interactions with other people.

Denied voice and most other forms of communication in the digital text-based online classroom, participants interact through writing. In the online classroom contexts I observed, although not as comfortable with this method of communication as they would have been with face-to-face conversation in a traditional classroom, participants considered their discourse real enough to promote a sense of an engaging and interactive community. One 5-week course conducted almost entirely online pro-duced 1,394 separate replies, or approximately 178,432 words shared between its participants. As Scott Free (all participant names are pseudo-nyms), the teacher, said, "I see (read) 17 engaged people working at something that seems to be interesting to them and that I would judge to be of personal and professional value. That is sufficient for me to think that we are being successful [at engaging and communicating with each other]" (Barber, 1995, p. 463).

Text-Based Discourse May Create Communication Problems

Discourse in the online classroom, conducted and displayed entirely as lines of typed text on computer screens, removes the physical interaction as well as what Farb (1973) called paralanguage characteristics of face-to-face conversations. By paralanguage, Farb meant voice intonations, body language, and facial expressions. These features of nonverbal communication are often used by both the sender and the receiver in a communication situation to assure that the intended message has been clearly communicated and understood by the other party. Loss of these communication clues can promote misunderstanding.

For example, Leo and Kelly interacted in a lengthy online discussion that seemed to be emotionally heightened by their misreading of communication clues. Both Leo and Kelly are middle-aged women. Both are successful writing teachers—Kelly in a mid-Atlantic state, Leo in a Latin American country. Leo, responding to another participant's contention that literacy can be defined however we want, wrote, "There are political-economic systems here that are against class structure" (Barber, 1995, p. 308).

Kelly responded to Leo by saying, "Tell me more about the political-economic systems that are against a class structure. Are you referring to ideologies or to actual working systems?" and started this exchange.

Leo: I am referring to economic systems like, for example, socialism. What I mean is that society does not need to have economic classes as we know them but it requires a different mentality where the few are willing to sacrifice for the mass, and that doesn't happen very easily nor happen, most of the times, voluntarily.

Kelly: I thought that you were referring to a system in the abstract. But we do not live in the abstract—is there a society now existing (or one from the past) that did "not need to have economic classes as we know them"?

Leo: I do not understand your question. As a matter of fact, I am not referring to a system in the abstract but to a system that is not allowed to flourish by the power structure. Even though there are very good examples that are functioning very successfully there isn't much "advertisement" in the U.S. media. I do not think I have as much information on this topic as I would like to have, and we are moving farther and farther away from the readings. What do you think? It is also something that I do not think I can continue discussing through the computer screen.

Kelly: I disagree that my question is getting too far off the readings. If you are going to make such statements about economic systems in a public forum, I think it perfectly appropriate that you provide us with one (I'd be happy with one) system that is functioning in the way you are talking about. We wouldn't let our students off the hook when they overgeneralize, would we?

Leo: I am not one of your students remember? And I think that I have given you some examples already. Maybe we should go back to some of the previous responses and read carefully before jumping to reply mode. I think we are sometimes doing more responding than reading. (Barber 1995, pp. 308-310)

Leo and Kelly miss the points the other is trying to make and may be guilty, as Leo suggests, of "jumping to reply mode" before reading and carefully considering what the other is writing. These problems may have been addressed within the context of the traditional classroom where both speakers would have been able to hear the message conveyed by the speech rhythms and vocal emphasis of the other or seen the messages conveyed through body language. But here, in the online classroom, lacking these forms of communication feedback, the effectiveness of their ongoing dialogue is compromised. As a result, they end up talking past each other, each intent on making her own points, neither really "hearing" what the other is trying to say through typed messages displayed on computer screens.

Another problem is what Selfe (1992) called "grammars associated with virtual environments—the grammars of computers, of computer screens, operating systems, and networks" (p. 27) that replace the familiar grammars of the printed page and make navigating through text on computer screens quite different from turning pages in books or journal articles.[2] The computer screen itself, which offers a smaller view of text than we are used to in print-based media, poses an additional problem. The view of text on computer screens is generally limited to 16 to 25 lines of text. Longer text-based discussion, then, consists of multiple screens of small, often hard-to-read text. Zora Lake, another teacher involved in my online classroom study, cleverly expressed the difficulty and frustration of reading and responding to a seemingly endless scroll of glowing text dis-

[2]For some interesting examples and suggestions about how text might be presented and utilized online, see the online electronic journal *Kairos: A Journal For Teachers of Writing in Webbed Environments* <http://english.ttu.edu/kairos/>.

played on her computer screens: "Help! I'm suffering from 'carpal tunnel vision.' Has anyone studied the long-term effects of looking at a computer screen for extended periods of time?"

The problem, of course, is a lack of familiarity with the context of the online classroom. Zora Lake and other participants were unfamiliar and uncomfortable with using computer screens as a medium for reading text. Her identification of "carpel tunnel vision" led, interestingly, to a negotiation concerning shorter formats for posted messages rather than a discussion about how one might more effectively write or display written messages. Also, Zora Lake and the other participants never discussed navigational and search features of the conferencing program itself that promote easier manipulation of the text messages on their computer screens, as well as easier access to desired information within these messages.

In addition to being unfamiliar with the context of the online classroom, Zora Lake and her colleagues were also relatively unfamiliar with the computer hardware and software they were required to use in this course. Learning from this experience, teachers can address problems associated with electronic environments by teaching students how to use the navigational features of word processing or conferring software programs, by helping them become comfortable with the virtual grammars of computers, computer screens, and operating systems, and by encouraging them to practice and perfect these skills.

Discourse Is Ongoing

Despite problems associated with the reliance on typed text as the primary mode of communication, the online classroom can effectively demonstrate the fluid nature of writing—Faigley (1992) contended that online discourse is "a hybrid form of discourse, somewhere between oral and written" (p. 168)—as well as the changing relationships between writer, reader, and language, and can help participants envision writing as something more than a collection of rules for the construction of sentences and paragraphs. This, combined with the asynchronous archiving capabilities of most commercial collaborative or conferencing software programs and the opportunity for tele-access, means that the online classroom is available to both students and teachers beyond and outside the time, space, and structural boundaries of the traditional classroom.

The result is a multivoice, multivalent discourse in the online classroom that can continuously evolve within what Bakhtin (1981) called *heteroglossia:* the dynamic interactions between speaking individuals and the word meanings they employ. For Bakhtin, words are never fully owned by a speaker. They are half owned, he said, by the listener, the receiver, who uses his or her socially constructed knowledge to place meaning on the words he or she hears. Bakhtin contended that meaning is made through dialogic InterChange at the point where multiple word definitions overlap. And because any speaker is a member of multiple discourse communities, there are multiple voices, multiple forms of language usage, and multiple meanings potentially present in any dialogic InterChange.

As Cooper and Selfe (1990) suggested, this opportunity for ongoing and simultaneous discourse can promote the opportunity for participants to "learn from the clash of discourses, to learn through engaging in discourse" (p. 867). For example, participants in my study connected and engaged in discourse with someone's posted comments every day of the week, and at all hours of the day except from 2 a.m. to 5 a.m. Save for this time period, class was always in session and the interaction was ongoing. From what I observed, the benefits of this situation included the opportunity for participants in this online classroom to enter the ongoing discussions at any time, and within contexts they found personally comfortable. For example, Pisces, another Latin American teacher, "attended" class from her off-campus apartment and often prefaced her comments with the remark that she was reading and responding from the comfort of her bed! Other participants remarked that being able to always respond gave them more opportunities to reread and reflect on points made by their colleagues or more carefully craft their own responses.

Perceived Loss of Traditional Face-To-Face Learning Contexts

The notion of education has long been based primarily on the paradigm of personal interaction in an environment enclosed and defined by four walls, the traditional classroom. The online classroom may help transcend these boundaries of the traditional classroom and help create new sites for teaching and learning. But this move to the online classroom can be disconcerting as participants feel they are missing essential human contact by not meeting face to face. Some promoters of the online classroom attempt to address these concerns by saying "someone is always online," meaning that because of the perceived ease of communication, and the interactive relationship between writer and reader, a participant in the online classroom should be able to receive quick, albeit text-based, response or reassurance. But this reassurance may be of little help offsetting what Moran (1992) described as a sense of loss and dislocation as there is a move away from traditional contexts of teaching and learning writing, an experience that may be upsetting for many. Pisces, for example, was always uncomfortable with the online classroom, arguing poignantly in many of her messages that even the comfort of attending an online class from her bed was no substitute for face-to-face interaction, social collaboration, and community-building in the traditional classroom:

I'm still sitting in the lab and it's almost empty. I know everyone is out there in virtual space, but I kinda miss them here. Not sure if the sense of community which I've read about can develop as strongly as when we're looking at and "hearing" each other. It can get awfully silent here. Over and Out. (Barber, 1995, p. 295)

When Pisces wrote about knowing "everyone is out there in virtual space," she was saying she knows her online classmates are reading and responding to each other's written comments rather than talking with each other face to face. For Pisces, the computer lab, which functions as a portal to her online classroom, is empty, lonely, and quiet, as is the online classroom itself. Her closing, "over and out," speaks to the sense of detachment she feels in this unfamiliar and uncomfortable context.

Participation Varies

Beside the notion of community, one of the most commonly touted benefits of the online classroom is that it increases the participation of voices often silenced in the traditional classroom. As Hiltz and Turoff (1978) reported, because all participants in a computer-mediated context like the online classroom can talk simultaneously, no one person can dominate, no one can be interrupted, and multiple leaders are likely to emerge. This may encourage participants in the online classroom to express controversial or unpopular opinions and to consider those expressed by others based on "their merit rather than the status of the proponents" (p. 27). Priscilla is a good example of this. A middle-aged woman working toward a doctorate degree as a way out of her perpetual part-time teacher status, Priscilla found a sense of comfort and freedom in the online classroom not available in the traditional classroom. As she said:

I feel much more satisfaction with participation in this course since I have *EXACTLY* the same opportunity as the next person to have my say heard and reacted to. When certain ones have tried to discredit my contribution, the absence of the vocal and visual language have made the retort less personal. Therefore, I feel more freedom to be the REAL me online. (e-mail communication)

On the other hand, the online classroom can also decrease participation. For example, despite Priscilla's feeling that her opportunity to "have my say heard and reacted to" is increased in the online classroom, there is no guarantee that comments prefaced by her name would not be ignored by other participants, thus excluding her completely.

Paradigms Change

There are enough similarities between the traditional classroom and the online classroom, between working in physical space and in computer-augmented space, to foster the thought that successful pedagogical practices in the traditional classroom can be transferred unchanged into the online classroom. In fact, a great deal changes in the online classroom and successful practices in the traditional classroom may not work. For example, Scott Free, the teacher in this online classroom, consciously tried to remove himself from the center of focus and create a more student-centered environment in his traditional, face-to-face classes. He made sincere attempts to limit the number of times or ways in which he inserted his voice into the ongoing discourse, often sitting along the walls of the classroom listening but not speaking. Even though he did not speak, he was always present and students knew that they could turn to him when needed.

In the online classroom, however, teachers who do not speak are essentially invisible or, worse, nonexistent. As a result, students may feel alone and adrift in a strange place and consequently do not participate on a regular or increased basis. When Scott Free tried to duplicate his traditional classroom demeanor in the online classroom, he dropped out of sight and left his students feeling abandoned and bewildered. Only after receiving several pointed e-mail messages did he reenter the online conversation and address his students' concerns.

Teachers who prefer to foster social interaction and collaboration in the traditional classroom may find, in the online classroom, that students, feeling anxious and confused, actively desire some indications from the teacher about how they should act, what they should say, and how they should conduct themselves. While waiting for protocols or models on which to base their interaction, these students, feeling that they lack clear indications from the teacher about how to be successful in this new environment, exhibit disappointing levels of engagement and productivity.

Of course, it is argued by many that these situations are good, that they foster a much needed decentering of authority and that they give students a tremendous amount of power with which to direct their own creating and sharing of knowledge. However, the point is not whether the changing paradigm is good or bad, but that it can change when we move from the traditional to the online classroom, from the familiar to the unfamiliar. As I discuss further, teachers desiring to use the online classroom need to be aware of this potential for paradigm shift and be willing to adjust their personal pedagogy accordingly.

THOUGHTS AND RECOMMENDATIONS

Based on these characteristics of the online classroom I briefly outlined, I suggest the obvious conclusion: Teachers should experiment with ways to effectively and productively utilize the online classroom as a site for teaching and learning. Teachers should, as Lemonick (1993) suggested, learn to inspire, motivate, and referee the human-to-human discussion teaching and learning can promote. What follows are some brief thoughts and recommendations that, rather than providing complete answers, should be read as invitations for further critical thinking.

Rethink Pedagogy

The online classroom is not an electronic duplication of the traditional classroom. It is an extension into new and challenging dimensions. Educators cannot simply transfer or transpose theory, techniques, and teaching from the traditional classroom into the online classroom and expect consistently positive results. The online classroom requires that they create and conduct their pedagogies and curricula in different ways.

Three obvious pedagogical components of the online classroom that might be rethought are reading assignments, pedagogical style, and evaluation. Reading assignments that may seem appropriate in terms of length or difficulty for the traditional classroom may balloon in size and complexity in the online classroom. Remember that interaction and collaboration in the online classroom is conducted through a dialogue of typed text that must be read on computer screens. Lacking familiar grammars and techniques for navigating multiple screens of text, participants in the online classroom may find themselves awash in glowing characters. This sense of information overload may hinder engagement and may provide a focal point for unproductive resistance. Teachers alerted to this potential problem may consider scaling back their course reading assignments and modeling the production of shorter, but more succinct, written responses.

Teachers should also rethink their individual pedagogical styles. Although the use of networked computer technology to augment the teaching of writing is a relatively recent focus in the computers and composition arena, one consistent contention appearing in research and anecdotal reports is the democratizing or decentering model it brings to teacher-student and student-student relationships. Despite well-touted benefits, this "leveling" may require teachers to change their pedagogical styles. Teacher-centered teachers may have to move toward a more student-centered position in the online classroom, one that accommodates a new status for themselves, that of co-learner. On the other hand, student-centered teachers must realize that the newness and strangeness of the online classroom may be disconcerting to participants. This may mean that on occasion they should adapt a more active and directive role. In either case, the decentering of traditional models of authority in the online classroom may create what Pratt (1991) called contact zones, "social spaces where cultures meet, clash, and grapple with each other, often in contexts of highly asymmetrical relations of power" (p. 34), places where multiple voices can be heard and encouraged to learn from one another. In order to be most effective, teachers should be aware of this fundamental feature of the online classroom to foster multiple centers of authority and reconsider their personal pedagogy accordingly.

Evaluating the efforts, the work, and the learning of participants in the online classroom also requires rethinking. Many of my colleagues argue that the online classroom encourages students to become aware of the immediacy of their audience and the rhetorical situations from which their writing emerges or to which it is directed. This fluid nature of writing in the online classroom, according to the argument, will promote new compositional forms (which may, for example, contain multimedia or hypertextual/hypermedia links) based primarily on collaborative, interactive writer-reader relationships that concentrate on the issues of audience, content, and style. How do teachers, as evaluators, adapt to these process or product changes in writing produced in the online classroom? How do they evaluate writing produced in the online classroom? Given the relative ease with which participants can produce writing, as well as the ease with which they can continually revise and edit their writing, should the basis for evaluation be quantity? When participants can contribute writing to the online classroom essentially at any time, should they be expected to do so? Should daily contributions be expected? Twice a week? Once a week? And should teachers, if they are evaluating based on quantity of writing, differentiate between writing that addresses the course topics versus writing that, for example, explores topics of personal interest? How will they determine this differentiation? Or, if they intend to evaluate on the basis of quality, rather than quantity, how will they determine quality? And whatever the criteria for evaluation, do they/can they/should they give comparative letter grades? Why/why not? Should this even be a problem?

Plan Ahead

A basic strategy for teachers moving into the online classroom is to plan ahead. They should allow time to become comfortably grounded in the appropriate theoretical and pedagogical backgrounds. They should not assume that the online classroom will work with just the flip of a switch. It is necessary to become familiar with the technical and physical components of the online classroom in advance and then check everything before using it for teaching. Are all the computers connected and operating correctly? Is the necessary software installed and working correctly? If someone else previously uses the online classroom and changes some of its settings, can they be restored to the teacher's desired status quickly and easily? And what about the actual mechanics of the course? For example, what course components will be introduced, and when? How will they be introduced in such a way that they will be engaging for students of all levels of technological expertise? One answer might be handouts explaining or demonstrating the points the teacher is trying to make. A good test for effectiveness is for the teacher to personally walk through each handout, ensuring the instructions are clear and lead to the desired results, before it is actually turned over to the students. And, finally, in planning, teachers should also ask themselves how they will deal with problems.

Have Alternate Plans

Again and again, I observed teachers unravel as they were unable to follow their lesson plans when the online classroom failed. This vulnerability, coupled with the fact that they had no alternate plans, made their classes as dead and lifeless as the failed computer technology. The lesson here is straightforward: Teachers must not assume that the online classroom will always work. Numerous technical problems beyond the ken of the composition teacher can, without warning, turn the online classroom into a room full of technological tombstones. In these situations it is wise to have alternate plans. For example, if there is a problem with the computer technology associated with the online classroom, a return to paper-based work or face-to-face collaborative reading and discussion of writing is recommended. Many of the computer-based activities in the online classroom can be done just as successfully in the traditional classroom. The loss or malfunction of its computer technology means that the online classroom reverts to the traditional classroom, and there are many successful strategies for teaching and learning there.

As part of the alternate plans, teachers must realize the tendency of participants in the online classroom to interact with the technology, or with each other, in ways teachers may not expect. For example, the ability to send anonymous messages may encourage some participants to voice comments normally left unsaid. How should such situations be addressed? The new environment of the online classroom may also encourage participants to play rather than to work on task. This sense of play, although seemingly not a good attribute, may actually help online classroom participants feel more comfortable in an unfamiliar context, one devoid of the expected forms of connection and interaction found in the traditional classroom. The ability to play allows online classroom participants to make connections with each other that mask the perceived sterility of this environment.

Provide for Hands-On Training

The technological aspects of accessing and participating in the online classroom can be disconcerting to newcomers. Remembering the new and unfamiliar grammars and navigational commands can be very confusing and frustrating. Easily made mistakes can soon have participants stuck in unproductive attitudes, feeling stress over their inability to work productively. Simply talking about the theoretical perspectives behind the online classroom, demonstrating navigation through and utilization of its various components, and saying, "Here's what you can do" is not sufficient or effective. Teachers need to realize these implications and build in sufficient orientation and training opportunities for participants to become comfortable with the concept and utilization of the online classroom. Because participants are being asked to enter and utilize a new teaching and learning environment, sufficient time for them to learn the technological and virtual grammars necessary to navigate and be productive within this new space will help facilitate their transition. Participants (both teachers and students) in the online classroom, especially those with little or no experience with computer technology, want (require/demand) time to learn to use the new medium effectively and efficiently.

The most effective type of training may be hands-on where participants can see and feel what results are produced by the invocation of different commands at the keyboard. At my study site, students pressed me into explaining some of navigational features and textual strategies of the conferencing program they were using in their class. As I explained and drew pictures on the chalkboard, they sat and looked at me blankly. When we moved to the computers and they could see changes occurring on their screens as a result of the commands they entered, their expressions became more animated.

But where will the time come from to provide this hands-on training? One recommendation is to devote the first meetings of the online classroom to becoming comfortable with, and working within, the computer classroom. Will not an initial, intensive hands-on training period end up as an individual problem-solving situation for the teacher as he or she helps individual students with their particular problems? And will not such proceedings detract from a carefully prepared lesson plan? Probably so. But the opportunity for each student to learn individually by doing far outweighs, I believe, any perceived loss of teacher control. Furthermore, the time spent encouraging individual participants to practice what they are learning will be time well spent for both teacher and student. For the teacher there is the opportunity to assess individual learning progress and to anticipate future problems. For the student there is the opportunity to gain confidence using new navigational and textual strategies helpful in addressing a context for teaching and learning where all interaction occurs on the computer screen.

Address Modeling of Expected Participation

Should teachers provide models for participation in the online classroom? Feenberg (1989) asserted that computer-augmented communication requires context building, which can be provided by what he called "the teacher-moderator" whose role is "to summarize the state of the discussion and to find unifying threads in participants' comments" (p. 35). In other words, a teacher using Feenberg's model might moderate the ongoing discussion in an online classroom by summarizing important or interesting points and, then, using them as prompts for further discussion. The teacher might also synthesize the common threads of multiple exchanges, perhaps following common discussion threads, and use these prompts for further discussion in specific directions. Finally, the very way a teacher constructs on-screen messages in the online classroom—the word choice, the length, the use of subject lines or keywords—could model some expected or desired manner of participation. All of this is not so different than what a teacher normally does in the traditional classroom, with the exception that in the online classroom the teacher, like the students, must do all his or her interaction and collaboration through typed text displayed on computer screens.

On the other hand, a more successful strategy might be a laissez-faire approach promoted by Godwin (1994) that encourages letting participants hash out their disputes in public and develop their own community norms and system of discourse with relatively little modeling or direction. When, for example, information overload pervaded the online doctoral studies classroom I observed, participants, on their own initiative, negotiated the consistent use of names (real or pseudonymous) to identify parties in communication interchanges. They also negotiated focusing their interactions around specific topics instead of attempting to address every point made during their ongoing discussions. And finally, they negotiated shorter written messages, using a style they called "chunking," where they attempted to confine their discussion of separate points to a block of text approximately 16 to 20 lines in length.

These blocks or chunks of text were, by agreement, separated by a blank line. Although their written interactions with each other, and with the readings they were responding to, were often much longer than 16 to

20 lines, participants felt chunking their writing in this manner allowed readers easier access to ideas by displaying one important point or idea on a computer screen at a time. The blank lines between their points were thought to allow resting places for readers' eyes. This very interesting, and accurate, awareness of the difficulties of reading and interacting with text displayed on computer screens encouraged these teachers to rethink the interconnectedness of the needs of their audience and the purpose for their writing in the online classroom.

Each participant in this online classroom was a reader as well as writer, and each learned of the necessity to write for his or her readers with no direct imposition of models by the teacher. The advantage of this hands-off approach is that participants can effectively, and democratically, develop their own collaborative models for communicating with each other within the online classroom. The disadvantage of Godwin's suggestions is that the participant-generated evolution of collaborative models for dialogic interaction can be slow, resulting in missed opportunities for productive work when frustrated participants, unable to communicate effectively, withdraw.

In short, teacher-supplied models for format, style, or length of written interactions can help promote more effective communication within the online classroom from the outset but run the risk of being resisted if they are perceived as being imposed. As the examples from my observations suggest, students in the online classroom are just as capable of developing and utilizing their own models for interaction. So which approach is best? Perhaps neither alone, but instead both in the form of a compromise. For example, teachers could supply models for interaction in the online classroom (either through their own messages, posted templates, or private e-mail messages) that include header information like the author's name, name of person with whom the author is interacting, and the reason for the interaction (to respond to a previous statement, to ask a question, or to make a connection). The body of written interactions could be left to individual participants to design and write as they will.

Provide Channels for Productive Work With Topics

Interaction within the online classroom can be like a conversation at a party where everyone is talking at once, often talking past each other instead of with each other, and not always talking on task. But, like party conversation, or a discussion in a Burkean parlor, the seemingly chaotic discourse in the online classroom can be the very lifeblood of creative teaching and learning. And, unlike the ephemeral nature of party conversation, the conversation within the online classroom, or any online community, can be recorded and preserved, forming, according to Rheingold

(1993), a database that, through its organizational structure, can become a living guide for specific information.

At a party, the mental model that helps one make sense of multiple conversations involves focusing listening on conversations that hold immediate interest. In the online classroom, topics help focus discourse threads by defining particular areas of inquiry. Rheingold said topics serve as intelligent community filters "where people seeking information can be directed to the specific part of [the online classroom] where their area of inquiry is a topic of discussion" (p. 61).

Defined topics, then, can serve as useful and productive pointers to spaces within the online classroom where particular discussions can take place. The question of whether topics should be defined or created by either teachers or students, or both, is probably best left to negotiation as there are benefits either way. Teacher-defined and maintained topics may provide more definitive direction, definition, and focus to the ongoing discourse. They may also help maintain control over potential information overload and time spent off-task. Topics defined and maintained by students may provide them the opportunity to pursue their own interests, especially with regards to course projects.

Encourage Collaborative Course Projects

It seems counterproductive to encourage collaborative community-building within the online classroom for the duration of the course and then allow course projects to be created individually and privately outside the online classroom, aloof from the direct collaborative input of the classroom community. By pursuing course projects outside the online classroom, and not sharing them with others, participants effectively deny themselves a very real opportunity to explore the implications of working collaboratively to create meaningful knowledge within the socially oriented discourse community engendered by the online classroom. Students should be encouraged to engage in collaborative projects with fellow students, perhaps even students from other sections of the same course, or other students in similar courses taught at other institutions.

Allow for Face-to-Face Interaction

Earlier, Pisces spoke eloquently about how she felt the community building in the online classroom did not develop "as strongly as when we're looking at and 'hearing' each other" in the traditional classroom. For Pisces, and surely for other students, the ability to meet face-to-face is important for them to really "know" each other, a notion supported by

Godwin (1994) when he said a sense of community develops when "you see the same faces, know the same personalities, and have ongoing relationships" (p. 74). In the traditional classroom, students have the opportunity to get to know one another as the course proceeds. They see each other each time the class meets. The same is not always true in the online classroom. Therefore, to achieve balance, teachers might plan for the first class meetings, even if they are held in a computer-augmented classroom, to concentrate on face-to-face dynamics. Initial assignments in the online classroom might include writing and sharing biographical details. Responses from other participants could help develop the discourse of the online classroom. As the course progresses, scheduling regular face-to-face meetings might contribute to the maintenance of this sense of community, as well as fostering the development of collegial relationships and the opportunity to discuss topics of interest in more detail, and perhaps even more easily, than in the online classroom.

Allow Sufficient Time

Finally, new environments and new paradigms take time to accept and adapt to personal productivity. Teachers should not expect effective teaching and learning to begin immediately in the first days of the online classroom. Nor should they think that the opportunities for further learning will not continue beyond the duration of a course conducted in the online classroom. As Pisces said of her online classroom, "It ended when everyone was just getting the hang of it" (e-mail communication). Despite all our efforts at rethinking pedagogy, planning ahead, encouraging active participation in an ongoing dialogue, and providing models and topics for productive, collaborative work, the one consideration teachers may not be able to overcome is the lack of time in the online classroom in which to bring all their plans to fruition. The answer to this problem is, of course, inherent within the nature of the online classroom. As long as students can have access to the online classroom and continue talking with one another, class will be in session and the opportunities for teaching and learning will continue to evolve. With the online classroom, class does not end at the end of the hour, or day, or semester. It is always there, always waiting for someone to connect and interact with others.

CONCLUSION

In conclusion, the online classroom produces a context of great flux, a context where everything is infused with new meaning, tension, and great opportunity. I have tried to show some of this tension and opportunity through this compilation of insights garnered from my participant-observer ethnographic studies of writing teachers coming to grips with the implications for using computer technology in their own teaching of composition. Rather than report on the studies themselves, I have tried through this metatext to point out that the liminality of the online classroom is, for some teachers and learners, unsettling in that it replaces familiar paper with unfamiliar electronic text, verbal with visual orientation, oral with print interaction, and face-to-face with virtual context. But using the online classroom may outweigh these unsettling considerations and, in fact, may be of substantial benefit in that it promotes collaborative learning in socially constructed discourse communities available to all participants at all times. Teachers can successfully utilize the online classroom to promote these benefits but to do so requires planning and preparation that may be different or more extensive than what is required for the traditional classroom. In addition, teachers must, as Mayher (1990) suggested, develop the "capacity to learn from their teaching by being in continual conversation with it" (p. 283). Further critical yet creative investigation of using the online classroom as a site for teaching and learning composition will, I'm sure, prove interesting and productive.

REFERENCES

Allwright, D., & Bailey, K. (1991). *Focus on the language classroom.* New York: Cambridge University Press.

Anderson, D., Benjamin, B., Busiel, C., & Paredes-Holt, B. (1996). *Teaching on-line: Internet research, conversation and composition.* New York: HarperCollins.

Bakhtin, M. (1981). *The dialogic imagination.* Austin: University of Texas Press.

Barber, J. F. (1995). *Talking around the electronic campfire: An ethnography of writing teachers investigating computer-assisted composition within a computer conference.* Unpublished doctoral dissertation, Indiana University of Pennsylvania, Indiana, PA.

Barthes, R. (1972). *Mythologies.* London: Paladin.

Berlin, J. (1982). Contemporary composition: The major pedagogical theories. *College English, 44,* 765-767.

Cooper, M., & Selfe, C. (1990). Computer conferences and learning: Authority, resistance, and internally persuasive discourse. *College English, 52,* 847-869.

Curtis, M., & Klem, E. (1992). The virtual context: Ethnography in the computer-equipped writing classroom. In G. Hawisher & P. LeBlanc (Eds.), *Re-imagining computers and composition: Teaching and research in the virtual age* (pp. 155-172). Portsmouth, NH: Boynton/Cook.

Eldred, J., & Fortune, R. (1992). Exploring the implications of metaphors for computer networks and hypermedia. In G. Hawisher & P. LeBlanc (Eds.), *Re-imagining computers and composition: Teaching and research in the virtual age* (pp. 58-73). Portsmouth, NH: Boynton/Cook.

Faigley, L. (1992). *Fragments of rationality: Postmodernity and the subject of composition.* Pittsburgh, PA: University of Pittsburgh.

Farb, P. (1973). *Word play: What happens when people talk.* New York: Knopf.

Feenberg, A. (1989). The written world: On the theory and practice of computer conferencing. In R. Mason & A. Kaye (Eds.), *Mindweave* (pp. 22-39). New York: Pergamon Press.

Geertz, C. (1973). *The interpretation of cultures: Selected essays.* New York: Basic Books.

Godwin, M. (1994, June). Nine principles for making virtual communities work. *Wired,* pp. 72, 74.

Herrmann, A. (1990). Computers and writing research: Shifting our "governing gaze." In D. Holdstein & C. Selfe (Eds.), *Computers and writing: Theory, research, practice* (pp. 124-134). New York: Modern Language Association of America.

Hiltz, S. R. (1986, Spring). The "virtual classroom": Using computer-mediated communication for university teaching. *Journal of Communication, 36,* 95-104.

Hiltz, S. R., & Turoff, M. (1978). *The network nation: Human communication via computer.* Reading, MA: Addison-Wesley.

Jorgensen, D. (1989). *Participant observation: A methodology for human studies.* Newbury Park, CA: Sage.

Klem, E., & Moran, C. (1991). Computers and instructional strategies in the teaching of writing. In G. Hawisher & C. Selfe (Eds.), *Evolving perspectives on computers and composition studies: Questions for the 1990s* (pp. 132-149). Urbana, IL: National Council of Teachers of English.

Lemonick, M. (1993, Fall). Tomorrow's lesson: Learn or perish. *Time,* pp. 59-60.

Lincoln, Y., & Guba, E. (1985). *Naturalistic inquiry.* Beverly Hills, CA: Sage.

Mayher, J. (1990). *Uncommon sense.* Portsmouth, NH: Heinemann.

Moran, C. (1992). Computers and the writing classroom: A look to the future. In G. Hawisher & P. LeBlanc (Eds.), *Re-imagining computers and composition: Teaching and research in the virtual age* (pp. 7-23). Portsmouth, NH: Boynton/Cook.

Postman, N. (1992). *Technopoly: The surrender of culture to technology.* New York: Vintage Books.

Pratt, M. L. (1991). Arts of the contact zone. *Profession,* 33-40.

Rheingold, H. (1993). *The virtual community: Homesteading on the electronic frontier.* Reading, MA: Addison-Wesley.

Roszak, T. (1986). *The cult of information: The folklore of computers and the true art of thinking.* New York: Pantheon.

Selfe, C. (1992). Preparing English teachers for the virtual age: The case for technology critics. In G. Hawisher & P. LeBlanc (Eds.), *Re-imagining computers and composition: Teaching and research in the virtual age* (pp. 24-42). Portsmouth, NH: Boynton/Cook.

Stoll, C. (1995). *Silicon snake oil: Second thoughts on the information highway.* New York: Doubleday.

Talbot, S. (1995). *The future does not compute.* Sebastopol, CA: O'Reilly & Associates.

Van Maanen, J. (1988). *Tales from the field.* Chicago, IL: University of Chicago Press.

Zuboff, S. (1988). *In the age of the smart machine: The future of work and power.* New York: Basic Books.

PART · III

FOCUS ON ADMINISTRATION

This final section examines the work that needs to go on behind the scenes to contribute to good writing classes: what kinds of teacher-training programs are needed, what kinds of departmental supports are needed, and what kinds of workshops, attitudes, and materials are needed. The contributors to this section, however, do not offer prescriptive approaches to these issues; rather, they articulate a broad range of concerns, from the most theoretical to the most practical, that administrators and teachers should plan for. Integrating technology into teaching is a time-consuming, sometimes frustrating, always unpredictable process, and good programmatic support will enable individuals and departments to develop courses and teaching practices that support student learning in myriad ways. The complex interactions in any classroom can never be fully anticipated, but sound teacher training programs, and sound departmental rationales for computer-supported classrooms will make it much easier for faculty to take risks, solve problems, and explore the possibilities of computers in writing classrooms.

Kemp starts the discussion with a controversial account of common mistakes in the creation of computer-based writing programs and suggestions for ways technological pioneers can build their electronic skills without sacrificing the esteem of colleagues who may not understand their attraction for computers. Kemp argues that many, if not most, computer facilities arrive in English departments without broad-based support, and he further argues that the challenges to traditional notions of literacy and classroom practice that can arise from new electronic teaching practices can set up great divides between departmental revolutionaries and departmental advocates of the status quo. Drawing on his years of experience as a writing program administrator and software designer, Kemp charts a political and pedagogical course for innovative writing teachers.

Coffield, Essid, Lasarenko, Record, Selfe, and Stilley offer a more optimistic take on the practical and political problems Kemp describes. This chapter enacts the collaboration it argues for, bringing together voices from a range of institutions. Pooling their diverse experiences, the authors describe how both local as well as long-distance efforts support curriculum development, personal growth, and program development. Their sharing of classroom disasters—and inventive recovery strategies—will help newcomers feel able to make their own mistakes, and their sharing of online collaboration will help inspire newcomers to use electronic resources. They argue that planning must take into account individual, departmental, institutional and even community needs, and they provide a clear strategy for making the journey into the information age an exciting one.

While Condon's chapter explores the work that a group of experienced teachers produced, Mirtz and Leverenz offer a generative approach to faculty development for new teachers of writing. Drawing on their experiences with workshops for new teaching assistants, Mirtz and Leverenz argue that all teachers (not simply those who will be teaching in a computer room) need exposure to information about teaching with computers. Their thoughtful chapter offers multiple models for providing training to new teachers, and argues that introduction to computer technologies will "encourage teachers to be flexible, to take risks and move beyond the familiar." Their chapter argues as well that experiences in a computer-supported classroom allow teachers to create a critical distance from their teaching philosophies and thus critique their own practice more effectively. Their comprehensive guide to the concerns of program administrators will be a useful guide for those seeking to support new teachers.

Yagelski suggests that online components in teacher training courses help introduce preservice teachers to the use of critical reflection in theory and practice. His rich description of the use of a computer conference throughout the semester of an English methods course illustrates both how a thoughtful teacher can use conferencing to help students learn, but also how students can help each other learn about the complexities of teaching English. The voices of Yagelski's students mingle with his own in this lively account of a group of students at work. The computer conferencing helps support careful reflection, even as it challenges students to push their reflections further.

Chapter • 13

Surviving in English Departments: The Stealth Computer-Based Writing Program

Fred Kemp

When I began advocating the use of computers for writing instruction about 10 years ago, I had the naive idea that the principal concern in teaching was "functionality," a concern for continually increasing one's teaching effectiveness, no matter the means. I presumed, in the best logical-positivist tradition, that whatever one was doing in the classroom could be improved, and all that was necessary in order to convince one's colleagues about this method or that was to demonstrate improved functionality. Although I myself was no youngster at the time and was certainly not new to the classroom, I was quite innocent regarding what I have come to realize are stronger currents influencing how people decide what it is they do or do not want to do in their English departments.

My loss of innocence in this regard occurred in May 1987 when I was visiting a small southern campus as part of a grant to enhance faculty understanding of what was then called "computer-assisted instruction." It was the first time I had ever been paid to go to a campus and talk about computers. My host showed me about the English department and introduced me to various faculty we encountered along the way. In the faculty lounge, she introduced me to a rumpled sort with a peering way about him as "our visitor who has come to tell us all about computers." We shook hands, and then my host glanced at her watch and said, "Oh, I think we should go." The gentleman I had just met, who had already

267

turned away, said back over his shoulder, "Yes, you should." It was clear by his tone what he meant.

As insults go it wasn't particularly virulent, but it caught me off guard as I was proceeding dutifully to help a group of people who had asked for such help. My host dismissed the comment with, "Oh, he's a poet," as if by so identifying the gentleman she both explained and excused his attitude and treatment of a guest. I received, in a burst, a view of what I have since called "the Resistance" (capital R), my perhaps overly dramatic characterization of certain anti-technology attitudes thriving in many English departments among the "over-my-dead-body" faculty. The Resistance as I am defining it is not amenable to logic or demonstration or any sort of "proof" in the loose way we use the term in writing pedagogy. It composes a quite serious set of perspectives on academic values and what it means to teach and work in English departments, usually implicit and regarded as an improper topic for open discussion, but undoubtedly ignored at considerable peril by those who seek to shift the instructional paradigm by means of computers and networks.

Since that day I have visited more than 30 campuses in the United States and beyond for the purpose of reviewing local computer-based writing programs and suggesting means by which such programs could be established or improved. Although I hope that those who invited me have learned something from my visits, it is certain that I have learned a great deal from them about how computer-based writing programs are usually initiated, the archetypal mistakes that practically everyone makes, and the nature of the problem in persuading colleagues and administrators of the value of using network technology in their instructional efforts. I hope, in this chapter, to extract from my experiences a set of subtle understandings and practical guidelines for writing instructors who would like to see their students using networks and the Internet more, without risking their professional standing among colleagues.

HOW MOST COMPUTER-BASED WRITING PROGRAMS COME TO BE

My own experiences helping to establish a computer-based writing program at the University of Texas at Austin in the mid-1980s were rife with misconceived ambitions, hunches, serendipity, and no little subterfuge. What eventually became the highly successful and professionally supported Computer Writing Research Lab was actually more the result of a low-level comedic chaos than the sane and sober calculations we usually discover in retrospective publications. As more and more equipment flowed into what began as a diversion for several graduate students and faculty members, I began to realize that whatever the English department felt about using computers for teaching (and it didn't particularly care for it), the world at large was serious, in its own complex and chaotic way, about computers and changes in the way societal knowledge would be stored, transmitted, and used. Most of my friends and colleagues perceived signs of the impending change as pointing to nothing less than an intellectual apocalypse. But for reasons I have never fully understood but that I presume arose from a prior 13-year idealistic, and ultimately frustrating, teaching experience, I welcomed the possibility of radically transforming what we did for, and to, students. Accordingly, I set out to formalize my own understanding of how such facilities should be started and supported. I began my inquiry by reading Cynthia Selfe's (1989) *Creating a Computer-Supported Writing Facility: A Blueprint for Action.*

The book sets out an admirably clear agenda for proceeding from concept to fruition by including all relevant administrative and pedagogical elements in an open discussion of what writing is, what technology is, what learning is, what pedagogy is, and the importance of consensus regarding these vital elements. Selfe made three primary suggestions:

1. Plan computer-supported writing labs or classrooms so that they are tailored to writers, writing teachers, and writing programs, not computers.
2. Ground daily lab or classroom operations and instruction in the best of current writing theory, research and pedagogy.
3. Improve labs or classrooms by focusing on the writing programs and the writers' communities they support. (pp. xx-xxi)

She also said that "once a faculty has identified a set of instructional goals that will inform the educational activities of a computer-supported writing facility and a set of operational goals that shape the daily operations of that facility, other design decisions become increasingly simple to make" (p. 26).

Indeed. In fact, the entire book, although containing important specifics regarding implementation of computer facilities and instruction (and which I recommend as necessary reading even now), emphatically begs the central question of how to get the faculty to agree in the first place as to what the principal tenets of writing instruction should be, something that 20-plus years of pressure from the "New Rhetoricians" has not accomplished. It is on this need for such a facultywide agreement and the utter unlikelihood of achieving it that the central problem of establishing computer-based writing instruction hangs. In my years of teaching writing I have seldom seen even a group of PhDs in rhetoric and composition agree on instructional theory, goals, and implementation of methods. Technology introduces a whole new world of conceptual (and emotional) baggage into the matter.

As I visited campuses, I began to realize that the messy beginnings of the Computer Writing Research Lab were not an exception but practically the rule. I have never seen a computer facility based on a previously shared understanding of what instructional goals it was to serve, even when the proposed participants of such "sharing" are limited to those who would teach in the facility. Almost always an administrator makes what amounts to an isolated decision to introduce computers, usually for one or more of the following reasons:

- one or two important faculty have been relentlessly hounding him or her.
- the administrator has attended a conference session or read an article that promises obsolescence for administrators who do not "prepare for the twenty-first century."
- the administrator has undergone a personal epiphany regarding belief in computers through a sudden discovery of e-mail, multimedia, or desktop publishing (often accidentally through a son or daughter, a spouse, or a colleague).

If a consensus is achieved among those principally concerned, it probably has arrived after the decision has already been made and usually to go along with authority. Often several levels of administrators are bypassed by grant money that establishes a computer-based classroom (as happened at the University of Texas), but again such money is almost always the result of one or two people's efforts, either those of the grant writers or of those who decide, at some invisible level, that such and such a department should enter the computer age, and never (in my experience) from a desire among teachers to support a shared understandings of writing instruction. The importance of a single, perhaps even single-minded, advocate for the technology cannot be overstated, no matter from what motivations that advocacy arises.

Once a facility has been established and a group of people begin teaching in it, certain shared understandings about writing instruction do arise, not so much because the instructors have openly negotiated such understanding but because teaching in a computer network environment offers very clear paths of least resistance toward distinct curricular emphases (which I would characterize as collaborative, peer-critiquing, and student-centered). The instructional environment itself, for those who continue to work in it, shapes attitudes toward teaching and student-to-student interactivity that eventually, more or less, cohere. Subsequent facilities, therefore, often are proposed and supported with the honest and open sense of purposefulness that Selfe described. This is not to say that such common instructional attitudes or shared understandings inevitably arise from the initial facility. To be successful both politically and pedagogically, an initial computer-based classroom must overcome a discouraging array of often hidden dangers, most of which I try to cover in this chapter.

For most of the faculty (and in the case of grant money, for administrators too) the computers suddenly appear, a room is appropriated, and a search commences for those full- or part-time faculty who will engage, in some entirely unforeseen fashion, with the computers. In other words, computers and networks are acquired not because they will allow the implementation of a commonly agreed-on pedagogy but because of outside social and commercial forces and the universally vague (and undoubtedly correct) belief that our students need them if they are to "compete" in that gloomy domain, the "modern world." Selfe's insistence that the pedagogy should come first is proper, but such doesn't normally happen. In fact, computers are usually introduced into a department for what—from a writing instructor's point of view, anyway—are the wrong reasons and by the wrong people, and this usually leads to a series of decisions that tend to work against the immediate success of a computer-based writing program. Those who support the instructional use of computers must be aware of this realpolitick and prepare alternative Plans B through Z.

There are fears, reasonable enough, that producing a computer-based instructional facility for the wrong purposes supported by people with presumably reductive intentions will lead to instructionally harmful implementations. For instance, many people worry about using computers acquired by administrators who seem dangerously intrigued with automating instruction or reducing teachers to the role of technicians. But the facilities themselves, the networked computers themselves, militate against such retrogressive tendencies, once they are in place and being used by teachers. Actual experience dramatically revises expectations and prognostications, both good and bad, and encourages a student interactivity and motivation that tends to self-structure good pedagogy. This dynamic, frankly, does not make sense to those schooled in positivistic attitudes toward planning and prediction, which is one reason why the whole issue of introducing technology into classroom instruction in English departments engages such a mix of uncertainties and even fear.

THE ROMANTIC TRADITION AND DEPARTMENTAL ELITISM

English departments traditionally have not looked with favor on technology. Such disfavor probably stems from attitudes established in the 18th and 19th centuries when aestheticism, most particularly romantic literature, developed antipathies toward science and industry and especially the notion of utilitarianism, seeing in them forces that challenged humanist tendencies and a transcendent, even mystical, communion with nature. As a result, a bifurcation came to exist in the minds of many humanists that drew the line between the techniques and technologies of mankind and its aesthetic efforts, one that aggressively asserted that a person could not live in both worlds without compromising humanist sensibilities. Teaching itself, to many faculty who often vocally eschew pedagogy and "educationists," is seen as something of an art and consequently foreign to articulated processes. The presumed sheer mechanistics of computing threaten in many people's mind to reduce an art to little more than a procedure. Then too, language itself is usually presumed impervious to the analytic codes and formulas on which, it is also presumed, a machine must depend (as witnessed by the continuing inability of even the most powerful computers to hold a simple, intelligible conversation). The introduction of computers into the "art" of teaching writing seems to many faculty to be yet one more move to strip language of its sublimity.

The romantic rejection of technology has, at its heart, however, an elitism that often masquerades as a core concern for human values. And within that elitism, as within all elitisms, exists a resistance to the mutability of the human condition, to the *transitoriness* that defines humanity much more than does any stasis on which elites establish and defend their authority. Although at one level exists an undoubtedly sincere love for the cultural artifacts on which a particular elite has staked its claim to special knowledge, at a darker level such cultural artifacts become the anchors for privilege. Knowledge of books, for instance, of the "texts" that frame academic success within English departments, sets the pecking order. Publications and research grants merely provide tangible validation of a knowledge of texts; they are the "meters" that score the academician's value to the scholarly community.

Those who determine the elements of value in such communities are those who, in short, set the criteria for who gets published and who gets grants. In the crudest terms, these people pick and choose which members of the community best demonstrate special knowledge of the artifacts on which the community chooses to stake its reason to exist. The process contains a neat circularity that tends to confirm those already in authority and to resist any challenge to either the artifacts that anchor authority or to the criteria that judges merit. There is nothing in this description that should surprise or appall any educated person. Complex interactions among any group of people tend to resolve themselves this way, allowing social order to emerge.

The problem arises, as Kuhn (1962) made clear, when social or technological change (and they are really perspectives on the same thing) force a re-evaluation of the artifacts of value themselves, in effect bringing outside pressures to bear on the closed circle of value that the elite, usually with the uncritical acquiescence of the nonelite, has been able to maintain. In science, this occurs when progressively acute means of observation begin to make certain explanatory paradigms suspect and new explanatory paradigms begin to form. The elite typically engage in a heated rear-guard action, ridiculing new and unproved frames of meaning all the way to the citadels of professional organizations and standard-setting bodies, whose role is to maintain "purity" or "clarity" within the principal knowledge domain. Eventually, however, the old ideas sink, revealed as little more than the fixations of older colleagues, and a new elite assumes authority, usually proclaiming that it will never fall into the mindless conservatism of its predecessors. A new set of artifacts are trotted out, new patterns of reverence are established, and guards and checkpoints again are set up along the paths to special knowledge. The process is not always readily visible, but an example in English departments might be the overthrow of philological criticism by New Criticism, or New Criticism itself by poststructuralist critical stances. Nobody lowers the flag and marches out of the garrison into the desert, but the professional effect is undeniable.

This review of human nature is not intended as criticism of a process that is quite beyond criticism, but rather as a foregrounding of the rules of engagement for those who, perhaps quite innocently and idealistically, have accepted the role of revolutionary. The struggle, in other words, will not be easy. Those who would use computer technology in significant ways in English departments are not simply combating ignorance or technophobia. The struggle does not hinge on educating the senior personnel or demonstrating how well this or that works. Although we bring our colleagues into our networked classrooms, let them see our students' Web pages, shower them with Interchange and MOO transcripts, and spend sincere hours detailing patiently the marvelous learning that we see going on in computer-mediated student interaction, the unconvinced remain unconvinced, the Resistance remains intact. The issue is not functionality, but rather fears of transition, of loss, and of the unthinkable invalidation of the work of lifetimes, and so much of it occurs unconsciously, beneath a presumption that instructional effectiveness is the only issue on the table.

This is not to say, of course, that all faculty divide on so serious a fault line, or that even most faculty engage much one way or the other. Most faculty will simply ignore the whole issue of computers and writing, and when queried will exhibit a mild approval or disapproval depending on the circumstances and the audience. But often the fortunes of a computer-based facility are influenced, sometimes profoundly influenced, by the hardened attitudes of a few senior faculty, and it behooves the computer advocate to remain aware of why such attitudes arise and persist.

THE PSYCHOLOGY OF ADVOCACY AND ITS PERILS

Actually, the struggle to achieve consensus on writing theory, or even the grudging acceptance of computers in the classroom by most of our department or campus colleagues, is not necessary. Computer aficionados should free themselves of the notion that they are the principal agents of change in the department, and especially free themselves of any self-conceived nobility for being such agents. Change, in fact, will occur with or without them, although possibly more slowly. Even if the computers are improperly assembled, the wrong software purchased, and a pedagogy implemented that fights the computers rather than uses them, change will occur. The computers will eventually be upgraded, the right software purchased, an effective curriculum will evolve, and all the wrinkles in a plan that poor initial decisions cause will smooth themselves out, eventually.

The important thing for those who encourage such changes is survival. They must ride the transition in such a way so as to influence important decisions without confronting the Resistance openly or dwelling on its presumed ignorance or technophobia. Teachers are all missionaries of a sort, and they have a tendency to seek and even need the publicly proclaimed conversion of those who do not have their vision, whether the issue be great literature or computers in the classroom. Far too many teachers are not averse to converting by the sword. But the demarcation between those who encourage change and those who resist it usually falls between those on the margins of authority and those at the center, for reasons I presented earlier. Even when the computer enthusiast succeeds in a confrontation, wins a close faculty vote, secures a dean's override of a faculty committee's recommendation, that person may well have lost the larger issue. Far too much of what is needed to make computer-based classrooms succeed to a large extent depends on the benign neglect of the faculty at large over a period of years.

What the computer enthusiast should do, rather than press the issue openly, citing commonsense and Alvin Toffler, is read everything there is about using computers in English departments, good and bad, pro and con. The principal understanding that should be encouraged to ferment is that using technology in humanities instruction is an incredibly rich and messy subject, practically uncharted despite the profusion of academic articles like this one, and certain to take a form on any one campus unlike anyplace else. As academics we resist the idea that solving a problem is not simply a matter of bringing to bear an irresistible theory and chopping it down to size until it fits our situation. But in fact, computer technology and especially the Internet is rebuilding the nature of distributive learning in this country in models that are morphing too quickly to be captured in any grand scheme.

Too many of our idealistic pro-computer colleagues argue from principle, heatedly bemoaning the always obvious fact that what takes place in the teaching profession too often subverts real learning among students in favor of individual career advantages and institutional perquisites. They spend great effort and no little time attempting to tweak the bureaucracy openly, perhaps reveling in their identity as unappreciated saviors. What should count, however, is neither legitimacy nor prophecy, but rather the ability to encourage effective change and extract students from the stifling grip of current traditional writing instruction that, as long as the traditional classroom environment exists, will most likely continue to dominate general instructional practices.

The flip side of aggressive idealism is premature discouragement. Many messages on e-mail discussion lists (such as ACW-L) describe abortive attempts to persuade colleagues and administrators of the validity of computer-based instruction and the bewilderment when one encounters those who "simply refuse to listen." A malady common to most computer-instruction enthusiasts is the presumption that their sudden and total conversion to the use of computers is characteristic of all or most teachers, if only those teachers were provided a proper demonstration of what computers and networks do. Not understanding the Resistance, sometimes clotheslined by sudden negativity in the midst of a presumably triumphant presentation, these enthusiasts often slip as quickly into despair as they leaped into advocacy.

What is required is time, strategy, and humor.

THE "STEALTH" COMPUTER-BASED INSTRUCTION PROGRAM

I recently visited a mid-sized university in which English department administrators spoke aggressively about their determination to employ computer technology in instruction. Money was apparently no object, nor would tradition or seniority be allowed to stand in the way. Later that afternoon I managed to wrangle a meeting with the writing faculty by itself in an informal setting. As usual, the representatives of the writing faculty were predominantly women, youngish, and disturbingly earnest, and as usual, they told a different story from what I had heard in the morning.

As we huddled around a small table, I heard the real story, which in my experience has become something of an archetypal narrative. Massive pressure from above, a provost in this case, had profoundly shaken the department chair out of a 5-year lethargy regarding computers, and he had called in the usual star chamber of departmental authorities and informed them that despite their misgivings, the department would be networked and a computer-based classroom would be installed. Furthermore, the writing program would manage the room because a computer-based instruction would obviously be too reductive for literature. The director of the writing program was called in, given the good news, and told to find people to manage the new equipment. The chair obviously expected profuse gratitude from the director of the writing program, and she supplied it.

But she was not sure the gratitude was deserved. For one thing, neither she nor any of the senior members of the writing program were especially excited about using computers to teach writing nor, outside of their own use of word processing, knew much about computers at all. For another, it meant she would have to deal more closely with the notorious campus computing authority, a group of techno-warlocks sealed in a concrete building across campus with infamous and open disregard for the humanities. But most important, her long-time efforts to establish writing as a valid area of scholarly investigation were seriously threatened. Computers, she knew, carried with them the taint of commerce and technocracy; she and her associates would be guilty by association, and years of trying to validate the academic study of writing and pedagogy among her noncomposition colleagues would be subsumed in the florescent glow emanating from the computer "lab."

What I recommended for that writing program was what I call a stealth computer-based program, a departmental jujitsu for encountering the Resistance. Expectations for what the computer lab would accomplish should be ratcheted down to floor level. No immediate high-level determination should be made about scheduling the room or developing instructional methods or even which personnel should do these things. Above all, no individual should be arbitrarily assigned to manage the computer-based classroom by people above him or her in the hierarchy.

Why? Within every assembly of personalities and ambitions that informs an English department, there exists at least one person who will respond with delight to the instructional possibilities of computers. "Delight" is the operative word here. The central trick of administrators who honestly wish to develop a computer-based instructional effort is to find that person, or rather, to allow that person to come forth. The problem is that such people are often, almost by definition, of otherwise little consequence to the department. One of the usual characteristics of people who demonstrate a fascination with computer-based instruction is that they have little stake in the status quo: They are usually young or late-starters in the profession, have achieved little currency in the profession's credit mechanism, and (because of the student-based nature of networked instruction) tend to be advocates of teaching and of revising authority structures in the classroom.

Perhaps the most straightforward way of determining who should or would sponsor a computer-based instructional effort is to call a meeting of those "interested" in working with computers in some undefined fashion, emphasizing that everyone in the department may attend on an equal footing, and then, during the meeting, to offer the directorship of the department's computer-based instructional effort to whoever presents the best case for himself or herself. A usual departmental assumption that militates against this "open" policy of determining who will spearhead the department's computer effort is that the computers are too valuable and the possibilities for "irresponsible" teaching too great to entrust it all to a volunteer, someone who quite possibly might not be a team member (outside the department's intimidation structure). But the chances are slim to nil that somebody assigned involuntarily to the job will put in the effort or demonstrate the instructional flexibility to make the technology work. The wise senior administrator must be aware of this, or his or her efforts to "bring the department into the 21st century" are likely to produce an expensive white elephant and embarrassingly unused facilities.

The main operating principle here, and it is a cumbersome one to get across to suspicious devotees of hierarchy, is that people who can make magic with computers and teaching quite often have not found a prior niche in academia and have therefore developed little previous clout or reputation. Although this itself is a romantic notion, most of the people I know in the tiny field of computers and writing who have assumed the lead in theory and practice have seemed almost destined for the field and for little else within the reward structure of English departments. To say this is not to saddle them with limitations or lack of ability, but to underscore that some people do not shine competitively until it is their game that is being played. It is the senior administrator's job to recognize that with computers a new game is being proposed for his or her department.

Once the stealth program is in place, which means little more than having a networked computer-based classroom actually working and an eager volunteer guiding its activities, the operation should go gently underground. People who want to teach in the room will gravitate toward it, over time, and if provided enough time, will be sufficiently robust in their intentions to overcome the inevitable initial series of frustrations (both technological and curricular). Advertising the room to the faculty at large, on the other hand, and generating workshops "to get them to use the computers," simply emphasizes to some people the raw character of what seems to them intimidating changes, seems to propel a number of people into computer-based methods before they have resolved their own motivations, and stiffens the Resistance. Then too, a stealth computer-based writing program downplays, for a while at least, the link between composition and technology that can dismay writing program administrators and writing center directors who have sought a different ethos.

The two major programs I have been involved in, the Computer Writing Research Lab at the University of Texas at Austin and the Computer-Based Writing Research Project at Texas Tech University, were essentially stealth programs, for several important years practically invisible to all but the few teachers and curriculum developers who sought them out on their own. The number of sections taught grew slowly over those years, but experience over time was allowed to guide the development of syllabi and instructional tasks, and frustrations were ameliorated without the stress of publicity. By the time both programs cast off their stealthy guise, they were rock-solid, confident, with accumulated patterns of success that could attract innovative and competent teachers and defuse criticism relatively easily.

DOING THE RIGHT THING FOR THE WRONG REASONS

Kemp (1987) challenged the "robotics assumption" regarding computers, the almost intuitive belief that computers can indeed do some of the things workers already do, and indisputably do them faster and more precisely. The robotics assumption assumes that computers are efficiency devices and that those parts of life that do not respond well to efficiency—art, music, and just about anything that a humanist would consider a valued activity—are, or should be, outside the realm of computer influence. "Efficiency," as we must all agree, in some areas improves lives and in other areas reduces lives. What I argued then and continue to argue is that the robotics assumption is a convenient pigeon hole for anti-technologists to use in disposing of unpleasant notions, and puts computers in a "damned-if-they-do, damned-if-they-don't dilemma.

Most people who do not understand the real value of computers to an instructional program and yet continue to advocate them fall under the spell of the robotics assumption. They assume that bringing computers into an instructional effort will reduce the need for an expert teaching staff, speed up (in some undefined way) the "learning" that students are supposed to be ingesting, and assert more central control over the whole business. In other words, computers will bring efficiency to a system that seems to need it.

But in learning, as in many important activities in life, efficiency is not necessarily a productive characteristic. The pursuit of efficiency as it is commonly defined may indeed be reductive, and even destructive, for certain learning goals. Therefore, the reason for which many administrators seek to include computers and networks in their instructional programs may be precisely the same reason for which anti-technologists reject out-of-hand the use of computer technology in classroom instruction: efficiency. The central irony is that the robotic assumption, which defines personal computers as basically engines of efficiency, completely mischaracterizes computers in writing instruction.

Actually, computers and computer-mediated communication (CMC) in writing instruction are not efficient at all, and in some ways are much less efficient than a current traditional instruction that relies on lectures and teacher-centered discussion. As a classroom teacher of more than 20 years experience, I know that few classes run as smoothly as those in which I fill the time simply talking at my students. No homework assignment is as efficient as assigned exercises from a handbook. If efficiency in the classroom and throughout a writing program were a principal criterion of instructional success, then what has evolved through a century of prescriptivist lore and classroom control in the oral classroom must be considered the epitome of success.

The same reasoning confronts the argument that computers provide greater administrative control. In truth, computer-based classrooms liberate both teachers and students from the deeply ingrained expectations of behavior that dominate almost every teacher and student who enters that rectangular room of desks, blackboards, and "stage," where the teacher rules. What controls the usual classroom is not Big Brother monitoring class sessions through computer screens, but rather an overwhelming set of practically irresistible assumptions about what is and is not supposed to happen in a U.S. classroom. The robotics of U.S. education were in place long before Neumann and Bush and Turing ever conceived of the computer.

In accordance with the nature of the stealth computer-based writing program, however, it may not be necessary to disabuse senior administrators of their expectations that the computers will provide greater efficiency, a lower payroll, and more program control. Once a cadre of experienced instructors has evolved and the nature of computer-based writing instruction has been well developed locally (which may take several years), firm arguments can be made from experience that will counter the intuitive belief that computers automate instruction and bypass the human element. Once a department has built a solid history of computer-based instruction, the true value of such instruction—better learning—will become common knowledge, gained not through rhetorically charged memos and speeches in faculty meetings, but through the most powerful opinion-changing medium of all, casual hallway conversation.

ANSWERING THE TOUGH QUESTIONS

The resistance to technology, I have discovered, presents a series of tough questions that remain remarkably similar among campuses and across a variety of instructional levels. At the most functional level of change, the computer enthusiast needs to be prepared for such questions. Here are my rejoinders to the toughest questions.

Why Change What Already Works?

There is a tendency to believe that whatever pedagogy is currently in place has somehow proven itself in some way, as if it had undergone at a time in the past a standard of proof that we now ask (sometimes zealously) of newer pedagogies. In fact, no primary pedagogical emphasis—formalist, expressivist, cognitive, or social—has ever been proven more effective than any other, and no method ever shown in any objectively verifiable way to produce better writing than any other, regardless of claims.

Those who wish to stick to the tried and true are simply giving tradition and time more due than they deserve, having succumb to the honored human tendency to validate the familiar for simply being familiar.

Where am I Going to Find the Time to Learn How to Use Computers?

The question presumes that whatever current activities fill the schedule are necessary, that learning about computers will require "finding" additional time. But if one values what computers can do to assist instruction (in other words, if one becomes steeped in the literature over time), then much previous activity begins to pale in importance and become replaced by work on and with the computer. People who have defined important scholarly and instructional activity as a particular set of tasks, say, making up and grading quizzes, begin to discover that interactive learning behavior on networked computers slowly assumes an increasingly important role relative to making and grading quizzes. "Making time" for the computer becomes no more or less an issue than "making time" for reading or "making time" for grading.

Aren't Computers Too Expensive for Our Modest Program?

Computers are too expensive for English departments only if they are assumed to be "add-ons," or peripheral to the main instructional mission of the department. Once those in English studies recognize that their principal activity, working with words, is in this day and time an activity clearly dependent on word processing, network information access, and electronic publishing, then computers and networks stop being glamorous and start becoming essential, in much the way that microscopes and

Bunsen burners are essential to chemistry studies. The level of acquisition may always be in contention, but the prohibitive cost of computers at all is a presumption built on the notion of computers and networks as peripheral to what English departments do. That presumption is changing rapidly

Don't you Spend Too Much Time Teaching How to Use Computers and Not Enough Time Teaching Writing?

One might as well ask if maybe the first or second grader is spending too much time trying to form letters and not enough time learning to write. The distinction between learning to write and learning to use a computer to write is fast disappearing in a society that increasingly realizes the liability of doing any extensive writing without a computer.

Responsible teachers learn quickly when computer and software instruction extends beyond a general writing and email functionality and enters into a level of training unnecessary for the genre of writing the course supports. General composition classes would not need training or practice in 90% of what a powerful word processing program like Microsoft Word can do, but a technical communication class may indeed need sophisticated instruction in esoteric desktop publishing features. If time is "wasted" learning unnecessary aspects of the equipment and software, then the teacher has not developed a sense of what is and is not necessary to support the goals of a particular course, an eternal problem of course preparation.

Isn't "Teaching With Computers" Just Another Instructional Fad Like Open Classrooms and Sentence Combining That Will Eventually Fade Into the Long Sunset of Trendy Practices?

No phenomenon in the history of the world has gained such an immediate influence on people's daily lives as had computer technology and the Internet, including all major religions, the industrial revolution, the cinema, and television. It is estimated that if the current exponential rate of growth for access to the Internet were to continue, by the year 2001 every individual in the world would be connected. The sheer social force of computer technology not only makes it impossible to characterize as a mere "fad" of any sort, it makes the avoidance of computers in any meaningful area of human endeavor practically futile. Writers in various publications commonly see our world in the throes of a "third revolution," an "information revolution," following on the Neolithic agricultural revolution and the late 18th-century industrial revolution. The principal technology of so momentous a change can hardly be discounted as a "fad" nor rejected as simply an irritating distraction.

Won't Administrators Take the Increased Use of Computers as an Excuse to Increase Class Load and Reduce Tenure Faculty?

This will not happen if an informed and experienced group of teachers in that department demonstrate the absurdity of the "efficiency" argument based on a solid history of successful instruction and the vitalization of composition. It will certainly happen if teachers reject all engagement with the issue.

One must address such questions carefully, for as described here, the resistance to the use of technology is often a deep-seated matter of epistemological proportions, and questions thrown in the path of the would-be paradigm shifters are often delaying tactics in service of unspoken and less civil opinions, not open queries seeking real answers. But such questions must be responded to, or the game goes no further.

CROSSING THE BRIDGE EVEN AS WE BUILD IT

An engineer plans and builds a bridge before he or she sends people across it. New pedagogies, however, and especially those enhanced by emerging technologies, must engage in a process apparently far less sensible, one that engages a complex of human and technical factors in a largely unpredictable mix. It is a troubling and even outrageous fact that in developing new computer-based instructional processes, all we can build on each day is what we learned the day before, and this constructive process requires a faith in what we are doing that flies in the face of modernist presumptions of cause and effect. We must cross the bridge even as we are building it, or as one techno-wag described how distributive development of the Internet was occurring: "the equivalent of modifying a 747 while it's in the air" (Steinberg, 1996, p. 206).

It is easy enough to explain why. Mechanical systems are designed according to well established principals in which highly directed and unique elements are integrated to produce a single, clearly measurable function. Witness the automobile, or indeed, any machine. Allowing Mumford's (1967) expansion of the term *machine* to apply to any rigorously hierarchical human organization, consider a national militia or a factory of the 1950s, or an "ideal" national curriculum. Much of our desire to apply tough standards of "proof" to alternative pedagogies (although exempting our current pedagogy) arises out of an uneasy alliance between those who wish to avoid foregrounding pedagogy at all, considering teaching to be an implicit and transparent skill of all properly educated people, and those who see formal instruction as mechanical systems that can be disassembled for objective analysis. Mechanical systems can be designed, built, and used, and they can be fairly easily analyzed.

Organic systems, on the other hand, arise from an evolved, interactive mix of elements that "self-structure" their cooperative functions through growth, intense communication, trial and error, and feedback. Ironically, the Internet, the greatest technological achievement of modern times, more closely resembles organic than mechanical systems, to the great consternation of some and the delight of many. The Internet is universally recognized as an "evolved" rather than a designed system. Instructional environments that support high student interaction and feedback likewise seem more like organic than mechanical systems. Much of the strength of computer-based classrooms accrues from human behavior that has been enabled by the instructional environment, but not channeled by it.

So the pedagogy that arises out of CMCs defies the wisdom of both the humanists who eschew mechanical systems as dehumanizing and reductive, and the social scientists who seek mechanical designs and measurable functionality. For one the computer-based classroom is too mechanical, and for the other it is not mechanical enough. The stealth pedagogy, therefore, tries to avoid both radar screens, exhibiting a stealthy mode of accomplishment that can only be described as "postmodern," although without most of postmodernism's ideological trappings. It is as inaccessible to a positivist's usual perspective as is fractal geometry, and therefore resists the usual cognitive processes by which intelligent people perceive and evaluate behaviors and outcomes.

So why do people continue struggling for highly dialogic computer-mediated forms of instruction against the considerable odds described here? The Resistance is often maddening, arising as it does from a complex soup of personal and professional motivations that defy straightforward understanding, but no less maddening are the reasons people pursue the computer alternative. All would like to reduce their positions to an irresistible functionalist argument, but the context will not allow it, and so sawtooth feelings continue to exist, even as administrators and peacemakers try to mitigate any evidence of "we-they" dichotomies with soothing descriptions that never quite take.

CMCs in the future may well frame most (but not all, of course) formalized instruction, simply because the basis of knowledge is language and communication, and no medium comes as close to providing the general advantages of significant and highly interactive communication as computer-mediated networks do, including the heretofore default medium of face-to-face orality—especially under the authority constraints of the traditional classroom. Many teachers will agree that this is so and yet find themselves swimming in a sea of challenges, most of which seem irrational, their very terms and conditions hidden and apparently inaccessible to productive debate.

At the heart of what appears to be a gloomy scenario, however, exists an exciting and compelling phenomenon that in its very refusal to bend to grand designs and mechanical projections promises to respond more effectively to current problems in education than instructional designs left over from the last century. Centering learning on human contact, upon a richness of learner-to-learner interactivity inconceivable a few years ago, promises to foster new learning behaviors that can thrive in a rapidly evolving world. Much of the disconnect and unhappiness many teachers feel arises, I think, from classroom methods and infrastructures that conform more to traditional expectations and administrative perquisites than to how people actually learn best. Ironically, networked computers are introducing a more distinctly human character to what has been for decades an increasingly closed-ended curriculum, but the peculiar strains of this transition call for a subtlety of understanding seldom addressed professionally.

REFERENCES

Kemp, F. (1987). The user-friendly fallacy. *College Composition and Communication, 38,* 32-39.

Kuhn, T. (1962). *The structure of scientific revolutions.* Chicago: Chicago University Press.

Mumford, L. (1967). *The myth of the machine.* New York: Harcourt.

Selfe, C. (1989). *Creating a computer-supported writing facility: A blueprint for action. Advances in computers and composition studies.* Houghton MI: Computers and Composition.

Steinberg, S. (1996, October). Netheads vs. bellheads. *Wired,* pp. 144-147, 206-213.

Chapter • 14

Surveying the Electronic Landscape: A Guide to Forming a Supportive Teaching Community

**Kate Coffield, Joseph Essid,
Jane Lasarenko, Linda M. Record,
Dickie Selfe, and Hugh Stilley**

On August 29, 1995 a message leaped from the monotony of everyday e-mail like a primal scream:

> H E L P ! I've got six computers down, a workshop to teach in twenty minutes, a CMC training seminar to conduct later this afternoon, two committee meetings regarding how this lab will be used, a campus technology review committee meeting, a thesis chapter to finish by tomorrow, a grant proposal due in two weeks—and there are still 28 lab orientations to do for the composition classes.

A primal scream such as this one could have come from anyone who has taken on the challenges and responsibilities of computer-mediated communication (CMC) program development. As teachers explore new online technologies, they soon discover that there is more involved than "mere" enthusiasm. Early adopters, by choice or otherwise, are faced with the burden of creating a path where none existed before. They are often alone, or nearly so, traveling Frost's "road not taken" into a world of postmodernism, decentering, master directory blocks, and extents b-tree headers, with "miles [of ethernet cabling] to go before they sleep."

Even if you are not an "early adopter" of anything, you may face or soon see one or more of your colleagues caught in the scenarios we describe. Reading this book implies that you are at least thinking about venturing into CMC instruction. Our goal here is to share both the rewards and the challenges that this entails. Concrete, practical strategies such as those offered here may help reduce the primal screaming that all too often accompanies the journey from chalkboard to cyberspace. We hope this chapter will serve as a "virtual map" for teachers who have a dream but have yet to start, for those who are just beginning their journey, and for all who are constantly in the process of revitalizing their approaches to teaching writing and communication courses.

This chapter itself is a product of CMC. It arose from a workshop at the 1995 Computers and Writing Conference in El Paso, Texas, a national conference that is the most significant professional gathering for college writing teachers in the United States who are working with computers in their teaching or research. At the 1995 conference, we presented a workshop with the same title as this chapter, which was our preliminary interactive exploration of the issues we discuss here. At that workshop, those in attendance—most of whom had never met face to face—shared their experiences in computerized classrooms. In the workshop room we used both group discussion and synchronous computer conferencing to discuss teaching, and we used a MOO to involve participants outside of El Paso to join the discussion. Our goal was to compile strategies for survival in the often-wild world of the computer classroom, and we have continued that workshop's conversation on national electronic discussion groups, as well as on World Wide Web.

What we offer, then, is not a static set of guidelines, but rather an evolving model for supporting ourselves and other teachers, that draws on our experiences. Our underlying premise is that online writing courses and classrooms are more than instructional spaces; they exist in a complex web of institutional, professional, and technological forces that influence the lives of all who work in them: students, teachers, administrators, and technical personnel. We also assume that even though dedicated individuals can make a difference, we need fellow explorers and pioneers to sustain us and help us progress in computer-intensive instruction. The ideas here are not empirical findings, but points of departure meant to provoke some response. We hope readers will empathize with, wonder about, perhaps reject, and certainly refine our discussions and suggestions.

Our opening quotation and subsequent suggestions could lead one to believe that CMC instruction is simply too much work, requiring too much expertise, for one person to do alone. That is true. However, with the help of CMC technologies themselves, these challenges need not be faced alone. Survival in this discipline is an ongoing project among those willing to share information and experiences. Ultimately we will all be part of multidisciplinary teams working toward commonly developed goals, but this is a gradual process.

CHARTING A COURSE

Planning is crucial to a successful long-range outcome in any technological environment, although there is a temptation to skip this step because of the fear that it will add to your workload, and divert effort from teaching or publishing. It should be remembered, however, that basing dreams on a pedagogically sound plan will help reduce the sense of panic that comes with the realization that no matter how hard you try, it is impossible to keep up with the pace of all technological change. Gilbert (1994), director of technology projects for the American Association of Higher Education, said that technology changes on an 18-month cycle, whereas college curricula change on an 18-year cycle. Without a plan, the changes will still happen—and no doubt happen quickly—but they may have nothing to do with your curricular dreams. Written curricular goals provide a base from which to explore where you want to go technologically, and why, and will bolster the promotion of your project for those who do not see things your way.

CMC planning is complex. Early decisions will influence and be influenced by not only your own department or program but also by your institution and community. The standard college or university is embroiled in the forward and backward pressures of disciplines, people, money, policies, and politics. All must be part of your plan, and you may find that many demands are contradictory or even mutually exclusive. The fear of making mistakes should not interfere with your vision, but it is important to understand how project goals will be viewed within this larger framework. Diplomacy is of the utmost importance here; and occasionally a combative mentality is required.

From the beginning, you should insist that technical negotiations focus on theory and pedagogy as well as on standard issues of compatibility, costs, and technical resource conflicts. Even the choice of an operating system has serious ethical and pedagogical consequences. Formulating a strongly supported plan will help avoid long-term disasters. LeBlanc (1994) noted that technology decisions exert "a relentless influence on the success or failure of computers in achieving one's literacy goals" (p. 23). The lab, program, or curriculum you design today is the one you and your students will have to live with. Basing design, hardware, and software choices on pedagogical goals will help ensure maximum educational functionality and maximum flexibility in a rapidly changing technological environment.

It is impossible to convince nontechnical audiences to support expensive technologies without making instructional goals clear to them. And a highly technical audience must be made to see how a particular operating system, network set up, lab design, or piece of software makes a crucial pedagogical difference. In the case of a program that is writing-intensive, you must show that CMC is not just "typing" and that collaboration is not "cheating." Concepts such as *networked writing classroom* and *collaborative software* are still foreign to many top administrators, technical support people, and budget review committees. For that reason, establishing a set of goal statements that are useful in a number of rhetorical situations is recommended. Appendix A contains a list of sample goal statements from R. Selfe (1997a). Selfe's selections are drawn from a survey of 55 postsecondary institutions and presented at a 1997 Epiphany Institute.

You will need to collect some unique marketing information at this point. First, it will help to have a bibliography or a small set of professional publications that encourage technology practices in the college writing classroom—resources included in this book are a good starting point. If you are designing a new facility or redesigning an existing one, your collection should include information on plans and layouts; otherwise your online writing classroom may materialize as rows of tightly packed workstations facing an instructor terminal and whiteboard. Quantitative data is very convincing to administrators and technology specialists, as are testimonials from other administrators with successful programs at well known institutions.

The next step after establishing goal statements is to examine the technological resources at your institution, and find out who is responsible for them. Have technology goals been developed to go along with the long-term goals at your campus? Who developed them? Read the long-range plan, and meet with senior-level administrators to determine their stances on technology. The information technology director, if you have one, may cooperate with deans and department heads in setting up small stipends or equipment grants for early adopters who are willing to act as scouts on the journey. If your campus has a writing-across-the-curriculum program, those involved may be able to offer leads and co-sponsor projects. Advocate for technology use across campus, not just in your own department; otherwise you lose influence and momentum. Unless you become part of a larger team with a larger vision, you may quickly be dismissed as an advocate for only your department or program.

Once you have written your dream, plan in terms that are accessible to academics, administrators, and technicians, the next step is to establish connections. Be careful not to limit your range; begin within your program or department and then branch out to the college, the campus at large, and the local community. You can, for example, present your case to the local board of education, present at conferences and publish in journals, make connections in the local newspaper. Aim to make your program and your cause visible and viable in the minds of those who make decisions.

Further your education by volunteering to attend technology committee meetings, if your institution has them. Some campuses may have several such committees attempting to set overlapping (or even contradictory) policies. You may not be able to intervene directly, but by attending you will at least come to know the agenda of these groups and be able to report back to your colleagues. At Michigan Technological University, for example, there are several key computer committees across campus. The Humanities Department has ensured its representation (by students, faculty, or staff) on all of them, which means that it is in touch with, and can influence, the campus' technological trends and policy. Most of these committees should be conducting open meetings. If not, make your interest known and work to open them up. If no technology committee exists, talk to senior administrators about creating one.

Above all, get to know your computing support people—the ones who actually run your network, keep you connected to the Internet, and send you arcane messages about disk quotas, rebooting systems, and backing up servers. Even if you initially speak different languages, it is important to remember that technical support folk are highly skilled—and they will be the leaders of the rescue team each time you get lost in the jungle of technology. Learn their language and share yours, and you may find yourself on more solid ground with the support staff than you are with the managers and administrators who control them (and with whose policies they may actually disagree). They can become good friends and valuable allies in convincing the less knowledgeable that "X" is a better piece of software despite its seemingly high cost, or that a powerful server is more important than someone's favorite spreadsheet program for your writing lab.

Whether or not you are a lone visionary, expand your horizons to include colleagues around the world. Strong advocates for campuswide technology planning exist at the national and international levels and can help you in your efforts. Questions that might be unanswerable on your own campus can benefit from the thought of experts who willingly share their advice electronically. The personal benefits that can arise from such contacts are invaluable. Kate Coffield credits Internet contacts with helping her change the way she teaches writing, her ability to get a writing classroom set up at her university, and her involvement in scholarly activities like this chapter.

If all this seems complex and time consuming before you have hardly begun the journey, it is. The most important thing to remember is that change takes time and effort. Continually revisiting your written dream plan can sustain you in times of doubt and ensure that you are constantly assessing the value of CMC technology in pedagogical terms. Rethinking the issues, revisioning the path, can lead you toward new exploration and new alliances with administrators, technologists, colleagues, and students—it may even lead to that new facility or a long-awaited upgrade!

FINANCING THE EXPLORATION

If you can't pay, you can't play. Financing technology at even a small college is a very complex matter. As corporate and government funding requirements demand tighter control over projects, simultaneous demands for computing skills and technological muscle bring in funding. This means that you will need to approach funding at multiple levels: general funding from the university, student or parent technology fee increases (not tuition that normally goes directly to the general fund), grants and corporate sponsorship or partnerships, and alumni support. You need to have plans for making your efforts clear and valuable to all. Convincing funding entities—internal or external—of the value of computer-mediated classrooms, labs, writing centers and even entirely virtual environments like OWLS, MOOs, and Web sites is a multifaceted task. However, the most important activities fall into two major categories: (a) providing a convincing illustration of the short- and long-term monetary demands of a CMC program, and (b) convincing decision makers of the value technology can add to the educational experience of students—in all disciplines.

One of the most effective ways to demonstrate the financial needs of a classroom/lab is to provide a realistic, comprehensive budget. Too often, this practicality is glossed over when proposals are being made. It should have as much detail as possible including salaries, wages, service contracts, and equipment costs amortized over each item's lifetime. Plan for maintenance and obsolescence from the very beginning, but remember that money for replacements often comes from different sources. Plan for replacement of existing equipment, even when it means extra effort to change the opinions of the public and administrators. Based on the model developed at Michigan Tech in 1997, Appendix B will help you develop a financial needs analysis tailored to your situation. There are many models for financing; gathering experiences from other institutions can add valuable perspective to your proposal.

In 1993, computing operations at the University of Richmond, were taken over by a corporation. This type of arrangement, known as *outsourcing,* at first seemed popular with faculty and staff. According to the contract with the firm, administrative and academic computing services merged under "university computing." The university built new labs and centralized support staff while the corporation hired more support staff and provided and supported a range of software and hardware. In 1995, the arrangement with the corporation was popular and progress in integrating technology seemed good. In 1998, however, the provost surveyed faculty about computing services, and the survey revealed near universal disapproval of the way computing was being handled. Specific findings of the survey have not been released, but as a result of the findings the university decided to take all computing operations back "in house" when the corporation's contract expires. As of early 1999, many centralized services, and some labs, were in the process of being relocated to academic departments. The experience at Richmond demonstrates the need to negotiate carefully all agreements paying close attention to issues such as how much support will be provided to faculty, staff, and students; how the corporation will balance academic and administrative support; what software products will be provided; and what type of assistance with instructional design will be included. Faculty usually lack experience with such issues, but their input is essential to the success or failure of outsourcing. And of course, the same careful attention is important to in-house negotiations for technology support.

As a profession, educators are just beginning to gather information about the value that CMC instruction adds to students' learning experiences. Therefore, arguing this point requires some creative thinking because empirical evidence of this type is still difficult to come by. To demonstrate the growing importance of CMC to program viability and vitality, you might collect personnel needs analyses from large organizations, small businesses, and independent contractors. These can be used to supplement your own primary teaching objectives so that students graduate with quality educational and working-world experience. Integrating appropriate business goals is likely to enhance the appeal of corporate proposals for support. Compiling job descriptions, salaries, and postgraduation managerial evaluations of graduated students will help show the necessity of providing computer experience as part of the educational process. An observational, ethnographic research agenda that looks into the actual behaviors, perceptions, and learning patterns of those using your facilities may interest software and hardware developers who are keenly interested in and will often fund collaborative ventures. Student testimonials (both graduated and onsite) also are important.

Finally, in the category of unusual supportive data, you should prepare concise statements of your own agenda as a humanistic educator. Your agenda should promote the growth of technologically sophisticated learning and work environments that de-emphasize the technology as an end in itself and instead forefront (a) comfort (drinking and eating, ergonomic chairs), (b) gestures toward the humanist tradition (machines named after authors and characters), (c) an emphasis on face-to-face support, and (d) a critical attitude toward CMC technologies. Technicians, senior administrators, and even corporate representatives are surprisingly accepting of educational goals that are clearly defined. A well-prepared package of corroborative evidence will become a keystone for many proposals. Information technology is a bandwagon now. "Jump on with your eyes open," agree experts with heavy lab-building experience. Combine savvy positioning and marketing efforts with visionary "wish lists" that help justify student activities, increased technological budgets and know-how. Positioning yourself carefully is critical and well worth the time it takes to get the answers. An added benefit is that the process of gathering this information helps to clarify priorities for your CMC program, priorities that take into account the unique political, economic, and academic situations at your institution.

With a clear vision mapped out, a support network set up, a comprehensive needs assessment made, and evidence of the growing importance of technology to pre-professional preparation of students, you will be fully outfitted for repeated forays into the world of funding sources.

Now is the time to be creative. Be aware of the larger climate, such as any technology planning committees that can make decisions that will affect your work. A transcription of board activities relating to technology could be posted to all manner of electronic (or paper) environments—e-mail or newsgroup discussion forums, World Wide Web pages, or plain old bulletin boards—to elicit wider discussion that can be brought back to the committee for its consideration. As the Internet transcends geographical and temporal boundaries, there will be more multi-institutional activity and probably funding for it. So you need to keep pressing to find parallels in other fields (e.g., science and math) where the National Science Foundation, computer manufacturers, and other corporate entities may furnish partial support. For starters, you will need to know the major players and where to start looking for funding sources. A substantial, albeit far from comprehensive, list of funding agencies and Web-based information sources is provided in Appendix C.

Granting: "Always Connect"

It is impossible to speak of funding sources without touching on the obvious opportunities of grants. If your campus has a grant writing office, the people in it should become an integral part of your support network. If no office exists, you will need to put together a grant writing team comprised of representatives from all potentially affected areas, including the technical support people, on your campus. By discussing your ideas with faculty and administrators in other departments, you may well be able to enlarge the original scope and develop collaborative ventures that are likely to be more successful than solitary proposals.

There are other steps you can take to further increase the likelihood of a successful grant proposal. First, collect sample successful grants from other universities or directly from the funding agencies. Before beginning to plan or draft, obtain specific grant requirements from funding agencies. When writing, compose the draft exactly to agency guidelines. More grants have been denied based on nonadherence to grant specifications than you would imagine. Successful proposals are often marked by ongoing, long-term, often oral conversations with corporate and government granting agencies. Don't be afraid to contact someone in the granting agency's office, even if that agency is a large national agency like the National Endowment for the Humanities. Successful proposals are political, stressing mutual benefits, and they are practical. Funding objectives must be accurately tracked and assessed, so include a plan for this in your proposal. And remember the adage to be careful what you ask for: A grant that provides for thousands of dollars in equipment but none for the staffing and support of that equipment may create enormous problems for a department. Finally, in growing a program, remember that facilities and communication systems rarely spring fully formed from a one-shot approach, one sympathetic administrator, or a single massive grant, although these are all worth cultivating if the chance arises.

ATTRACTING AND TRAINING NEW EXPLORERS

Integrating online activities into an existing program is something best done with company, although that may not be possible in every situation. Still, you will have a better experience from the start if you can begin your journey with fellow explorers. With companions, you can share successes and failures, talk over new ideas, and evaluate new technologies; you will feel supported as you implement changes. In some cases, you may find yourself charged with recruiting fellow teachers. Whether you are a newly hired junior faculty member, right out of a program with a strong technical reputation, or a long-term member of the department who has just been assigned to CMC development, others on your campus may look to you as a leader. Sometimes, the first person to express an interest in a new technology is expected to lead its introduction. Depending on local circumstances, you may be expected to generate enthusiasm for computer use, the Internet, and the new modes of electronic instruction. Or you may have to implement a vague charge like getting faculty "capable of instruction for the 21st century."

Whatever your local situation, you will find that the process of reconsidering pedagogies and technologies is made less daunting by a supportive community. We hope that novices and veterans alike will benefit from the survival tactics recommended in the next section.

Starting Out

Many people picture themselves walking into the computer classroom and just teaching. After all, they may have had many successful years in a traditional classroom setting. But the transition to CMC is not always simple. No matter how well organized you think you are and how smoothly your facility seems to be running, the unexpected in a computer lab can take on dramatically different dimensions. It is important to be honest with yourself and with other teachers about some of the things that can and do happen in computer classrooms:

- On Jane's first day, the entire network crashed.
- The power went off during Kate's first orientation; in her first synchronous conferencing session with combined classes, the server went down.
- Linda arrived 1 hour before a class to find no power to any of the lab computers because a maintenance crewman wanted to know what the big red "emerg. stop" button did so he pushed it a few times, and but it didn't do anything—except cut off power to the lab. The electrician arrived to reset the power connection with only 3 minutes to spare before class.
- As Joe scrambled about assisting a teacher and her students on the first day of a specially funded project, an international student called him over to explain that her monitor was "sparkling." It was on fire.
- The regional director of the Society for Technical Communication was to visit Dickie's class. For that event he prepared a technology-intensive class session. Minutes before she arrived, the server went down and class members were unable to access any of the software they needed. He quickly switched gears and orchestrated face-to-face discussions, which became the focus of subsequent electronic conversations once the server was rebooted.

These experiences became valuable landmarks in the journeys we took into new CMC terrains. Beyond the moments of terror they fostered, successfully meeting these challenges helped strengthen those who experienced them. The stories also demonstrate opportunities for collaborative learning made possible in a lab where students are actively engaged in constructing knowledge rather than simply receiving it from an omniscient teacher (Barker & Kemp, 1990; Freire & Macedo, 1987). An axiom among CMC teachers is to "always have an alternate plan." This is sound advice, especially if you are inexperienced as a troubleshooter. But if you are both the technical support person in the classroom and the teacher, it is often just as useful to turn technical difficulties into a collaborative problem-solving exercise. It lets students know you are human, and it gives them something from which to learn about and which to write. We advise gathering students around as you investigate what went wrong and showing them problem-solving techniques they might use in similar situations.

What's wrong with this picture? Well, many faculty are simply not ready for the scenarios just described. They feel insecure, and justifiably so. They are out of their element; they know it and the students know it. Insecurity is contagious, and educators must also understand their students' desire for a teacher-centered classroom. What does this translate into? Teacher insecurities and those of their students suggest that we need to be prepared not only with alternative plans each day, but with a clear description of why they are using these technologies, and what added value they bring to the content or process of the course. If you are the trainer, you can prepare colleagues for many of the most common and often negatively perceived experiences. It is almost always a shock for an instructor to bring a class into a lab for an initial session of real-time computer conferencing, only to discover that students immediately begin to appropriate the unique communication spaces afforded by computers. It is no less distressing to find that every real-time conference, whether it is done on a local-area or wide-area network, will involve not only the active work of the class but also the "underlife" (Brooke, 1987) that we commonly tune out in traditional classrooms.

Technology aside, the transition from a structured secondary school environment to the independence of university life may already have disoriented many students. Some panic if they cannot count on instructors for confidence and guidance. Trying to help her already intimidated students recover from the shock of the system collapse, Jane made jokes, laughed, pounded on the walls—anything and everything to help students (and herself) realize and accept that things can and will go wrong in the classroom. Fortunately, the problem was a small one, easily fixed by a change to the network configuration file, and the class soon returned to discussing the syllabus.

Not all problems are so easily resolved, but what can be done in a "traditional" classroom if the lights go out? Climb the nearest power station with Swiss Army knives? No, we move outside and sit in a circle on the grass, or we cancel class—which is exactly what Linda had to do when a thunderstorm caused dangerous surges and brownouts during her fully online composition class. Strategies that have worked well in the traditional classroom, with some modification, are readily transferable to the computer classroom, providing that adequate groundwork has been done.

For these reasons, it is important to address a wide range of technology issues clearly in relation to the syllabus. At the very least, students should know why they are being asked to use computers in their writing class, in both practical and theoretical terms. We realize that some faculty, particularly in large first-year composition programs, have little control over their syllabi or even the texts they use, but they still have the responsibility of explaining the syllabus or texts to students. However, to the extent possible, technology itself should be part of the class agenda or syllabus. Consider devoting a 2- or 4-week unit on readings about technology, or having students write about their relation to the technology used. Kate and one of her colleagues had great success using the computer classroom with a unit on liberal arts education. The more ways teachers and students can connect and relate to such issues, the faster everyone will become comfortable.

Comfort and security can also come in the form of a simple paper handout. We advocate distributing plenty of information to help students and faculty learn the technologies we plan to use. One of Jane's students nicknamed her "the handout queen" by the end of the first week of classes. Still, they acknowledged that the handouts were necessary, and often the only thing that kept them "hanging in there." Some teachers do not endorse such handouts, and argue that they are counterproductive. In one online discussion, Rhinehart (1995) of Syracuse University stated:

> both the anecdotal evidence I have and the formal research we've conducted suggest that this kind of help [instructor-designed handouts] does not work like training wheels on a bike—users do not cast it aside as they pick up speed. Instead they frequently hang on to it and are still doing what it teaches and nothing else over a year later. Inquiry does not grow out of a state of comfort—it frequently requires some teacher-constructed confusion/frustration to make it happen.

Still, for timid or new users, and especially for complex processes, such aids can be indispensable in helping students and faculty to adapt to the strange new world of the electronic classroom. Not all handouts need be in paper form; to combat printing and photocopying costs, Joe (like many authors in this volume) has placed his syllabi and most of his handouts on the Web, a technology that has proven simple enough to lure his novice computer users to try other software.

Variety is a goal in any course plan, and you should aim to include a variety of interactive and collaborative activities into your work. But there can be too much interactivity, too much variety in your planning. Depending on your own familiarity with the technologies available, plan to incorporate only one or two new activities at a time. You may want to begin by adding a simple e-mail component to your courses. If you are already comfortable with e-mail, and the level of work it can generate, you might add the Web, or investigate a different technology such as a synchronous forum like a MOO or a chat room. If you don't feel comfortable with these (or if your students don't have access), you may want to experiment with the features of software like Daedalus Group's Daedalus Integrated Writing Environment, CommonSpace from Sixth Floor Media, a Houghton Mifflin group, Connect.net from Norton, or other programs designed to support writing classes. There are supportive people online who already use these products, and they are usually willing to share their experiences and ideas.

Finally, don't be afraid to observe and learn from your students and then use them as teachers. They quickly learn the new technologies and many come to love them—although not all students react the same way to all learning situations. But don't be afraid to let your students bring new technologies into your lab. In the traditional classroom, we find it rewarding and delightful when our students raise a question or make a connection that we have overlooked. This attitude should carry over into the computer-mediated classroom.

Recruiting Colleagues: Strategies and Cautions

The first, most general, and most significant question to ask about faculty involvement with technology is whether we have an ethical responsibility to become technically literate. The answer is a resounding, "Yes!" Our students compete for jobs in technologically saturated professional arenas, and are expected to demonstrate an ability to communicate well using different technologies. Even in the academy it is becoming rare to face an interview that does not require some demonstration of technological expertise. So the real issue is not whether, but to what degree, we must enter this "brave new world," and that answer is determined partly by institutional circumstances and partly by personal inclination. If there is a strong technical support system at an institution, then the teacher may only need to become comfortable with whatever software will be used in course work. If there is little or no technical support, a lab coordinator or teacher may need the skill of a system administrator just to keep the lab running and to offer assistance to other faculty. The decision about the degree to which one should become techno-literate will also be affected by the amount of resistance present in local departments and later by success and by ethical concerns unique to this revolution.

Ironically, student motivation and initiative can actually work against efforts to bring technology into the classroom. Some faculty feel threatened, if not by the technology itself, then by the implied challenge to their authority when students quickly appropriate computer capabilities for class and social activities that are outside the technical capability of faculty. Kate recalls working on a conference proposal with a colleague who was definitely "pro-tech" but who dug in her heels when Kate referred to computer-based instruction as a positive move away from the "traditional relics . . . of instructor-centered learning." The colleague was all for CMC, but far from willing to accept decentering as a "positive move." At another school, a graduate-student committee worked for an entire semester, producing a proposal for a student-run program of volunteer lab staffing, recruitment, and training, which was initially rejected by the department chair. Only the intervention of an administrative colleague from outside the department, who helped satisfy the chair's security concerns, made it possible for the students' project to move forward.

This seems a good place to caution that sometimes people who have discovered the value of technology can get a bit fanatical when describing it to colleagues, and this can be counterproductive. Evangelical rhetoric can be off-putting. As we explain to others what we do, we should consider how deeply entrenched ideologies affect the way we are perceived. Even faculty who are truly interested in incorporating technology may be put off if the process is seen to involve their being "born again" as postmodern technologists.

Before we insist on a convergent theory of writing pedagogy, we must examine theories critically and enable our colleagues to do so as well. Such a pedagogy "asks teachers to participate in a range of identity-changing, ideologically-situated assumptions about language and learning" (Welch, 1993, p. 388). The pedagogies of the networked writing classroom, such as Barker and Kemp's (1990) "Network Theory" and other social constructivist models of knowledge, also call for such changes of identity on the part of teachers, not all of whom are social constructivists. Some faculty teaching composition have little or no grounding in writing theory, period; even those who do may be professed "agnostics" when it comes to applying theory to teaching practice. And there are others who discover—after they enter the computer-mediated instructional environment—that they are not as firm in their desire for decentering as they thought. In any case, evangelizing will do little to convince those who doubt the pedagogical benefits of computers in the classroom (see also Hawisher & Selfe, 1991).

So, where should recruiting begin? Certainly not with the resistant. It seems more promising to focus efforts on those colleagues who have already shown interest and who may be willing to collaborate with the more experienced and courageous in exploring the computer classroom, at least on a limited basis, and especially if they receive adequate support. The best recruits will be those already comfortable with collaborative activities in traditional classrooms. Such teachers are less likely to feel threatened by the epistemology of social constructivism. They already practice it in every class. For more on this point, see Kemp (chap. 13, this volume).

Recruitment works well if it is linked to colleagues' current interests and professional needs. Does the Victorian literature specialist know about the excellent mailing list in that subject or an online archive of pre-Raphaelite art? Has your Shakespearean found the Web sites for the newly discovered elegy or the Shakespearean insults? Taking the time to find a few useful sites for colleagues can generate good will of much greater value than the few minutes it takes you to find them. Once faculty become familiar and comfortable with the uses and benefits of the Web and other Internet resources, they may be more willing to participate with their students, in part, because their personal level of emotional risk has been reduced.

Still, it is crucial to make changes cautiously. Honesty is essential to successful recruitment and retention. If only the benefits of CMC are used to attract colleagues, they may abandon their efforts when reality contradicts an overly optimistic picture. They may feel they are being asked to convert too quickly to using techniques that they have come to view as disrupting rather than enhancing their classes. Faculty need incentives to change deeply entrenched ideas and beliefs about teaching and "professing." Our seemingly enthusiastic colleagues may not be prepared for the longer class preparations required to make the transition to CMC or the technical hurdles that invariably bedevil new instructors in computer-assisted classrooms. For example, colleagues may well recognize the value of e-mail in their personal work and wish to incorporate it into their teaching, but they probably have not considered the implications of reading 100 students' e-mail responses weekly. Without sufficient help, they can sour very quickly on classroom technology.

A good faculty training program can alleviate many frustrations (see Mirtz & Leverenz, chap. 15, this volume for such a program). These programs work best when they emphasize the importance of taking things gradually, one at a time. For example, it is best to provide numerous small workshops on using the existing software before encouraging colleagues to teach in a computer-classroom environment. Workshops can introduce faculty to resources like textbook supplements that include online guides and linked Web pages. Those in the know should share; otherwise, CMC newcomers are likely to "bail out" before they have a real chance to learn how to use new types of resources.

Once faculty are comfortable with the technologies, additional workshops can help them discover new ways to use them in the classroom. Invite faculty to participate in producing their own Web pages; start an e-mail list for the department on technology issues; have people give short presentations on some aspect of their field using resources primarily from the Internet. Faculty, like everyone else, learn better by doing than by hearing people talk about doing. Specific training and workshops also need to address such teaching issues as lesson planning, out-of-class student resource availability, and student-based teaching.

As colleagues become more enthusiastic about teaching with the technologies they are learning, we must again try to convince them not to overdo it. They may not be able to get as much lab access as they would like, or they may burn out if they do. Faculty need to be aware that although students may have computer access during class time, requiring out-of-class computer-based assignments may not be feasible at your institution. One of the most frequent student complaints is that campus open-access labs are unavailable due to the limited number of students they can accommodate.

Gaining Additional Support and Visibility

Integrating courseware takes time and effort, but the results can be impressive as colleagues share their success stories with chairs and deans. The advice given in the earlier parts of the chapter, if successful, will go far toward alleviating some of the resistance you may encounter. However, visibility and credibility alone are generally not enough. It is important to work with senior administration to create faculty incentives, whether in the form of merit increases, release time for course preparation, small stipends or honoraria, or simply recognition.

Convincing the faculty of the importance of technology is a big issue in many English departments. It is clear that keeping track of successes, current literature on national trends, and generating assessment models are some of the more important challenges that the Computers and Writing community now faces. If the prospects seem bleak locally, there is no need to limit your recruitment efforts to your own department. You may want to consider whether your program shares common ground with other innovative CMC programs on campus. Investigate ongoing grants involving technology, even those outside your own academic discipline. See if these projects include goals to attract wider participation, then volunteer.

Organizing your own classes, recruiting your colleagues, and making yourself and your program visible to the outside world is far from simple. But we are not talking about a passing fancy here. Green (1996) stated that we are experiencing increases of 50% to 100% per year in the use of information technology. The demand for electronic services is not likely to decrease according to the demographic trends found in R. Selfe's (1995) "Surfing the Tsunami." How we help manage and institute that growth will have an immediate and important impact on our professional lives. As seen earlier, demand is likely to exceed supply.

NAVIGATING THE BYWAYS

The initial journey into an online classroom—or even a partially online classroom—can be overwhelming for institutions as well as individuals. While students queue for lab access, institutions—many of whose long-range plans failed to predict the Internet explosion—are fighting to keep up with demands for technology and technoliteracy. Not all are succeeding. Many schools are struggling with huge leaps in the number of Internet users. Here are some sobering statistics for us to consider: A campus computing 1995 survey recorded a 1-year leap from 15.8% to nearly 24% of classes being held in computer classrooms; e-mail was being used in 20% of courses, up from 8% during the previous year (DeLoughry, 1996). The signature of one e-mail enthusiast reads, "There are only two kinds of e-mail users: those who have sent and received a message and those who are about to."

It is easy to see how teachers can be overwhelmed. When that person is given responsibility for integrating CMC techniques into firmly established curricula, many more problems, both practical and ethical, arise. Over time, solutions, but many potential disasters can be foreseen and forestalled. In this section, we raise questions and offer examples from our own experiences, which may help to allay some of the most pressing problems.

Resistance

Despite the extraordinary growth of CMC, resistance to its use for teaching remains high at many schools. Many teachers feel overwhelmed by new technologies, or campus policies restricting the use of particular technologies like Usenet groups or MOOs and MUDs. Others face unsupportive administrators who block the use of available technologies. Many have trouble learning new technologies. Already, some depend on their children at home to teach them how to use their own computers, or they don't even have a computer at home and feel completely out of their "natural" element when they must use technology on campus. No wonder they are reluctant to enter a teaching environment as foreign to most as hiking in the wilderness without a compass. When students are more comfortable than the teacher with the technology, the threat to the teacher's emotional safety can be quite real. Learning where and why there are points of resistance in a particular institution is an important step toward countering it. You might start this learning process by asking yourself a few questions; we offer some illustrative answers that we have received when we have asked these questions at our own institutions.

- Are faculty or administrators fearful that technology will somehow make them obsolete?

A literature professor confided, "I feel like computers are taking over and soon all teachers will be replaced by them. This would be horrible for students."

- Is there a strong "we've done it this way forever" attitude?

An English department chair, who acquired a computer for office use, remarked, "It's great for memos and letters to my kids, but I can't imagine using it to write anything creative." Other faculty say they cannot compose on the computer—they still hand write a draft and then "type it into the computer." Still others refuse to use a computer at all, feeling that it's "anti-humanistic," and hoping for the return of the quill pen.

- Are restrictions on gaming and other marginalized software and hardware born of the belief that play should not be part of academy learning, or are they based on resource allocation concerns?

At Michigan Tech both attitudes are present. MOOing students are regularly kicked off dial-up modems without warning because of the demand for remote access to campus. MOOing on campus, however, is regulated primarily by local departments. So we are able to allow MOOing for academic purposes in our lab. There is also strong support in some units, both academic and administrative, to ban all gaming software from workstations and networks regardless of its therapeutic or educational value.

MOOs and MUDs are considered "gaming" by some computing staff, so you should carefully consider ways to show that a particular piece of software has "academic merit" and serves the ends of a particular class or curriculum (see Matthews-DeNatale, chap. 4, this volume, for more on this issue). Daisley (1994) noted that "the problem with the idea of on-line speech or writing as play is that we tend not to value play in academic settings. One point I would argue here is that play, within the framework of playing with language, is an essential part of all discourse communities, especially in formation stages, and as such should have its acknowledged classroom space" (p. 109). Playful activities can be helpful for community formation, but they can also further academic goals. For instance, Joe was able to use a simulation program, Sim City 2000, with the full cooperation of computing staff and recognition of colleagues, as part of a set of scholarly readings about the social, ecological, and architectural issues of metropolitan areas. Other campuses, however, may be less accommodating.

It is easy to understand why playful activities can attract questions or create some resistance. In other instances, the causes of resistance range from obvious to elusive. It is important to adopt a generous attitude toward resistance, and to take the time to understand it. Joe and Kate use an electronics metaphor to explain various attitudes toward technology: *adaptor, transistor,* and *resistor.* Although these terms are not value-free, they avoid the stigma of pejorative terms like *geeks, followers,* and *Luddites.* In this model, we can imagine new classroom technologies arriving on a campus much like alternating current through a wire. Those who are enthusiastic about technology, the *adaptors,* create conditions and make changes under which a new classroom technology will continue "down the line" for others to use. The *transistors* join in at their own pace, using the adaptors' methodologies or adding their own. Transistors are fragile and vulnerable to points of resistance; they need voltage regulators, surge protectors, and above all, grounding. Finally, and to various degrees of strength, *resistors* reject the process or even actively fight it. Theirs are the handwritten memos you still receive in your mail pigeonhole. But they also serve a purpose in the system by challenging and controlling what can become rapid and uncontrolled technological change for its own sake.

It is important that we understand all these roles in technology discussions and planning. The diversity of views and experiences of faculty are likely to be reflected in our students, and we must take seriously critiques of and fears about technology. In a role-playing exercise designed for the original El Paso workshop, Simone (1995) drew more complex portraits of colleague types, with such characters as "'Polly Anna Blue,' a lecturer and promoter of computers and composition, and 'Gloria Bee,' a long-time member of the department who teaches 19th-century American literature, and a member of the committee that picked the current freshman text . . . [which] is incompatible with the teaching/learning context of the computer classroom." Simone situated these and other characters in a large composition program at "Big Technology State University," at a meeting of the "planning committee for Technology and Curriculum," the purpose of which was to come up with a few "concrete recommendations" for the dean. Participants in the workshop were to assume roles and carry on a "virtual" meeting, maintaining the integrity of the characters while showing "a genuine effort on the part of the group to get this over with."

The value of Simone's exercise lies in its realism: We see colleagues not only as types, but as individuals, with different interests, levels of security, hidden agendas, and above all, varying degrees of investment in the status quo. At the same time, when viewed within a larger institutional setting, in the context of administrative pressure and accountability (and those pesky weekly committee meetings!), the issue of resistance takes on sociopolitical as well as individual overtones. For some colleagues, levels of enthusiasm or resistance may in fact have nothing at all to do with technology, or even with pedagogy, and everything to do with keeping their jobs, maintaining or increasing their status, or simply getting out of meetings and on with their lives.

We advocate including all types of colleagues in discussions about technology, even if many of them never choose to teach in a lab. As noted in the previous section, teaching with technology takes a great deal of time and effort, and the learning curve is both steep and continuous. In an informal survey, Kate, a lab coordinator, found that resistance had little to do to with technophobia and much to do with lack of incentives— release time, overload pay, lab access, more training, freedom from the confines of a program syllabus in order to experiment, and others. Under these sorts of conditions, it is no wonder that faculty are sometimes unwilling to make the necessary investments. The local answers to these questions will help you navigate this difficult terrain. They, and others like them, can help you choose your battles carefully.

Unfortunately, the running of new labs is often left to part-time faculty, full-time junior faculty on release time or as an overload, or even graduate students who have little power within the academic political structure. This marginalization prevents the most effective implementation of CMC. If possible, have tenured faculty in charge of the computer classroom; such faculty are often in a better position to run interference for untenured or part-time faculty. Another idea is to use professional staff, even though, as many have observed, they have less political clout on university committees. Although desirable, these solutions are not always feasible. But the important message here is to form alliances with others who share your vision and can provide practical and emotional support.

We need to position ourselves to be in on decisions that will affect the implementation of CMC and especially those that may lead to active faculty support. As mentioned earlier, one way is to get on the committees that make these decisions. If they don't exist, agitate for them. If they are cumbersome and useless, form active ad hoc committees. Although it is essential that instructors try to understand the constraints on network systems technicians and administrators, it is equally important that there be instructor input to help counter decisions solely based on economics or efficiency. Despite costs, educators have an ethical responsibility to expand access for student users and most especially for those who lack the resources for meeting their own computing needs. This may mean lobbying for alternative resource allocations to support departmental computer labs or even including personal computers as part of the requirements for attending college, so that some of the cost can be supported through financial aid programs.

Success

The creation of a computer lab or a virtual, online environment does not mean all forms of resistance have been overcome, but it does mean that an important first step has been taken. Once the resistance hurdle is cleared or circumvented, the next greatest challenge may be your success! It is difficult to imagine, while you are still the isolated explorer, that blazing trails can lead to even more stressful, possibly dangerous, adventures. And it may. Successful innovators may be swamped with requests for support and facility use from faculty who previously shied away from whatever techno-territory exists at your institution. A full-sized, well-staffed lab is quickly overwhelmed; those with smaller facilities reach the limits of their resources even more quickly. Many ask, "What if there is simply not enough time in the lab to teach?" Rather than explorer and proponent, you may find yourself in the uncomfortable role of gatekeeper. Who will have access to the lab? What will be the criteria for use and distribution of limited technological resources? Will you be forced to attend mostly to the "squeaky wheels," or will you be prepared to make decisions based on the sound ethical, theoretical, and pedagogical considerations.

If lab facilities are limited, rotating access can be designated based on proposals describing well developed plans for teaching with technology. This has the advantage of foregrounding the importance of teaching over technology—and it guarantees a much higher likelihood of success for those attempting computer mediation for the first time. Another idea, as noted in the recruiting section, is to double up teachers and have each one/teach one; the "train the trainer" model is becoming increasingly popular. It allows those with experience to share class time and expertise with others who are just learning, and may also lead to mentoring partnerships that relieve the heavy burden that can fall on the individual who is perceived as the one to turn to with technical questions. Even a first-come, first-served sign-up sheet helps to manage flow and also can be used to track lab use. This is the time to document the impact of growing interest and use by faculty and students. Carefully collected data can help convince administrators and granting agencies to develop enough facilities to go around.

There are many alternate paths on the CMC road map. Mentoring is a successful strategy being used at many institutions, including California State University (CSU), Chico, where the Technology and Learning Program for faculty uses instructional computing consultants and interns to help faculty learn a variety of computer-assisted instructional techniques. They have the freedom to work with groups or individual instructors, teaching how to use hardware and software, brainstorming strategies for using the computer lab for course work, and even helping to design assignments and Web pages. This flexibility and personalized support is having a significant impact on the number of faculty even willing to consider CMC. At the University of Richmond, each academic department now has a "Technology Fellow," a faculty member who teaches with technology and who provides mentorship similar to that provided by CSU Chico's consultants. National models are beginning to emerge and may already be familiar to senior administrators. For example, the Teaching and Learning with Technology Roundtable (TLTR) and the Epiphany Project provide materials and guidance for getting faculty to integrate technology into their classes. Both projects offer faculty workshops, and TLTR sponsors retreats for administrators interested in change.

Another challenge seems to be coming from new types of educational approaches. That is, at some point institutional budget constraints, social pressure, and enthusiasm for CMC are likely to raise interest in distance learning alternatives. Although computer mediation offers seductive and exciting options, the dangers of "mass" distance learning education must not be allowed to become transparent. Instead, we need to establish clear educational goals first, then approach pedagogy and planning.

Getting Recognition for CMC Efforts

A 1996 discussion on CHORTT-L@MTU.edu, an electronic discussion group, carried the subject line, "Bony Fingers," a reference to an old song: "You work your fingers to the bone, and what do you get? Bony fingers." As seen earlier, early adopters of CMC in the classroom, and even those coordinating the programs and facilities, are often junior faculty, graduate students, or adjuncts who, although motivated, may also be overworked, underpaid, often unrecognized, and frequently are making the extra effort in the hope of some distinction or reward. Unfortunately, even within supportive departments and schools, their contributions may go unnoticed or be glossed over, simply because nobody understands what they are really doing. Applications for grants, promotion, tenure, contract renewal, or even release time may fall through if review committees cannot evaluate CMC-related work in comparison with more familiar teaching and research projects. Such failures are demoralizing and, unfortunately, far from infrequent.

Some CMC explorers find that they and their work fall outside the "mainstream" of their schools' disciplines. Some programs, not knowing quite what CMC is all about, may view it as neither pedagogy nor research, but instead dismiss it as "service." You can try to avoid such problems by working from the start to document the work that you do and illustrate its value to the program. Harrington (1996) offered the following general suggestions for CMC instructors and administrators:

- Have a job description (get your department to help you construct one if you don't have one already).
- Get advice in advance from others about how to document what you're doing
- Get external reviews of your work. These are especially important if you are the only one in the department in your field.
- Do not let technology-related things get catalogued under "service" only—if you're supporting other teachers learning how to integrate technology and teaching, you are teaching, too. And other aspects of your work might be called "research."

Who are we? What are we called, and by whom? Where are we heading? How can we justify our existence to our institutions? These questions cannot be directly answered outside our own contexts, but they must be addressed, nonetheless, if we wish our explorations recognized for what they are. CMC pioneers have produced a decade of impressive writing and research, both print and electronic. Obtaining these resources, getting them into our libraries, and making them visible to our colleagues is only a first step in showing that CMC is "real" pedagogy, that it is academic, not just technical, administrative, and service. As we teach writing, we must also write, sharing our travelogues with fellow explorers. In doing so, we strengthen our discipline, and in turn strengthen ourselves.

CONTINUING THE JOURNEY: SOCIAL ACTION THROUGH E-MEDIA

"You aim to 'grow a program' and try to enjoy and survive the growth spurts" (R. Selfe et al., 1995).

Getting yourself and colleagues on technology committees won't necessarily be easy, but if you are willing to do the hard work of presenting a student-centered pedagogical perspective over and over, projecting a clear idea of what to do with the technologies pedagogically, programatically, and politically, talking to those who make decisions and award grant proposals will often work. In order to create meaningful change, we need to lead the culture, not follow it blindly. We can do this by shaping critical questions that those out ahead of the general trends should be asked to answer. Our maps and suggestions so far have been an indirect method of trying to get out in front with some of the survival tactics are often lost in instructional theory discussions. We close our chapter with some direct commentary about our social responsibilities.

We need to argue for educating students who will be able to act ethically in a social sphere, which includes electronic venues. We need to be able to show them the value, complications, dangers, and rhetoric of electronic communication systems. After all, not all revolutions are liberatory. And we are watching, advocating, and participating in a social revolution.

We advocate making room for students in the decision making processes of our technology centers. Interaction among students, faculty, technicians, and administrators in our labs and on committees will enrich the educational experience we are trying to offer. Actively participating in the mundane institutional mechanisms where policy statements, budget discussions, and ethical conundrums are negotiated will enable students to gain practical rhetorical experience. This grounding the pragmatic decision making will better preparing them to become successful technology leaders even at the earliest points in their professional careers. Including them will help develop a deeper technological literacy that can be both reflective and critical, and it justifies many of our technological dreams. The elements necessary to this vision include the following:

- A comprehensive technological commitment from the institution.
- A strong commitment to supplying technology for those who are least able to afford it.
- Unfettered student access to Internet audiences, largely through networked communication technologies.
- Software and hardware that make self-publishing easy and inexpensive.
- Student access to highly sophisticated media development tools for transactional, playful, and aesthetic projects.

This vision is our attempt to help define the effort that this book advocates: provide students and teachers with the means to effect social action. The philosopher Arendt (1958), in *The Human Condition,* lamented the demise of a rare type of experience in the world. She noted that social action "has become an experience for the privileged few, and these few who still know what it means to act may well be even fewer than the artists, their experience even rarer than the genuine experience of and love for the world" (p. 324).

She feared that social trends—not just in education, but those that began in the 1940s and before—are limiting most peoples' abilities to "act in the world." Arendt's call for renewed social action is reflected in our efforts to build collaborative teams of teachers, students, student workers, administrators, and technicians, all of whom are committed to and have a stake in the success of our technology-rich educational environments. We would like to suggest that CMC programs are well worth the trouble it takes to establish and maintain them. For faculty and students alike, they open new discourse communities, new ways of interacting in the social world, that not only reflect individual cultures but also enrich them.

APPENDIX A[1]

Techno-Centric Goals

Techno-centric goals are those focused on the technologies themselves and understanding their importance. They include such items as our ability to

- Improve basic technical literacy.
- Make technology accessible to as many students and faculty as possible.
- Stay current with an expanding range of new technologies.
- Provide technical working-world skills for students.
- Increase students' technical facility on multiple platforms.

Educational Goals

Next, educational goals are those that we want to accomplish within these facilities. Among them are items like the following:

- Critical thinking skills.
- A student's sense of audience and the writing process (revision).
- The fluency or amount of writing/communicating taking place in classes.
- Lifelong learning skills.
- Collaborative skills, both in the sense of collaborating on writing projects and collaborating synchronously or asynchronously in discussions with local audiences and audiences world wide.
- Our understanding of the influences that communication technologies have on our working and writing processes so that we graduate thoughtful users (and consumers) of communication technology.
- Our sense of the aesthetic or humorous uses of these technologies.

Technology-Rich Facility Goals

These are useful goals for the facilities themselves that will help efforts to teach with technology. We need to provide the following:

---

[1]From R. Selfe (1997a).

- User-centered consulting, tutoring, or coaching for both students and teachers.
- A range of "publishing" opportunities and environments for communicating with "live" audiences.
- Sites for social action: opportunities for students to manage and maintain communication technologies.

Departmentally-Oriented Goals

These goals focus on the departmental use of technology-rich facilities as well. That is, they enable us to do the following:

- Conduct research into innovative technologies.
- Attract young, active scholar/teachers.
- Improve communication-across-the-curriculum programs through these facilities and the sharing of technology-rich pedagogies.
- Provide a site for synergy and community development for current degree programs (composition, literature, technical communication, ESL, and graduate rhetoric/composition programs, among others).

Each of these sets of goals are useful not only to sharpen our own educational direction but also to help colleagues new to the use to computers and to educate administrators who can help make technology happen. The process of identifying such goals can also help us convince technicians to work with us in our efforts and convince university and departmental committees to value the work innovative teacher/scholars working in these facilities as they come up for promotion or tenure.

APPENDIX B

An Amortized Budget[2]

The following is an adaptation of an amortized budget and lab fee increase proposal developed for the Center for Computer-Assisted Language Instruction (CCLI) in the humanities department at Michigan Technological University (MTU). It was prepared for the Student Lab Fees Subcommittee of the Computer Advisory Committee at MTU. In preparing a needs analysis, no element should remain transparent—invisible—to those you will be approaching for support. Yet, newcomers to the field are rarely able to envision all possible costs.

At MTU, which has a relatively long history of CMC education, a financial assessment was created to reveal the true cost of supporting the CCLI. It showed an annual operating cost of about $120,000—larger than some entire department budgets. With that information, the lab was able to negotiate a lab fee increase that brings in about $100,000 per year. The shortfall was an inducement to seek outside matching funds and in-kind donations.

The following list is based on MTU's self-assessment. The figures and specific equipment choices have been left off because they change so rapidly and vary from one institution to another. An estimated life expectancy has been provided for most equipment so that an amortized schedule for replacement can be figured. For example, if a workstation costs $2,500 and must be replaced every 4 years, the yearly amortized cost would be $2,500 ÷ 4 = $625. This amount needs to be saved per workstation each year. If a facility administrator wants to replace 25 machines, he or she should be collecting $15,625 per year just for workstation replacement. The value of volunteer staffing hours must be included. Volunteers should receive the proper recognition.

Personnel (yearly expense that accounts for approximately 1/2 of our budget)
- System Administrator
- Student Consultant(s)
- Workstudy student(s)
- Volunteer hours

---

[2]From R. Selfe (1997b).

Network Server Equipment (replace every 3 years)

- Server(s)
- External backup device
- Removable storage device
- External hard drive(s)
- External CD-ROM drive(s)

Workstation Equipment (replace every 4 years)

- Workstations
- Operating system
- RAM
- Hard drive
- CD-ROM

Periferals and Furniture

- Network Interface Hardware (replace every 3 years)
- Printers and Peripherals (replace every 3-5 years)
- Software (upgrade every 2-3 years)
- Support utilities (upgrade every 2-3 years)
- Furniture (upgrade every 7-15 years)

Consumables (yearly expenses)

- Paper toner
- Cartridges
- Service contracts
- Cleaning supplies

APPENDIX C

Financial and Grant Starting Points

Guide to Financial Aid: The Smart Student™: http://www.finaid.org

CPB Grants: http://www.cpb.org/grants/index.html

Fund for Improvement of Postsecondary Education (FIPSE): http://www.ed.gov/offices/OPE/FIPSE/

National Telecommunications and Information Administration (NTIA) grants: http://www.ntia.doc.gov/otiahome/otiaact.html

A   Guide   to   Department   of   Education   Programs: http://www.ed.gov/pubs/index.html

Major Department Programs (Financial Aid, Research and Statistics): http://www.ed.gov/programs.html

Listserv Resources

GRANTS-L To subscribe, send an e-mail message to listproc@listproc.gsu.edu with the message: subscribe grants-l YOUR NAME

FINAID-L To subscribe, send an e-mail message to listserv@psuvm.psu.edu with the message: subscribe finaid-l

Other Financial Resources

Bellsouth Foundation, 1155 Peachtree Street, NE, Room 7H08, Atlanta, GA 30367-6000. Telephone (404) 249-2396. Fax: (404) 249-5696. Offering project, training, and seed-money grants in Alabama, Florida, Georgia, Kentucky, Louisiana, Mississippi, North Carolina, South Carolina, and Tennessee.

Fund for Improvement of Postsecondary Education (FIPSE), 7th and D Streets, SW, ROB-3, Room 3100, Washington, DC 20202-5175. Telephone (202) 708-5750. Fax (202) 708-6118.

National Foundation for the Improvement of Education, 1201 16th St., NW, Washington, DC 20036. Telephone: (202) 822-7840. Fax: (202) 822-7779. Learning Tomorrow Program. Offering funding for "Teacher-Led, school based initiatives that use technology to improve learning . . . among students at risk."

National Telecommunications and Information Administration (NTIA) grants, Herbert Clark Hoover Building, 14th St. & Constitution Ave, NW, Washington, DC 20230. Telephone (202) 482-1551.

Resources Especially for Graduate Students

National Academy of Education, Stanford University School of Education, CERAS 507, Stanford, CA 94305-3084. Telephone: (415) 725-1003. Fax: (415) 723-7235. Spencer Postdoctoral Fellowships. Intended "to promote scholarship on matters relevant to the improvement of education."

National Association for Core Curriculum, Inc., 404 White Hall, Kent State University, Box 5190, Kent, OH 44242-0001. Telephone (216) 678-0006. Fax: (216) 672-3407. Bossing-Edwards Research Scholarships. Intended "to encourage research on core curriculum and other interdisciplinary/integrative approaches to education."

The Grants Register: 1995-97, ed. Lisa Williams, published by St. Martin's Press. This publication contains listings for thousands of general as well as institution- or discipline-specific grants.

ACKNOWLEDGMENTS

Our thanks to the participants in "Surviving the Journey: Practical Strategies for Computers and Writing Program Development," a workshop held at the 1995 Computers and Writing Conference with on-site and online participants. The workshop discussion has informed and inspired this chapter. The contributions of David Owen, Andrew Henry, John Slatin, Sharon Cogdill, Susan Romano, Sandra Lee, and Peg Syverson were particularly valuable.

REFERENCES

Arendt, H. (1958). *The human condition.* Chicago: University of Chicago Press.

Barker, T., & Kemp, F. O. (1990). Network theory: A postmodern pedagogy for the writing classroom. In C. Handa (Ed.), *Computers and community: Teaching composition in the twenty-first century* (pp. 1-27). Portsmouth, NH: Heinemann-Boynton/Cook.

Brooke, R. (1987). Underlife and writing instruction. *College Composition and Communication, 38,* 141-153.

Daisley, M. (1994). The game of literacy: The meaning of play in computer-mediated communication. *Computers and Composition, 11,* 107-120.

DeLoughry, T. J. (1996, January 26) Reaching a "critical mass." *The Chronicle of Higher Education,* p. A17.

Freire, P., & Macedo, D. (1987). *Literacy: Reading the word and the world.* South Hadley, MA: Bergin & Garvey.

Gilbert, S. (1994, November). *If it takes 40 to 50 years, can we still call it a revolution?* Paper presented at Teaching and Learning in the New Academy Conference, Richmond, VA.

Green, K. C. (1996). *Use of instructional technology jumps on college campuses.* Claremont, CA: Office of Public Relations, Claremont Graduate School.

Harrington, S. (1996). Posting to <ACW-L@UNICORN.TTU.EDU> on 20 February.

Hawisher, G. E., & Selfe, C. L. (Eds.). (1991). *Evolving perspectives on computers and composition studies: Questions for the 1990s.* Urbana, IL & Houghton, MI: The National Council of Teachers of English and Computers and Composition Press.

LeBlanc, P. J. (1994) The politics of literacy and technology in secondary school classrooms. In C. L. Selfe & S. Hilligoss (Eds.), *Literacy and computers: The complications of teaching and learning with technology* (pp. 22-36). New York: Modern Language Association of America.

Rhinehart, G. (1995). Posting to <ACW-L@UNICORN.TTU.EDU> on 12 December.

Selfe, R. (1995). Surfing the tsunami: Electronic environments in the writing center. *Computers and Composition, 12,* 311-322.

Selfe, R. (1997a, January). *Making progress within local contexts: Human and technical infrastructures behind teaching with technology.* Presentation delivered at George Mason University, The Epiphany Institute: Astride the Divide, Washington DC.

Selfe, R. (1997b, February). *Unpublished internal document: Proposal for lab fee increase, Humanities Dept., Michigan Technological University.* Prepared for the Student Lab Fees Subcommittee of the Computer Advisory Committee, MTU.

Selfe, R., Heaps, A., Kitalong, K., Coffield, K., El-Wakil, S., Gillam, J., Henry, A., & Suchman, S. (1995). *Surviving the journey: Practical strategies for computers and writing program development.* Paper presented at the Computers and Writing Conference, El Paso, TX.

Simone, S. S. (1995). *Exercise prepared for Selfe et al. Surviving the journey: Practical strategies for computers and writing program development.* Paper presented at the Computers and Writing Conference, El Paso, TX.

Welch, N. (1993). Resisting the faith: Conversion, resistance and the teacher. *College English, 55*(4), 387-401.

Chapter • 15

A Mediated Coexistence:
The Case for Integrating Traditional and
Online Classroom Training for New
and Experienced College Teachers

Ruth Mirtz
Carrie Shively Leverenz

The rapid escalation in computer use in the workplace and in the home has led to a perceived need for increased computer literacy, a need that many college and universities are responding to by investing in computer-supported instruction. Writing programs that serve a large percentage of the student body are often targeted to benefit from this investment. However, the new computers and software rarely replace all the traditional writing classrooms and rarely come with money to keep the equipment repaired, let alone to pay the costs of developing appropriate curriculum and a coherent, thoughtful teacher-training program. In some colleges, this gap in training is filled when a few technologically adventurous teachers train themselves to teach in online environments and then offer to help their less proficient colleagues. In other universities, the responsibility for training teachers for both online and traditional teaching may be "tacked on" to a writing program director's other administrative responsibilities or delegated to an overworked, underpaid graduate student.

As writing program administrators responsible for supervising 80 to 90 teaching assistants each year, 30 to 40 of whom are in their first year of teaching, we have struggled to provide adequate training and support for teachers of writing in both traditional and online classrooms. Both kinds of teaching are, and we expect will remain, highly visible in our program. Although we have a long-standing, well-structured training program for traditional classroom teaching, providing adequate training for online teaching has been a particular struggle because we did not initially understand how we viewed the potential of the online classrooms or their relation to the traditional classrooms. Because we now believe that online writing instruction should go beyond mere word processing to include attention to the ways in which networked communication challenges traditional notions of authors, readers, and texts, we also believe that teachers must come to see the online classroom as fundamentally different from a traditional classroom and must be given support for developing a pedagogy that makes the most of those differences. Given our high hopes for online writing instruction, the continued strong presence of traditional writing classrooms, and our lack of resources for totally individualized teacher training, we developed an alternative: the integration of online training into the training we provide for all teachers, most of whom will teach in traditional classrooms. Although our integration of these two kinds of training was initially motivated by our very practical need for a larger pool of teachers prepared for online teaching, we believe that because online teaching can disrupt and challenge conventional notions of classroom discourse and authority, teacher training is at its best when traditional and online classrooms are seen as provocative influences on each other and when all teachers are given the chance to experience that provocation. In addition to helping computer classroom teachers use the full potential of the available technology, we believe that experience in an online classroom can encourage teachers to be flexible, to take risks, and to move beyond the familiar. The online classroom can also provide a lens through which to examine and critique more "traditional" classroom practices. Although a teacher may still prefer teaching in a traditional classroom, having the opportunity to experience a radically different classroom setting can help him or her see the familiar classroom with new eyes. New teachers must be willing to interrogate their unexamined assumptions regarding teaching, learning, writing, and technology, and experienced teachers must be given opportunities to reflect on the relation between traditional and online teaching and to share their reflections with the whole teaching community. For such an integrated training program to provide the greatest benefit to all, administrators must be prepared to articulate a clear philosophy of computer-supported writing instruction, a philosophy that includes the special, disruptive, challenging relation between traditional and online classrooms.

The special kind of integration that enacts this philosophy is called a *mediated coexistence* of the two kinds of teaching. We begin by describing some of the other philosophies we have propounded, tacitly or consciously, as we worked to develop a provocative training program. Later, we explore the gamut of reactions to teacher training that new and experienced teachers describe and how those reactions can be used to move a training program toward this mediated coexistence.

TOWARD A PHILOSOPHY OF MEDIATED COEXISTENCE: HOW WE GOT WHERE WE ARE

For several years we did not see a reason to change our existing teacher-training program, even when the addition of a second computer classroom and a major software upgrade (to establish networked computers rather than stand-alone word processors) created the need for twice as many teachers to teach in these newly networked spaces. The existing training program consisted of two graduate-level training courses offered during a 6-week summer session and an additional 1- or 2-day workshop focused on how to use the classroom's software offered the week before classes start. Our own lack of experience led us to believe that teachers could move unproblematically from traditional to online teaching, with only a few hours of such practical instruction. However, a concrete problem appeared when the volume of problems and questions from teachers struggling in the online classrooms suddenly increased. Something was amiss because fewer teachers wanted to teach in the online classrooms and some teachers were using the computers less and less in their daily instruction.

We realize now that our former training program, which included no discussion of online writing or teaching practices in the required training classes and only limited software instruction for those teachers assigned to a computer classroom, reflected an unstated but powerful message: "Computers are just a tool that help you do what you would ordinarily do in a traditional classroom. You don't need to change. Your pedagogy doesn't need to change. Your students don't need to change."

Our lack of experience with online teaching, both as teachers and administrators, made it easy for us to think of training for the traditional classrooms as training in the "basics" and to see training for online teaching as "supplemental" but not necessary, something to do at a later date. Although we had done some reading about the effect of computers on composition, we had no experience with the disequilibrium that networked classrooms can create in teachers who expect to stand at the front of the room and command students' attention, who routinely initiate and manage class discussions, or who are accustomed to intervening, even unobtrusively, in small group workshops—all practices that can be difficult for teachers to perform online. Without firsthand knowledge of these difficulties, and with limited time and resources, we believed that the "basic" issues of writing instruction—how to construct a good writing assignment, how to handle the paper load, and how to evaluate writing— would be most pressing for new teachers. We took it for granted that training focused on these basic teaching skills would easily transfer across teaching situations, even though a decade ago Bridges (1986) urged that "[h]elping prospective teachers redefine the basics . . . should be the focal point of any comprehensive training program" (p. 15). Our training program was not allowing teachers to redefine classroom dynamics, the nature of authority in writing classrooms, and the changes that technology brings to the classroom.

Even when administrators recognize the special demands of teaching in a networked classroom, they may minimize the differences between online and traditional classroom teaching in an effort to lessen the anxiety many new teachers feel when assigned to a computer classroom for the first time. Assuring new computer classroom teachers that they do not need to know anything special to be able to teach writing online can give them the confidence all teachers need. Although workable because of its practicality, this "another way of doing the same thing" philosophy of online teaching comes dangerously close to the "replacement fallacy" Kemp (1987) described and that characterized a lot of early computer and composition programs. When classrooms were first furnished with computers, they were expected to be little more than word processors and were expected to do little more than make the physical act of writing easier. Although such a limited and limiting view of the computer's potential effect on writers, readers, and texts has been challenged in the literature on computers and composition teaching, many teachers have not had the opportunity to read this literature, and thus have not had their assumptions about computers and composition questioned. As one teacher in our program said, "The traditional [teacher] training counts for everything I do—the computers just change how I do it. I see the computers as a tool to do the same thing we do in the traditional [writing class]." Although this teacher's view may seem naive, we recognize that our focus on training in the "basics" of traditional classroom teaching and our treatment of online teaching as supplemental, something laid on top of one's existing teaching practices, reinforced rather than challenged this view. The philosophy of "another way of doing the same thing," although seemingly comforting, can be, in fact, discouraging to students and teachers. Teachers anxious to explore the potential of the online classroom to challenge their students and their own teaching practices may feel unsupported in their efforts. There is no encouragement to try something in the online classroom that does not have a paper-and-pencil equivalent for a traditional classroom. Just as dangerous is the likelihood that teachers who go into an online classroom, expecting everything to be the very minimally differ-ent from a traditional classroom, may come to blame their students or themselves or computers in general—rather than their lack of adequate training—for whatever unpleasant surprises they find. We need to listen to those teachers and theorists who warn that "(t)he unproblematic corre-spondences between process pedagogy and word processing software . . . have to be questioned" (Faigley & Romano, 1995, pp. 48-49); Hawisher and Selfe (1991) also warned us to "develop the necessary critical perspec-tives to help us avoid using computers to advance or promote mediocrity in writing instruction" (p. 62). And when we listened to our teachers explain why they were struggling in the online classroom, we realized that our initial philosophy was not enough. As one of our teachers said, "The style, pace, and dynamics are all very different for me in the [online class-room]." Another teacher acknowledged the value of her traditional train-ing but found herself needing more: "Because I had taught several years prior to teaching in the [online classroom], I knew what types of papers I would assign, but that was all that really remained consistent between the two types of classrooms."

Our recognition that online classrooms require different teaching strategies led us to consider briefly a shift from a philosophy that sees com-puter classrooms as another way of doing the same thing to one in which traditional and online classrooms are seen as "completely different but just as valuable." We were tempted to deal with the differences between the two types of teaching by establishing separate teacher-training programs, a prac-tice that may convey to new teachers that although the two kinds of teach-ing writing are completely different, one is not superior to the other, and a teacher's preference for a particular teaching space is merely that, a personal preference. At those universities with a specialist in computers and composi-tion, such a division may seem natural, and the obvious benefit of this "sep-arate but equal" philosophy is that it gives each administrator a more man-ageable arena in which to gain expertise and a more reasonable circumfer-ence of responsibility. However, we recognized an inherent limitation in establishing entirely separate training programs. When only some teachers, usually those who volunteer to teach in a computer classroom, are given the opportunity to experience the difference of online teaching, they become a "captive audience" for computer-related theory and pedagogy, and the teacher-trainer is merely preaching to the choir. If Klem and Moran (1994) are correct that computer classrooms have "redefined the 'work' of teach-ing" (p. 84) and that teachers' "familiarity with the software and an under-standing of the network . . . are prerequisites to, but not sufficient condi-tions for, successful and gratifying teaching in the new workplace" (p. 85), then those teachers who do not elect to or who are not chosen to teach in a computer classroom miss the chance to expand and complicate their teaching repertoire. Another detriment of this separate but equal philosophy is that it segregates teachers into two camps, often into the computer "whizzes" and everyone else. Teachers who are uncertain about or resistant to online classroom teaching will not have the benefit of a risk-free space to try something new. And the challenges to classroom discourse and teacher authority made possible by online teaching stay within the group of teachers who are familiar and comfortable with such challenges, leaving those teachers who might most benefit from the challenge—those threatened or discouraged by technology—free to ignore the whole issue. In addition, given the increasing number of jobs requiring experience with computer-mediated writing instruction, we concluded that preparing teachers either for only traditional classrooms or for only online classrooms was not only impractical in our local situation but irresponsible as well.

All of these forces led us to ask whether all teachers who go through our training program might benefit from some exposure to the issues raised by online teaching, such as those Faigley (1992) outlined. For example, Faigley argued that "electronic discourse explodes the belief in a stable unified self, it offers a means of exploring how identity is multiply constructed and how agency resides in the power of connecting with others and building alliances" (p. 199). If it is true that using computers to write and to teach writing raises important questions about the nature of readers, writers, texts, and contexts, then all writing teachers should have the opportunity to ask themselves those questions. If computers make these and other issues more evident, all teachers should benefit from the experience of online classroom dynamics. Partly for practical reasons and partly for philosophical ones, then, we decided to include exposure to online writing and teaching as part of our 6-week summer training courses required of all new graduate student teachers. More specifically, we scheduled approximately half of the training meetings in a online computer classroom, where the new teachers were asked to participate in activities such as writing informal responses online, sending e-mail, and participating in small-group and whole-class online discussions of teaching issues, including current issues in computer-supported writing instruction. In particular, we wanted to be sure that all new teachers had the opportunity to consider whether the online classroom—a virtual classroom where paper could be obsolete, where authors are anonymous or collaboratively constructed, where texts are less fixed—can indeed lead to a radical shift in what it means to teach writing. Although an emphasis on the differences between traditional and online classrooms could make an integrated training program seem self-contradictory, we believe these differences can be mutually informing and can lead to a constructive dialectic of the sort demonstrated by Lanham's (1993) dialogue with himself at the end of his book about online literacy, *The Electronic Word*, a dialogue in which the resistant, book-loving self challenges the revolutionary, pro-digital self. Such a dialogue provides an important counterpoint to the otherwise monologic training program and provides a way to resist confrontational opposition in the two methods of teaching writing. Perhaps because the issues raised by online teaching are new to us, too, opening up these issues to conversation and debate is one way for us to illustrate the degree to which teaching writing is always an ongoing process of experimentation and re-thinking, rather than a practice that a teacher can quickly master once and for all, something that many new teachers are anxious to do. Two additional advantages of thrusting online classroom issues on all new teachers are that the entire community of teachers sees technology, the nature of authority, and changing discourse practices as important concerns to everyone, no matter where they teach or who they teach. And again, although teachers will have different responses to their online experiences, having shared that experience is important to the community building that is a goal of most teacher-training programs. Although for every teacher excited about online teaching there is another teacher who would avoid it at any cost, both of these teachers will at least be informed enough about online teaching to talk about their differences.

THE ASSUMPTIONS AND ATTITUDES OF NEW TEACHERS OF WRITING

In addition to articulating a clear philosophy regarding what we see as the relation between traditional teaching and online teaching and inviting new teachers to contribute to and question this philosophy, administrators must also be aware of the attitudes toward teaching, learning, and technology that new teachers bring to their training and find ways to help teachers uncover and complicate those attitudes. Uncovering one's assumptions about computers and writing and bringing them into conversation with others' ideas can yield important insights into one's teaching values in both traditional and networked classrooms. Perhaps ironically, it was the difference in teachers' responses to online teaching—particularly the negative responses—that taught us the most about the benefits and challenges of integrating our training program. We realize now that we had tacitly assumed that providing new teachers with experience in an online classroom would automatically lead to increased interest in and enthusiasm for online teaching. However, the new teachers' journal responses, surveys, and group discussions of computer-supported writing instruction revealed that their attitudes toward their experience with the online classroom varied widely, from unrestrained enthusiasm to absolute rejection. After having carefully supported initial experience in an online classroom, a few new teachers did request to teach in one. But just as many voiced a desire not to be assigned to an online class, and still others expressed indecision or anxiety about online teaching. Although few of our new teachers have teaching experience in computer classrooms, almost all of them have personal experience with computers that affects their attitudes toward online writing and teaching. Among the teachers we surveyed, many thought that computers had helped them become better writers, but just as many had horrifying tales of losing chapters of a thesis because of a bad diskette or because they did not know the software. We discovered a broader range of experience than we expected, as well: One teacher had a younger brother who had recently withdrawn completely into cyberspace; another teacher had never used a computer until the training session. However, the majority of these teachers used computers for almost all of their own writing and a similar majority believe that students need to know how to use computers to succeed in college and in the workforce.

Not surprisingly, for most teachers, the degree of their enthusiasm for computers was positively correlated to how much they enjoyed or tolerated computers in their own work and how much they believe their students need to be computer literate. When teachers are less reliant emotionally and academically on computers for their own work, they are less interested in technology in general and less worried about their students' need for computer experience. Obviously, new teachers' personal enthusiasm or dislike for computers will affect their response to training for online teaching, but the relationship between teachers' feelings about computers and about teaching in a computer classroom is more complicated, for it is often teachers' assumptions about what makes for good teaching or a productive classroom environment that most affects their attitudes toward online teaching. As Welch (1992) suggested, one benefit of being confronted with a radically different approach to writing and teaching is that we come to a better understanding of the teaching values we currently hold. When we consider the possibility of teaching in a paperless classroom, for example, we are forced to explain our preference for reading texts written on paper and responding to them using a favorite pen or pencil. If we resist the idea of using e-mail or chat groups to foster student discussion during class, we should ask ourselves what is so important about face-to-face teacher-student conferences and class discussions. Similar questions need to be asked by those with the greatest enthusiasm for online teaching: What is lost and what is gained, for example, when we freewrite on the computer instead of in a notebook? Although we recognize that writing programs and the teachers who teach in them can differ greatly, we believe that many of the attitudes our new teachers expressed are fairly common.

One attitude that has the capacity to affect both writing teachers and their students is a fear of technology in the classroom. Despite their own use of computers for academic work, some teachers actually expressed an apocalyptic, Orwellian view of technology in the classroom as the precursor to a society of computeroid humans who do not have any reason to move away from a monitor. More specifically, these teachers expressed a belief that computer-generated writing and classroom discussion were somehow less valuable than the writing and discussion that happens in a traditional classroom. For example, according to one teacher, "writing somehow becomes trivial when you write on the computer with a bunch of other people." Another teacher summarized an online discussion of computer-supported writing instruction like this: "We agreed that [online] teaching is impersonal and that we don't want to do it. . . . We agree that computers are wonderful for many personal deeds—but not for instruction." Behind these arguments against online writing lies an important if unarticulated assumption that writing needs to be personal and individual in order to be meaningful—an assumption held by many teachers who want to see their students come to love expressing themselves in writing. Teachers benefit from uncovering and interrogating this assumption regarding the inherent value of personal, expressive writing early in their teacher training, if only to soften the disappointment many of them feel after a semester of teaching required writing to students who do not see the value in expressing themselves to teachers for a grade.

Other teachers worry about a loss of intimacy and connection in the classroom that might occur if students regularly face a computer screen instead of each other. They seem to fear that students will become seduced by or addicted to technology and lose their "selves" or that they will come to prefer computer interaction to human interaction. In contrast to the claims of many proponents of online teaching, some teachers believe the computer classroom is antithetical to a process-oriented, collaborative pedagogy. They see the computers as tools designed for individual use and find that the arrangement of computers along the outer walls of the classroom reminds them of orderly rows of students all facing one way and doing "one's own work." In a network interchange, one new teacher summarized her small group's online discussion of computer-supported writing this way:

> We discussed all of your questions and came to the conclusion that NONE of us wish to teach in an [online] classroom, for pretty much the same reasons: We feel that the computer is dehumanizing and detrimental to the relationship between a teacher and a student. . . . We aren't very impressed with the whole notion of [online classrooms], actually, and do not covet the opportunity to teach in one. Computers are the antithesis of intimacy and socialness, two characteristics desirable in a first-year writing class.

One assumption revealed in this statement is that the teacher-student relationship is very important and should be characterized by "intimacy" and "socialness." Such an assumption is not unusual among new teachers, many of whom are quite idealistic about the impact they believe they can have on students and their writing. But as many experienced teachers know, this longing for intimacy with one's students can be problematic when teachers have to make hard decisions about how much of their time they can afford to give to students or when to enforce a tough attendance policy or how to evaluate writing that has not met their expectations. The articulation of this assumption about the importance of teacher-student intimacy provides an opportunity to talk about the potential of a networked classroom to build student to student relationships even as it de-emphasizes the teacher. But it is also important for new teachers to talk about why teaching and learning seem to require intimacy and whether this intimacy is beneficial or even possible in an institutional setting where teachers inevitably have more power than students. Related to the issue of power is the problem of teacher authority in the classroom, which concerns all new teachers and which experience in a networked classroom seems to foreground. For example, some of the new teachers we surveyed expressed concern that they would not be able to control what their students were doing. As one teacher wrote, "How do you cope with authority in a class where everyone faces a computer?" Another teacher seemed to see authority as a zero-sum game: If the computer has authority, then the teacher doesn't. And if the teacher isn't in charge of the class, he or she isn't really teaching. In this teacher's words, teaching with computers "means that you can not instill an authoritative approach to teaching—thus you act as a non-teacher . . . then we are back to the problem which *2001* and the Nixon tapes teach us—the machine takes over."

An obvious assumption here is that the machines—rather than the students who are operating them—are really in charge of a computer-supported classroom. This assumption leads us to ask whether it is student authority rather than the authority of the technology that is the real (and realistic) threat for these teachers. This is a question all teachers need to explore, whether or not they will go on to teach in a online environment. The challenge to teacher authority represented by the computers was vividly played out when these new teachers were given the role of students and asked to participate in online discussions. Like most students when first introduced to this new form of classroom conversation, the new teachers engaged in off-topic talk, told jokes, and wrote playful insults. Some used inappropriate language and purposely broke rules they would not have been brave enough to break in face-to-face discussions. The following discussion occurred among four new teachers trying to discuss online the advantages and disadvantages of teaching in an online classroom:

A: Probably the turning technological point in my life was learning to play Space Invaders in 1981.

B: Agreed, That was a challenge. You can't find any good games like that today.

C: On Atari, right? I hate video games now, though.

A: Yeah, video games are a real waste of time.

B: My son is five and can whip me in every Nintendo game he owns. This is an advantage in that expertise can easily switch to unexpected places. (Like how I tied that back to topic??)

D: "Everyone" tells me that the internet is great fun. I don't know if I believe it. I just call the mouse, meese, the rodent. I could think of other things to call it, but I don't want to sound anymore depraved than I already maybe do.

A: Alright we got off track there for a minute. Why do we want to teach in this classroom? Someone tell me.

B: You don't have to do all the talking.

C: Do we want to teach in this classroom? I think I would just for novelty, variety. Anybody ready to go get a brew?

B: Virtual beer, oh, the horror!!!!!

D: I dated a guy once that played a lot of "Galaga." Do any of you remember that one? It was about invaders from space and you advanced from cadet to general or something?

A: Did anybody see that episode on MAD TV when they gave homeless people virtual reality helmets for "virtual homes"?

These teachers are rightly concerned that their students would act similarly when writing online, but expressing these worries gave them the opportunity to talk about how much authority a teacher should assert in controlling any kind of classroom discourse—traditional classroom discussions or small group discussions, which typically include the kind of off-topic socializing exhibited in online discussions. Another result of teachers' experience with online writing was a recognition that students' attitude toward the activities they would ask them to perform was likely to vary. Some teachers loved online discussions; others hated them. What would teachers do if their students had similarly diverse reactions? This problem is not unique to a computer-supported classroom but is one that all teachers must face, especially those teaching a required course that students will inevitably have differing attitudes toward. Grappling with the fact that not all students will love us or our assignments is an important part of all teachers' preparation for the classroom. These new teachers' responses to the online classroom also remind us of how frightening teaching can seem to new teachers and how important it is to feel confidant that one can succeed. As Selfe (1989) pointed out, it is especially hard for English teachers "to surrender the role of expert teacher and assume the role of naive learner" when having to learn new skills, new software, and new ways of acting in the classroom (p. 50). Such confidence is more easily achieved if teachers can imagine themselves in the classroom, doing what they think teachers should do, which in their experience does not include giving students instructions about using software or sending e-mail. Not surprisingly, these new teachers express a resistance to adding any more to the complex work of teaching writing. Especially for brand new teachers, the traditional classroom is familiar and imaginable, whereas an online classroom seems risky and threatening, a place where they are more likely to fail. One new teacher reflected, "I think teaching for me will change if I teach in the [online classroom] because I think I would feel threatened by the technology and my own ignorance of it. This would undoubtedly affect my enthusiasm for teaching." Another teacher expressed a similar fear: "I'd give computer assisted teaching a try if my skills were up to par. At the moment I'd be afraid of bombing out on something obvious in front of the computer masters in my class." Of course, all new teachers are afraid of "bombing out" in front of their students, but it is easier to admit that one is not an expert on teaching writing with computers than it is to admit that one is not yet an expert on teaching writing in general.

Although we have been emphasizing the value of interrogating the assumptions behind teachers' negative responses to online writing classrooms, we also see a need for teachers who are ambivalent about or enthusiastic toward online teaching to have their assumptions challenged. One teacher admitted that being forced to confront his own resistance to computer-supported writing instruction made him more open toward its benefits. In his words, "In spite of my anti-computer stance . . . I must admit that I am buying into the things I read about them being better suited for the English classroom. This is an idea that intrigues me. I guess computers are here to stay and maybe we better learn to deal with them first as learners, then as teachers, then as both." Giving teachers the opportunity to share their concerns in an online forum makes it possible for all participants to speak, whatever their attitude, and this expression of multiple views is crucial to the process of community building that is one of our primary goals for teacher training. Implicit in the following online comment is the value of sharing one's fears with others:

> [Our group] discussion kept regressing to our personal fears and vendettas toward computers, but we all admitted that they can be of benefit inside and outside the classroom. We are all a little hesitant about teaching in a less-than-human computer classroom. Computers are expanding in their range of influence, and we'll be ready, just not so ecstatic as others might be.

From our perspective, a teacher's experience-based enthusiasm for online writing is far more instructive than any complex rationale we as administrators might have given him or her.

WHAT EXPERIENCED TEACHERS TELL US ABOUT TRAINING FOR THE ONLINE CLASSROOM

We have been arguing that conversations about teaching, especially those among new teachers during initial teacher training, are enhanced when these teachers share the experience of being in a computer-supported classroom. However, all teachers—newly experienced or thoroughly experienced, in both traditional and computer-based classrooms—need continued opportunities to learn new teaching skills and to problematize their assumptions. A survey of experienced teachers confirmed our sense of the value of continuing to discuss online issues throughout the years a teacher works in our writing program. In the survey, our teachers described the relation between traditional and computer-supported teaching in ways that reinforced our sense that teachers benefit from thinking about this relation rather than assuming that there is no difference or an unbridgeable difference. One teacher remarked that the computer classroom helped him do better what he was trained to do in his traditional classroom training:

> Most of what I know as a teacher is enhanced by the presence of the computers. It is easier to get students to help each other, to collaborate, and to respond to each other's work.

But these experienced teachers also reminded us that whatever we as administrators might hope to accomplish during teacher training, there is no substitute for actual classroom experience—both traditional and online.

> As a novice computer teacher, I was far more reliant on my usual methods transferred rather than incorporating the computer into class differently. . . . Experience enabled me to admit my novice-ness and allow computer-proficient students to be more authoritative. (I don't think you can risk that kind of authority shift in your first year of teaching.)

Experienced teachers who have taught in an online classroom do gain additional insight into their teaching personality and values. In contrast with many of the inexperienced teachers who tended to blame the computers for usurping writing instruction or dehumanizing the intimate act of teaching, experienced teachers recognized that an individual's personality can affect one's experience in the online classroom:

> [After one semester] I have not taught in the online classroom again, and I'm not sure if I want to. I suppose I'd like to give it one more try, but I think that it doesn't particularly match up with my teaching personality. I like chalk. I like faces, not backs. I like talking and writing, not typing and double-clicking.

For teachers who have rejected online classroom teaching for personal reasons, it is especially important to provide opportunities for ongoing discussion, not with the intention of changing their minds, but with the hope that other teachers will feel challenged by the questions these reluctant teachers raise and so that those reluctant teachers will not feel shut out of the teaching community. As one teacher who taught a semester in the computer classroom and decided not to return cautioned,

> Like many innovations in comp theory and practice, one sensed that all the world's problems and kinks had been solved by computerized teaching. In meetings, I never felt like my problematic encounters in the [online classroom] were taken very seriously by others who seemed to view the computer classroom as some kind of miracle.

Perhaps what is most important about these experienced teachers' comments is the reminder that teacher training does not end when teachers are no longer required to enroll in teacher preparation courses or when they step into a classroom for the second or third or tenth semester. These teachers continue to struggle—as do we—with issues of teacher authority, with the question of what kind of classroom community to create, with the problem of how best to teach students to care about their writing enough to want to make it better. Teaching in an online classroom does not resolve these issues for teachers, but continually reopens them, and that, we believe, may be the ultimate value of giving all teachers experience working online.

COMBINING PHILOSOPHY WITH PRAXIS: WHAT A MEDIATED COEXISTENCE LOOKS LIKE

Designing a teacher preparation program that includes both online classroom teaching and traditional classroom teaching requires a clear philosophy toward the relation between the two teaching contexts, but this training program philosophy needs to be more than integrative. In fact, an integration is not as important as continuous contact and space for disruption and difference which a cooperative, but incompletely integrated, coexistence allows. As Faigley and Romano (1995) reminded us, a "unified and coherent" program is always "fiction" (p. 46), and we cannot afford to preserve old dichotomies or assume computers are a short-term problem easily ignored. Teacher preparation needs to be ongoing—before, during, and after teaching; dialogic with traditional classroom teaching; sensitive to resistances among new and experienced teachers; and consciously philosophical about how networked classrooms are and are not the same as traditional classrooms. In other words, a mediated coexistence gives teachers the knowledge and understanding of two approaches to writing instruction and the room to discover for themselves what the two approaches say to each other. Although each school must generate its own training activities based on the needs of teachers and administrative limitations, we have developed five forums for teacher training that successfully mediate the kind of co-existence between traditional and online classrooms we advocate here. These include the following (see details in appendix):

1. Graduate course work in writing pedagogy that includes experience in online writing as well as close attention to traditional classroom teaching methods.
2. Separate "expert" or "advanced" training for teachers who are most enthusiastic or most likely to do well, at both the theoretical and experimental level and the concrete classroom problem level, generally in the form of 2 to 3 day workshops outside of the semester schedule.
3. Ongoing support of a specialized, practical, and therapeutic nature for those who have chosen freely or who are forced by circumstances to teach in an online classroom, generally in the form of regular staff meetings or problem-solving meetings during the semester
4. In-service workshops for all teachers where those who have withdrawn from online writing issues are in contact with those with other attitudes and where all teachers are challenged to reconsider their traditional classroom methods.

5. Listserv and other online forums for largely unmoderated, voluntary discussions of any and all teaching issues, an online equivalent of hallway and shared office teacher talk.

Our own philosophy into practice is to introduce networked classroom teaching to all new teachers, to provide a series of other ways for some teachers to become more expert in networked classroom teaching, and to let all the versions of networked and traditional classroom training influence and interact with each other. We generally try to use all five forums in a calendar year, in order to reach as many of our large staff as possible and to meet the myriad needs of the teachers. Those needs are determined in large part by the constant gathering of feedback from teachers and students in each forum. Assuming a certain kind of activity will produce certain results will lead to less and less effective time spent in teacher training. Quick surveys at the end of staff meetings, lengthier responses to specific questions at the end of a graduate pedagogy course, mid-semester self-evaluations of students and teachers, end of semester teacher evaluations, and of course, informal hallway interviews are all valuable sources for determining which of the forums will fit other writing programs.

In our own program, we are not yet sufficiently skilled as teacher trainers nor are our new teachers sufficiently confident of their teaching to use online teaching as the mechanism to complicate and interrogate any and all teaching ideas. We continue to separate completely some teacher preparation activities. We believe that we are able to reach and influence a larger percentage of our teachers by enabling them to choose their level of involvement in online teaching and yet, with each choice, to push them to take some risks with their teaching. A mediated coexistence, then, looks like a well-planned, productive chaos, perhaps what our classrooms look like in mid-semester when new peer response groups are forming and students are finding ways to work together on their papers. There is a lot of noise, lots of negotiation and compromise, not everyone is equally happy at every moment, not everyone agrees on what the task is, some are waiting for help, but everyone ends up talking about their papers. A training program that enacts a mediated coexistence between online and traditional classrooms is one where both kinds of teaching support and mirror, intercede, and provoke each other. This kind of teacher-training program may be an intermediate stage while we wait for online teaching to become the standard, but it may also be the kind of interaction of philosophies and practices that teachers decide they always want.

APPENDIX: FIVE TEACHER-TRAINING FORUMS

The five descriptions here are the ways we design occasions for teacher interaction and dialogue among all the aspects of our large writing program. Some of these forums have counterparts for training in the writing center and for professional preparation for the job market. They are also the result of a very practical need to do as much teacher training in groups as possible; few writing programs can afford to provide one-on-one preparation for teachers, even in simple knowledge of software. Some forums are required for all teachers on our staff; others are voluntary.

Graduate Course Work in Writing Pedagogy

Many schools have a required or optional graduate course that introduces important composition and pedagogical theories and conducts discussions of teaching issues. Some of these courses are regular graduate courses in the graduate program and some are practicums or "supervised teaching." Although the physical complications of holding a graduate course in an online classroom may cause logistical challenges, the philosophy of the course can include technological issues, changes in teacher-student roles, and practice being both student and teacher in the online environment. The best introduction to online teaching is in the context of learning to teach writing, rather than outside of that context. Graduate pedagogical courses tend to generate a sense of community, too, among new college teachers, and their interaction during the stress of encountering new technologies helps encourage the less aggressive computer users.

When redesigning a pedagogical course, at a minimum, articles on technology and teaching are added to the reading list, some activities are moved from oral discussion to online exchanges, and some teaching demonstrations are located at the computer monitors. When possible, the entire course takes place in the online classroom and the software is used in the same way that a writing teacher would for writing students. Whether locating the entire course in the online classroom makes teachers less prepared for traditional classrooms is still a question, but we believe it to be an unlikely event, as long as the course is truly mediated by computer technology and not an e-mail correspondence course.

Separate "Expert" Training

These intensive 2- or 3-day workshops are usually planned outside the school calendar, either before or after the semester, and generally include only the teachers who are most interested or have already been assigned to the online classroom. These workshops have a set agenda and are often the location for group decisions about policies and sharing teaching ideas. A simplified schedule is often as follows:

Day 1: Introductions, guest speakers on philosophies of online teaching, discussion of policies and practical issues, a series of teaching demonstrations to acquaint or re-acquaint teachers with software features or upgrades.

Day 2: Discussion of trends in technology and how teaching changes in the online classroom, advanced instruction in specialized software functions.

Day 3: Sharing and responding to drafts of course syllabi and writing assignments, hands-on practice with expert teachers, more teaching demonstrations, evaluations of the workshop

Ongoing Support for Problem Solving

Meetings for ongoing problem solving are designed for only those teachers assigned to the online classrooms. A 2- or 3-hour block of time is ideal, but 1 hour may be all that can be wrenched from the schedule during the semester. In these meetings, teachers do the most trouble-shooting and how-to oriented work because the participants are faced, often the next day, with students in front of computers in their classrooms. Policies and recent software changes have to be covered, and specific job assignments and duties are discussed. Follow-up meetings are essential because, in many cases, both new and experienced teacher feel abandoned by mid-semester when things are not going well. Even very experienced teachers discover unanticipated problems after several weeks of class. They or their students might be having problems with the software or hardware, but it is equally likely that they will have questions about pacing activities, about student interaction during online discussions, or about facilitating peer response groups. A short staff meeting agenda might look as follows: Introductions and announcements (5 minutes); demonstration of new software, new solutions to a problem (30 minutes); discussion of recent problems and concerns (30 minutes); question and answer period (30 minutes); hands-on time with the expert teachers (as time allows); and quick surveys to evaluate the meeting (5 minutes). A follow-up mid semester staff meeting might be structured only with announcements first, followed by questions and answers.

In-Service Workshops for All Teachers

We required our teachers to attend at least three of six substantive teaching workshops each year, one of which is entirely devoted to an online classroom issue. All teachers need preparation for the possibility of teaching in an online classroom, whether at their present school or another in the future; all teachers need to think about how to support their students' use of word processing and Internet research in their traditional classrooms. We purposely design these sessions for discussion of issues rather than hands-on experiences, partly because our facilities will not accommodate hands-on practice and because we want to attract the computer-phobic teachers, who need to start thinking about their role in a technology-rich future. For example, we recently offered a workshop on using the World Wide Web as a research tool for students in first-year writing classes. The purpose of this workshop was not to convince teachers that they should be requiring cybersources in student research papers. Nor was our intention to show teachers how the computer classroom can facilitate online research. Rather, our hope was that teachers would bring to the table multiple perspectives on the goal of the "research paper" in first-year writing and that as a result of the conversation that ensued, they would think hard about their assumptions regarding the uses of the Web for students' research. A 1-hour in-service workshop for a general audience of teachers might be planned as follows: introductions and goals for the workshop (5 minutes); read two or three short, provocative texts, possibly including students texts when possible (10 minutes); discuss three or four pertinent, challenging questions or have a short free write session for individual responses (15 minutes); small-group discussion to share responses and raise new questions (15 minutes); small groups report to the entire group about questions and concerns (15 minutes); one or two guest speakers describe a related teaching activity that involves some of the theme questions discussed earlier. With more time, teachers might write the actual activity or assignment just as their students would (15 minutes); and wrap-up discussion and short free write evaluating and describing what participants learned from the workshop (15 minutes).

Writing Teachers' Listserv and Other Online Forums

We offer a closed-subscription online forum for the teachers who are presently working in the online classrooms and our own listserv open to all of our teachers on staff and all topics in writing instruction. The forum available only in the online classroom itself is vital for technical matters and specific classroom questions and provides constant access to the expert knowledge of the director and his or her assistants. The open discussion listserv is an opportunity for teachers more gradually and successfully to experience an online writing environment, that is, to enact technology on one level while discussing teaching issues on another level.

REFERENCES

Bridges, C. W. (1986). The basics and the new teacher in the college com-
    position class. In C. W. Bridges (Ed.), *Training the new teacher of
    college composition* (pp. 13-26). Urbana, IL: NCTE.

Faigley, L. (1992). *Fragments of rationality: Postmodernity and the sub-
    ject of composition.* Pittsburgh, PA: University of Pittsburgh Press.

Faigley, L., & Romano, S. (1995). "Going electronic: Creating multiple
    sites for innovation in a writing program. In J. Janangelo & K.
    Hansen (Eds.), *Resituating writing: Constructing and administering
    writing programs* (pp. 46-58). Portsmouth, NH: Boynton/Cook
    Heinemann.

Hawisher, G. E., & Selfe, C. L. (1991). The rhetoric of technology and the
    electronic writing class. *College Composition and Communication,
    42*(1), 55-65.

Kemp, F. (1987). Getting smart with computers: Computer-aided heuris-
    tics for student writers. *The Writing Center Journal, 9,* 3-10.

Klem, E., & Moran, C. (1994). Whose machines are these? Politics,
    power, and the new technology. In P. A. Sullivan & D. J. Qualley
    (Eds.), *Pedagogy in the age of politics* (pp. 73-87). Urbana, IL:
    NCTE.

Lanham, R. (1993). *The electronic word.* Chicago: University of Chicago
    Press.

Selfe, C. L. (1989). *Creating a computer-supported writing facility.*
    Houghton: Michigan Technological University.

Welch, N. (1992). Resisting the faith: Conversion, resistance, and the
    training of teachers. *College English, 55*(4), 387-401.

Chapter • 16

Asynchronous Networks for Critical Reflection: Using CMC in the Preparation of Secondary Writing Teachers

Robert P. Yagelski

Not long ago, Lynn, a former student teacher of mine, invited me to visit the high school where she now teaches in central Indiana. The visit was a rare pleasure for me, an opportunity to catch up with a former student in her first year as a full-time classroom teacher and to talk with her new colleagues about teaching writing. At an after-school meeting of English department at Lynn's school, I found myself at the center of a vigorous discussion about the role of literature in the high school English curriculum. I argued, as I have elsewhere (Yagelski, 1994), that literacy and not literary studies should be at the center of the secondary school English curriculum, a position to which most of Lynn's new colleagues took strenuous exception. For Lynn, it was uncomfortable to watch her new colleagues and a former professor engage in heated debate about what and how to teach in high school English classes. For me, however, what was most remarkable about the visit was that we had such a discussion at all.

That discussion was part of a monthly English department meeting at which Lynn and her colleagues share ideas about teaching or discuss issues in English with guest speakers. Notwithstanding Lynn's discomfort, the debate about English curriculum in which we engaged during my visit was an opportunity for Lynn and her colleagues to address complex issues in the teaching of secondary school English. Unfortunately, my visits with former student teachers are more likely to leave me with the "disquieting sense of familiarity with the school, the classroom, and the assignments" that Kutz and Roskelly (1991, p. 3) described in their book about transforming the teaching of English. The classroom activities, the reading and writing assignments, the content of the lessons, even the arrangement of the room are often deadeningly similar to any number of other high school classrooms I have been in—including those where I have taught. It can be dismaying to see how readily some of my former students adapt to the conventional practices of their new professional communities and, in the face of often overwhelming teaching loads and a rigid prescribed curriculum, abandon approaches to teaching writing that I hoped they had learned as preservice teachers. Even more dismaying is the realization that many of these young teachers have adopted what I believe to be problematic attitudes toward teaching writing that continue to drive the English curriculum in secondary schools. For many of these teachers, the kind of discussion in which I engaged with Lynn's colleagues is not part of their professional practice. Covering the prescribed curriculum, managing the paper load, and maintaining order preclude the kind of critical attention to teaching that enables them "to reflect critically on their education and society" (Kutz & Roskelly, 1991, p. 8).

Like Cochran-Smith (1991), I believe that "[p]rospective teachers need to know from the start that they are part of a larger struggle and that they have a responsibility to reform, not just replicate, standard school practice" (p. 280). And so to visit a former student teacher and see a classroom that replicates standard school practice highlights a difficult challenge facing teacher educators: how to introduce new or prospective secondary school English teachers to effective writing pedagogies in a way that fosters the kind of ongoing critical reflection advocated by Cochran-Smith, Kutz, and Roskelly, and other proponents of critical pedagogies. Mayher (1990) argued that in order to avoid constructing makeshift approaches to teaching literacy and replicating problematic existing practices, teachers need to develop the "capacity to learn from their teaching by being in continual conversation with it" (p. 283). That effort must begin with teachers' preservice training as student teachers. Because they are almost certain to face the kind of working conditions Kutz and Roskelly described and because opportunities like those at Lynn's school to reflect on their practice will likely be limited, student teachers must learn while in their teacher-training programs to become what Schon (1987) called "reflective practitioners." As such, new teachers may be more likely to construct theoretically grounded pedagogies that result from careful, critical reflection in the face of often overwhelming daily responsibilities that might otherwise encourage them to abandon whatever approaches to teaching writing they may have adopted as a result of their training.

In an effort to foster the kind of reflective practice described by Schon (1987), I incorporated into a sequence of required methods courses for English education majors at Purdue University several elements designed to provide opportunities for critical reflection on the theory and practice of teaching writing in secondary schools. The most important of these elements were extended, carefully structured field experiences in local high school and middle school classrooms, a series of projects that encouraged critical reflection on the students' experiences in those classrooms, and the use of asynchronous computer-mediated communication (CMC) as a vehicle for ongoing discussion and reflection.[1] I began using asynchronous CMC as a way to extend classroom discussion beyond the weekly class meetings in order to leave more class time for students to work on their writing assignments. Eventually, however, as I explored the potential of this medium as a teaching tool, I came to see CMC as integral to my students' preparation as secondary school English teachers. Despite a number of problems that often accompany attempts to use CMC in teaching, asynchronous CMC became the central vehicle by which I encouraged these preservice English teachers to reflect critically on the teaching of writing in schools.

This chapter describes how I used asynchronous CMC as a vehicle for reflective practice in the training of secondary school English teachers. My discussion, however, is not about the wonders of computer technology in the teaching of writing; rather, it is about one way in which computer technologies can be employed in the ongoing effort to transform practice in English classrooms. I begin with Freire's assumption that "literacy becomes a meaningful construct to the degree that it is viewed as a set of practices that functions to either empower or disempower people" (Friere & Macedo, 1987, p. 141). Ultimately, my goal is for my students to begin to conceptualize literacy as a social practice, as a potentially "transformative act," in Freire's words. The more immediate goal is to help them develop a critical stance toward literacy and its teaching in schools. Furthermore, I assume that technology is not neutral but that, as Selfe and Hilligoss (1994) put it, "technology, along with the issues that

---

[1]*Asynchronous* CMC refers to electronic communication that does not happen in "real time." In other words, those communicating electronically are not "speaking" to each other at the same point in time. E-mail is the most obvious example of asynchronous CMC. An e-mail message may be read by the receiver days or even weeks after it is sent. Electronic discussion groups, or newsgroups, another common form of asynchronous CMC, are the focus of this chapter. Such asynchronous forums allow students to "participate" in discussions without all of them being logged onto the computer network at the same time. Real-time, or synchronous, CMC, by contrast, requires participants to be logged onto the network at the same time in order to "talk" to one another via their computers. This chapter does not address synchronous forms of CMC.

surround its use in reading and writing-intensive classrooms, both physically and intellectually disrupts the ways in which we make meaning" (p. 1). My purpose, then, is to use technology to disrupt my students' received notions about literacy and its teaching and to employ that technology as a vehicle for encouraging critical reflection.

ENGLISH 391 AND THE PROBLEM OF TEACHING CRITICAL REFLECTION

As one of three "methods" courses required of English education majors at Purdue University, English 391, Advanced Composition for English Teachers, is intended in part to prepare preservice teachers to teach writing to secondary school students. But it is unique among the methods courses in Purdue's program in that it is also a writing course taught in a networked computer lab equipped with 24 Apple computers linked to the university's mainframe system, so that each machine also has Internet access. For many students, the lab environment is intimidating; they tend to associate their English classes with less technological settings. Nevertheless, most expect the course to "teach" them something about computers and writing. The course thus foregrounds the students' writing in unconventional and sometimes challenging ways that, for many students, has not happened in previous writing courses. For instance, the ease with which students can change their drafts and distribute them to classmates over the network can highlight the ongoing nature of revision and make them more aware of various social factors they tend to consider when revising; the network can also complicate such issues as audience and authorship. In short, these elements of the course—its focus on methods of teaching writing, its focus on the students' own writing, and the use of technology in writing—work together to draw student attention to writing and its teaching in what I hope will be useful ways.

But these elements by themselves do not necessarily foster the kind of critical reflection that Mayher, Schon, and others advocate. In moving from the college classroom, where they are student writers, to a high school classroom, where they become student teachers, students often are overwhelmed by the many challenges of classroom teaching and quickly revert to more familiar traditional practices in their teaching. Some evidence suggests that many student teachers readily abandon the methods and theoretical frameworks that they learned in their college methods courses when faced with the difficulties of managing a secondary school English classroom of their own. A group of student teachers in one study, for example, rejected much of the content of their university methods courses in as little as 2 weeks after they began student teaching (Richardson-Koehler, 1988). My own experience with student teachers corroborates such a finding. Too often I have seen student teachers jettison techniques for teaching writing that but a few weeks earlier they had enthusiastically advocated in their methods course. I recall one student teacher who was a vocal proponent of process-oriented techniques such as the regular use of peer editing groups as a vehicle for helping high school students improve their writing. During class discussions and in her written assignments for English 391, this student teacher enthusiastically embraced these techniques as more effective than more traditional "product-centered" approaches. The following semester, after only a few weeks of student teaching, I asked her why she had not used peer groups in any of her lessons. She replied that there wasn't time to work on her students' writing because she was under pressure to "finish" Romeo and Juliet by a specified date. Besides, she added, the students don't work well in groups.

None of this is surprising, given the pressures of classroom teaching and the constraints on new teachers. What is most disheartening, however, is the lack of careful, critical reflection on the part of new teachers in such cases. For this student teacher, the pressures of "delivering" the prescribed curriculum were real, but those pressures seemed to preclude any questioning of that curriculum or the conventional methods by which it was "delivered." She did not examine the ways in which her daily lessons, constructed to "finish" Romeo and Juliet by a certain date, might actually conflict with her broader goals for her students as writers and readers and even inhibit effective group work. In such instances, "student teaching [can] become simply an exercise in adapting new personnel into old patterns" (Salzillo & Van Fleet, 1977, p. 28), and the student teacher a vehicle for a curriculum that may remain unquestioned and unaltered. The goal of teaching literacy as a "transformative act" is quickly lost in the frantic attempt to stay on schedule.

Many scholars have critiqued school practices and teacher-training programs for the ways in which they tend to replicate existing practices (e.g., Giroux, 1988). And many argue that encouraging teachers to adopt a critical stance on their own work is a key to transforming those practices. Schon (1987) wrote eloquently about the need to foster in new teachers what he called "reflection-in-action," that is, teachers' ability to think critically about what they are doing as they face unfamiliar or difficult situations in their practice as teachers. For Schon, such critical reflection results from a constant moving between practice and critique, so that a beginning teacher first learns a method and its theoretical underpinnings, experiments with that method in a classroom situation, then reflects on the experience—usually in conjunction with a mentor—returns to the classroom to make adjustments and try again, then engages in further reflection. The goal is to encourage new teachers to understand reflection and critique as an integral part of their practice. For Schon, the key to achieving this goal is the opportunity for ongoing reflection and critique;

the problem, of course, is how to provide those opportunities within institutional contexts that can work against them.

In the English education program at Purdue, I worked closely with local teachers to incorporate carefully defined field experiences into two methods courses and to provide regular opportunities for reflection on those field experiences, which took place in middle and high school classrooms.[2] In addition, English 391, which did not have a field experience component but was required of English education students, became a forum for discussion of those field experiences because many (and sometimes most) of the students in the course each semester were also enrolled in one or both of the methods courses. The goal in these courses was to create the kind of regular opportunities for critical reflection that Schon described. But the practical constraints we faced in scheduling field experiences and coordinating the other requirements associated with the methods courses became significant obstacles. Often, there simply was not time within the confines of a three-credit course to schedule the reflective sessions that we felt were essential in helping students develop a critical stance toward their teaching. Additionally, we needed time simply to introduce students to the theory and methods of teaching writing that we hoped they would take into their classrooms. Such constraints eventually led me to see the use of asynchronous CMC, in the form of a Usenet newsgroup that I set up for English 391 and for a related methods course, as a crucial element in our effort to help students become reflective practitioners.

STRUCTURING THE ASYNCHRONOUS ONLINE ENVIRONMENT FOR REFLECTION

CMC as an instructional tool is by now nearly two decades old. Distance-learning educators have been using asynchronous applications on computer networks since the late 1970s to teach every imaginable kind of course with varying degrees of success (see Wells, 1993, for a good review).[3] And

[2]In Yagelski (1997), I described this collaboration between Purdue's English Education program and the English Department at Lafayette Jefferson High School in Lafayette, Indiana. Although the members of the Jefferson English Department, especially Joy Seybold, were not directly involved in the development of English 391, they were instrumental in helping design and mentor field experiences we collaboratively developed for another methods course in the Purdue program. I also wish to acknowledge the assistance of Sarah Powley of McCutcheon High School in Lafayette, Indiana, who worked with me in trying to link her high school students and my university students through the Internet (Yagelski & Powley, 1996).

[3]As indicated in footnote 1, discussion here focuses on asynchronous forms of CMC, such as newsgroups, listservs, and e-mail. It is important to note that syn-

as such asynchronous CMC applications as e-mail, newsgroups, and list-servs become increasingly common elements in conventional college courses, we are benefiting from a growing body of literature on the uses of CMC in teaching and especially in reconfiguring classroom discourse. We know, for example, that when used in carefully structured ways, CMC can encourage students to become more active participants in class discussions and can counteract some of the constraints that are inherent in teacher-led, face-to-face classroom discussions (Hiltz, 1990; Levin, Kim, & Riel, 1991; Quinn, Mehan, Levin, & Black, 1983). Additionally, some studies indicate that CMC can have a significant impact on student writing (e.g. Cohen & Riel, 1989) and on student learning generally (e.g., Cheng, Lehman, & Armstrong, 1991; Hiltz, 1990). Such findings are compelling to writing teachers who wish to create in their classrooms more egalitarian spaces for critical discourse among students.

These potential benefits of CMC represented a way to address some of the constraints I described earlier in my attempts to foster critical reflection among preservice English teachers at Purdue. For example, one of the first characteristics I noticed in the online discussions I initiated in my early attempts to use a newsgroup in English 391 was the potential for much greater participation by students than was typically possible in conventional class discussions. The newsgroup meant that I could devote more class time to student writing and collaborative work without giving up what I believed were crucial discussions about teaching writing and about the students' work in local schools. But simply getting students "talking" on the newsgroup about teaching writing was not enough; their "talk" had to be critical and reflective. As a growing number of studies and my own research indicate, using CMC for educational purposes is complex and potentially problematic (e.g., Kremers, 1990; Romano, 1993; Yagelski & Grabill, 1998).

Although many accounts from teachers who use CMC as a forum for discussion tout the potential of CMC to promote more egalitarian and less teacher-centered discourse, a number of studies indicate that how CMC is employed in specific classroom contexts can determine the nature of online student discourse. For example, Quinn et al. (1983) concluded from their study that a course employing CMC "should be structured to take advantage of the multiple threads of course discussion possible in non-real time media" (p. 325). Other studies have indicated that setting requirements for online discussions and even grading such discussions can

---

chronous forms of CMC, especially programs like Daedalus, have become increasingly popular among many writing teachers; however, as the following discussion makes clear, the characteristics of asynchronous CMC made the newsgroup a particularly appropriate tool for my purposes in English 391. See Butler and Kinneavy (1991/1994) for an interesting discussion of the use of a synchronous program to encourage an "interactive electronic discourse community" in a writing course.

significantly influence the rates and nature of student participation (McCreary & Van Duren, 1987; see also Wells, 1993). Moreover, as teachers well know, what works in one classroom may not be effective in another. In order to be effective, CMC must be used in ways that are appropriate to the context of a particular course and that match course instructional goals

In English 391, my primary purpose was to encourage student participation in online discussions in ways that would promote careful reflection on the issues we were discussing and on the experiences students were having in local secondary school classrooms. I was interested in lively exchanges that would engage students in the online discussions, but only to the extent that such exchanges fostered critical reflection on their work. Thus, it was as important for a student to post messages regularly—as a way to encourage reflection on the student's own work—as it was for that student to discuss the issues with her or his classmates. Accordingly, I required that students log in weekly and read all messages posted to the course newsgroup; in addition, students were required to post at least one message each week on some aspect of their work in the course or in the related methods courses. Ideally, these requirements would encourage students to take time each week to think in careful and focused ways about their work and the issues we were addressing; and they would do so in the context of discussions with peers engaged in similar reflection.

I also set clear guidelines for our online discussions. Initially, I did not describe the newsgroup conversations as "discussions"; rather, I assigned weekly "commentaries" in which students were to explore issues relevant to the course, pose questions, identify problems, and share their thoughts and insights. At the outset of the semester, before the students were online, these commentaries were written and submitted to me in hard copy. After the second week of the semester, I instructed students to post their commentaries to the newsgroup instead of submitting them in hard copy. In presenting the online discussions in this way, I achieved three purposes. First, the newsgroup was not initially presented to students as a forum for open discussion but as a place for exploring and sharing ideas. Second, students were given clear guidelines regarding what to discuss on the newsgroup. Third, a timetable requiring regular participation was established at the outset.

In my experience, such a structured approach to using CMC helps avoid some problems that some researchers have identified with the uses of CMC for course-related discussion. Perhaps most important, such structure helps eliminate student confusion about their purposes of CMC in a course and the students' online roles. In summarizing potential disadvantages of educational uses of CMC, Hawisher (1992) emphasized "the importance of integrating the conference fully into coursework, or the students will not use it" (p. 93). This assertion was supported in Yagelski and Grabill (1998). In that study of the uses of CMC in two undergraduate writing classes, we found that students' unfamiliarity with online discussions, together with a lack of clear expectations for online work set by the instructor, led to inconsistent student online participation and to discussions that deviated widely from the course topics. Online discussions were most likely to be deemed ineffective by the instructor and students when the students were unclear about the purposes of those discussions in the course. Our research also underscored the importance of the instructor's online role in influencing student participation. We found that students in the two writing classes we observed took their cues for online participation from the instructor. In one course, the instructor's online presence provided a model that in some ways seemed to limit student participation; in the other course, the instructor's lack of an online presence seemed to result in confusion on the students' part about their roles in the online discussions. Our findings reinforce some previous research suggesting that an instructor's "discourse style" influences students' online participation rates (Ahern, Peck, & Laycock, 1992). As Hawisher (1992) aptly put it, CMC applications like newsgroups "can be every bit as ineffective as traditional forums for learning" (p. 93).[4]

The newsgroup for English 391, then, was integrated into the course with clear goals in mind. It was to be a vehicle not just for discussion but for the students' critical reflection on their work in the course and their experiences in local secondary schools. From the outset each semester, I established guidelines for its use as well as (what I hoped would be) a clearly articulated purpose. I also established my role not simply as a "moderator" of discussion, as it were, but as a fellow participant and catalyst who tried to engage students critically, to push them and challenge them, to reinforce their attempts to be reflective about their work. The following examples of newsgroup discussions from the fall of 1994 illustrate the ways in which the newsgroup functioned as a vehicle for critical reflection.

---

[4]Some recent research suggests the complicated ways in which online discussions can be subject to some of the same problems associated with conventional teacher-led class discussion. For example, Thompson (1988) described how she dominated online discussions in the course she taught much as she had in face-to-face classroom discussions, producing 60% of the number of lines in online messages. Additionally, scholars have increasingly begun to explore the ways in which electronic discourse may replicate racial, sexual, and other inequities that can affect traditional face-to-face classroom discussions (e.g., Romano, 1993).

THE ENGLISH 391 NEWSGROUP DISCUSSION: "MOTIVATION AND POSITIVE COMMENTS"

In the fall of 1994 there were 19 students enrolled in English 391, all but 2 of whom were English education majors or elementary education majors seeking middle school language arts endorsements. As was usually the case in this course, the newsgroup discussions began around the third week of the semester, after I introduced students to the newsreader program and instructed them to begin posting their weekly commentaries to the newsgroup instead of submitting them in hard copy. The required once-per-week posting quickly evolved into the kind of lively discussions familiar to readers of Usenet newsgroups, with the multiple interactive threads reported in some studies (e.g., Levin et al., 1990) and with many students posting several times each week in response to each other's comments and questions. During the course of the semester, the students posted 258 messages to the bulletin board for an average of 13.6 messages per student. Seventeen (89.5%) students posted at least one message per week to meet my minimum requirement of 11 messages during the semester; however, 10 (52.6%) students posted at least one message more than the required minimum.[5] Three students posted 20 or more messages during this time; I posted 17 messages (see Table 16.1). These numbers convey a sense of how active the newsgroup became and they mirror the findings of some studies of CMC indicating that required minimum participation and clearly defined parameters for online discussions can result in high rates of student participation in online asynchronous discussions. But these numbers do not reflect the often critical nature of the newsgroup discussions in the course.

By the middle of the semester, students in the course were engaged in a number of discussion threads on the course newsgroup, including debates about evaluating writing, employing student peer editing groups, managing large paper loads, "standards" in English, and constructing writing assignments. In these discussions, students drew on their work in local middle and high school English classes. In effect, the online discussions were not just about the specific issues we were addressing in English 391, but also about the teaching of English—especially writing—in secondary schools more generally. More important, however, these discussions enabled students to pursue issues arising from their field experiences, assigned readings, and course assignments that they would have

---

[5]My requirement of one post per week meant that students were to post at least 11 messages during the semester. The minimum of 11 messages was a result of the fact that the first messages were not posted until the third week, when the students' accounts became active, and a fall break week when I did not require students to post.

Table 16.1. Online Participation Rates English 391, Fall 1994.

Student	Total Posts	Posts/Week
Rebecca	16	1.45
Janis	11	1
Kit	11	1
Ann Marie	11	1
Holly	12	1.09
Kristin	18	1.64
Mindy	21	1.91
Jacque	11	1
Stacy	20	1.82
Debbie	15	1.36
Kristi	17	1.55
Becky	13	1.18
Brent	16	1.45
Amy	11	1
Sue	10	.91
Emma	11	1
Sherelle	10	.91
Kristine	20	1.82
Christine	4	.36
Bob (instructor)	17	1.55
Totals	275	25

had little or no opportunity to address in any depth during face-to-face classroom discussions. From my point of view, what was most compelling about these online discussions is that they encouraged all students in the course to reflect on the teaching of writing in secondary schools in ways that would simply not have been possible during our twice weekly class meetings.[6]

Consider the following excerpts taken from the newsgroup discussions that occurred in November and December of that semester. In

---

[6]The one exception was Christine, who posted only four messages during the semester and none after the seventh week (see Table 16.1). But the case of Christine is illustrative, in that she was not an English education major and took the course for reasons that were not typical of students in the course. She was a senior journalism student, involved with the student newspaper and preparing to graduate and find employment in journalism rather than education. She told me that she took the course because she had heard that it was a "good writing class." But it became clear quite early that Christine was not interested in the focus of the course on teaching writing. Indeed, she helps support the point I make in the concluding section of this chapter that the use of CMC must be structured in ways that take into account the specific student population being served in the course.

this first set of exchanges, several students pick up on a topic that had been vigorously discussed both in class and on the newsgroup for several weeks: the challenge of motivating adolescent student writers and the related problems of managing class time and responding to student writing. The topic had initially been introduced a few weeks before by Jacque, who shared some concerns about motivating adolescent students after observing a class at a local high school in which a number of the students had not completed their writing assignments. In the first post, Kristi picks up the discussion by relating Jacque's original concerns about motivation to her own experiences in a program for at-risk students at the same high school. Several other students follow up with their own responses.[7]

> I would like to make a few comments about teaching students, not a subject. I tutor in the literacy lab at the high school. When I first started working with these students, I was nervous because a lot of them have behavior and attention problems. I came to realize over the past 2 months that all that some of these students need is a little extra attention, and to be treated like respectable students. I know that sometimes I feel as if the teacher of this class treats the students like small children, or kids in a special education class. These students are all capable students. I found that if I treat them like any other students, giving them the respect and attention that they deserve, they try a lot harder than if I treat them like they are stupid. I really think that it is important that teachers try to establish good relations with all students, no matter what their level of learning might be. If we show respect for them, they will be more likely to respect us. (Kristi, 11/18)

> The big discussion going on is time and how do we manage time for our students. Well, I would have to say that we need to help our students manage their time, but we can only do that with our class and are unable to manage their time with their other classes. I guess that is the problem. How can we help our students manage time with every thing else that is going on in their life? That was the biggest problem I had because I had everything due at the same time. (Stacy, 11/18)

> I wanted to comment briefly on Jacque's commentary about motivation and deadlines. It's true, I remember students in a lot of my classes not turning in notecards, outlines, or rough drafts because they were not worth much in the overall grade. I think that part of the reason was because they (as some of us still do) considered writing in terms of products instead of a process. Those little steps just seemed like hoops to jump through and extra points for the report card. Maybe teaching

---

[7]My contributions to the discussion reproduced here are signed, "Bob." I quote at length in this excerpt and the one that follows to convey the flavor of the online exchanges. I also reproduce the messages as they were originally posted, including errors, although I have deleted some material in order to protect the students' privacy.

writing as a process would change that a little. I think, though, that there would still be a problem with deadlines if they were created by the teacher and not the student. Jacque, you said that you make your appointments in this class early to motivate you to get your writing started. But I think that that's just it—you made the appointment. You agreed to a date and took responsibility for it. That seems to be important, don't you think? If the student is supposed to be in control of his or her own writing, doesn't it make sense that the student be in control of the writing process? Just a thought. (Kristin, 11/18)

What else can I say in regards to time management that hasn't already been said? It is something that we definitely need to stress the importance of. In my opinion, managing time appropriately has something to do with one's organization of their life. Maybe that is not true for all people, but it is for me. Unfortunately, I don't think I learned any organizing skills while in school. I attribute them all to my mom. We both run our lives in similar ways. Hopefully, I will one day be able to pass these skills on to other students. I believe they will help. (Mindy, 11/18)

I'm glad that everyone has commented on the procrastination-time management issue because I think that it affects everybody, no matter what the course. As I mentioned in my previous commentary, I still feel that it is our job as teachers to teach the students how they can manage their time more effectively, which will decrease some of their last minute rushes. Someone mentioned that it was nearly impossible to teach this for all of their classes since we will only have them for one class period. I think that if we can teach them in our class then they will be able to implement what they have learned for their other classes. That is the whole idea of teaching (in my opinion anyway)— teach the students a concept in which they can apply it to their lives at a later time. (Emma, 11/18)

I can relate to the commentary posted by Kristi. I agree that some students benefit greatly from a little extra attention. I, too, have been working in the Lafayette Jeff[erson High School] Literacy Lab this semester. For most of the last several weeks, the experience has been mixed; I have some positive, productive days there, and there have been a couple of very frustrating days as well. One of my main priorities in the lit. lab has been to LISTEN to the students that I am working with, and show them the kind of respect that they deserve. (After all, many of these kids have been told that they're stupid or lazy or doing things wrong for the last several years of their public schooling.) I show interest in them, and try to be encouraging and supportive. Just lately, some of the students have begun to respond very positively to my being there. We're getting through the lessons with fewer problems. Last Tuesday, one group requested that I work with them (a miracle)—and one of the students that I have been working most closely with, a boy who is extremely creative, but supposedly reads at a second grade level, told me that HE thinks his reading is improving. This made me feel great! He said, "I'm going to prove my parents wrong." (Kristine, 11/18)

I hate to say it, but I still have questions about time management. I just can't seem to tell how long things are going to take. How do I know how long an assignment should take? I recently forced a group of comp students at the high school to write a persuasive paragraph. I watched them write in class, so I knew relatively how long they spent on them. Some students spent a lot of time and some did not, but more time did not necessarily mean a better product. It seems like the little piece by piece prewriting activities and planning guides and note card checks would not only help them manage time, but also keep them working on the project. No one could just write up something quickly if they had to show the steps to get there.

I also made them do the peer feedback and revision thing. Not everyone revised. I felt guilty about taking away points for that until I noticed that their peer feedback giver had suggested some great improvements which were not made. Now I'm ruthless.

I'm not sure about my method of assessment, but at least they can look at the sheet and see why I removed points. But overall they were really creative and funny paragraphs.

The main thing I have learned about assessment is that it takes a long, long, long time. =)

On a different note, I want to share a quote from our last Murray reading. He discusses the pressure of "so much evaluation, so much self-criticism, so much reading" on the student. He writes, "The pressure must be there, but it should never be so great that it creates paralysis or destroys self-respect." On one hand, a lot of prewriting and revision help relieve the pressure of the deadline by making sure a lot of work is done before the paper is due. But it shouldn't be a lot of negative self-criticism and none positive. How can I make sure that my students have "respect for the potential that may appear" and "faith in the evolving draft"? positive comments on drafts? stickers? encouraging them to work until they have something they can look back on for a little self-confidence and pride in past accomplishments?

It seems that in this class and methods, yes, I have learned a lot, but I have found out about so much more that I do not know. Oh well, have a good day, everyone. See you in class. (Janis, 11/20)

Kristin, I thought that you made an interesting point in your commentary. You stated that you thought part of the reason that students don't turn in note cards, outlines, and rough drafts is because "they . . . [consider] writing in terms of products instead of a process. Those little steps just [seem] like hoops to jump through and extra points for the report card." (I hope that I quoted you correctly. I'm sorry if I didn't.) This statement brought another question to my mind: Could part of the reason that some students don't hand in this preliminary work be that these techniques don't coincide with their own writing processes? I handed in these assignments because I felt that it was part of my responsibility as a student: I was given an assignment; I was expected to do it; I did it. However, the note cards and outlines were almost like a separate entity from my paper. It was almost as if the note cards and outlines were one assignment and the actual writing of my paper was another assignment—they just happened to be assignments that shared the same topics and resources. When left on my own to write papers, I don't fill out note cards and write out a physical outline; I use different techniques. Maybe this means that I don't use the proper methods to write my papers. On the other hand, maybe these preliminary assignments end up forcing students to conform to writing processes that stifle their own writing processes, processes which may work better for them. (Jacque, 11/20)

Kristi, I think you're right on target with your comments about respecting the students you are working with in the Literacy Lab at the high school. As you point out, these kids are so often treated as if they're stupid that they may come to believe it themselves. Many will wear their label as a badge because it can give them status among their peers. But they all want to feel good about themselves, and as teachers we can help them do so. We have to remember that we're dealing with human beings—even when those human beings do and say things that we don't like. And it's worth remembering, as Kristine aptly pointed out, that it can take a long time to get through to some of these kids. Patience can indeed be a virtue for a teacher. (Bob, 11/21)

Janis, you asked an important question in your latest post: How can we as teachers make sure that students will have faith in their evolving drafts, as Donald Murray suggests in his article? The suggestions you offer make sense: making positive comments on their drafts on post-it notes, for example. But there's one crucial rule of thumb here: Be interested in *what* they write. If students see and hear your interest and enthusiasm for what they're writing, they are much more likely to have that faith in their work. It can be astonishing to see a kid get excited about his or her essay just because you, as the teacher, reacted with interest to a story or essay that he or she submitted. This may sound obvious, but as teachers we become accustomed to looking for problems in a draft (I know *I* do!), and we forget to let students know that we are actually reading *what* they are writing. Even simple little questions can do wonders: "Really? Did this really happen to you?" "That's amazing." "I was there once, too!" Such comments and questions let students know that you're responding to their ideas and not just to their prose.

And I think you're right, Jacque, to suggest that often students go through the motions when we ask them to complete specific steps in their writing. As you so correctly point out, students may use different strategies than we want them to use. We have to be flexible enough to accommodate the differences in the ways that students go about their writing—and we have to have a little faith that they'll do what works for them. This goes hand-in-hand with what I said above. If you give them some room to do what they believe is best at the same time that you express interest in their work, they're much more likely to stick with that work. (Bob, 11/21)

In the first post, Kristi extends the discussion of motivating students by referring to her experiences in the "literacy lab" at a local high school. She concludes after 2 months of working with at-risk students that a key element in her pedagogy must be respect for her students. In this instance, Kristi's conclusion about the importance of treating all students with respect arises directly from her experiences in the high school rather than from a text or class discussion. The newsgroup discussion provides her with a forum for sharing this experience with her peers. But it is in the context of the online discussion of such issues that Kristi examines and shares her experience; the online discussion, in effect, provides a context for ongoing reflection on and critical examination of her experiences. A few messages later, when Kristine responds to Kristi's post, she extends that examination by relating Kristi's assertion about respecting students to her own experiences in the literacy lab with similar students. In this instance, Kristi's comment provides a context for Kristine's reflection on her own experience and a framework (in this case, seeing at-risk student writers as people deserving respect rather than simply as students exhibiting "remedial" problems) for making sense of that experience. In this way, the newsgroup provided a critical space not just for sharing experiences but for re-examining them in the context of an extended discussion about teaching writing.

It is important to emphasize here that this critical online space differed in important ways from conventional classroom discussion, which is often constrained not only by time but by the instructor's agenda for each discussion as well. The newsgroup enabled students to pursue questions arising from their experiences that they might not have had the opportunity to pursue in face-to-face class discussions; perhaps more important, they pursued such questions in the context of their field experiences and related course assignments. For instance, Janis takes the discussion of "time management" in a different direction from Kristi's concern about respecting students. She relates an experience she had with adolescent writers in a local high school classroom and poses a practical question: How much time should we spend on a particular writing assignment? After describing the rather disappointing results she had with an assignment she gave her students, she draws an obvious but important practical conclusion about assessment (that it is very time consuming). She then relates her experience to one of the assigned readings by Murray (1972/1982), quoting Murray as she raises further questions about motivating student writers. In this case, Janis attempts to make sense of some difficulties she encountered in her field experience by drawing on ideas she encountered in the course readings. In sharing her experience on the newsgroup, she doesn't simply describe the difficulties she faced or pose a question to her classmates about those difficulties; she attempts to analyze those problems within a frame of reference provided by Murray's process-oriented ideas about teaching writing. This sort of self-reflection about her teaching is precisely what Schon (1987) advocated in his proposals for teacher education programs. Ideally, this reflection will lead to tentative explanations and ultimately to adjustments that Janis can make to address the problems she sees in her approach to responding to her students' writing.

Jacque engages in the same kind of theorizing in a follow-up to another student's post about motivating students. Like Janis, Jacque attempts to analyze the problems Kristin described by using the idea of the writing process as a theoretical frame. She explains the students' lack of interest in such prewriting activities as making outlines and developing notecards in terms of the students' own writing processes. And like Janis, she integrates ideas from the assigned readings, her own experiences (as a student writer), and the questions posed by a classmate as she participates in the ongoing discussion; in doing so, she reflects on her experiences and those of her classmates in an effort to explain a problem that she and other student teachers have encountered in working with adolescent writers.

My experiences in teaching writing in a variety of settings have convinced me that although it is certainly possible to foster this kind of critical reflection without the use of asynchronous CMC technologies, these technologies offer the potential for more in-depth and extended engagement with important course-related issues than is easily accomplished in a conventional classroom discussion. In their newsgroup discussions the students examined and tried to make sense of their experiences as writers and as preservice teachers of writing. Moreover, they did so in a collaborative online environment in which they engaged complex issues and problems as peers, as pre-professionals facing similar obstacles and striving toward similar goals. In this way the newsgroup functioned as something other than a formal collaborative project or assignment; rather, it became a place for collective inquiry into writing and the teaching of writing. The highly interactive nature of the newsgroup discussions and the potential for a less leader-centered conversation online facilitated that inquiry.

My role in this inquiry was, admittedly, an important one because I determined the course agenda and established the policies for participation on the newsgroup. But the brief exchange reproduced here reveals that I did not "manage" the discussion in the way I would manage a conventional classroom discussion. The issues discussed were raised by the students as a result of their field experiences or their engagement with course readings, and the discussion developed as students responded to each other or as they introduced new questions or issues into the conversation. My contributions served largely to reinforce several of the ideas offered by the students. At other times, however, I played a more vigorous role, challenging students' assertions or posing questions to extend their comments. In the following excerpt, for example, Emma rejoins the issue of responding to student writing, which Jacque had raised earlier, and relates this issue to the problem of motivating student writers. Initially, several other students pick up the thread, and then I join in by challenging some of Emma's assertions, which leads to further exchanges.

> I just wanted to respond to the commentary on positive responses (I forgot who wrote it—sorry!) I had an instructor during high school who ALWAYS gave back positive feedback on the papers so that it took the "challenge" away from writing the paper because you knew she would always like it. So the students assumed her class was the blow-off class and hardly prepared for it. Her class started to become unmanageable and the principal was called in to intervene. This was never done at my school unless there was a real problem.
>
> I agree with giving positive reinforcement on papers, but I believe there can be some kind of improvement (even in an A paper.) When I assess papers, I will point out their strengths, but only really praise a part if it is excellent. What I am trying to say is that I will be a hard grader, yet my students will "cherish" those praises that are hard to attain. I hope I don't sound like I'm bragging, but some of the best classes I have taken have had teachers who were hard graders and I worked so hard to get a good grade. That grade felt like an accomplishment and was remembered more than the A I got from the class where everyone seemed to get good grades. In the hard class, I knew that was the grade I REALLY deserved. The teachers of those classes were respected more by the student body and the catastrophes that the teacher had in my first paragraph were avoided.
>
> My final comment is that even though you establish yourself as a "strict grader," you must remember to keep the writing process open for the student. I mean that you shouldn't grade the student in a way that the student gives up completely. In your comments (even negative) always give suggestions that will help the student progress and not just slam the door. This is especially important for at risk students. I think this will only come with time and experience in the classroom. (Emma, 11/22)
>
> I just wanted to spend my last few minutes before break chatting on the bb. In particular, I wanted to respond to what Jacque posted about positive feedback. (You know, Jacque, you always bring new and good ideas to the bb!) I also like to give a lot of positive comments to the kids that I have been working with out at Jeff[erson High School] this semester. Positive comments really can bring positive results, I think. This is only true, however, if those comments are GENUINE. I also agree that a teacher who is TOO positive all the time can be perceived as being less than genuine (for lack of a better word.) Personally, I find people that are overly positive about every-

thing to be positively nauseating. So, you just have to be true to yourself, and be fair in your praise. Positive feedback may sometimes make all the difference in a student's learning, but too much may come off as sounding phoney. (Kristine, 11/22)

I just wanted to make a few comments about positive comments. I think that giving too many positive comments isn't beneficial. I am not saying that you shouldn't give them, but teachers shouldn't give positive comments just to make their students feel good about their work. Does that sound right? I really don't know what I want to say. . . . Last year, I observed a teacher at [Jefferson High School]. She never gave positive comments, and told me that when I graded papers just mark what was wrong without explaining what the students did wrong. I wasn't even allowed to tell them Good Job. I should tell this was a French class I think that you should help the students discover what they did wrong on the assignment, but she never let me do that—though I did. (Stacy, 11/22)

Jacque has raised further questions about making positive comments on student work, and many of you have responded with good advice. Of course, as Kristine and Emma and a few others have pointed out, making gratuitous positive remarks on student work is useless, since students will quickly realize that your comments are meaningless. We must, as Kristine reminds us, be genuine in the comments we make on our students' writing.

But let's not be too simplistic here. "Positive" is a relative term, and we can praise a piece of writing that is not well done, if there is good reason to. For example, let's say a student who is having real trouble with sentence boundaries hands in an essay that is superficial and poorly organized but which has no run-ons or fragments. That's cause for praise, and those positive comments about his or her success with sentence boundaries are doubly important if we (as we absolutely should) point out the problems with organization and development. Each student is different as well. And comments that might encourage one student may very well discourage another. Responding to student writing is no straightforward matter. It is simply not a matter of making positive comments or being "tough"; rather, it is a complex matter of evaluating and encouraging and teaching our students, who are complex individuals.

With that in mind, I'd caution against thinking that teachers perceived as "hard" or "strict," such as the teacher Emma describes in her post, are always the most effective. I wonder whether all students in her classes worked as hard as you did, Emma. One of my colleagues at the high school where I worked in Vermont was a history teacher who was among the strictest and "toughest" I've known. He never praised students, and he was legendary for his hard tests and high standards. The students almost universally believed him to be a "good" teacher. Yet if you looked at what his students were learning, there was good reason to question his effectiveness. For the most part, he allowed little or no room for careful, critical thought, and students could do well on his "tough" exams only by memorizing a great deal of information (which they likely forgot soon after the test). His pedagogy was based, in my view, on a limited and faulty notion about what counted as learning. Yet everyone believed he was a "good" teacher. We need to remember that societal attitudes are at work here. We are conditioned to believe that tough is good, that someone who fails a lot of students has high standards. I think it's rarely so clearcut. (Bob, 11/25)

Of course positive feedback can be meaningless. Even in this class people have read my paper and just simply said "Great paper!" My response to that is "So what." I choreograph for the Purdue Repertory Dance Company and members of the company are never overly critical of my pieces. My directors are, they tear things apart and many times I have left a conference very upset because they had nothing good to say. That was very discouraging for me and it was very hard to keep pushing on. I really wanted them to say what had worked in my piece but that was rare. This semester has been the exact opposite of the last two semesters. Everyone can only say good things. This works, that is great and I love the costumes. That is nice but almost just as devastating. I have worked so hard to get to this point and now I get no helpful comments. I think this is very similar to any writing as well. Students need both sides. All negative is depressing and all positive is worthless. If the student really wants to work negative comments or maybe more appropriately helpful comments, can help them pin point trouble spots. They also need some encouragement too. I think who ever said that all positive comments can make the student more likely to work much less for the teacher is right. If the student gets an A on every paper chances are that the students effort and quality will go down. Why should they work so hard if they are sure that they will get an A. I think a good mix of both. This is what you did well, you improved on this but you can still work on this. . . . (Rebecca, 11/28)

I hope everyone had a good break and managed to waddle back to Purdue in time for classes. I just wanted to comment on a few of the comments that have been posted (imagine that!) In response to Dr. Yagelski's response to my commentary I understand where you are coming from. However, I still felt I learned more from this teacher because the teacher was "stricter" and had higher standards. This was a challenge for me. I knew I had to actually work in order to get a high grade and even harder for an A. I think the challenge motivated me more than if I had an average teacher because even if I did poorly in the average teachers class I probably wouldn't have tried hard to do better. I would have settled with the B or C. But with the strict teacher, I was ALWAYS trying to do better whether I got a D or a B. Does this make sense? For example, for our portfolio at the beginning of the semester, I worked hard on my first draft. After our first conference I realized that you were going to be grading harder than I had anticipated! Therefore, I spent more time on my revisions than I would have if you had just put positive comments on my paper like, "Good job" or "Well organized." (Emma, 11/28)

Emma, you say in your latest post that you worked harder for that "strict" teacher. What about the rest of your classmates? Were they the same as you? Did every other student feel the same motivation as a result of this teacher's "strictness"? My guess is that the answer is no. Once again I want to stress that this is an enormously complex issue. We're just a little too willing to settle for easy answers: tough is better; easy is bad. As I've already said here, it's never quite so straightforward. What worked for you as a student likely did not work for every other student in your class, and a teacher who is inflexible in her approach will lose those other students. Moreover, don't fall into that old trap of believing (as I did as a first-year teacher) that your students are like you. I tried to teach like the teachers I had who seemed to reach me. While it's a good idea to borrow from "good" teachers, my mistake was in believing that what worked for me as a student would work for all my students as well. I was very wrong. You are not your students. Most of your students will not be English majors. Most will probably not even like English. Your challenge as a teacher is to find ways to connect with those kids—and that may mean adopting approaches that would not have worked with you.

And I don't believe that teachers represent the primary source of motivation for our students. Rebecca says that we can't expect our students to have the same kind of discipline she has. Why? If we assume at the outset that their only motivation will derive from grades, then we will likely miss opportunities to motivate them in other ways. I don't think most of my high school students were motivated primarily by grades. Many were motivated by the desire to succeed, to express their views, to feel valued. Many of my students knew they had little chance to earn an A, yet they worked even harder than many students who could earn A's. Why? I hope we won't sell our students short. It worries me when we begin to generalize about students in ways that limit our expectations of them. Don't forget what you felt like—and feel like—as a student.

Thanks for these good comments. (Bob, 11/29)

I would like to respond to the comments about what motivates students. As Dr. Y commented, all students are not motivated in the same way. I am motivated by a number of things, including grades, personal growth, and interest in my topic. Other students are motivated by an entirely different set of values. For example, I have a friend who works hard on papers, but if she gets a bad grade or disagrees with the teacher, she works even harder. In my case, I would probably get a bit discouraged. But she thrives on this feeling to succeed, and surprise the teacher with a great paper. This relates to our future as teachers. We need to get to know our students, and use a variety of techniques to see what motivates them. I plan on giving the students the option of rewriting essays. I feel that this is a motivator for some students. (Kristi, 11/29)

I would like, I suppose to comment briefly on motivation. I agree that we are all definitely motivated by different things. I can't assume that what motivates me motivates everybody else. Like Emma, I like challenging teachers—but only if I think that I can meet there challenges. There is no way I would be motivated to achieve The Impossible Dream. I went to the Kappa Delta Pi (education stuff) meeting last night and a guest speaker gave a speech about teaching. She said to always aim your objectives one step higher than you want your students to achieve (at least that's what I think she was saying.) At the time it reminded me of our discussion of motivation. (Ok, not really, but it did a second ago.) Anyway, I thought that this was kind of interesting. I took from this that your students are never going to be quite as motivated, or as successful, as you would like them to be. How sad. I really don't think that this is always true. If this formula works, are you ideally supposed to trick students into doing the work? Is this kind of like a pre-determined curve that will be used for end-of- the-semester grading? Ick. What does everybody else think about this? Happy commenting. (Kristin, 11/30)

This discussion that has been going on about positive comments is certainly an interesting and complicated one. Emma—I understand what you're saying about your "stricter" teachers having more of an impact on you. I have experienced the same type of thing, even at the college level. For example, this semester I have a class that feels like such a waste of time for me (Kristin—you know what I'm talking about!!). I can't seem to get anything out of the class because I can't dedicate myself too it. I don't have to. The professor expects so little of us that I usually do just enough to satisfy him. I thought my midterm was close to one of the worst pieces of writing I have ever turned in for a grade. To my surprise and delight—I got a A. I wonder how much studying I'm going to do for the final!!?

But, as has been pointed out by many people, being to hard of a grader can tend to "turn the students off," which is something that none of us want to do. I do believe that there is a happy medium between being too easy and too hard. It is up to each of us, as individual teachers with a variety of INDIVIDUAL students, to find that middle ground that works for our classrooms. Of course, this might be difficult, but I think it is something that will come with experience. (Rebecca, 11/30)

In this example, I move the discussion forward by challenging Emma's argument that teachers need to be "strict" in their grading policies in order to motivate their students. Kristine and Stacy seem to reinforce Emma's concerns about too much positive feedback on student writing, but their contributions somewhat complicate the issue. My purpose in my first message in this thread is to complicate the issue further and try to encourage the students to problematize the practice of motivating adolescent students through the use of strict grading policies. Emma's response to my challenge is to defend her initial position; she offers as illustration her experience with my own responses to her essays in the course. But in my follow-up, I don't let her—or Rebecca, who argued in support of Emma's position—off the hook, and I push my point about the complexity of the issue. My concern here was not to let students get comfortable with easy answers to complex questions, particularly since their own experiences as successful and motivated students often reinforce those easy answers. Like Schon (1987), I want students to think critically about their experiences as they try to make sense of them and draw implications for their pedagogy; like Freire, I want students to problematize their received versions of the world. Note that in their follow-up comments, Kristi, Kristin, and Rebecca draw on their own experiences as writers as they address the problem Emma has raised. I see this kind of explicit reference to and reflection on those experiences as akin to Freire's argument that in order to foster what he calls "critical consciousness," a teacher must begin with students' concrete experiences in the world, and I try to reinforce it where possible.

There are several further points to make about this excerpt. First, I view this online discussion as a productive attempt by the students to engage complex and sometimes difficult issues that will also become increasingly important as they move into positions as full-time English teachers. In discussing these issues on the newsgroup, the students are engaging in a kind of professional discourse about their work as student teachers and their future work as full-time teachers of writing. The newsgroup provides a forum in which the students can engage these issues more fully than they likely would in a conventional classroom discussion, because it enables them to think about the issues and their responses over time, rather than at the moment, as they would have to do in a face-to-face classroom discussion.

Furthermore, I argue that this kind of "pre-professional discourse" can be undercut by the complex dynamics of a conventional, face-to-face classroom discussion. In my attempt to push Emma's thinking and to problematize her assertions, I was aggressive in a way that could be uncomfortable for students when they engage in a discussion with an instructor, particularly a professor. Emma, in fact, tended to be a very quiet student in class and did not often participate actively in our class discussions, though she was more active in small-group discussions. To push her in this fashion in a conventional classroom discussion would, I think, have been intimidating to her as her classmates looked on (especially, as in this case, with a male professor arguing with a female student). The newsgroup offered Emma the chance to think about and respond to my challenge without having to do so "on her feet" in a face-to-face class-room discussion.

It also enabled other students to join in as they saw fit without having to wait to be acknowledged by the instructor. It is noteworthy that although my two comments in this brief thread were long and somewhat aggressive, they were only 2 of 10 comments involving Emma and five other students. These students enriched the discussion by directly address-ing Emma and each other and not just responding to my comments. Although some of these comments can be read as the students deferring to me, this discussion, like the previous example, was interactive in a way that can be difficult to accomplish in a face-to-face classroom discussion involving 20 or more people. For instance, Kristine responded to Jacque; Stacy and Rebecca joined in the discussion to respond to comments posted by other students; and after my comments were posted, Kristi, Rebecca, and Kristin responded both to Emma and to me. In short, asynchronous CMC allowed all these students to contribute to the discussion without waiting to be acknowledged by the teacher and without worrying whether or not their comments were still relevant or "timely" as the discussion progressed. In face-to-face discussions, it is often the case that by the time a student gets a chance to speak, his or her comment is no longer relevant because the topic of conversation shifted. Asynchronous CMC to some extent mitigates this "conversation drift" by stretching out the time of the discussion, as it were, and enabling students to post comments in response to comments that were posted a few days—or even weeks—before.

This kind of extended, interactive reflection in the online discus-sions in English 391 goes beyond what is typically possible in convention-al, teacher-led classroom discussion. Schon (1987) emphasized the impor-tance of a mentor in the process of reflection-in-action, one who can guide preservice teachers in re-examining and making sense of their experi-ences—in conceptualizing the problems they have identified, critiquing their own actions, and devising alternative strategies for addressing those problems. To an extent, I acted as mentor in English 391; in addition, the students were all paired with mentor teachers in the classrooms where they worked. But the newsgroup allowed for this process of reflection to become a community process, so that students re-examined their experi-ences in collaboration and discussion with their peers, who were engaged in similar work and reflection. Moreover, the newsgroup provided the possibility of regular response from those peers—and from the instruc-tor—in a way that is not possible with written observations that might be submitted in journal form, say, once each week or so. At their best, these discussions were not just opportunities for sharing experiences and problems in teaching writing or voicing opinions about those problems; instead, they complicated and problematized the students' experiences as they thought about what it means to teach literacy. In short, the newsgroup provided a virtual space for these student teachers to come together to reflect critically on their experiences throughout the semester; it facilitated a shared reflection on experience that (ideally) encouraged the kind of critical consciousness necessary for them to become the kind of transformative agents in schools in ways that Cochran-Smith (1991) described.

THE COMPLEXITIES OF CMC FOR CRITICAL REFLECTION

Like many teachers of writing and teacher educators, I am enthusiastic about the possibilities that technologies such as asynchronous CMC promise for us as we work to create new and more effective ways to teach writing and foster critical literacy. But I share the concerns of scholars like Hawisher and Selfe (1991), who cautioned that "if electronic technology is to help us bring about positive changes in writing classes, we must identify and confront the potential problems that computers pose and redirect our efforts, if necessary, to make our classes centers of intellectual openness and exchange" (p. 56). The results described in this chapter are exciting in what they promise for training critically reflective teachers of writing; But there are also significant problems, both practical and political, that can accompany our attempts to employ technologies such as CMC in teaching writing.

Research on the uses of CMC in teaching indicates that a wide variety of factors, many of them embarrassingly obvious, can influence student participation in online discussions and thus the effectiveness of efforts to use CMC for pedagogical purposes. For instance, in her review of such research, Wells (1993) identified the amount of time students must devote to such tasks as log on procedures as one of three important factors that can affect rates of student online participation. My experience in English 391 and in similar writing classes supports Wells' conclusion. Like many teachers of writing who use computers, I have found that even such mundane factors as the times when campus computer labs are open can shape how students participate in the newsgroup discussions. Additionally, teachers often need to devote extra time to ensure that students understand the technical procedures necessary to use technologies such as CMC. And as noted earlier, some studies indicate that factors such as grading policies and a teacher's discourse style can significantly influence students' online participation. Clearly, teachers who wish to employ CMC technologies to encourage critical reflection need to account for such factors if CMC is to become a productive space for such reflection.

Simply getting students online can be a formidable challenge in itself. In addition to the practical obstacles I described here, access to computers can be a thorny issue. At Purdue, students are blessed with many well-equipped computer labs where they can work outside of class during rather generous open lab hours. Even so, many students in my English 391 classes had difficulty, because of their class and work schedules, finding their way to a computer to complete their work. In short, participation in online discussions can be determined in large part by how easily students can get to a computer.

These problems of student access to computers raise broader, more complex issues related to using computer technologies in the ways I have described in this chapter. For one, students in different institutional settings do not have equal access to computer technology. Although a burgeoning literature on the uses of computers in teaching writing extols innovative pedagogical applications of such exciting technologies as multimedia programs and the World Wide Web, many students and teachers simply do not have access to even the most basic technology required for simple CMC operations such as email (see Piller, 1992). The English Education program at Purdue, which depended on collaboration with local schools, was hampered by the limited access teachers and students in those schools had to this technology (see Yagelski & Powley, 1996). And even as these technologies become increasingly available to users nationwide, students in underfunded teacher-training programs may find themselves excluded from the uses of these technologies. All this suggests that whatever university instructors are able to do to introduce new writing teachers to new pedagogical possibilities represented by computer technologies, those new teachers are often likely to encounter very different situations in schools. In short, what is possible in one context may not even be available in another. The unsettling irony is that although I hope to employ computer technologies to help promote a critical literacy that I believe is essential to democracy, I am a participant in an educational (and economic) system that continues to be characterized by the very inequalities that I hope a critical literacy can help eliminate.

This problem of inequality relates to yet another set of issues that should be addressed here: the role of socioeconomic factors in the use of CMC as a means to critical reflection. It is crucial to bear in mind that the students who participated in the newsgroup discussions in my classes at Purdue were a relatively homogeneous group: mostly white, mostly middle-class undergraduates enrolled in an English education program that would lead to state certification to teach English in secondary schools. In many ways, the homogeneity of my students made it easier for me to establish the newsgroup discussions as a vehicle for critical reflection. Not only were most of the students motivated to do well in a course that was required for teacher certification, but they also shared similar experiences in the English education program. In addition, because their socioeconomic and racial backgrounds were so similar, they found it relatively easy to engage with each other in the kind of critical dialogue I encouraged. At the same time, their homogeneity made it difficult at times to confront issues of diversity in the teaching of writing, and the presence of one or two minority students each semester only highlighted the homogeneity of the students. Different and more diverse groups of students in other institutional contexts would, I believe, present different challenges for instructors trying to use CMC in the ways described here.[8]

It is also worth noting that all of the complexities that attend efforts to foster a Freirean sort of critical consciousness in students apply to online spaces as well as classroom spaces. Recently, some teachers have written about the ways in which online discussions can undermine our best efforts to create open, egalitarian online spaces for student discourse (e.g., see Faigley, 1994; see also Gruber, 1995; Kremers, 1990; Romano, 1993). Although one benefit of CMC can be its potential to decenter the classroom and encourage greater student participation, freewheeling discussion of the kind described by these scholars can present teachers with difficult problems of authority and does not necessarily engender the kind of critical reflection I hope to see students engage in online. It is clear that simply getting students online is not enough to achieve that kind of critical reflection.

Nevertheless, despite the difficulties I have cited here, which relate to larger, systemic problems, asynchronous CMC can be effectively employed in writing courses as a vehicle for fostering critical reflection. What is perhaps most compelling about applying technologies like CMC to teaching is that such efforts can create new opportunities to examine pedagogies and consider new ways of addressing the problems confronted in teaching writing. As Selfe and Hilligoss (1994) pointed out, "computers and the issues they raise provide teachers with new, and increasingly uncertain, perspectives: on the existing theoretical problems, on our pedagogical approaches, and on the social systems that influence our instruction" (p. 1). If writing teachers are to be prepared to become reflective practitioners who will teach literacy as a potentially transformative activity, then we will do well to use computer technologies, such as CMC, not

---

[8]Another factor to consider here is class size. English 391 was a writing workshop course that was capped at 20 students. In my experience, enrollments of 15 to 30 work especially well for the kind of online discussions I described here, which are carefully integrated into the regular class meetings and course assignments. Smaller numbers of students can lead to very different kinds of online discussions, which can be difficult to sustain; conversely, much larger student enrollments present different challenges for instructors as they conduct online discussions.

only to foster critical reflection but also to disrupt our received ways of thinking about literacy and to explore new ways to understand what it means to write.

REFERENCES

Ahern, T. C., Peck, K., & Laycock, M. (1992). The effects of teacher discourse on computer-mediated discussion. *Journal of Educational Computing Research, 8*, 291-309.

Butler, W. M., & Kinneavy J. L. (1994). The electronic discourse community: God, meet Donald Duck. In G. Tate, E. Corbett, & N. Meyers (Eds.), *The writing teacher's sourcebook* (3rd ed., pp. 400-414). New York: Oxford University Press. (Original work published 1991)

Cheng, H., Lehman J., & Armstrong, P. (1991).Comparison of performance and attitude in traditional and computer conferencing classes. *American Journal of Distance Education, 5*, 51-64.

Cochran-Smith, M. (1991). Learning to teach against the grain. *Harvard Education Review, 61*, 279-310.

Cohen, M., & Riel, M. (1989). The effect of distant audiences on students' writing. *American Educational Research Journal, 26*, 143-159.

Faigley, L. (1994). *Fragments of rationality.* Pittsburgh, PA: University of Pittsburgh Press.

Freire, P., & Macedo, D. (1987). *Literacy: Reading the word, reading the world.* Westport, CT: Bergen & Garvey.

Giroux, H. (1988). *Teachers as intellectuals: Toward a critical pedagogy of learning.* Granby, MA: Bergen & Garvey.

Gruber, S. (1995). RE: Ways we contribute: Students, instructors, and pedagogies in the computer-mediated writing classroom. *Computers and Composition, 12*, 61-78.

Hawisher, G. E. (1992). Electronic meetings of the minds: Research, electronic conferences, and composition studies. In G. Hawisher & P. LeBlanc (Eds.), *Re-imagining computers and composition: Teaching and research in the virtual age* (pp. 81-101). Portsmouth, NH: Heinemann.

Hawisher, G. E., & Selfe, C. Y. (1991). The rhetoric of technology and the electronic writing class. *College Composition and Communication, 42*, 55-65.

Hiltz, S. (1990). Evaluating the virtual classroom. In L. Harasim (Ed.), *Online education: Perspectives on a new environment* (pp. 133-183). New York: Praeger.

Kremers, M. (1990). Sharing authority on a synchronous network: The case for riding the beast. *Computers and Composition, 7*, 33-44.

Kutz, E., & Roskelly, H. (1991). *An unquiet pedagogy: Transforming practice in the English classroom.* Portsmouth, NH: Heinemann.

Levin, J. A., Kim, H., & Riel, M. (1990). Analyzing instructional interactions on electronic message networks. In L. Harasim (Ed.). *Online education: Perspectives on a new environment* (pp. 185-213). New York: Praeger.

Mayher, J. (1990). *Uncommon sense: Theoretical practice in language education.* Portsmouth, NJ: Boyton-Cook/Heinemann.

McCreary, E. K., & Van Duren , J. (1987). Educational applications of computer conferencing. *Canadian Journal of Educational Communication, 16,* 107-115.

Murray, D. M. (Ed.). (1982). Teach writing as process not product. In *Learning by teaching* (pp. 14-17). Portsmouth, NH: Heinemann, (Original work published 1972)

Piller, C. (1992, September). Separate realities: The creation of the technological underclass in America's public schools. *Macworld, 9,* 218-230.

Quinn, C. N., Mehan, H., Levin, J. A., & Black, S. D. (1983). Real education in non-real time: The use of electronic message systems for instruction. *Instructional Science, 11,* 313-327.

Richardson-Koehler, V. (1988). Barriers to effective supervision of student teaching. *Journal of Teacher Education, 39,* 28-34.

Romano, S. (1993). The egalitarian narrative: Whose story? Which yardstick? *Computers and Composition, 10*(1), 5-28.

Salzillo, F., & Van Fleet, A. (1977). Student teaching and teacher education: A sociological model for change. *Journal of Teacher Education, 28,* 27-31.

Schon, D.A. (1987). *Educating the reflective practitioner.* San Francisco, CA: Jossey-Bass.

Selfe, C. L., & Hilligoss, S. (Eds.). (1994). *Literacy and computers: The complications of teaching and learning with technology.* New York: Modern Language Association of America.

Thompson, D. (1988). Conversational networking: Why the teacher gets most of the lines. *Collegiate Microcomputer, 6,* 193-201.

Wells, R. (1993). *Computer-mediated communication for distance education: An international review of design, teaching, and institutional issues.* State College, PA: American Center for Distance Education.

Yagelski, R. P. (1994). Literature and literacy: Rethinking English as a school subject. *English Journal, 83,* 30-36.

Yagelski, R. P. (1997). Portfolios as a way to encourage reflective practice among preservice english teachers. In I. Weiser & K.B. Yancey (Eds.), *Situating portfolios: Four perspectives* (pp. 225-243). Logan: Utah State University Press.

Yagelski, R. P., & Grabill, J. T. (1998). Computer-mediated communication in the undergraduate writing classroom: A study of the relationship of online discourse and classroom discourse in two writing classes. *Computers and Composition, 15*(1), 11-40.

Yagelski, R. P., & Powley, S. (1996). Virtual connections and "real" boundaries: Teaching writing and preparing writing teachers on the internet. *Computers and Composition, 13*(1), 25-36.

Glossary

Compiled by Michael J. Day and Susanmarie Harrington, based on the Epiphany Project's Glossary of Terms from The Field Guide to the 21st Century

With additional contributions from
Richard J. Selfe
Gail Matthews-DeNatale
Zane Berge
Mauri Collins

Alliance for Computers and Writing (ACW): An organization that brings together educators and publishers to advance the teaching of writing with technology. The ACW is a network of regional organizations. Contact Fred Kemp (f.kemp@ttu.edu) to find out about the ACW nearest you, or visit ACW's Web site (http://english.ttu.edu/acw/). The ACW also sponsors an electronic discussion group, so you may hear about discussions on ACW; that refers to the mailing list, ACW-L. Anyone can subscribe; see the ACW Web site for more information.

ACW-L: The Internet discussion group of the Alliance for Computers and Writing. To subscribe, send the message subscribe ACW-L your name to listproc@ttacs6.ttu.edu.

Anonymous FTP: A form of FTP (see entry for FTP) that allows unregistered users (those without passwords to the account) access to files on a remote computer. When using FTP, one logs in as "anonymous" and uses one's e-mail address (e.g., MDAY@SILVER) as the password. Sometimes users will be instructed to use a generic password, such as "guest," instead of their e-mail addresses.

ASCII: An acronym that stands for the American Standard Code For Information Interchange and is pronounced ASKEE, this term is generally used to refer to "plain vanilla" text (or other data) that can be easily transferred from one computer to another because it is stripped of all the control and formatting characters that are particular to a specific software or hardware environment. Examples of formatting that will be lost if a file is "saved as" ASCII include boldface, underline, and special font designations. Most word processing packages now have the ability to save files in ASCII format so that users can send them to other users who work on different hardware and software systems. Authors may choose to save an ASCII version of their articles and use these files for e-mail attachments and when sending text to graphic designers who work with programs and systems that are different from the one in which the file was originally created.

Aspects: Group editing software that allows up to 12 users to share and edit files on a local network, or even across a wide area network. Within the writing classroom, such a program might be useful for small-group editing exercises and peer critiques. A convenient "chat box" window allows participants to have real-time written conversations as they edit. For more information, see http://www.grouplogic.com.

Asynchronous: Not occurring in real time or simultaneously. E-mail is asynchronous communication.

Asynchronous Communication Networks: Networks that allow the exchange of information or written messages, but in a slightly delayed fashion. Messages are exchanged among computers on a network much like letters are exchanged within a postal system, only faster. E-mail is an example of "asynchronous" communication. This is in contrast with synchronous communication, such as Internet chat rooms, in which exchanges take place in "real time" (see also Synchronous).

Authoring Systems (or Languages): This term refers to computer languages (like HyperCard, SuperCard, ToolBook, or Inkway) that use "real" language (in limited sense) to represent programming commands. The intent of such systems is to make it easier for users to program their computers without having to learn the more obscure terms and syntax of most programming languages such as FORTRAN, Pascal, and C.

Beta version: A preliminary version of a program, distributed to a small group of users who will test the program and find the remaining bugs, so that the producers can fix them before distributing the commercial version on a wide scale.

Browsers: Software that allows a networked computer to connect to other Internet sites. Some browsers (such as Netscape Navigator or Mosaic) are graphical, and allow formatting, images, and even sound and video; and others (such as Lynx) are text only.

Bug: A problem with software, that can cause the program to crash, or give unreliable results.

Bulletin Boards (BBs): BBs are virtual "spaces," located within some computer's memory, that are used to post and receive messages of interest to various groups of people, hence, the analogy to traditional bulletin boards. The messages on BBs are generally directed at people with something in common (a hobby, a profession, a chronological age, a problem) and are transmitted and received within minutes for relatively little expense. Users generally get access to these BBs through personal computers equipped with modems and connected to telephones—users pay the phone costs. Frequently, BBs can also be accessed through educational, governmental, or some business computer systems. BBs are popular because they provide virtual spaces for users to talk about topics of general interest (e.g., problems with specific computer platforms or software packages), a variety of academic and scholarly projects (e.g., cold fusion research, the use of computers in composition instruction), areas of personal commitment (e.g., abortion, environmental news), or personal concerns (e.g., computer dating, vampires, alternative sexual practices).

CD-ROM: Compact disks (CDs) are used as mass storage devices that allow users to store large quantities of information (i.e., 100 megabytes to 1,000 megabytes currently) on one surface. These disks are read by a light beam, and the information fed into a computer. Although new technologies are making writeable CD-ROMs available to users, unlike floppy disks, conventional CDs can only be read by a user: Users cannot write information on them, erase it, and write other information. Hence, teachers may come across the term CD-ROM, referring to CDs that provide only "read-only" memory. Soon, however, the profession may have access to CDs that can be both written and read by teachers, much like large floppy disks. Some companies supply multiplatter machines that allow users to access (usually relatively slowly) more than one CD. For instance, a user could employ such a device to access an encyclopedia, a graphics database, and a listing of government documents during one work session!

Central Processing Unit (CPU): The brains of the computer that contains the internal storage, processing circuitry, and the control units of the computer. CPU refers to the components of a computer that control and make sense of the directions that users and programs give to the computer.

CHORTT-L: An e-mail list maintained by Michigan Technological University. CHORTT stands for Computing in the Humanities: Overcoming Resistance to Teaching with Technology. To subscribe, send e-mail to majordomo@mtu.edu, with a blank subject line and the following in the body of the message: subscribe chortt-l.

CMC: See **Computer-mediated communication**

CommonSpace®: A program that allows writers and readers to share and respond to texts. Multiple columns can be added to any text, so more than one reader can see other readers' comments; comments can be linked to a particular spot in the students' text. Teachers can create a library of frequently used comments, which can be pasted into responses. Some synchronous communication is possible. For more information, see http://www.hmco.com/hmco/college/newmedia/sixthfloor/CS1.html.

Computer-Based Instruction (CBI) or Computer-Mediated Instruction: Using computers to instruct human users. CBI includes computer-assisted instruction (CAI; tutorial, review and practice, simulation, etc.); Computer-managed instruction (diagnostic and prescriptive testing functions); and electronic messaging, which is generally associated with networked computer classrooms.

Computer-Mediated Communication: Any communication conducted over computer networks.

Connections MOO: A text-based virtual reality that seeks to provide an alternative learning environment for classes and other groups. Currently, the Netoric Project's Tuesday Café is held at Connections MOO. http://web.nwe.ufl.edu/~tari/connections/ (see also **MOO**).

Courseware: Software, including documentation and workbooks, that is marketed for educational purposes.

Cross-Post: Posting a BBS or discussion group message to multiple subject groups or conferences. It is a good idea to be judicious about cross-posting because people who subscribe to several thematically related conferences or lists will become annoyed when they receive the exact same message many times from the different lists (see also **Netiquette**).

CU-See Me®: Software for live video and audio conferencing on the Internet. For more information, see http://www.wpine.com/Products/CU-SeeMe/.

Cyberspace: A general term for the space created by computer networks. Cyber, like virtual, has become a handy modifier, for everything from cyberpunk fiction to cyberclassrooms.

Daedalus Integrated Writing Environment (DIWE): A suite of programs, available for both Macintosh and IBM computers, designed for writing classrooms. A simple word processor allows students to compose text; a mail program allows students to send e-mail on the local network; invention and response programs guide students through the process of generating ideas or responding to drafts; a conferencing program, InterChange®, allows synchronous discussion; and a bibiography-building program, Bibliocite®, formats bibliography entries in multiple formats. For more information, see http://www. daedalus.com/.

DaMOO: A text-based virtual reality for teachers and students of writing and communication. DaMOO hosts the real-time discussion segments and sessions of the Teaching in the Community College Conference, a completely online conference. For more information, see http://damoo.csun.edu/.

Desktop Publishing (DTP): The use of personal computers and the appropriate software to produce publications that approach typeset quality (1200 DPI). GenerallyDTP systems use word processing software, graphics software, and a page-layout program (to combine text and graphics on the same page) as well as a laser printer for high quality output.

Distance Learning: Using computers hooked to WANs (see Wide-Area Networks) and equipped with telecommunications software, learners can attend "classes" offered at sites distant from their own. Sometimes, distance learning involves an exchange of video or television images.

Diversity University (DU): A nonprofit instructional organization and one of the earliest educational MOOs, where many important educational events take place. Distance education is a priority. For more information, see http://www.du.org/ on the Web.

Download: The electronic transfer of information from a remote computer to a local one. Upload refers to the transfer from the local machine to the remote one.

EDUCOM, EDUCAUSE: An organization that seeks to transform higher education through the use of information technology. EDUCOM, which recently merged with CAUSE to form EDUCAUSE, sponsors the e-mail-based newsletter *Edupage*, a summary of news about information technology, is provided three times a week. To subscribe to *Edupage* send mail to: listproc@educom.unc.edu with the message: subscribe Edupage yourname.

Electronic Discussion Groups, or Lists: Groups of people with similar interests hold discussions via e-mail. These lists, sometimes called lists or listservs, cover a dazzling array of topics. Some of the lists germane to computers and writing are ACW-L, and Rhetnet-L (Discussions related to Rhetnet, an online publication). List members can send one message to the host computer, and that message is then delivered to everyone participating on the list (see also **LISTSERV**).

Electronic Journal (e-journal): An electronically distributed publication, which, like a print journal, includes a table of contents, numerically defined issues, and an ISSN number. Recipients can reformat text as they wish, and print only what they need to print.

E-Mail: Refers to electronic mail, or mail sent by computer from one person to another or from one person to many people. E-mail can only be sent from one computer on a network to another computer on the same network or from one computer on a network to another computer on a linked network. E-mail works much like the postal system (only much faster!) in that messages are forwarded to individuals or groups who have addresses—the name of the computer at which one receives or sends mail. To use e-mail, a user also needs a communications software package that allows one computer to speak to other computers. These programs also allow users to set the communication protocols (the settings and the parameters) for their machines to match the protocols for the machine they are sending information to. Some people access e-mail with GUI software programs such as Eudora. Internet browser software packages (e.g., Microsoft Internet Explorer and Netscape) also include e-mail capabilities.

Emoticon (smiley): Electronic text likenesses of human faces used in mail and news to indicate a variety of emotions and reactions. In the Inited States, you read the "face" from left to right, as if it were rotated 90 degrees counterclockwise. The most common smiley is :-), indicating happiness. You will also often see :-(,meaning disappointment and ;-) meaning, wink, irony or sarcasm. However, other cultures have their own smileys. In Japan, the smiling face is (^_^).

ENFI (Electronic Networks For Interaction): A real-time writing environment for the networked computer classroom, in which synchronous communications software allows teachers and students to explore, collaborate, and expand on ideas in class in writing. They see each other in the process of developing ideas; they write for each other and not just to "the teacher."

Epiphany Project: Originally supported by Annenberg/CPB, Epiphany supports teacher initiatives nation in the field of computers and writing at universities across the nation. Faculty development is a primary focus. http://mason.gmu.edu/~epiphany/docs/descrip.html http://mason.gmu.edu/~epiphany/.

File Server: A file server is a computer, hooked to a hardware network and using network software, that stores files centrally so that they can be shared by many users. File servers are the machines that run networks and determine many of their operating characteristics. Be sure to back up file servers frequently!

Filesharing: Exchanging files from one computer to another on a networked system of computers.

File Transfer Protocol (FTP): A protocol and program that permits files to be transferred over the network.

Flame: To express a strong opinion to, and/or criticize someone (or something), usually in a frank inflammatory statement, in an electronic message. Because e-mail seems ephemeral, it is usually composed spontaneously, and quickly sent, writers may "say" things that they would have kept to themselves were they communicating face-to-face or in a publication. This problem with the medium is further exacerbated by the fact that its inherent lack of attitudinal signifiers, such as a smile or a wink, creates a context in which humor and irony are sometimes mistaken for serious criticism. One way to avoid misunderstandings is to use emoticons when joking or teasing another person (see also **Emoticon** and **Netiquette**).

Freeware: Microcomputer software available on the Internet for free. All you have to do is download it. Many companies make a bare bones version of their software available as freeware, in hopes of attracting customers into buying full-featured versions, at a price.

Frequently Asked Question File (FAQ): Pronounced "fack", A FAQ is a document containing information about some service, application or function. FAQs contain answers to the most common questions and generally are updated as users gain experience with the service, application or function. When you join a discussion group on Usenet or the Internet, be sure to ask for the FAQ file before asking questions others in the group might think are self-evident. It is considered common courtesy to look for and read all FAQ lists before requesting software technical assistance or asking questions of a listserv. Not all programs or lists provide FAQ lists, but those that do are annoyed when newcomers ask questions that have been asked by others hundreds of times and are already answered in the FAQ list (see also Netiquette).

Gopher: An information management tool that allows users to search for specific kinds of information over a wide-area network by using a series of menus. Gopher was developed by the University of Minnesota and is freely available in client and server form. Many Gophers serve as useful front-ends to Internet databases, FTP archives, OPACs and CWIS. Gopher's widespread use and popularity has largely been eclipsed by the increased use of World Wide Web browsers.

Groupware (Group Conferencing Systems): Programs (often marketed for business) that permit simultaneous work on a common file by more than one networked user. All the users can see the changes made by any other person as they occur.

Home page: See also **Web site.** A site, or home page, on the Web is a document stored on the Web. Home pages are typically introductions to an individual or group; university home pages, for instance, have links to other documents about academic opportunities, admissions, and so on. More and more teachers are finding that home pages for their classes give them an easy method of making information available to students without making lots of handouts.

Hyper Text Markup Language (HTML): Allows all network browsers to see (nearly) the same formatting when they access a URL. HTML is a series of commands that are placed at the beginning and end of text. For example, in the following text: <p>type your text here</p>, the p's within the brackets tell a browser that the text in-between is to be treated as a single paragraph. For more information on learning HTML, see any of the books available in the computer section of your local bookstore, or visit Jeff Galin's quick start pages at http://139.182.93.107/jrgst7/newbie.html.

HyperCard: An authoring language developed by Bill Atkinson at Apple Computer in1984, HyperCard allows authors to create hypertext stacks, or files, that contain text and graphic components. Using HyperCard, authors can create hypertext stacks without knowing traditional programming languages. The software uses a card metaphor to organize itself. Readers move from card to card, using the mouse to click on buttons in a card to select the next card to be seen. SuperCard is another version of an authoring language that allows for enhanced hypermedia applications.

Hypermedia: A hyperdocument that mixes all or any one of the following: text, still photography, video, sound, and synthesized voice-in a hypertext environment. Various nodes in a hypermedia document about Virginia Woolf's life, for instance, may contain a video clip about education in Victorian England, a speech from the suffrage movement during the time that Woolf was writing, photographs of a number of Woolf's original diary pages, and several published chapters from *A Room of One's Own*, among many other potential items.

Hypertext: A term coined by T. H. Nelson in the 1960s, hypertext refers to the nonsequential arrangement of text-based information. Hypertexts can be broken down into nodes, or small units of text (screens of text or of text and graphics, or scrolling screens of text and graphics, for instance), which are linked, or connected, to other nodes in webs, or connected sets of information (a web of nodes may be a set of critical essays on existentialism, a set of poems by Emily Dickinson, or a set of definitions of terms from a single page). In most hypertexts, each node will contain several "hot" words. If readers select one of these words or icons, they jump to a node containing related information. In a pure hypertext, every node is connected to every other node, so each reader must choose which nodes to view and the order in which to view these nodes. Typically, hypertexts present readers with alternative paths through a document; as a result, each reader creates his or her own path through a hypertext.

Internet Relay Chat (IRC): A worldwide synchronous multiuser chat protocol that allows one to converse with others in real time. IRC is structured as a network of servers, each of which accepts connections from client programs, one per user. Jarkko Oikarinen, a Finnish programmer, created IRC. IRC is a free program, which means that anyone with access to the Internet can get a client program and use it to talk with others. IRC allows users logged in to "chat" with other users around the world. IRC uses separate channels to keep discussions identified (#hottub for discussions of hot tubbing; #baseball for baseball, etc.). IRC is still popular, but not every campus has the software to permit IRC, and some campuses may forbid IRC, viewing it as "nonserious" and therefore "nonacademic" use of resources. Many teachers have switched to using MOOs rather than IRC. For more information, see http://www.hut.fi/~jlohikos/IRC.html (see also **MOO**).

Interchange™: See Daedalus Integrated Writing Environment.

Internet: A collection of computer networks interconnected by a set of routers that allow them to function as a single, large virtual network. The Internet is often referred to as a "network of networks."

Internet Explorer: A popular multimedia browser for accessing the World Wide Web.

Intranet: A network of computers whose contents are not open for all to see on the Internet because it is designed to be used locally within a specific site or organization (see also **LAN** and **Server**).

Kairos: *Kairos: A Journal for Teachers in Webbed Environments*, takes its name from the classical rhetorical term for situational context. It is one of the first peer-reviewed Web-based journals for teachers, researchers and tutors of writing at the university level. For more information, see http://english.ttu.edu/kairos/.

Liquid Crystal Display (LCD): This term refers to the screen displays used for laptop computers. These screens are flat and, thus, take up little room, but they also can cause eye strain because the image they produce is not as bright as many users would desire.

Lingua MOO: A text-based virtual reality for teachers and students of writing and communication. The C-Fest real-time discussions surrounding the Conference on College Composition and

Communication occur on Lingua MOO. http://wwwpub. utdallas.edu/~cynthiah/start.html.

Links: Built-in connections between texts, used in hypertext (such as the World Wide Web or StorySpace). A link takes you from one document to another, or from one place in a document to another place in the same text, allowing for reader-directed information retrieval. On the WWW, links are identified by underlining or by the use of different colors in the text; links can be followed by using arrow keys, or pointing and clicking.

LISTSERV: LISTSERV® is a software packages used to create and manage electronic discussion groups. These discussion groups are often called "lists" (or listservs) because the software sends a single message to a list of many subscribers. Participants subscribe by sending a message to a central listserv account; list discussions are conducted by electronic mail over the Internet. Many lists have a moderator who manages the information and content. Programs such as Majordomo and Listproc provide similar services (see also **electronic discussion group**).

List: See **LISTSERV**, electronic discussion group.

Listproc: See **LISTSERV**.

Local Area Network (LAN): A network connecting machines at one site. Networks that are internal to an organization are increasingly referred to as intranets so that they can be distinguished from the Internet, a network connection that has the capacity to communicate with people and broadcast information outside the organization (see also **Intranet** and **Server**).

Logs: Records or transcripts of online work.

Lurking: Reading or "listening" to a mailing list discussion or USENET newsgroup without actively participating (i.e., without contributing to the discussion). Lurking is encouraged for beginners who wish to learn the history and habits of the group (see also **Netiquette**).

Majordomo: See **LISTSERV**.

Media MOO: A text-based virtual reality for media researchers. Netoric's Tuesday Café meetings for writing teachers met on Media MOO 1993-1997 (see also **Netoric**).

Megabyte: The amount of stored data equal to 1 million characters (letters, numbers, symbols) of text. It is equivalent to 1,000 kilobytes, commonly referred to as 1,000 "KB" or 1,000 "K". The word *megabyte* is often abbreviated as meg or MB.

Megabyte University (MBU-L): One of the earliest and most prolific Internet discussion groups for computers and writing. MBU-L ended in 1997.

Mhz: Stands for "megahertz," a unit of measurement equal to 1 million electrical vibrations per second. Megahertz is the unit of measure that describes the rate at which computers process instructions. It is used to compare the speeds of very similar computers but is not a very good measure of computer speeds between platforms. As of 1998, personal computers commonly work at 200 and 300 MHz, and sometimes even up into the 500+ MHz range.

Modem: MOdulator/DEModulator—a device that converts the digital signals in a computer to analog signals, and vice-versa, to enable computer communication through analog telephone lines.

MOO: MUD, object oriented. A multiple user dimension which, in addition to text-based communication, allows users to construct and manipulate "objects" and move from textually described room to room. MOOs (MUD, object oriented) emphasize objects created within the virtual space; in a MOO, users move from "room" to "room," using objects. It is possible to read a newspaper, or slides in a MOO. Great resources for learning more about educational uses of this technology are Jeff Galin's Web page, MOO Central (http://139.182.93.107/jrgst7/MOOcentral.html) and the Kairos coverweb on writing classes on the MOO (see **MUD, Netoric**).

MUD: Multiple user dimension. A synchronous (real-time) text-based virtual reality in which "players" interact. MUDs are remote login-based environments; users telnet from their local computer to interact with others. Also known as MOOs, MUDs, and MUSHes (or MU*, M**), these acronyms refer to virtual spaces that permit discussion and other activities. MUDs are associated with gaming (Dungeons and Dragons, etc.), and many MUDs and MOOs are socially oriented; MUSHes are similar spaces.

Navigate: The process of moving about purposefully within a virtual environment. For example, readers of a hypertext or hypermedia document navigate from node to node via links, and Web surfers click on links in pages to navigate from site to site. Each reader chooses his or her own path of navigation, depending on interests, curiosity, associations, directions, and so on. The term *navigation* suggests the wide-open spaces involved in virtual environments and the need to find one's way with the help of navigational devices (nodes, links, Web maps, files, menus) that are particular to electronic environments.

Netiquette: A contraction of "network" and "etiquette" referring to proper behavior on a computer network, such as reading FAQs, newcomer listserv lurking, using emoticons, avoiding cross-posts, not flaming, and so on.

Netoric: The Netoric Project, created by Greg Siering and Tari Fanderclai, is a regular gathering of computers and writing teachers at Connections MOO, in the Tuesday Café, a room constructed on that MOO. Meetings are held, unsurprisingly, on Tuesdays, 8 p.m.

eastern time. Meetings of computers and writing teachers began in 1991 on IRC channel #cw, and in 1993 moved to MediaMOO, where the first Tuesday Café was held (see also **Connections MOO**).

Netscape: A popular Web browser, used for viewing and searching the World Wide Web.

Network: Collections of computers that are linked electronically so that they can exchange information and share peripheral devices such as printers and scanners. Local area networks (LANs) link computers in a single location (e.g., a classroom, a building, or a campus) by some kind of cabling system. Typically, LANs are used when computers are located within one to two miles of each other. Wide-area networks (WANs) link computers in different and more far-flung locations via high speed, long distance communications networks or satellites. ARPANET, and Internet are WANs that connect people in various locations for various purposes. ARPANET is a WAN supported by the U.S. Defense Advanced Research Projects Agency (DARPA) and is intended to support defense research (see also **Internet**).

Newbie: A slang term that is often used in reference to persons who are new to a particular program, group, machine, listserv, and so on. The term is often used affectionately, but sometimes is considered to be derogative.

Newsgroups: See Usenet.

Node: A computer that is attached to a network; also called a host.

Online Writing Lab (OWL): A virtual environment that uses e-mail and web pages to provide support for writers. The Dakota State University OWL (http://www.dsu.edu/departments/liberal/owl/) provides a good overview of the services provided by many OWLs and links to other Internet resources.

Platform: A unique and complete computer system. Each platform, such as the IBM, UNIX, or Macintosh, approach the solutions to computer-use problems from different perspectives. Each computer configuration generally has both advantages and disadvantages.

Plug-in: Multimedia (e.g., audio, video, graphics) and protocols (gopher, telnet, HTML) are changing so rapidly that software companies find it difficult to create programs in a timely manner that recognize all new formats. Plug-ins are a way of avoiding having to write a whole new software program each time an additional protocol or file format becomes popular. Programs like Netscape and Adobe Photoshop have a "preferences" option that users can modify to include additional "associated" plug-ins. A "plug-in" is a small program that has a specific function and is designed to work in companion with another, primary, software program. For example, if a user comes across an Internet page that includes MacroMedia Schockwave files, Netscape will display a message informing the user that plug-in is necessary for this portion of the page to be viewed. Users have the option of downloading the plug-in, which will become an associated program will automatically open each time the user visits a site that includes Shockwave files in the future. Common plug-in programs include RealAudio, Telnet applications, and Adobe Acrobat Reader.

PowerPoint®: Presentation software by Microsoft that creates slides to accompany a lecture or other formal presentation.

RAM: An acronym that stands for random access memory, the memory of the computer that can be accessed by users, filled with information (e.g., text, graphics, data), and easily changed.

Real Time, or Synchronous, Discussion: Discussion held on-line among participants who are active at the same time. Some software programs allow such discussions in class; IRC and MOOs allow it anytime.

Remote Access: The ability to access another computer. Remote access requires communications hardware, software, and actual physical links, although this can be as simple as common carrier (telephone) lines or as complex as a telnet login to another computer across the Internet.

Rhetnet, Rhetnet-L: Rhetnet is an experimental, online journal about rhetoric, writing, and technology, scholarship on the World Wide Web about the World Wide Web. Rhetnet-L is an electronic discussion group for For more information, see http://www.missouri.edu/~rhetnet/. To subscribe to Rhetnet-L, send the message subscribe rhetnet-L Your Name to listproc@lists.missouri.edu.

Scanner: A peripheral device that digitizes images (e.g., line art or photographs) and text copy, and stores these in a file so that users can work with them. Using a scanner, students can take a drawing that they have produced, digitize it, store it on a disk, and import it into a paper they are writing. Similarly, with scanners that allow for optical character recognition (OCR), a teacher can use a scanner to digitize the best and the worst examples of a set of essays and store them in computer files so that students can refer to them (see also Digitizer and OCR).

Server: In LANs, the server manages the traffic on the network at a given site, orchestrating demands on peripheral devices and central files so that multiple users' requests get responses in a timely and efficient manner. This internal or local network is known as an intranet. Some servers are designed so that they can be hooked up to the

Internet by a phone line or other form of wired connection. Web pages (HTML files) must be stored or uploaded via ftp onto an Internet server before they can be read by persons browsing the Internet (see also **LAN, FTP,** and **HTML**).

Shareware: Microcomputer software, distributed through public domain channels, such as FTP, for which the author expects to receive compensation.

Signature: The three or four lines at the bottom of a piece of email or a Usenet article that identify the sender. Often contains addresses, telephone numbers, and e-mail addresses. Large signatures (more than five lines) are generally frowned on.

Snail Mail: Mail delivered by the postal service.

StorySpace: A hypertext authoring program that can be used to create fiction, nonfiction, classroom exercises, etc. For more information, see http://www.eastgate.com/Storyspace.html.

Syllaweb: A class syllabus on the World Wide Web.

Synchronous: Data communications in which transmissions are sent at a fixed rate, with the sending and receiving devices synchronized. Synchronous communication occurs in real time (e.g., with two or more users communicating online at the same time to one another).

Synchronous Communication Networks: Networks that allow users to exchange written information at very high speeds so that written conversations take place in "real time," much like regular conversations, rather than in a delayed, or asynchronous, fashion, such as e-mail (see also **Asynchronous**).

Techno-rhetorician: A term coined by members of the computers and writing community to refer to people in the composition and rhetoric field who use computers and the Internet.

Telnet: Remote login, or remote terminal connection service. Telnet, a basic service on the Internet, allows a user to interact with another computer as if she or he were directly connected to the remote computer.

Teaching Teaching, Learning, & Technology (TLT) Roundtable Program: Sponsored by the American Association for Higher Education, the Teaching, Learning roundtables help faculty at participating institutions coordinate and stimulate their uses of technology to improve teaching and learning. The TLTR Program provides a conceptual framework, guidelines, information, training to help educational institutions, and also hosts both national conferences and regional workshops for information exchange and training. For more information, see http://www.aahe.org.

Textra Connect: A program, similar to DIWE, which allows students to word process (using Norton Textra), share texts, and send local e-mail. Textra makes possible a paperless classroom. For more information, see http://www.wwnorton.com/connect.htm.

Thread: A series of postings to an electronic BB, or other electronic discussion group (e.g., listserv), that have a common subject heading. A thread normally consists of responses to an original posting to a discussion, or an offshoot of another thread (see also **Listserv** and **electronic discussion group**).

286, 386, 486, and Pentium: These numbers or names refer to the different microprocessor chips found in DOS (IBM-compatible) personal computers. In this series of Microprocessor chips, all manufactured by Intel Corp., the 286 chip is the older, less powerful chip, and the Pentium chip is the most powerful and most recent chip.

UNIX: An operating system developed by Bell Laboratories that supports multiuser and multitasking operations. That is, this operating system allows many people to share the processing capabilities of the computer on which it is running, and allows those people to use several programs at once.

Upgrades: Most software programs are revised periodically, to take advantage of new technological developments and to stay current with hardware improvements. An upgrade is a new and presumably improved version of a program.

Universal Resource Locator (URL): A term used to designate the address for a site located on the Internet. URLs are typically WWW sites that indicate the host's domain, subdirectory, and HTML filename: <http://www.thedomain.edu/theuser/filename.htm>. But URLs can also designate gopher sites: <gopher://gopher.hu.mtu.edu> or anonymous FTP sites: <ftp://something.somewhere.edu>. If the user has previously associated a Telnet program plug-in with a browser such as Netscape, then clicking on a Web page link to <telnet://telnetaddress> will also automatically begin a Telnet session (see also **Plug-In**).

Usenet (NETNEWS, Newsgroups): A distributed computer BB system in which some computers on the Internet participate. It is not strictly an Internet service; many computers not on the Internet also participate. Usenet consists of thousands of newsgroups (somewhat like lists electronic discussion groups except that they are not distributed by e-mail) that anyone with access to Usenet can read and respond to. With the number of groups growing daily, there is truly something of interest to everyone on Usenet. Most Web browsers, such as Netscape and Internet Explorer, have a "news" button or menu item that allows users to access Usenet newsgroups after setting their "news" preferences.

UserID: The name used to log in to a computer, such as the one on which e-mail is stored and sent. UserIDs are usually the first part of an e-mail address.

VAX: Computer produced by the Digital Equipment Corporation in wide use on the Internet.

VAX Notes: VAX Notes is essentially a computer BB. It is structured like a two-dimensional matrix with a set of topic notes on various subjects. Replies to each topic get attached to each topic note. Topics are numbered 1, 2, 3, etc. Replies to Topic 3 would be numbered 3.1, 3.2, etc. It permits users to have several different discussions simultaneously. It also saves all topics and replies, permitting readers to connect at any time, even several days late, and still catch up on the entire transaction.

Videodisk: These are optically scanned disks that can store large quantities of video and graphic data (both images and sounds) and retrieve them for playing back on a monitor. They are currently read only, meaning information can be retrieved from the disc, but new information cannot be added to the disc.

Virtual: Refers to things that are stored in the digital domain of a computer and are thus not physical entities. Hence, classes held via computer, which never meet in a traditional classroom, are termed *virtual classrooms*. Text which exists only in the computer's memory has been called *virtual text*.

Virtual Reality: Systems that transform the computing environment by immersing the user in a simulated three-dimensional world, which also can include movement and tactile control. Virtual reality systems permit users to interact with computer systems in a manner that more closely mimics how humans naturally operate in the real world.

Webfolio: A portfolio of work submitted on the World Wide Web.

Wide-Area Network (WAN): A distributed network spanning hundreds or thousands of miles, connecting a number of local area networks (see also **LAN** and Intranet).

World Wide Web (WWW, "the Web", or W3): A hypertext-based, distributed information system created by researchers at CERN in Switzerland. It allows users to create, edit or browse hypertext documents that include images, sound, and video. The World Wide Web is one of the most popular and useful information sharing tools on the Internet. The Web is usually accessed using a Web browser; the two most popular multimedia browsers are Netscape and Microsoft Internet Explorer. However, for those with limited, low-speed, or low bandwidth access, lynx is a widely available text-only browser.

Author Index

Subject Index